Trends and Issues in Distance Education

International Perspectives, Second Edition

A Volume in
Perspectives in Instructional Technology and
Distance Education

Series Editors:
Charles Schlosser and Michael Simonson,
Nova Southeastern University

Perspectives in Instructional Technology and Distance Education

Charles Schlosser and Michael Simonson, Series Editors

Trends and Issues in Distance Education

International Perspectives,
Second Edition

edited by

Lya Visser
George Washington University

Yusra Laila Visser and Ray J. Amirault
Florida Atlantic University

and

Michael Simonson
Nova Southeastern University

Information Age Publishing, Inc.
Charlotte, North Carolina • www.infoagepub.com

Praise for *Trends and Issues in Distance Education: International Perspectives*

The first edition of this book, which I studied in my educational leadership program, is both eye-opening and essential reading for anyone interested in global distance education. The various perspectives presented are at the same time an introduction to the current state of international distance learning and a prescriptive vision of how the future of this crucial area of world development could progress. Through scholarly chapters and interviews, leaders in the field have a platform to voice their views to readers, who will be immediately engaged and inspired by the many possibilities available to lead distance learning successfully into a bright future. I look forward to the second edition of this book, which will surely update readers on recent developments in the field, and enhance the visions for international distance education.

—Gamin G. Bartle
(Director of Instructional Technology Services at
Drew University, Madison, Wisconsin)

This book gives a general overview of distance education, covering concepts, trends, strategies and obstacles. The wealth of the book lies in the geographical, cultural, and social contexts represented by the authors, who cite a number of experiences that go well beyond the theory of distance education. In spite of the differences in contexts, one can recognize a similarity in the challenges faced in working with distance education. As a doctoral student in the field, I appreciated having a text that documented and systematized the processes of distance education beyond the U.S. context. The book provides insights and inputs for the dialogue on the existing strengths and opportunities for different distance education methodologies and approaches. The challenge for future editions of the book is to make the book available in other languages (e.g., Spanish) and to increase the incorporation of lessons learned from other countries in Latin American and the Caribbean. It is with pleasure that I welcome the second edition, which has made great strides toward both of these recommendations.

—Rosita Ulate
(Academic Assessor for the School of Natural Sciences at UNED, Costa Rica)

Reviewer Comments for Second Edition of *Trends and Issues in Distance Education: International Perspectives*

This book draws on the rich experience of the authors in a wide variety of contexts—from Brazil, through Malaysia and Mozambique to Wisconsin. It explores vital issues in the conceptualization and practice of distance education in an increasingly globalized and technological world. The dangers of viewing knowledge as a commodity and the pitfalls of rapidly expanding transnational education are presented. Promising examples of distance education in refugee camps, prisons, a manufacturing company, and the airline industry are analyzed. In an important enhancement, the collection stimulates further reflection of each chapter through the provision of "comprehension and application" as well as providing resources for further exploration.

—Jennifer Glennie
(Director South African Institute of Distance Education, South Africa)

(See back cover for more Reviewer Comments)

Library of Congress Cataloging-in-Publication Data

Trends and issues in distance education : international perspectives /
edited by Lya Visser ... [et al.]. -- 2nd ed.
p. cm. -- (Perspectives in instructional technology and distance
education)
Includes bibliographical references.
ISBN 978-1-61735-828-9 (pbk.) -- ISBN 978-1-61735-829-6 (hc) --
ISBN 978-1-61735-830-2 (ebk)
I. Visser, Lya.
LC5800.T74 2012
371.35--dc23

2012011510

Printed in the United States of America

CONTENTS

SECTION II: APPLIED DISTANCE EDUCATION INITIATIVES IN DIVERSE SETTINGS

SECTION III: DISTANCE EDUCATION IN UNIVERSITY AND OTHER FORMALIZED HIGHER EDUCATION SETTINGS

**SECTION IV: DISTANCE EDUCATION IN THE WORKPLACE AND
IN NONFORMAL SETTINGS**

FOREWORD

Lya Visser

There are few things of value that can be accomplished without the dedication and support of others. This also holds for this book, which has been written by over 30 authors guided by a team of four section editors. As lead editor, I have done much of the coordination, planning, and administrative work, and of course the usual "chasing around." However, I also had to make the difficult decision on the sequence in which the editors would appear on the cover. This decision was particularly difficult because we, the editorial team, have worked as just that: a team. Yusra Laila Visser, the lead editor of the first edition, has again been very instrumental in the conceptual development of the second edition and has, by taking on the first section of the book, ensured a solid foundation for the subsequent three sections. Ray Amirault has contributed in very important ways to the high quality of the book, not only through having taken on the largest section of the book, but also through timely, systematic, and excellent feedback. Michael Simonson has shaped the section on secondary education and teacher training, an often undervalued segment of distance education. A word of thanks also for the editors of Information Age Publishing for their comments and advice. I thank my editorial team member colleagues for their hard work, their dedication and patience, and most of all for their care. I am very happy that this teamwork has resulted in a book that we are proud of, and that you will certainly find interesting, informative, and at times challenging.

INTRODUCTION

Lya Visser and Yusra Laila Visser

FROM COVER TO COVER

It has been nearly 6 years since the first edition of *Trends and Issues in Distance Education: International Perspectives* was published. In the foreword of that book, we wrote that it represented a "moment-in-time" snapshot of the breadth of perspectives regarding the trends and issues in distance education. Some 4 years after the publication of the first edition, we realized that the field of distance education had become significantly broader, stronger, and more international. In short, we recognized that there was a need for a second edition of the book. It is with great pleasure that we offer you the result of the collaborative efforts of the books' editors and chapter authors.

This book has been written for all of us. It has been prepared for students studying *about* distance education, and for those studying *through* distance education. It has also been written for practitioners working in training and education, providing them with insights about distance education research and practice in a wide variety of settings. Likewise, the chapters in the book have been written for instructors who recognize that it is important to help learners to look beyond the boundaries of their own environment so as to increase their understanding of, and appreciation for, different cultures, circumstances, learners, and leaders who may face both similar, and radically different, opportunities and obstacles in relation to learning and education. Finally, the book has been written for researchers, providing them with insights on some of the key issues and

Trends and Issues in Distance Education:
International Perspectives, Second Edition, pp. xiii–xv

questions preoccupying practitioners and researchers in distance education worldwide.

When deciding on the format and scope of this book, we deliberately chose to ensure that the book would represent distance education in a *truly* broad spectrum. We have sought to represent a diverse set of viewpoints on the globally relevant issues affecting distance education. In the chapters, the various authors explore both relatively small-scale initiatives and large-scale distance education initiatives. The chapters span the globe so as to provide an opportunity for the reader to get a true sense of the diversity of "flavors" represented in international distance education. With regard to the use of technology, the chapters explore everything from the application of some of the most advanced technologies (e.g., 3-D technologies) to the highly effective use of some of the more rudimentary technologies (e.g., crank radios).

ORGANIZATION OF THE BOOK

In the second edition, we again provide a coherent structure for presenting international perspectives on the state of the field by examining and discussing specific trends and issues currently faced by the community of distance education practitioners and researchers. For this edition, we have divided the book into four separate sections, each with its own assigned section editor. At the beginning of each section, the section editor will provide a brief introduction to the section, providing an overview of the chapters in the section, and sharing some insights on how the section has been developed.

Section I, "Perspectives on Global Trends and Issues in Distance Education," presents six unique approaches to exploring what are perceived to be some of the key trends and issues of relevance to the distance education field globally. This section tackles such issues as the fundamental definition (and understanding of) the construct of "distance education," the implications of an international distance education research agenda, gauging short-term possibilities and challenges with the integration of commercial technologies into distance education, the place of postsecondary distance education in a time of globalization, and the lessons to be extracted from the concrete and rich case of distance education in Brazil.

Section II, "Distance Education in Primary and Secondary Education Settings," focuses on the design and development of a virtual secondary school, discusses e-learning in an ample sense in Portugal, shows us how interactive radio instruction helps students and teachers to learn more effectively when assisted by radio lessons, and in its last chapter analyzes and critically reflects on the often positive results of 30 years of distance education experience in Mozambique.

Section III, "Distance Education in University and Other Formalized Higher Education Settings," includes six chapters that focus on distance education in university and higher education settings. This is the largest section of the book, its chapters addressing themes such as the impact of e-learning on the historical trajectory of the university, current research on distance education at the tertiary education level, issues related to quality and accreditation in transnational distance education, opportunities and lessons learned with teacher education programs, the use of personal learning environments for distance education in postsecondary settings, and issues with setting up distance education support systems. The wide range of topics and the challenging comprehension and application questions will surely broaden and enrich the reader's understanding of international distance education in higher education settings.

Section IV, "Distance Education in the Workplace and in Nonformal Settings," focuses on the increasingly significant topic of how distance education is being used to meet learning needs outside of the primary, secondary, and tertiary education systems. In other words, this section explores the use of distance education for just-in-time or on-the-job learning in both the public and private sectors, as well as the use of distance education for reaching hard-to-reach and traditionally underserved audiences. Chapters in this section cover topics including online corporate training, the use of wikis in informal education, and two different chapters on using distance education to enrich the lives of often forgotten segments of society: refugees and prisoners.

For us, as editors, one of the most attractive attributes of the book is the impressive diversity represented in the collection of chapters. At the same time, just as in the first edition, we recognize that the text does not present an exhaustive review of all the international perspectives that might come to bear when seeking to achieve an exhaustive review of international perspectives on the trends and issues in distance education. The latter is, in our view, not only likely unattainable, but perhaps undesirable. Part of the task in serving as a team of editors is to determine which of the themes and topics being identified are likely to be of greatest relevance and interest in light of the main purpose of the book.

We wish to thank the many people who helped us write this book. The second edition is the result of hard work and the efficient, challenging, and effective cooperation among more than 30 people. Through the unique collection of contributions, the authors of the chapters have made it possible for you, the reader, to extend your horizons.

SECTION I

PERSPECTIVES ON GLOBAL TRENDS AND ISSUES IN DISTANCE EDUCATION

Yusra Laila Visser, Section Editor

INTRODUCTION

The unifying theme for Section I is *perspectives on global trends and issues in distance education*. This section consists of six chapters, each of which tackles a substantively different theme (often addressing more than one trend or issue) and makes the case for its perspective in a unique manner.

Section I is introduced by LaPointe and Linder-VanBerschot, whose chapter focuses on distance education research (Chapter 1). The authors elucidate recent distance education research findings of global relevance. This chapter draws from an especially broad array of sources, recognizing that the literary foundation for the field is growing rapidly as the number of open access online journals increases. LaPointe and Linder-VanBerschot make a dedicated case for the importance of a coherent international distance education research agenda. The chapter explores how the field of distance education might benefit from such an approach, and realistically explores the barriers to the field's adoption of such an agenda to date.

In Chapter 2, Jan Visser makes a carefully crafted case for why traditional conceptions of distance education are increasingly unaligned with the needs of learners in the twenty-first century. Jan Visser explores reasons for distance education's historical failure in impacting those audiences which the field could have served best but failed to reach. He concludes with a discussion of the unique role that distance education (when properly conceptualized and leveraged) can play in the development of the "metacompetencies" that will become increasingly important for living in an evermore complex world.

In Chapter 3, Brent Wilson introduces the concept of *nowcasting* (making predictions for the more immediate future and constrained to a particular set of conditions) to explore trends and issues impacting distance education within 2 or 3 years. For this chapter, Wilson examines distance education from an economic lens (e.g., the investment, development, and marketing of educational products and services and quality-improvement measures required to use public and private resources in an accountable way).

Chapter 4, authored by Lya Visser, looks at postsecondary distance education in an environment of increasing globalization and internationalization, citing several high-quality sources to analyze opportunities and challenges associated with international postsecondary distance education. Further, she explores the risks inherent in the commercialization of higher education, as well as the pressures toward commercialization resulting from the economic impacts of both globalization and internationalization. Lya Visser emphasizes both the crucial future role of postsecondary distance education *and* the threats to its future success. She concludes her chapter with a discussion of the conditions required to assure a successful role for postsecondary distance education in the future.

Next, Frederic Litto explores the trajectory of distance education in Brazil, beginning in the 1940s (Chapter 5). He gives due attention to the impact of Brazil's colonial history on systemic educational issues and challenges to educational reform, something likely familiar to those working in other postcolonial contexts. He provides a rich picture of the current state of distance education in Brazil and uses a broad selection of statistical data to familiarize the reader with the complex web of variables promoting and hampering distance education efforts in this rapidly developing country. Litto's chapter, while focused on a specific country context, identifies trends and issues which merit careful attention, as they replicate themselves globally, across low- and middle-income countries (and indeed, some high-income countries too).

Chapter 6, the final chapter of Section I, came about as a result of J. Michael Spector's willingness to review a prepublication version of the book with the goal of critically analyzing the chapters in Section I. As a result of my collaboration with Spector, Chapter 6 presents a brief analysis of each of the chapters in Section I, the collective of Section I chapters (i.e., the integrity of the Section), and the extent to which Section I aligns with the broader themes and goals of the book.

The chapters in this section range in orientation from highly conceptual explorations of the fundamental definition of the discipline to deeply contextualized discussions of unique barriers to distance education initiatives. What unifies these chapters, however, is the common focus on identifying and analyzing those trends and issues that are of global scope and relevance in distance education. As such, the authors in this section provide the foundation for an important dialogue in the distance education field. It is a dialogue which recognizes that in spite of all of the diversity in its theory and implementation, distance education confronts certain trends or issues in a more or less consistent manner at a given time in the field's history. This dialogue can be the foundation for a more in-depth exploration of additional global trends and issues or the implications of the specific trends and issues already identified in this section. As LaPointe and Linder-VanBerschot suggest in Chapter 1, it can also be a dialogue that establishes the framework for a common, collaborative research agenda informed by global trends and issues.

CHAPTER 1

INTERNATIONAL RESEARCH

Responding to Global Needs

Deborah K. LaPointe and Jennifer A. Linder-Vanberschot

The purpose of this chapter is to provide an overview of the current state of research in distance education. Distance education helps respond to an international need of providing instruction to a growing population of diverse learners around the world. Examples of great international distance education programs are provided as insight for leaders in the field. Additionally, advances in international research are offered, including culture, language, tutoring and mentoring, social software, and retention of students. Although ideally researchers in the field would proceed with a unified research agenda, the authors encourage a simple awareness of the different voices shaping the field of international distance education. The chapter concludes with a list of current questions, as well as useful recourses.

INTRODUCTION

In most corners of our world, education is the means by which the building of human capital occurs. Yet education symbolizes more than economic development. Education is a conduit for facilitating the knowledge construction of individuals—individuals who hold the potential to solve the world's global problems and promote human rights. Thus education

Trends and Issues in Distance Education:
International Perspectives, Second Edition, pp. 5–22
Copyright © 2012 by Information Age Publishing

is crucially important not only for its direct beneficiaries—individuals—but also for society as a whole.

No country has been able to meet these critical educational goals and development needs solely through face-to-face classroom instruction (Ryan & Fitzgerald, 2009). In many countries, distance education offers the sole opportunity for citizens to gain access to education. The widespread accessibility of distance education is perhaps its most remarkable character, as it increases the opportunity for employed adults, school leaders, and the less-advantaged to obtain higher education (Ding, 2001). To continue to provide such open access, distance education has always been responsive to new technologies and media, striving to provide access and autonomous learning, as well as new teaching and learning methods.

While education can be justified as a human right and has increasingly provided more access for more people, recent evidence suggests quality has taken a back seat to quantity (Wright, Dhanarajan, & Reju, 2009). The relation between investment in education and economic growth is distressing, according to Hülsmann (2004). Hülsmann's work suggested that a conflict exists among the demand for education, the available budgets for funding, and the calls for cost-effective resource allocation. While more people have access, what they learn is not always useful, and dropout rates are high.

Additional problems substantiate Hülsmann's (2004) warning. Evaluations of online learning environments frequently reveal that, after the necessary expenditures are made on web technologies and infrastructure, the courses offered online tend to mimic the conventional classroom. Similarly, in the absence of a unifying research agenda, there is increasing academic cacophony. This chapter navigates recent advancements in open and distance learning, as well as addresses the challenges of creating an international research agenda for this continuously evolving field.

BELIEFS ABOUT LEARNING AT A DISTANCE

Quality in design and learning outcomes has long been a goal in distance education. It was foremost in Moore's theory of the structure and dialog of transactional distance (Moore & Kearsley, 1996). The basis of this theory rests on approaching learners where they are (i.e., at their learning level, in their own environment, and with the specific technology at their disposal) and interacting with them in ways that help them meet learning outcomes. Effective learning environments, including those in the distance paradigm, acknowledge individual differences and contexts, motivate the student by mindfully engaging learners through complex yet authentic tasks, avoid information overload through chunking, provide hands-on activities, and encourage student reflection. In a quality learning environment, students complete tasks with relevant cognitive tools in interaction with other students, instructors, tutors, or expert members of the learning community. Learners search for information, publish results, and create products to solve problems; teachers provide structure, monitor progress, and assess accomplishments. All the while, the technology is a constant, yet transparent, component of the course design. LaPointe (2006) even suggested that distance education, if structured correctly, has the capability of being a transformative learning experience for the students.

We have always had isolated examples of effective distance education environments. The Speak2Me online synchronous English as a Second Language program offered by Ladder Publishing Ltd. in Taiwan was an example of a distance education program that effectively harnessed technology to achieve learning outcomes. The Speak2Me program offered Taiwanese students a multimedia approach to learning conversational English. Learners purchased a monthly magazine that contained articles in English about American and Taiwanese culture, as well as an audio CD-ROM to which they could listen as they read the written text. Learners logged onto a website and conversed about the magazine articles in English with instructors from the United States as well as teaching assistants from Taiwan. A textbox on the website allowed learners, instructors, and teaching assistants to type out more difficult questions and answers as needed (LaPointe, Greysen, & Barrett, 2004). The program peaked with around 3,000 students, but ultimately failed after 4 years. Barrett (2008) suggested several potential reasons for the failure of the program, including poor marketing and lack of online course design. However, students and instructors alike referred to the program as a "tech trend and felt it was the future of education in their country" (p. 210).

Another case illustrates how meaningful online learning can encourage university-wide advancement. During the summer semester of 2007, Dr. Elena Barberà, a professor from the Universitat Oberta de Catalunya (UOC), visited the University of New Mexico (UNM) to collaborate on numerous research projects. Her time as a visiting professor inspired a group project for three students in an online course titled *Theory and Principles of e-Learning* in the fall of 2007. Using a project-based approach, they asked, "Can we share classes with other universities?" Over the next 2 years (long past the course requirements), three students from the Organizational Learning and Instructional Technology (OLIT) program at UNM spoke with numerous programs and units from both universities. In the spring 2008 semester, they initiated a pilot program to further refine goals and understanding between universities. Because of their efforts, UOC and UNM now offer a joint certificate in e-learning, which provides an opportunity for cultural and educational exchange to occur in a safe and structured online environment (OLIT, 2009). Furthermore, three additional research projects have been initiated as a result of Barberà's visit to UNM, leading professors at both universities to create a new program, update teaching approaches, and advance research in their field. This project, therefore, represents an exemplar of how distance learning research can drive changes to distance learning courses and programs, which in turn affect research.

ADVANCES IN INTERNATIONAL RESEARCH

With the proliferation of open-access journals, researchers from previously ignored areas of the world are being given a voice to advance the distance education research agenda. Topics such as culture, language, tutoring/mentoring, social software, and retention are gaining popularity in the international field of distance education.

Considering Culture and International Students

Distance education's ability to be delivered remotely comes at the expense of encouraging local initiatives, which value local culture and promote national beliefs, skills, and knowledge (Braimoh, 2001; Edmundson, 2007). Technology and course design typically embody elements of the dominant culture (Edmundson, 2007; McLoughlin & Oliver, 2000; Piecowye, 2003; Young, 2008). Current efforts to incorporate culture into the instructional design process notwithstanding (Linder-VanBerschot & Parrish, 2009; Thomas, Mitchell, & Joseph, 2002), online courses are overwhelmingly created by and for the dominant English-speaking cultures of the world. Albirini (2008) discussed the evolution of the Internet in developing countries and suggested that the Internet's adoption of Western culture and language has "facilitated the proliferation of alien cultural patterns at the expense of the social experiences of the local cultures" (para. 1).

Piecowye (2003), however, suggested that when international students enroll in courses designed or taught by people from different cultures, the students consciously choose what cultural elements, if any, they want to adopt. In the online courses he observed, Piecowye in fact found that the United Arab Emirate culture was reinforced by simulating the *majlis*, a traditional location where people meet to talk and seek guidance. Although distance education designers and researchers are beginning to include culture in their agenda, it is still too often discarded as an afterthought due to time or budget.

Language

When Wright and colleagues (2009) investigated distance education in developing and emerging nations, they found that one of the central challenges facing educators was language of instruction. Countries where several languages are spoken face the unique task of creating content and materials accessible to all their learners in that country. For example, Nigerians speak over 20 languages, 8 of which are official (Lewis, 2009). The challenge of providing content in the learners' native language is exemplified when one considers that there are almost 7,000 living languages in the world (Lewis, 2009). With the majority of online courses being developed according to Western standards, oftentimes these lesser-known languages and cultures are not even considered in the design process.

When nonnative English speakers join a course taught in English, they do not necessarily have the advantage of sharing culture and language with other members of the course. Hlas, Schuh, and Alessi (2008) investigated nonnative speakers' use of language in face-to-face and online learning environments using a mixed-methods analysis. Finding that nonnative speakers participated more consistently in online than in face-to-face discussions, they surmised that the difference might be due to these students having more time to reflect on the material and construct an argument when interacting in the asynchronous format. Linder-VanBerschot (2008) found that the asynchronous courses allowed nonnative English speakers an opportunity to lurk for a few days as they learned to navigate the course's structure and the communication conventions used by its participants. When the nonnative learners began to interact, they modeled their responses after those of native learners in the course. Language, like culture, is often overlooked in distance education research and design, but ignoring these factors impairs the effectiveness of educational efforts.

Tutoring and Mentoring

Tutor and mentor relationships are becoming increasingly positive in global online learning environments. Motteram and Forrester (2005) suggested that one of the essential components of a distance education program is to have tutors available to students. At the Universiti Tun Abdul Razak (UNITAR) in Malaysia, students taking distance education courses are required to attend face-to-face tutorial sessions at designated sites located throughout the country. Some degree programs also allow online tutorial sessions. Despite significant costs and scheduling challenges, UNITAR believes this model provides students with the support necessary for success (Alhabshi & Hakim, 2006). Stickler, Batstone, Duensing, and Heins (2007) provide tutors with several recommendations (including raising the tutor's awareness of the course expectations), and ensure their comfort level with working in an online environment.

Single and Single (2005) conducted a review of research on e-mentoring programs and found that the benefits of e-mentoring are similar to those of face-to-face mentoring, including impartiality and interorganizational connections. The government of Sri Lanka funded a 6-year Distance Education Modernization Project implemented by the Ministry of Higher Education. A training program was developed using a blended format of face-to-face workshops and online collaborative learning facilitated by e-tutors and e-mentors. The goal was to build the students' skills so that they could eventually teach in a problem-based online environment. Several studies have emerged from this work, including one that describes the transformative learning effects on the e-mentors (Gunawardena et al., 2007) and another that outlines the way in which e-mentors facilitated the social construction of knowledge within the group (Gunawardena et al., 2008). Mentoring and tutoring are especially valued when learners are from different countries and require additional support to succeed in the online learning environment.

Social Software

Learners today have more choices about how and where they learn (Greenhow, Robelia, & Hughes, 2009). Web 2.0 introduced platforms and services that increase the potential for developing community ontologies (Hatzipanagos & Warburton, 2009). Dalsgaard (2006) recommended that educators embrace these social software technologies as a means of actively engaging students. Social software allows for a safe and productive environment in which students can participate in real-time learning online. However, education providers remain tentative about such tools. Linder-VanBerschot and LaPointe (2009) created a model to outline the evolution of knowledge and sustainable innovation of community through the use of social software and knowledge management in an online environment. Although this model is based on current research, it has not yet been tested for usability.

When considering the bandwidth and censorship of different countries, not all social software is feasible or economical. For example, wikis may be accessible in countries where learners have limited Internet connectivity, but applications such as Second Life may not. The Australian Learning and Teaching Council used social software for supporting peer engagement and group learning (Ryan & Fitzgerald, 2009). Although

Australia has good bandwidth within the country, an increased number of international students who attend Australian online universities do not have the same luxury (Lanham & Zuou, 2003). Given increased demand for more flexible learning opportunities, Australian universities are using online and open learning to respond to their students' needs. Three Australian universities (University of Canberra, Queensland University of Technology, and Royal Melbourne Institute of Technology) created digital learning communities (DLCs) to enhance student community and peer engagement, to maximize accessibility, and to increase adoption by Australian university teachers. They suggest building social software technologies into programs to "engender a learning group ethos" (p. 171), allowing students to make their own connections between formal and informal learning opportunities. Like many new and emerging fields in distance education, a research framework is still very much needed.

Retention of Students

More conflicting information stems from retention studies. Research reports that distance education's isolating experience is frequently the cause of high dropout rates, ranging from 21% (Simpson, 2002) upward. Richardson (2000), however, found that dropout rates are frequently due to the characteristics of distance learners. These individuals are typically mature learners with family, work, and community responsibilities. Learners in developing countries often struggle to log on to online courses due to poor telecommunications infrastructure. Learners who fail to complete a course due to such conditions are "stopouts" rather than "dropouts."

Dahl (2004) identified three key strategies to increase retention in online programs. First, she recommended that all course content be timely, interesting, and relevant to the course objectives. Second, learners should have frequent interaction with and receive timely feedback from the instructor. Third, the instructor should minimize the feeling of isolation that discourages many online students by creating an interactive online learning community. Dahl suggests that these strategies promote communication and decrease online course attrition.

The hidden costs of dropouts and stopouts, once exposed, represent an opportunity to reexamine current mental models about education. Twigg (2003) reports that of 37,000 students enrolled in an introductory math class at one community college, but only 800 successfully completed their math requirement. Rethinking course design to alleviate unmet expectations and course repetitions could provide a significant source of funding for high-quality, high-touch investment in education. Equally important, a high dropout rate means that human preparedness remains globally underdeveloped, and the world's people are, therefore, limited in their capacity to deal with the issues they face (Maeroff, 2003).

AN INTERNATIONAL RESEARCH AGENDA

Meeting global learning needs and enhancing the learning experience by matching the learners' context with available technology remains an ongoing challenge in distance education (Panda & Mishra, 2007; Wright et al., 2009). Now that distance education is viewed as a reputable educational alternative for global development and human rights, and a respected partner to traditional face-to-face education, it is time to look at the field critically (Mason, 2006; Visser, 2003) and determine which lessons we have learned and should share.

At the turn of this century, Shive and Jegede (2001) suggested that research should be distance education's next important initiative, contributing to global economic development. There have been great advancements in distance education research during the past decade, yet leaders in the field still call for further research with more rigorous methods (Hannun, 2009; Zawacki-Richter, 2009), increased international focus (Uzuner, 2009; Wright et al., 2009), and operationalized key terms (Friesen, 2009; Raza, 2004). Garrison and Anderson (2003) summarized this concern for the field: "To date, published research and guides consist of innumerable case studies and personal descriptions and prescriptions, but little in the way of rigorous, research-based constructs that lead to an in-depth understanding of e-learning in higher education" (p. xi). Given the ubiquity of online and e-learning, leaders in the field are presented with enormous opportunities and risks. Thus, we need a cohesive approach to understanding the best methods for teaching and learning in an international online setting.

Garrison and Anderson (2003) recommended extending communities of inquiry (CoIs) for the purposeful sharing and conducting of research on distance education. CoIs may also increase the quality of standards adopted for the field. Tacchi, Foth, and Hearn (2009) took a similar approach by recommending the application of action research. They suggested a less formal method of research in order to give power to the people, especially those whose voices are often unheard, such as women, youth, people with disabilities, and people in poverty—people who constitute much of the world's population. In fact, Baggaley (2008) surmised that the greatest error of distance education is its failure to cater courses and research for the developing world that so desperately needs it. Friesen

(2009) similarly believed that multivocal research, or research that occurs in a wide variety of contexts and through a wide variety of means, "can make the difference between some research activity and none at all" (p. 230).

Raza (2004) explained the challenges in researching and obtaining data to assess the outcomes of online and distance learning. The research population often includes "students on the margin" (p. 210), who work full-time, live in geographically dispersed areas, and who are taking online courses because of life circumstances that do not allow for face-to-face instruction. Hence, it is more of a challenge to reach these students for research purposes. Furthermore, data management is a nominal priority in developing countries that are doing their best with the available resources. These should not be considered excuses, but rather mitigating factors that must be considered when conducting and critiquing distance education research (Bernard, Abrami, Lou, & Borokhovski, 2004). Researchers in the field "should aspire to the highest standards possible, given the limitations" (p. 170).

Because there are minimal standards in the field, it is nearly impossible to compare between institutions. Researchers are not using common descriptors such as means, standard deviation, and degree of reliability (Garrison & Anderson, 2003). Bernard et al. (2004) reviewed over 200 studies on distance education and concluded that overall they were "of poor methodological quality and severely lacking in critical information about research practices" (p. 175).

Given the lack of standard information, there are few meta-analyses in the field of distance education. Shachar and Neumann (2003) described the multiple hurdles they faced when they tried to complete a meta-analysis on the differences between traditional and online students. They documented profound differences in the reporting of treatments, settings, measurement instruments, and research methods. Bernard et al. (2004) added to the list a lack of experimental control, varied procedures for random selection and assignment, poorly designed dependent variables that lack reliability and validity, and failure to report on study and design.

The challenges facing distance education researchers are reflective of the field of education in general. Moss et al. (2009) engaged in a dialogue on the quality of education research. They suggested that educational researchers need to communicate across subfields and to recognize commonalities rather than constantly citing differences. They referenced a "breakdown in communication due to the 'multitude of tongues' within the field" causing researchers to "often 'talk past' each other, if they try to talk at all" (p. 501). They continued by highlighting genuine commonalities from which we can build. Similarly, Hine (2005) recognized that there are differences in the field of education, yet researchers should not be so naïve as to ignore best practices and lessons learned from other fields such as K–12 education. In reference to the war on qualitative versus quantitative research, Moss et al. agreed that both methodologies have standards of quality, utilize a strong chain of reasoning based on previous literature, and strive for genuine educational significance. Patton (2002) reminded us that "there are no perfect research designs. There are always trade-offs" (p. 223). However, he also called for enhanced standards for both designs, including providing theoretical underpinnings for qualitative research and more rigorous studying and reporting of results for quantitative research.

The purpose of this chapter is not to set an international research agenda, but instead to increase awareness of the different voices shaping the field of international online education. Improvements are being made in the field, and journals are largely to thank; they set guidelines and scrutinize submissions before sharing them with the larger audience. Perhaps Friesen (2009) expressed the most realistic approach in his statement that different types of research have different purposes, pose different questions, and thus yield vastly different contributions. Hine (2005) similarly suggested that the Internet means different things to different people and often reflects one's own concerns, thus driving research interests and approaches.

Regardless of the approach, good research is grounded in theory. Theory makes it possible to generate hypotheses about good practice, to frame experiments that will test these hypotheses and, as a result, develop more soundly based guides to practice (Perraton, 2000). However, despite the fact that distance education has been on the scene since the 1800s, research has not been central to its evolution. The field of distance education has been too busy meeting the teaching and learning needs of hundreds of thousands of off-campus students to make room for research activities, and the result has been detrimental.

LaPointe (2005) argued that distance education was a practice-driven rather than a theory-driven effort, drawing upon theories from other disciplines with little if any modification. As technologies and methods of teaching online advance, practice-driven research has continued to dominate the field. With the rapid advancement of tools, technologies, and social software, there is insufficient time to develop a theory that responds adequately to the day-to-day needs of online instructors; practice-driven research is more effective at responding to such direct needs. However, theory-driven research is necessary for generalizing findings and advancing the field; without it, leaders in our field cannot continue to create effective tools and practices for online learning.

Current Questions in the Field

When theory *is* absent, good research begins with a problem (Perraton, 2000). Perhaps the fundamental problem facing distance education is the question of how we can expand coverage, reduce inequalities of access and outcomes, and improve educational quality and relevance in financially sustainable ways (Daniel & Mackintosh, 2003). Addressing this problem through a solid research agenda will likely lead to improved, theory-based practice.

Zawacki-Richter (2009) invited all members of the editorial boards of four major distance education journals to respond to questions about research in distance education, including the most important and the most neglected areas in the field. Some 25 individuals from 11 countries, with an average of 27 years in the field, responded to his request. Unfortunately, the international voices were primarily from developed countries, thus eliminating an important population of distance educators from the conversation. Regardless, these scholars defined the most important areas of research to be interaction and communication in learning communities, innovation and change, and quality assurance. The most neglected areas included culture and cultural differences in global education.

Bernard et al. (2004) suggested several directions for future research, including

- developing a theoretical framework for distance education;
- studying student motivational dispositions for taking and completing online courses;
- studying student readiness for distance and online learning to better understand achievement and satisfaction;
- studying teacher and tutor skills and readiness;
- examining pedagogical features such as faculty development and the use of synchronous versus asynchronous learning tools;
- studying levels of learning and which instructional strategies are most appropriate for the different levels;
- examining inclusivity and accessibility for all learners despite differences in language, intellectual capability, location, etc.; and
- using more rigorous and complete research methodologies.

Uzuner (2009) conducted a review of research on culture in distance education literature by reviewing 27 studies, composed of qualitative, quantitative, and mixed-methods research. She suggested that future researchers investigate the culture of minority versus majority students.

Second, she recommended that researchers look beyond Asian learners and study the influence of culture on students from other countries, including among others, Germany, Iran, and India. Finally, she echoed Gunawardena et al. (2001) in recommending that researchers not overlook the individual differences within cultural groups.

New research questions emerge from research and literature reviews. How do distance education leaders set research standards when the field and tools are constantly emerging? Gulati (2008) documented how this is an extraordinary challenge for developing nations that devote extensive time and effort to bringing in distance education tools without referring to research on which tools are most effective. Does technology shape us as researchers or do researchers shape technology? With this perplexing question in mind, Friesen (2009) called for "approaches to research that are similarly flexible, multiple and differentiated" (p. 235). What will be the next form of open learning? Lenhart, Madden, Macgill, and Smith (2007) referred to multichannel communication as being an option, in which students communicate through multiple modes such as text messaging, instant messaging, and communication through social networking sites. To what extent do scholars need to reframe their research questions to respond to developing Web 2.0 issues? Greenhow et al. (2009) suggested that students need to be studied as producers, not recipients, of knowledge. They also provided lists of research questions for education researchers interested in understanding and shaping the Web 2.0 field. With all of these avenues ripe for exploration, researchers, graduate students, designers, and others invested in international online education should be energized to work together on pushing the field forward.

CONCLUSION

Leaders in distance education are working toward a systemic, theory-driven research agenda that captures the intellectual spirit of the field, incorporates the major issues attracting the attention of scholars and distance education practitioners (Roblyer & Knezek, 2003), and addresses human rights and economic development. Necessity is the mother of invention. The critical need has now surfaced for distance education to develop an international agenda that features systematic, longitudinal, in-depth component analyses; theoretical comparisons of strategies for fostering transformative learning of individuals and societies; and use of alternative methodological designs. Microscopic orientations on particular components that are known to be essential to distance education—including course design, culture, language, tutoring/mentoring, social software, and retention—are increasing demand. Large-scale, summative and formative evaluations are also needed, so that learning gains are empirically documented (Bork & Gunnarsdottir, 2001). To achieve that systemic theory of distance education, a set of reliable, consistent research results are essential.

Distance education should not be charged with solving all educational problems. It has become a recognized, valued partner in creatively meeting global learning needs, but is only a part of the larger educational system. By giving people the educational tools to address critical global problems, distance learning has the potential to promote economic development and higher standards of health and nutrition, reduce poverty, and foster cleaner and sustainable environments, mutual respect, and international peace and security. The development and implementation of a rigorous, systematic distance education international research agenda is critical, for without such, educational efforts may be met with continuing failure.

ACKNOWLEDGMENTS

Deborah K. LaPointe (1952–2009) wrote the first version of this chapter. Jennifer A. Linder-VanBerschot used her work and research as a foundation for writing this second version. This chapter is dedicated to the passion and drive with which Deb LaPointe adopted online technologies to provide educational opportunities to learners around the world. The author would also like to acknowledge Leanne Silverman, who asked great questions and provided the feedback necessary to create the chapter that you have before you.

COMPREHENSION AND APPLICATION QUESTIONS

1. Consider the statement: Distance education is a practice-driven effort. What evidence can you provide to support/refute this statement?

2. What do you consider to be the primary research questions in the field of distance education for your country? How might these questions differ if you were living in a more/less privileged country with a different set of resources?

3. What can you do to make distance education research have a more profound influence on theory?

RESOURCES FOR FURTHER EXPLORATION

Edmundson, A. (Ed.). (2007). *Globalized e-learning cultural challenges.* Hershey, PA:
Information Science.
Andrea Edmundson provides a collection of literature reviews, research, case
studies, perspectives, and lessons learned from authors around the world, thus
creating a set of issues and solutions for global online educators, administrators, and instructional designers. This book poses a strong case for moving outside of Western norms to develop more globally responsive online courses.

Evans, T., Haughey, M., & Murphy, D. (Eds.). (2008). *International handbook of distance education.* Bingley, England: Emerald Group.
With contributions from leading scholars, this comprehensive collection offers
useful information on improving course design and delivery. Instructors, policymakers, managers, and instructional designers will find much to consider in
terms of policy and advancement in the field of distance education.

Moore, M. G. (2007). *Handbook of distance learning* (2nd ed.). Mahwah, NJ: Erlbaum.
This edited book, one of the most comprehensive available, offers an excellent
overview of significant trends and topics in the field. The bibliographic references provide a solid list of resources for researchers or students developing a
particular topic. Chapters such as Gunawardena and LaPointe's on the cultural
dynamics of online learning remind the reader that culture should be a central
consideration for online and distance education programs.

Hatzipanagos, S., & Warburton, S. (Eds.). (2009). *Handbook of research on social software and developing community ontologies.* Hershey, PA: Information Science.
Recognizing that the rise of social software and social networking tools has
forced a cultural shift in the way we learn and communicate, the contributors
investigate the impact of these new technologies and how they are transforming our online behavior.

International Review of Research in Open and Distance Learning. Available at
http://www.irrodl.org/index.php/irrodl/index
IRRODL is an open-access international journal that presents original
research, theory, and best practices in open and distance learning. Both
authors and articles represent a global perspective, pushing readers to think
of the broader context in which they develop and deliver online courses.

REFERENCES

Albirini, A. (2008). The Internet in developing countries: A medium of economic,
cultural and political domination [Electronic version]. *International Journal of
Education and Development using ICT, 4.* Retrieved from http://
ijedict.dec.uwi.edu/viewarticle.php?id=360&layout=html

Alhabshi, S. O., & Hakim, H. (2006). Universiti tun Abdul Razak (UNITAR), Malaysia. In S. D'Antoni (Ed.), *The virtual university: Models and messages*. Paris, France: UNESCO.

Baggaley, J. (2008). Where did distance education go wrong? *Distance Education, 29*(1), 39–51.

Barrett, K. A. (2008). *An exploration of EFL teachers' and learners' lived experiences in a synchronous online VOIP-enabled cross cultural language learning environment.* Albuquerque: University of New Mexico.

Bernard, R. M., Abrami, P. C., Lou, Y., & Borokhovski, E. (2004). A methodological morass? How we can improve quantitative research in distance education. *Distance Education, 25*(2), 175–198.

Bork, A., & Gunnarsdottir, S. (2001). *Tutorial distance learning: Rebuilding our educational system.* New York, NY: Kluwer.

Braimoh, D. (2001). The effectiveness of distance education delivery methods in continuing education programs in Lesotho. In T. Evan (Ed.), *Research in distance education* (pp. 97-111). Australia: Deakin University Press.

Dahl, J. (2004). Strategies for 100 percent retention: Feedback, interaction. *Distance Education Report, 8*(16), 1, 6–7.

Dalsgaard, C. (2006). Social software: E-learning beyond learning management systems [Electronic version]. *European Journal of Open, Distance and E-learning, 2*. Retrieved from http://www.eurodl.org/materials/contrib/2006/Christian_Dalsgaard.htm

Daniel, J., & Mackintosh, W. (2003). Leading ODL futures in the eternal triangle: The mega-university response to the greatest moral challenge of our age. In M. Moore & W. Anderson (Eds.), *Handbook of distance education* (pp. 811–827). Mahwah, NJ: Erlbaum.

Ding, X. (2001). Information technology revolution and development of distance education in China. *Global E-Journal of Open, Flexible & Distance Education, 1*(1).

Edmundson, A. (Ed.). (2007). *Globalized e-learning cultural challenges.* Hershey, PA: Information Science.

Friesen, N. (2009). *Re-thinking e-learning research: Foundations, methods, and practices* (Vol. 333). New York, NY: Peter Lang.

Garrison, D. R., & Anderson, T. (2003). *E-learning in the 21st century: A framework for research and practice* London, England: RoutledgeFalmer.

Greenhow, C., Robelia, B., & Hughes, J. E. (2009). Learning, teaching and scholarship in a digital age. *Educational Researcher, 38*(4), 246–259.

Gulati, S. (2008). Technology-enhanced learning in developing nations: A review. *International Review of Research in Open and Distance Learning, 9*(1).

Gunawardena, C. N., Linder-VanBerschot, J. A., LaPointe, D. K., Barrett, K. A., Mummert, J., Cardiff, M. S., & Skinner, J. (2007, October). *Learning transformations through cross-cultural e-mentoring: Perspectives from an online faculty development forum.* Paper presented at the Seventh International Transformative Learning Conference, Albuquerque, NM.

Gunawardena, C. N., Nolla, A. C., Wilson, P. L., Lopez-Islas, J. R., Ramirez-Angel, N., & Megchun-Alpizar, R. M. (2001). A cross-cultural study of group process and development in online conferences. *Distance Education, 22*(1), 85–121.

Gunawardena, C. N., Skinner, J., Richmond, C., LaPointe, D. K., Barrett, K. A., Cardiff, M. S., ... Padmaperuma, G. (2008, March). *Cross-cultural e-mentoring to develop problem-solving online learning communities*. Paper presented at the American Educational Research Association annual conference, New York, NY.

Hannun, W. (2009). Moving distance education research forward. *Distance Education, 30*(1), 171–173.

Hatzipanagos, S., & Warburton, S. (Eds.). (2009). *Handbook of research on social software and developing community ontologies*. Hershey, PA: Information Science.

Hine, C. (2005). Virtual methods and the sociology of cyber-social-scientific knowledge. In C. Hine (Ed.), *Virtual methods: Issues in social research on the Internet* (pp. 1–16). Oxford, England: Berg.

Hlas, A. C., Schuh, K. L., & Alessi, S. M. (2008). Native and non-native speakers in online and face-to-face discussions: Leveling the playing field. *Journal of Educational Technology Systems, 36*(4), 337–373.

Hülsmann, T. (2004). Guest editorial: Low cost distance education strategies: The use of appropriate information and communication technologies. *International Review of Research in Open and Distance Learning, 5*(1).

Lanham, E., & Zuou, W. (2003). Cultural issues in online learning: Is blended learning a possible solution? *International Journal of Computer Processing of Oriental Languages, 16*(4), 275–292.

LaPointe, D. K. (2005). Distance education international research: What the world needs now. In Y. L. Visser, L. Visser, M. Simonson, & R. Amirault (Eds.), *Trends and issues in distance education: International perspectives* (1st ed., pp. 67–79). Greenwich, CT: Information Age.

LaPointe, D. K. (2006). The role of transformational learning in distance education: Becoming aware. In M. Beaudoin (Ed.), *Perspectives on higher education in the digital age* (pp. 91–109). New York, NY: Nova Science.

LaPointe, D. K., Greysen, K. B., &, & Barrett, K. A. (2004). Speak2Me: Using synchronous audio for ESL teaching in Taiwan. *The International Review of Research in Open and Distance Learning, 5*(1).

Lenhart, A., Madden, M., Macgill, A. R., & Smith, A. (2007). *Teens and social media*. Washington, DC: Pew Charitable Trusts.

Lewis, M. P. (Ed.). 2009. *Ethnologue: Languages of the world* (16th ed.). Dallas, TX: SIL International. Retrieved from http://www.ethnologue.com/web.asp

Linder-VanBerschot, J. A. (2008). *An exploration of communication conventions used by non-native learners in asynchronous online courses*. Albuquerque: University of New Mexico.

Linder-VanBerschot, J. A., & LaPointe, D. K. (2009). A model for knowledge and innovation in online education. In S. Hatzipanagos & S. Warburton (Eds.), *Handbook of research on social software and developing community ontologies* (pp. 254–268). Hershey, PA: Information Science.

Linder-VanBerschot, J. A., & Parrish, P. (2009, August). *We're in it together: Adopting a multicultural approach in online environments*. Paper presented at the Colorado Learning and Teaching with Technology Conference, Boulder, CO.

Maeroff, G. I. (2003). *A classroom of one*. New York, NY: Palgrave Macmillan.

Mason, A. (2006). The university: Current challenges and opportunities. In S. D'Antoni (Ed.), *The virtual university: Models and messages*. Paris, France: UNESCO.

McLoughlin, C., & Oliver, R. (2000). Designing learning environments for cultural inclusivity: A case study of indigenous online learning at tertiary level [Electronic version]. *Australian Journal of Educational Technology, 16*(1), 58–72. Retrieved from http://www.ascilite.org.au/ajet/ajet16/mcloughlin.html

Moore, M. G., & Kearsley, G. (1996). *Distance education: A systems view*. San Francisco, CA: Wadsworth.

Moss, P. A., Phillips, D. C., Erickson, F. D., Floden, R. E., Lather, P. A., & Schneider, B. L. (2009). Learning from our differences: A dialogue across perspectives on quality in education research. *Educational Researcher, 38*(7), 501–517.

Motteram, G., & Forrester, G. (2005). Becoming an online distance learner: What can be learned from students' experiences of induction to distance programmes? *Distance Education, 26*, 281–298.

Organizational Learnig & Instructional Technology (OLIT). (2009). Retrieved from http://www.unm.edu/~olit/index.html#olitUoc

Panda, S., & Mishra, S. (2007). E-learning in a mega open university: Faculty attitude, barriers and motivation. *Educational Media International, 44*(4), 323–338.

Patton M. Q. (2002). *Qualitative research and evaluation methods*. Thousand Oaks, CA: SAGE.

Perraton, H. (2000). Rethinking the research agenda. *International Review of Research in Open and Distance Learning, 1*(1).

Piecowye, J. (2003). Habitus in transition? CMC use and impacts among young women in the United Arab Emirates. *Journal of Computer Mediated Communication, 8*(2).

Raza, R. (2004). Benefits for students, labour force, employers and society. In H. Perraton & H. Lentell (Eds.), *Policy for open and distance learning: World review of distance education and open learning* (Vol. 4, pp. 209–223). London, England: RoutledgeFalmer.

Richardson, J. T. E. (2000). *Researching student learning: Approaches to studying in campus-based and distance education* (pp. 123–136). Philadelphia, PA: Open University.

Roblyer, M. D., & Knezek, G. A. (2003). New millennium research for educational technology: A call for a national research agenda. *Journal of Research on Technology in Education, 36*(1), 60–71.

Ryan, Y., & Fitzgerald, R. (2009). Exploring the role of social software in higher education. In S. Hatzipanagos & S. Warburton (Eds.), *Handbook of research on social software and developing community ontologies* (pp. 159–173). Hershey, PA: Information Science.

Shachar, M., & Neumann, Y. (2003). Differences between traditional and distance education academic performances: A meta-analytic approach. *International Review of Research in Open and Distance Learning, 4*(2).

Shive, G., & Jegede, O. (2001). Introduction: Trends and issues in open and distance education in Asia and the Pacific. In O. Jegede & G. Shive (Eds.), *Open and distance education in the Asia Pacific region* (pp. 1–24). Hong Kong: Open University of Hong Kong Press.

Simpson, O. (2002). *Supporting students in online, open and distance learning.* Sterling, VA: Stylus.

Single, P. B., & Single, R. M. (2005). E-mentoring for social equity: Review of research to inform program development. *Mentoring and Tutoring, 13*(2), 301–320.

Stickler, U., Batstone, C., Duensing, A., & Heins, B. (2007). Distant classmates: Speech and silence in online and telephone language tutorials [Electronic version]. *European Journal of Open, Distance and E-learning.* Retrieved from http://www.eurodl.org/materials/contrib/2007/Stickler_Batstone_Duensing_Heins.html

Tacchi, J., Foth, M., & Hearn, G. (2009). Action research practices and media for development [Electronic version]. *International Journal of Education and Development using ICT, 5.* Retrieved from http://ijedict.dec.uwi.edu/viewarticle.php?id=560&layout=html

Thomas, M., Mitchell, M., & Joseph, R. (2002). The third dimension of ADDIE: A cultural embrace. *TechTrends, 46*(2), 40–45.

Twigg, C. A. (2003). Quality, cost, and access: The case for redesign. In M. S. Pittinsky (Ed.), *The wired tower* (pp. 111–143). San Francisco, CA: Pearson.

Uzuner, S. (2009). Questions of culture in distance learning: A research review. *International Review of Research in Open and Distance Learning, 10*(3).

Visser, J. (2003). Distance education in the perspective of global issues and concerns. In M. G. Moore & W. G. Anderson (Eds.), *Handbook of distance education* (pp. 793–810). Mahwah, NJ: Erlbaum.

Wright, C. R., Dhanarajan, G., & Reju, S. A. (2009). Recurring issues encountered by distance educators in developing and emerging nations. *International Review of Research in Open and Distance Learning, 10*(1).

Young, P. A. (2008). The culture based model: Constructing a model of culture. *Education Technology & Society, 11*(2), 107–118.

Zawacki-Richter, O. (2009). Research areas in distance education: A Delphi study. *International Review of Research in Open and Distance Learning, 10*(3). Retrieved from http://www.irrodl.org/index.php/irrodl/article/viewFile/674/1294

CHAPTER 2

WHY DON'T WE SIMPLY CALL IT "ENVIRONMENTAL DESIGN FOR THE PROVISION AND USE OF DISTRIBUTED LEARNING RESOURCES?"

Jan Visser

Opportunities for learning vary greatly around the world. The author has been involved in educational development worldwide for more than 40 years. He discusses trends and issues in distance education against the backdrop of his experience of working in a world of great discrepancy in which the key problems now faced by humanity are increasingly intertwined and complex, requiring equitable human development on a global scale with a particular focus on the fourth pillar of education for the twenty-first century identified in the Delors et al. (1996) report, namely, "learning to live together, learning to live with others" (p. 91). He argues that the traditional conception of distance education, as currently defined by the majority of authors, is increasingly less helpful for envisioning a learning landscape that best serves citizens of the twenty-first century. He concludes that new visions of human learning are required and argues that the field of distance education is in a unique position to shape such visions in practical terms.

Trends and Issues in Distance Education:
International Perspectives, Second Edition, pp. 23–38
Copyright © 2012 by Information Age Publishing

MY VANTAGE POINT

Trends and issues exist in the mind of the beholder. To discern trends and issues requires having an overall vision that serves as a conceptual frame in which issues are embedded and against which trends become distinguishable. I therefore start off explaining where I come from.

I have worked around the globe for many decades, trying to contribute, however modestly, to improving the human condition, particularly where it is needed most: in Africa. I consider consciousness to be among the most human of human characteristics and thus care for its development. Consciousness is key to being able to improve one's condition. It allows us to look at our world and at ourselves as actors in the world—actors who have agency, who can ask themselves questions, think about alternative ways of intervening, imagining alternative futures.

Learning (not to be confused with memorization of facts) is a particularly important way to improve our capacity to consciously participate in collaboratively shaping the future. Distance education is one among many alternative ways through which human learning can be stimulated, structured, and facilitated. Its importance and relevance are thus best explored in the context of a more broadly defined learning landscape. This brings me to my first issue.

THE NEED TO BREAK THROUGH THE
BOUNDARIES OF THE FIELD

I define distance education as *any set of purposefully devised procedures and resources to support people's learning in ways that focus on the learners' ability to choose when and where to engage in a particular instance of learning*. This definition is wider than definitions employed by most other authors (e.g., Delling, 1987; Keegan, 1986; Moore & Kearsley, 1996; Perraton, 1988; Simonson, Smaldino, Albright, & Zvacek, 2006). Note that I make no reference, explicitly or implicitly, to the necessary presence of a teacher, in whatever guise. All other definitions do.

In fact, I no longer find the term *distance education* particularly useful. If I still use it, I do so because it has become a well-established term that vaguely binds together a community of practice that reads books like the one you hold in your hands. "Environmental design for the provision and use of distributed learning resources"—a notion proposed in the title of this chapter—comes closer to my vision of what is needed. No doubt, using the well-established term *distance education* places one within an important historical perspective, a perspective that goes from *correspondence education* via *distance education* to *e-learning* and *m-learning*. However, whatever name changes follow each other evermore rapidly as new technologies emerge, that same community of practice has now moved from being the innovative force it once was to becoming a well-established, rather inward-looking, field of expertise at risk of losing its creative spirit. Replacing old technologies with new ones for doing the same old thing is hardly creative; fundamentally changing the uses of existing or emerging technologies is. There is a need to break through the boundaries of the field.

UNFULFILLED PROMISES, PARTICULARLY FOR THE DEVELOPING WORLD

My interest in distance education is closely associated with the four decades during which I worked in parts of the world where going to school is a privilege rather than the exercise of the fundamental right defined in the Universal Declaration of Human Rights (1948; cited in UNESCO, 2000). Beyond the question that human rights are there to be upheld, I add to this the consideration that a large proportion of human potential to contribute to positive change is wasted as long as 101 million children in the primary school age around the world do not go to school (UNICEF, 2009), 49 million of them living in Africa and 40 million in Asia, the majority of them being girls. Moreover, the conditions in which hundreds of millions do go to school make it unlikely that their learning will profoundly touch their lives.

So long as the above situation perpetuates, any important advances in our understanding of the workings of nature and of the intricacies of human individual and social behavior are unlikely to come from those parts of the world where opportunities to engage in serious systematic learning are either absent or deficient. This means, for instance, that the chances that a major response will be found to urgent challenges the world is facing—think of a cure for AIDS or the development of truly workable mechanisms for sustainable and equitable development—remain limited to only a minor, privileged proportion of the available global brain mass. Consider in this context that, as the history of science shows, nothing whatsoever indicates that major advances in human understanding are predicated on a particular segment, be it race or any other subdivision, of the human species, and it will be immediately clear that humanity is seriously and stupendously foolishly shortchanging itself in opportunities to develop its so much needed shared wisdom.

Both for the sake of human rights and because it makes good common sense, there is a dramatic need to develop the learning capacity of our species integrally, everyone included. I believe that distance education has the potential to make its contribution to this goal. The assumed promise of distance education to make a major impact on the developing world has long been touted. It led UNESCO during the mid-1960s to undertake a major study concerning the potential of media to improve education (Schramm, Coombs, Kahnert, & Lyle, 1967); it was the premise for an influential book, *Distance Teaching for the Third World*, published a decade and a half later (Young, Perraton, Jenkins, & Dodds, 1980); it inspired the discourse that emerged from the World Conference on Education for All held in Jomtien, Thailand, in March 1990 (Inter-Agency Commission World Conference on Education for All, 1990); and it prompted a major UN initiative for the cooperative development of distance education in the nine so-called high-population countries, countries that are together home to more than half the world's population and the large majority of its illiterates (J. Visser, 1995). However, while gradual improvements can be gleaned from a comparison of data collected over time, no major breakthrough can, unfortunately, be reported. What went wrong? Consider the following possible reasons.

The desire to innovate, which drove the work of early distance education developers, led to thinking in terms of solutions found that could be plugged into identified problems elsewhere without much further consideration. The fact that contexts could be greatly different was often ignored. In fact, the need to take context into account, particularly as regards the huge differences that distinguish developing nations among themselves and that differentiate them from industrialized nations, while occasionally noted in the literature of the past, has only relatively recently received some serious attention in the instructional design field, thanks to a much-quoted article by Tessmer and Richey (1995). Arias and Clark (2004) pay attention to this matter with a view to the particular circumstances in developing countries.

A related issue is the gradual development in the distance education field of a sharp focus on cost-effectiveness and economies of scale. The fact that learning needs can be attended to through distance education at a reduced cost as long as high development costs can be spread over a large number of users has gradually become a major argument in defense of distance education over traditional modalities of educational provision. The argument is obviously valid, but its importance has sometimes been overemphasized to the extent that distance education has become attractive to politicians who wish to claim that they have at least done something to reduce deficits in schooling. A trend has thus emerged to document best practices and make information about such practices available to potential users in different parts of the world to adopt or adapt them. While there are obvious advantages to following this trend, the drawback is that it stifles creativity and innovation. A better balance between the desire to apply quick fixes and the long-term need to develop real solutions must be found.

In the above context, it is essential to go beyond superficial interpretations of what it means to learn. In fact, the opportunity offered by the advent of distance education (now often in the form of online learning) has, perhaps surprisingly, not led to asking any substantially deeper questions than the one regarding equivalency of experience between classroom learning and distance education (Simonson, 2000). Asking that question is only reasonable if one is convinced that classroom learning is the best of options and cannot be improved upon. But it's missing the chance for critical inquiry into current practice and experimentation with alternatives. Deeper questioning is called for.

What if the classroom weren't the best of all possible alternatives, and it would thus not be appropriate to consider the classroom as the standard of ultimate quality? What about the critique of the schooling culture (e.g., Shikshantar, [http://www.swaraj.org/shikshantar]) and the banking concept of education (Freire, 1972)? Can the possibilities offered by distance education help overcome, at least in part, the shortcomings of existing practice and the flaws of the schooling culture? Would it be possible to create something entirely better than what we currently have by taking a few steps back and first asking ourselves what we actually want when we create the conditions of human learning for the generations of the third millennium and only then start creating anew, and from scratch, the environments that are most propitious for achieving what we want? Doing so would avoid what now often is the trend, namely, that we adopt, without further ado, the same assumptions that underlie educational practice of the past and build around those assumptions distance education systems that surprisingly closely resemble the existing face-to-face practice. Considering that the brain, the seat of consciousness and the processing of information, plays a crucial role in how we learn, what is it that we now know about brain functioning and the growth of neural networks in ways that reflect our life's experience (Greenfield, 2000) that could relevantly inform the creative design of media-facilitated learning environments and "create a new science of learning that may transform educational practices" (Meltzoff, Kuhl, Movellan, & Sejnowski, 2009)? And as we rebuild the environments in which people learn, can they be built so as to allow those who participate in their processes to attain a truly deep and critical understanding and appreciation of their world (e.g., Bereiter, 2002; Bereiter & Scardamalia, 2003; Perkins, 1993, 1998)? These are but a few of the questions that ought to be asked if distance education is to remain true to its original inspiration to advance the state of learning through innovation rather than to merely replicate its current occurrences using alternative means.

COMMODITIZED EDUCATION OR DIGNIFIED LEARNING?

A trend has emerged to equate the creation of learning opportunities with the provision of commodities to consumers whose particular preferences, tastes, and styles of consumption can be made to match the items available on a limited menu. One finds this philosophy expressed, for instance, in an editorial note by Daniel (2002), in *Education Today*, the newsletter of UNESCO's Education Sector. Daniel's rationale is based on considerations of economy. It makes sense from that perspective.

However, the trend toward commoditization is also rooted in a rather limited, superficial, and simplistic vision of what actually happens when someone interacts with given learning opportunities. Certainly, part of what learning is (and that is the part covered by most conventional definitions of learning) can be understood in terms of delivery and subsequent consumption of a commodity. That part is not unimportant, but more is at stake. It all depends on what we do with consumable products. A more comprehensive and encompassing perspective on learning is needed. Such a perspective should ensure that the complexity of the world's problems is adequately reflected in the complexity of learning processes that evolve within a richly diverse learning ecology (see also J. Visser, 2001, 2003; J. Visser & Visser, 2002). Certain dimensions of the rich and complex reality of human learning can benefit from Daniel's vision. However, great care should be taken not to overemphasize this aspect and to be well aware of the great inherent risks of too strong a focus on learning as consumption of commodities.

The question of commoditization is linked to another trend, namely, to think of instruction as something that can be designed based on the use of reusable and scalable so-called learning objects. Learning objects are building blocks whose potential use to facilitate learning can be described in the form of metadata. They can be plugged in and out of a particular instructional context in any instructionally relevant manner. This allows instruction to be adaptable as well as generative. The assumed scalability of object-oriented instructional design makes this procedure attractive from an economic point of view in much the same way as discussed for the economies of scale concept that has pushed the development of distance education along. However, actual practice is often at odds with otherwise rational expectations. Why? Probably because we find it difficult, if not outright impossible, to simultaneously entertain different mindsets. By putting our focus on a particular technology, or some proven way of addressing problems, we are at risk of closing our eyes to other technologies or nontechnological (e.g., human) aspects. Thus, Parrish (2004) observes that "the problems of education are always more complex than technology alone can solve" (p. 51). Along with other authors, such as

Jonassen and Land (2000), Parrish draws attention to how a particular focus, in conjunction with the terminology in which it is expressed, sets one up in terms of attitudes and perspective that look at learning in only one way, ignoring alternatives.

The use of the commoditization metaphor is not innocent. Thinking of learning in terms of the provision of commodities creates a view of a world full of consumers. However, consuming is but one of the things humans do. While some may decide to limit their existence to mere consumption, others create meaning and dignity in their lives, transcending such basic behaviors. Learning can be greatly more dignified than the commoditization metaphor suggests. One of our greatest challenges is to restore its dignity. Technology may well be instrumental in meeting the challenge, provided we are able to look beyond the technology.

LEARNING AUTONOMOUSLY IN AN ENVIRONMENT OF DISTRIBUTED RESOURCES

The development of distance education and the rapid and pervasive spread of technologies have greatly diversified the conditions under which people learn. Little has changed, though, in how people are being prepared to reap the benefit of such diverse wealth. Where well-established education systems exist, people's first exposure to deliberately created learning opportunities occurs when they go to school or kindergarten, usually when they are between 4 and 6 years old. This is also their first opportunity to reflect on how they learn and what learning means to them. In countries with a less perfect school system, young people's initiation in such reflection will be more haphazard and therefore also more varied. However, for those who enter the world of learning via the school, their initiation into thinking about learning will naturally focus on the school context.

Sfard (1998) identifies two major metaphors that guide learners, teachers, and researchers in their thinking about what happens in the context of deliberately planned learning events. She calls them the "acquisition metaphor" (p. 5) and the "participation metaphor" (p. 6), and warns against choosing just one of those metaphors. Looking at learning from the perspective of the acquisition metaphor leads, according to Sfard, to a vision that

- emphasizes the individual learner and that person's individual enrichment as the prime goal of the learning event;
- interprets learning as an act of acquiring something;

- sees the student as recipient or (re-)constructor of a commodity that becomes the student's property and views the teacher as a provider, facilitator, and/or mediator in helping the students to acquire that commodity; and
- perceives knowing as having or possessing something.

By contrast, the perspective provided by the participation metaphor leads to a view of learning that

- emphasizes community building as the prime goal of the learning event;
- interprets learning in terms of becoming a participant in a social learning event and the environment that affords the event;
- sees students and teachers as co-participants with roles as apprentices and experts, respectively; and
- perceives of knowing as "belonging, participating, [and] communicating" (p. 7).

In her essay, Sfard (1998) draws attention to how the vocabulary associated with the acquisition metaphor pervades the discourse about learning. Those who enter the world of learning through the doors of the school thus easily end up being prepared for further learning in terms of that same metaphor. It is therefore no surprise that many of the distance education experiences, including the modern-day e-learning variety, simply replicate the traditional school model by different means. After all, most of those experiences were devised by people who are themselves the product of the acquisition metaphor. Somewhere the cycle must be broken to make way for a richer level of thinking, inspired by multiple metaphors, to understand the full complexity of learning. Our modern-day information and communication technologies and the experience gathered over the decades to build new learning experiences provide an excellent opportunity to do so. But where should we start?

The current trend in preparing learners for their participation in unfamiliar learning experiences, such as online learning, is to provide just-in-time advice, often in the form of checklists. The *E-Learning Companion* by Watkins and Corry (2010) is an example. So are the many dedicated web pages that online learning providers offer for the benefit of their students. A quick web search will turn up many good as well as bad examples. Such advice, if well-conceived, can be useful for online learners and face-to-face learners alike. De la Teja and Spannaus (2008) argue that "the specific set of competencies required in any setting for a particular learning event is driven by the strategy of the event, not whether it is online or face-to-face" (p. 187).

Given the great variety of learning opportunities people will encounter along the life span, more is needed. Current generations grow up in a continually changing learning landscape. Capability development to explore emerging learning opportunities should therefore start as early as possible in the family environment and continue throughout kindergarten and the school years. The skills to explore distributed learning opportunities, autonomously and collaboratively with others, should continue to be perfected as learners progress through life. To make this work, it will be necessary to make new generations think about learning by providing deliberate learning experiences that are varied in meaning and that can be described using vocabulary associated with multiple metaphors. And where better to begin than right at the start?

Research, rather than mere intuition, will be necessary to identify and validate the competencies today's learners must possess. Efforts continue to undertake such research, by, among others, the International Board of Standards for Training, Performance and Instruction (http://www.ibstpi.org/projects.htm). Ibstpi's effort recognizes that online learning environments currently provide the broadest range of challenges to learners. Thus, the complete set of competencies and related specific performance statements to be developed must be expected to also be relevant for other settings and circumstances in which people learn. It is important, though, that such research efforts be guided by visions of human learning that go beyond the traditional views. Work to establish such enhanced visions was initiated in the late 1990s by UNESCO, for example, in the framework of the Delors et al. (1996) report and the work of the Learning Without Frontiers (1999) initiative. The LIFE (Learning in Informal and Formal Environments) Center and the Learning Development Institute are among several institutions that carry this work forward.

STARTING ANEW OR BUILDING ON FOUNDATIONS ALREADY LAID?

There is a tendency throughout the history of the development of distance education to replace technologies whenever new ones become available rather than continuing to improve the use of existing technologies and enhance them through the inclusion of new ones while at the same time exploring the additional benefits such new technologies may offer. The tendency is understandable if one considers that most of those involved in developing educational alternatives are, by the nature of their trade, innovators in the sense defined by Rogers (2003). They are only too eager to try out anything new. It is one of the psychological traits present among a significant minority of humans that is necessary to lead others to eventually follow them. Without it, innovation would not diffuse the way it does. However, there is a costly downside to being innovative in too uncontrolled a fashion or rather, in a manner of being too much focused on the tools instead of the issues.

A typical example of the above phenomenon could be observed when the computer science community realized that its tools, which so perfectly allow everyone to communicate with everyone and stored information to be accessible across the globe, had great potential for building virtual learning environments. The term *e-learning* quickly emerged for electronic variants of learning settings that usually closely resembled the well-known school context, except that the teacher was not in the same location as the student. It took the computer science community some time to discover that something called *distance education* had preceded the invention of e-learning by decades and, though it had employed older technologies, was not conceptually very different from e-learning. There are advantages and disadvantages in such developments. The clear advantage of ignoring the past is that one will not be bogged down by it. The disadvantage, though, is that one cannot learn from past mistakes or build on past achievements. Rather than choosing between ignorance and slavishly persisting in patterns of the past, the greater wisdom lies in being critically aware of both past and present. Such awareness helps inventing approaches that are more profoundly innovative in that they go deeper than merely changing superficial detail. A back-to-basics approach is required, which asks questions about the kind of learning that best serves today's citizens and that explores the factors that facilitate such learning. Among those factors are technological ones, but not solely. Answers to questions about what technologies to use and how to use them will follow naturally from such prior considerations.

Consider this. During the 1990s, extensive discussions took place under the auspices of UNESCO about what education would be required for the twenty-first century. The international commission considering the question concluded that "learning to live together, learning to live with others" was "probably one of the major issues in education today" (Delors et al., 1996, p. 91). Only years before the Delors report came out, technologies had emerged uniquely suited to meeting the challenge of learning to live together. However, with few exceptions (e.g., Patarakin & Visser, 2003), little changed for those involved in designing virtual learning environments. Their major challenge remained to replicate as well as possible by different means (and if possible, to improve) existing models inspired by the traditional school learning practice, ignoring the opportunity to design something entirely new, based on a new conception of what it means to learn.

LEARNING BEYOND SKILLS DEVELOPMENT

My focus in this chapter is on trends and issues in distance education from a global human development perspective. The state of human development worldwide can be gleaned from the Human Development Report (http://hdr.undp.org/), published annually by the United Nations Development Programme. In addition to statistical data regarding different aspects of human development such as literacy, school attendance, life expectancy, access to water, poverty, and health-related indicators, these reports also focus, on a year-by-year basis, on issues of overall planetary import. The specific focus of the 2011 report, for instance, is on sustainability and equity. It looks at how people in general, but particularly the poor and disadvantaged, are affected by environmental degradation, calling for greater equity as part of the solution to this problem. Cultural liberty in a diverse world, human mobility, poverty eradication, deepening of democracy, and the impact of technological development are among the lead themes of past reports. Particularly during the 1990s, the United Nations system as a whole, together with bilateral partners and civil society organizations, organized debate around such planetary issues in the context of so-called world conferences, starting in 1990 with the World Conference on Education for All.

The above shift of attention to global issues has been timely. We live in an increasingly complex world, a world in which key issues can no longer be dealt with in ways that ignore that the world is one. French sociologist Edgar Morin's work increasingly focuses on this need. Implications of his thinking for education are expounded in his *Seven Complex Lessons in Education for the Future* (Morin, 1999). The need to take planetary issues seriously has critical implications for what and how we learn and for how we design the conditions under which people learn, including in distance education (J. Visser, 2007). There is a need to work concurrently on two fronts. One of those fronts is skill building. Successive Human Development Reports reveal great discrepancy in the various indicators that make up the Human Development Index across nations and geographical areas. Many of those discrepancies can be resolved by creating more equitable conditions for the development of specific skills in different parts of the world, provided such development goes hand-in-hand with developing facilitating contextual factors—for instance, in such areas as the development of economic conditions, environmental management, transparent governance, and the creation of legal and policy frameworks—that allow and encourage people to actually use their skills and, by doing so, enhance their own existence and that of their fellow human beings.

The trend so far in educational development, including in the development of distance education, has been to concentrate on skills development, something that is clearly demonstrated in how we decompose the purpose of educational efforts into specific learning goals, each of them specifying something the successful student will be able to do upon completion of the learning task. This is an obviously useful trend. It has allowed the instructional design discipline to develop into a mature science so that learning conditions could be deliberately created for specific learning needs, often in response to important social goals. However, the development of the aforementioned contextual factors, particularly in a worldwide perspective, depends on more than merely having skills, on more than the ability to do certain things. This "more than skills" area of concern is what I consider the second front that requires serious attention, alongside the first front mentioned above. It is an area that has to do with the development of the whole person, with all that is done to contribute to the continual building of the mind in the sense described by brain researcher Greenfield (2000). "Mind," says Greenfield, "is the seething morass of cell circuitry that has been configured by personal experiences and is constantly being updated as we live out each moment" (p. 13). She refers to this process as "the personalization of the physical brain" (p. 14).

I am not implying here that the brain is the only organ involved in human learning, or that human learning is a mere individual act. The brain is no doubt an essential organ in helping us learn. However, we learn, individually and socially, with everything we have and all we are. Our entire bodies are involved. Our entire life's experience counts in who we are and how each of us participates in this huge interplay, throughout human history, of complex interactions between members of our species as well as with the rest of the biosphere and our physical environment, at once producing and adapting to continual change while aiming at making existence progressively better for us all and for the planet as a whole. At that level, the level of what I called the second front, the immense diversity among us is not "an issue to be dealt with," which is typically what one does when designing skills-oriented instruction for a diverse population; rather, it is an issue to be embraced and exploited for the benefit of the species and the planet. This therefore requires a different vision of the development of human learning, appropriate for our era, a vision that focuses not so much on specific skills, but rather on how to live with the skills we have and those we are able to develop, that is, the metacompetencies that help us to better use our competencies. The seven complex issues identified by Morin (1999) form a good starting point. This is, I believe, an area in which the field of distance education, with its powerful potential to use media that connect people across boundaries, faces its next great challenge and opportunity.

COMPREHENSION AND APPLICATION QUESTIONS

1. In this chapter, the concept of *distance education* is given a broader meaning than by most other authors. What are the advantages of employing such a broader definition? Why might other authors object to broadening the concept beyond its usual definition? If you study this chapter together with colleagues, carry out a group exercise applying the techniques of concept mapping to elucidate the concept of *distance education*. Should you be unfamiliar with the techniques of concept mapping, do a web search to find out.

2. Comparing circumstances in the industrialized world and the developing world, give an example of a distance education application that may work well in one of those settings but less well in the other, due to the differences in context. If you would still consider transferring the chosen application from one setting to the other, how would you redesign it taking the new context into account?

3. Somewhere in this chapter, reference is made to two metaphors for learning and Anna Sfard's (1998) warning of the danger of choosing just one. Consider those two metaphors and their short description in this chapter (or, if you can, the longer version in the original article). Think back to your own learning experiences. Consider—or better, discuss with your colleagues—how they fit each of these metaphors or perhaps a mix of them. Then consider or discuss, based on your experience, whether you agree or disagree with Sfard's thesis that it would be dangerous to choose just one of the metaphors.

RESOURCES FOR FURTHER EXPLORATION

1. *Envisioning learning for the future*. There is increasing interest in generating new visions of learning that are better aligned with the human development needs of our time. Various institutions and research collectives are involved. I recommend exploring the websites of the LIFE Center at http://www.life-slc.org/ and the Learning Development Institute at http://www.learndev.org (particularly, but not solely, the Book of Problems at http://www.learndev.org/BOP-AECT2002.html). Also recommended are the following three print

publications, the first two of which are also freely available online:

(a)   Bransford, J. D., Brown, A. L., & Cocking, R. R. (Eds.). (2000). *How people learn: Brain, mind, experience and school.* Washington, DC: National Academy Press. Retrieved from http://www.nap.edu/openbook.php?isbn=0309070368

(b)   Morin, E. (2001). *Seven complex lessons in education for the future.* Paris, France: UNESCO. Retrieved from http://unesdoc.unesco.org/images/0011/001177/117740eo.pdf

(c)   Visser, J., & Visser-Valfrey, M. (Eds.). (2008). *Learners in a changing learning landscape: Reflections from a dialogue on new roles and expectations.* Dordrecht, The Netherlands: Springer. This book is also available electronically from SpringerLink.

2.   *Exploring the world in which we live.* This chapter is set in the world as a whole, a celestial body of planetary dimensions with planetary problems. You are invited to visit the following websites to develop an appreciation of our home in the universe (http://worldhistoryforusall.sdsu.edu/movies/flash_large.htm) and of what we have made of that home (http://www-personal.umich.edu/~mejn/cartograms/). Finally, browse through the statistics presented in the various editions of the Human Development Report (http://hdr.undp.org/) to appreciate what still needs to be done to create a better world. Consider that education, particularly with the help of modern technology, can contribute toward that goal.

3.   *Distributed learning resources galore.* There is an abundance of freely available educational resources that can easily be located on the World Wide Web. Providing references would not do justice to such abundance. Do a web search for phrases like "open courseware" (OCW) or "open educational resources" (OER) to start exploring such wealth. Another platform for access to free courses is Apple's iTunes U. Want to try your hand at contributing to what is already available? Try WikiEducator (http://www.wikieducator.org) or the OER website of Teachers Without Borders (http://courses.teacherswithoutborders.org/). Also of interest for exploring the ideas behind OER are the sites of the UNESCO OER community (http://oerwiki.iiep.unesco.org) and of the OER Foundation (http://wikieducator.org/OERF:Home).

REFERENCES

Arias, S., & Clark, K. A. (2004). Instructional technologies in developing countries: A contextual analysis approach. *TechTrends, 48*(4), 52–55, 70.

Bereiter, C. (2002). *Education and mind in the knowledge age.* Mahwah, NJ: Erlbaum.

Bereiter, C., & Scardamalia, M. (2003). Learning to work creatively with knowledge. In E. De Corte, N. Verschaffel, N. Entwistle, & J. van Merrienboer (Eds.), *Powerful learning environments: Unravelling basic components and dimensions* (pp. 55–70). Amsterdam, The Netherlands: Pergamon.

Daniel, J. (2002, October–December). Higher education for sale. *Education Today*, 1.

de la Teja, I., & Spannaus, T. W. (2008). New online learning technologies: New online learner competencies. Really? In J. Visser & M. Visser-Valfrey (Eds.), *Learners in a changing learning landscape: Reflections from a dialogue on new roles and expectations* (pp. 187–211). Dordrecht, The Netherlands: Springer.

Delling, R. M. (1987). Towards a theory of distance education. *ICDE Bulletin, 13*, 21–25.

Delors, J., Al Mufti, I., Amagi, I., Carneiro, R., Chung, F., Geremek, B., ... Zhou N. (1996). *Learning: The treasure within*. Report to UNESCO of the International Commission on Education for the Twenty-first Century. Paris, France: UNESCO.

Freire, P. (1972). *Pedagogy of the oppressed*. Harmondsworth, England: Penguin.

Greenfield, S. (2000). *The private life of the brain: Emotions, consciousness and the secret of the self*. New York, NY: Wiley.

Inter-Agency Commission World Conference on Education for All. (1990). *World declaration on education for all and framework for action to meet basic learning needs*. Paris, France: UNESCO.

Jonassen, D. H., & Land, S. M. (2000). Preface. In D. H. Jonassen & S. M. Land (Eds.), *Theoretical foundations of learning environments* (pp. iii–ix). Mahwah, NJ: Erlbaum.

Keegan, D. (1986). *The foundations of distance education*. London, England: Croom Helm.

Learning Without Frontiers. (1999). Learning Without Frontiers: Constructing Open Learning Communities for Lifelong Learning. *UNESCO* Retrieved from http://www.unesco.org/education/lwf/

Meltzoff, A. N., Kuhl, P. K., Movellan, J., & Sejnowski, T. J. (2009). Foundations for a new science of learning. *Science, 325*, 284–288.

Moore, M. G., & Kearsley, G. (1996). *Distance education: A systems view*. Belmont, CA: Wadsworth.

Morin, E. (1999). *Seven complex lessons in education for the future*. Paris, France: UNESCO.

Parrish, P. P. (2004). The trouble with learning objects. *Educational Technology Research and Development, 52*(1), 49–67.

Patarakin, E., & Visser, Y. L. (2003). *Creativity and creative learning in the context of electronic communication networks: A framework for analysis of practice and research*. LDI Working Paper # 4 [Online]. Retrieved from http://www.learndev.org/dl/Creativity&CreativeLearning.pdf

Perkins, D. N. (1993). Teaching for understanding. *American Educator, 17*(3), 8, 28–35. Retrieved from http://www.exploratorium.edu/IFI/resources/workshops/teachingforunderstanding.html

Perkins, D. N. (1998). What is understanding. In M. S. Wiske (Ed.), *Teaching for understanding: Linking research to practice* (pp. 39–57). San Francisco, CA: Jossey-Bass.

Perraton, H. (1988). A theory for distance education. In D. Sewart, D. Keegan, & B. Holmberg (Eds.), *Distance education: International perspectives* (pp. 34–45). New York, NY: Routledge.

Rogers, E. M. (2003). *Diffusion of innovations* (5th ed.). New York, NY: Free Press.

Schramm, W., Coombs, P. H., Kahnert, F., & Lyle, J. (1967). *The new media: Memo to educational planners*, with companion Volumes 1, 2, & 3 on *New educational media in action: Case studies for planners*. Paris, France: UNESCO.

Sfard, A. (1998). On two metaphors for learning and on the dangers of choosing just one. *Educational Researcher, 27*(2), 4–13.

Simonson, M. (2000). Making decisions: The use of electronic technology in online classrooms. *New Directions for Teaching and Learning, 84,* 29–34.

Simonson, M., Smaldino, S., Albright, M., & Zvacek, S. (2006). *Teaching and learning at a distance: Foundations of distance education* (3rd ed.). Upper Saddle River, NJ: Prentice-Hall.

Tessmer, M., & Richey, R. C. (1997). The role of context in learning and instructional design. *Educational Technology Research & Development, (45)*2, 1042–1629.

UNESCO. (2000). *World education report 2000—The right to education: Towards education for all throughout life*. Paris, France: UNESCO.

UNICEF. (2009). *The state of the world's children 2009*. New York, NY: UNICEF. Retrieved from http://www.unicef.org/sowc09/docs/SOWC09-FullReport-EN.pdf

Visser, J. (1995). International cooperation in distance education: The DE9 initiative, a case in point. In D. Sewart (Ed.), *One world many voices: Quality in open and distance learning. Selected papers from the 17th world conference of the International Council for Distance Education, Birmingham, UK, June 1995* (pp. 38–42). Milton Keynes, England: The International Council for Distance Education and The Open University.

Visser, J. (2001). Integrity, completeness and comprehensiveness of the learning environment: Meeting the basic learning needs of all throughout life. In D. N. Aspin, J. D. Chapman, M. J. Hatton, & Y. Sawano (Eds.), *International handbook of lifelong learning* (pp. 447–472). Dordrecht, The Netherlands: Kluwer.

Visser, J. (2003). Sense and nonsense of the McDonaldization of education: A response to John Daniel's "higher education for sale." In *McEducation for all? Opening a dialogue around UNESCO's vision for commoditizing learning*. Retrieved from http://www.swaraj.org/shikshantar/mceducationforall.htm#jan

Visser, J. (2007). Learning in a global society. In M. G. Moore (Ed.), *Handbook of distance education* (2nd ed., pp. 793–810). Mahwah, NJ: Erlbaum.

Visser, J., & Visser, Y. L. (2002). Undefining learning: Implications for instructional designers and educational technologists. *Educational Technology, 42*(2), 15–20.

Watkins, R., & Corry, M. (2010). *E-learning companion: A student's guide to online success* (3rd ed.). New York, NY: Wadsworth/Cengage.

Young, M., Perraton, H., Jenkins, J., & Dodds, T. (1980). *Distance teaching for the third world: The lion and the clockwork mouse*. London, England: Routledge & Kegan Paul.

CHAPTER 3

TRENDS AND ISSUES FACING DISTANCE EDUCATION

A Nowcasting Exercise

Brent G. Wilson

Weather forecasters often issue "nowcasts," that is, predictions of weather conditions for a specific location for the next hour or two. In this chapter, I conduct a similar "nowcasting" exercise for distance education, exploring some trends and issues that we believe will shape conditions in the next 2 to 3 year time frame. I highlight five key trends now shaping distance education: (a) an increasing capacity for people to generate and share knowledge and experience mediated, for example, through social media and open-access journals; (b) an increase in the evaluation of teachers and distance-education programs based on student performance on standardized learning measures; (c) and (d) a growing educational marketplace, simultaneously improving access to learning while increasing the digital divide; and (e) a shift in focus by educational researchers toward learning engagement and experience in distance education. I conclude the chapter by presenting three short examples of how these trends might impact those who teach and learn in distance settings.

Trends and Issues in Distance Education:
International Perspectives, Second Edition, pp. 39–54
Copyright © 2012 by Information Age Publishing
All rights of reproduction in any form reserved.

INTRODUCTION

A field of practice is best understood within a temporal context as ideas and practices change over time. This is what is meant by *trends*: changes over time within a field as well as changes in society and the larger environment that have an impact on the field. *Issues* point to unresolved concerns, questions, and tensions that arouse the interest of researchers and practitioners alike. The study of trends and issues can come in different forms, such as surveys of individuals, news sources, and panels of experts. The 2011 Horizon Report (Johnson, Smith, Willis, Levine, & Haywood), for example, is a good example of a trend analysis based on input from a panel of experts. The present chapter offers a more idiosyncratic view based on my perspective as a single observer situated in the United States, informed by working relationships with professionals in several locations worldwide.

Understanding trends and issues is especially important for a fast-changing field like distance education, which has continued an explosive growth trajectory that began earlier in the twentieth century. The pace of change in distance education has been so rapid that predicting conditions beyond more than 2 to 3 years has proven extremely difficult (cf. Allen & Seaman, 2010). So I title this analysis a "nowcasting exercise"; in weather terms, a *nowcast* is a very short-term forecast aimed at the next hour or two, based on the best information presently available, and often using models for guidance.

KEY TRENDS

I have organized the discussion below into five key trends:

1. Advancing forms of knowledge
2. Assessing learning achievement
3. Making learning convenient and accessible
4. Reaching all learners
5. Engaging learners through media and designed experience

Taken together, a picture emerges of a future with at least the potential to be more informed, engaging, and equitable for all learners. Shorter term, the same trends help establish a working agenda for distance educators.

Trend 1: Advancing Forms of Knowledge

The *information revolution* is changing how we represent, share, and formalize new knowledge. The modernist notion of progress, borrowing from Darwinian ideas of evolution, depends on innovating at local levels, noticing of the "differences that make a difference" (i.e., significant perturbations with the potential to change the system), and sharing and scaling up individual innovations for widespread adoption (Kelly, 1994; Miles & Huberman, 1994). Applying these ideas to society, human progress depends in part on noticing innovation and sharing knowledge, which lead to evolving practices that help us adapt to changing conditions and requirements encountered in the world.

Since distance education can be seen as a means of developing and sharing knowledge across time and space, its practice is directly impacted by developments in knowledge advancement. Whereas earlier in history, the *place* of innovation was critical to its dissemination (e.g., Silicon Valley), information and communication technologies (ICTs) are currently enabling innovators to traverse spatial and cultural boundaries on a more rapid time scale. Since it need not be either space- or time-bound, distance education is uniquely positioned to support (and leverage) this new economy of knowledge acquisition, production, and exchange.

Additional ideas related to knowledge advancement include

- *Wisdom of crowds*: The advent of the Web has made manifest the power of decentralized, complex adaptive human systems as an alternative to top-down control.

- *Scanning the terrain versus going deep*: Vast amounts of knowledge are shared on the Web, but often at a very surface level, consumed in small chunks rather than book-sized treatments. Web-savvy learners are very skilled at scanning this fast-changing terrain, but less skilled at the more patient, deep kinds of scholarships known in the academy.

- *Self-publishing*: Users increasingly disseminate knowledge through means of their own, thus maintaining more control over distribution of content. This leads to less filtering and editing, and more authentic voices, at the occasional risk of error and malicious intent.

- *Open access journals*: Academic scholarship is moving steadily toward openness and accessibility. Open-access journals tend to be freely accessible on the Web, with more transparent review processes (Siemens, 2007).

- *Sharing assets and resources*: With digital resources easily shared and disseminated, a number of trends are emerging:
  - o *Open-education movement*: Open Learning Resources (OLR) and global education initiatives
  - o *Expectations of free tools*: Embedding commercial interests under a façade of "free" tool access
  - o *Open-source movement*: Community, service-driven model of tool development that provides open-source code for tools and resources
  - o *Server-side applications/cloud computing*: Allowing station-independent access to tools and data
- *Commercial underwriting*: As part of their investment in, and marketing to, education, businesses are increasingly visible as underwriters of everything from curricular materials to scholarly production. An example is Microsoft's sponsorship of the distance education journal *Innovate*.
- *Filtering knowledge*: Collaborative filtering methods rely on users to help evaluate content. An example is Amazon's vast system of user reviews, a valuable complement to its quantitative search algorithms. In a similar way, many people are more inclined to take advice from a Facebook friend than trust an objective ranking when considering a distance education provider (Slaney, 2011).

Distance education has much to learn from information theorists such as John Seely Brown, who follow trends in knowledge development from a business perspective (as well as education).

Trend 2: Assessing Learning Achievement

The whole enterprise of education, like any other human enterprise, needs benchmarks of progress and achievement in order to be "domesticated" by governments and policymakers. In other words, distance education must ensure responsible use of funds and resources (e.g., taxpayer or the student financial contributions). For education, *learning* is the primary indicator (Rossett, 2009). In the United States, the primary and secondary education system has begun a major shift, which will evaluate *teacher* effectiveness based largely on their *students'* learning accomplishments (Balasubramanian & Wilson, 2010). This shift will not only impact primary and secondary education, but also the teacher training programs at colleges and universities (Crowe & Rhodes, 2009). "Outcomes-based assessment" of teachers and programs depends on standard metrics of student learning, often focusing on a few core subjects (such as reading, writing, and mathematics), administered at least annually, and based on standardized curriculum goals (which often result in more standardized teaching methods).

A whole range of issues relate to this shift toward outcomes-based assessment. For example, if only selected outcomes are chosen for assessment (e.g., math, but not art), increased pressure to narrow the curriculum to those targeted areas is likely to ensue. Or, if rewards are based strictly on student achievement on standardized assessments, teachers serving students with special needs, or those not yet fluent in the dominant language, may feel threatened since these students tend to perform poorly on standard assessments. Perverse incentives enter the system, discouraging teachers from serving those who may have the greatest needs. Teacher-training institutions may likewise suffer if incentives associated with advanced university study (e.g., a raise in salary) are displaced by rewards directly aligned with student performance measures.

In the near future, distance education programs may very well undergo the kind of scrutiny that primary and secondary schools have been undergoing in the United States in recent years. In the United States, accreditation agencies are already seeking evidence of learning for students enrolled in these programs, in the form of graduation and job-placement rates (e.g., Field, 2011). Simultaneously, universities are voluntarily seeking to demonstrate the credibility of their academic programs (both classroom-based and online) through participation in initiatives like the University and College Accountability Network (U-CAN). The bottom line is that seat time and completion of coursework will decline as quality indicators, while objective measures of learning will increase.

Trend 3: Making Learning Convenient and Accessible

Accessibility, convenience, and availability are the hallmark of distance education, often cited as the very *raison d'être* for its adoption. Complementing the traditional metaphors of education as *place* (i.e., a school) or as *experience* (with people, tools, and environment), education may also be seen as a developed *product*, especially with respect to distance education, which relies heavily on initial development of media and materials. If we accept the premise that we can commoditize educational programs through the creation of replicable curriculum and course materials and assessments, we can apply business models of productivity and efficiency and thereby gain more reliable outcomes.

A *product* metaphor may be difficult for some educators who are fully attached to the human element in distance education. While sympathetic to this stance, I invite the reader's forbearance as we explore some implications of distance education as an economic enterprise. We already understand how to think in objective, business terms in many settings, for example, the entertainment industry. Applying that same type of thinking to distance education presents some advantages. Free markets make products more accessible to consumers, which is generally a positive outcome. As educational choices proliferate (often in part due to advances in technology and distance education opportunities), more learners and investors enter the market, leading to an overall rise in the resources available, which is also a positive result. That said, it would be foolish to deny that in other ways, a market-based approach to education can lead to potentially severe problems (see the sections below on diversity and designing learner experience).

The last 20 years have seen a growing *disaggregation of the product* of education into pieces (e.g., instead of a graduate degree, a certificate; instead of a full plan of study, just a postassessment; instead of full-service on-campus living, only evening or remote access participation in the academic experience). Moreover, the *marketplace* for educational offerings has grown rapidly in many societies, leading to a more competitive environment with greater choice for consumers of education (Hemphill, Nauer, Zelon, & Jacobs, 2009). Even in countries with highly socialized education systems, the Web has created a platform for increasing educational choice and flexible engagement. The net result of these growing markets has been an overall growth in investment in education, particularly through the integration of remote learning experiences, which again, I believe to be a good development overall.

Trend 4: Reaching All Learners

Markets make products more accessible to consumers, but also tend to increase the divide between those who can afford quality products and those who cannot. Thus, as education becomes more market-driven in countries such as the United States, careful attention needs to be given to ensuring equitable access to educational opportunities. This issue is of particular concern when considering the proliferation of distance education programs offered by private and public institutions, on a for-profit and not-for-profit basis.

This is the "diversity" issue facing all countries in one form or another: facing up to the moral imperative created by new learning choices. Wherever free markets exist, some people will benefit and others will not, leading to potentially growing gaps between classes of people, gaps that are already a concern within society (Johnson, 2005). How can we create conditions in which education can serve the needed role of equalizer and opportunity-expander, rather than perpetuator of already established differences in class, access, and opportunity? Distance education can be consciously appropriated as an outreach to underserved groups and communities, aimed at reducing the difference in access and achievement. Without that specific commitment and carefully implemented programs, however, learning technologies could very well *increase* the digital divide rather than reducing it.

The age of learners is sometimes neglected when considering equity and diversity issues. Learners' age and experience with technology seem to differentiate their adoption decisions (Prensky, 2001). This has led to the concept of digital natives (younger learners adapting to ICTs and confident with diverse delivery platforms). Younger learners are often already fully familiar with mobile devices for communication and news access, and online access to games, media, entertainment, and social networking. A related issue is young people's lengthened transition to adulthood in postindustrial economies, with challenges of education, career development, self-regulation, and epistemological development playing key roles in that development (Arnett, 2000). Young people in a state of emerging adulthood need special support and educational experiences to help them make a successful transition to adult responsibilities.

The goal of reaching every learner is usually framed as a challenge to institutional indifference. Yet the institutions and delivery methods themselves can potentially be part of the solution. Christenson, Horn, and Johnson (2008) apply the model of disruptive innovation to distance education, seeing online learning as a means of addressing niche audiences and previously untapped markets, which over time will grow and become a major threat to traditional forms of schooling. Changes in delivery modalities (from traditional classrooms to more varied forms that include distance delivery) could either help or hinder the effort to better meet needs of individual learners. So much depends on how programs are designed and implemented.

Trend 5: Engaging Learners Through Media and Designed Experience

The question of learner engagement reflects a clear trend outside of school (particularly in marketing and entertainment, but also reflected more generally on the Web) toward richer interactions and experiences of very high quality and production value. Witness, for example, the emerging 3-D technology currently in movie theaters, but also in search of educational uses (Scrogan, 2010). The worlds of our children and grandchildren will differ markedly from our own, particularly in the fusing of virtual and embodied experiences. Within these new worlds, people's skill in using new media for communication, thinking, and work production will be highly valued as an educational outcome, an emerging area sometimes called new media literacy (Jenkins, 2006). As broadband delivery increasingly becomes the standard for distance education in the developed world, distance courses are becoming laboratories for testing out and applying innovative methods for learning engagement. Indeed, engagement from a distance can require particular attention, because online learners who feel disengaged can more easily choose to withdraw from participation.

In response to these changing conditions, new emphasis on *engagement and experience* seems to be taking shape in the field of instructional design (see, for example, the March/April 2011 issue of *Educational Technology* magazine with a special theme on transformative learning, edited by George Veletsianos and Brendan Calandra).

The scope of this chapter does not allow full treatment of engagement and the learning experience. Significant issues relating to this trend are outlined below.

- *Social media*: Gaming, blogging, tweeting, interest groups.
- *New media literacy*: Standards for becoming literate in reading and writing in a multiplicity of new media (Buckingham, 2003).
- *Attention economy*: The presence of various messages competing for learners' attention (de Castell & Jenson, 2004).
- *Kinesthetic engagement*: Designing learning experiences for full bodily senses, with the goal of achieving higher forms of engagement, such as the *Wii* entertainment system.
- *Aural engagement*: The use of audio for learning and instruction has many advantages, including mobility, affordability to produce and disseminate, and social characteristics.
- *Visual thinking*: Visual literacy, alternative representations for both thinking and learning (Roam, 2010).
- *Engaging content via online interactions*: Students learn when given opportunities for substantive interactions with content (Garrison & Anderson, 2003).
- *Aesthetic experience*: Learners can become deeply engaged in immersive experiences, similar to heightened aesthetic or spiritual experience (Parrish, Wilson, & Dunlap, 2011).
- *Designing for flow*: Flow refers to the highest levels of engagement in which the learner loses sense of time and becomes completely immersed in the task. Reese (2010) has led efforts to measure

immersive flow directly in educational games and showing how flow variations co-vary with learning insights as the game progresses.

- *Archetypes and ritual*: Teaching methods that draw on myth, ritual, and aesthetic principles can potentially engage learners more deeply and achieve lasting impacts (Wilson & Parrish, 2011).
- *Design as discipline*: Instructional designers are encouraged to draw on other design disciplines, e.g., industrial products, human-computer interface, graphics, games, movies, etc., for ideas for enhancing learning experiences.
- *3-D technology*: This is an emerging technology for potentially immersive environments in both distance education and classroom-based education (Scrogan, 2010).

Many of these points are not often articulated in the current distance-education literature. They will grow in importance as people's online experiences become more immersive and engaging. The technologies are ready; we need the ideas, models, and resources to create richer environments for learning.

THREE NOWCAST CASES

The three short cases below are intended to connect the trends outlined above to the kinds of problems and challenges facing the distance education world today.

Case 1: Improving a Course (Manuel's Commitment)

Manuel is a tenured psychology professor at a teaching university where he has been teaching online courses for the last 3 years. Not content with being a good teacher, Manual wants to be the *best* teacher his students have ever had, to the point that they switch careers and pursue psychology as a major. At first wary of online teaching, he now can't imagine going back to the regular classroom. "There's nothing I can't do online," he says with his usual enthusiasm. "I can create conditions online that I could never replicate in a classroom; and students experience things together they'll remember for a long time!"

Manuel's latest project is the Human Motivation class he took on last year at the request of his dean. "It's not where I want it to be, but give me time. I'll have them eating out of my hand." Eager for ideas and inspiration, Manuel sought out the instructional designers attached to the Faculty

Development Center at the university. They showed him some interesting instructional models and new technologies, which Manuel has played around with to determine their alignment with his goals for the Human Motivation course. However, the designers didn't seem quite prepared for the scale of Manuel's ambition. It appeared that the well-intentioned instructional design support staff knew how to help out a struggling teacher, but struggled themselves with a teacher who wanted to be *the best*.

What trends and issues relate to Manuel's situation? Clearly he is drawing on the power of media and distance learning technologies, and finding pedagogies to match these promising tools. The ideas and trends relating to media and designing learning experiences come to mind. Manuel understands how instructors must compete with outside media for learners' attention: he carefully crafts each weekly unit with the goal of leaving a genuine impact. And the overall arc of the course is a tightly orchestrated journey, challenging students to move beyond their comfort zones and to embark on an adventure (cf. Wilson & Parrish, 2011). Students buy into this because they see in Manuel all the qualities for a trusting relationship: enthusiasm, competence, and caring. While the immersive technologies are important, their full potential is only realized in the hands of a master teacher, and Manuel aspires to that role.

Case 2: Opening an Online School (Tyra's Opportunity)

Entrepreneurs are usually motivated by profit, but a worthy cause can also get their attention. Tyra is a career teacher/administrator who has seen the limitations of publicly funded schools, particularly in urban neighborhoods in the United States. Working with a team of parents, fellow educators, university researchers, and business partners, she is launching a charter secondary school connected with the state, but given separate funding and some waiving of standard policies. (Note: In the U.S. primary and secondary education system, a charter school is a publically funded school that is privately managed. Charter schools have specific accountability requirements, which are agreed upon when the school is established. Charter schools are not allowed to charge tuition. However, they are permitted to establish admission requirements.) This new school will be entirely online. What trends and issues should Tyra keep in mind as she and colleagues prepare for the school's first year?

The *open-learning movement* is part of what drives Tyra's whole effort. The school has a goal to use open-learning resources instead of textbooks. While initially this requires an investment to find and coordinate these resources, the effort will pay off within a couple of years as a growing body of resources is linked to courses and student activities and integrated into course environments. Those resources can grow steadily the intellectual and instructional offerings in the classes, as class technology resources and systems are revised and new resources become available.

The school would like to consider some commercial partnerships, but it does not want to strike any of those partnerships until it has fully defined its mission. Does it want to attract the elite, privileged student, and all the resources that such a student can bring? Or should the school prepare to admit the full range of students typically found in an urban neighborhood? The school's Advisory Board decides to launch the school by drawing on the energy of committed, wired-in parents and community members, tilting somewhat toward the elite side of the population. However, the school's mission has a strong commitment to diversity and community ties. Thus, over time the school plans to increase its diversity through its admissions policy and by strengthening ties to urban neighborhoods.

Tyra understands the power of school culture, and that the many interlinking parts of that culture, taken together, tend to resist change. Because of divested ties to a physical place, the school needs to carefully plan to support students' social and emotional needs. In the first year, a number of social outlets will be available, but beyond that, students will be regularly polled and consulted concerning ways to strengthen the felt connection with peers and staff.

A huge issue facing the startup of the school is preparing teachers for the different responsibilities required for teaching online. Selecting the right teacher is critical in this regard, but so is providing extensive support, training, and ongoing dialogue with teachers concerning the many challenges with starting an online school. Understanding how teachers' roles change when using constructivist strategies can also help ease this transition (Wilson, 2012). In short, attention to curriculum resources including technology and respect for people (including both students and staff) are key issues relevant to Tyra's agenda.

Case 3: Learning to Learn Flexibly (Hui Zhong's World)

For the last 9 months, Hui Zhong has been a trusted member of a working team within the Risk Management division of her firm. The team consists of three colleagues at her Shenyang office, two in Zurich, and one in London. Managing across time zones is a challenge, but the team members know each other very well and have come to depend on each other's roles and expertise.

Since joining the firm 2 years ago, Hui Zhong has been on a steep learning curve, absorbing the new corporate culture, roles, and expectations. She feels she has so much to learn! She had thought that finishing school would slow down the amount of learning she had to do, but the level of learning requirements seems only to have increased. While in-house training is available in some areas, more often she is left to fend for herself, relying on colleagues, connections, and her own capacity to adjust. "I need to be more systematic in my learning and professional development," she says. "The problem is, there is no graduate certificate out there that covers the most pressing things. I would have to invent a curriculum myself!" When asked about her team members, she replies, "The whole team is incredibly generous and helpful. It's just that we're all in the same boat; always looking for answers, half the time in crisis mode, it seems."

Hui Zhong's experience is increasingly common, but how does it relate to distance education? She may force us to reexamine some assumptions. Hui Zhong doesn't need a degree or certificate at this time, but what about *self-regulated, just-in-time,* and *informal learning* such as interest groups, webinars, professional conferences and organizations? Perhaps open-access journals or blog sites. Can she find some trusted professionals worth following on Twitter? Hui Zhong seems ready to take more personal responsibility as she reaches out for more learning opportunities online. If her firm doesn't yet have a learning management system for employees, she can create her own personal learning environment (PLE) in order to keep track of various learning opportunities and accomplishments. She may also be ready to establish a professional web presence herself and begin helping others in the same boat. Hui Zhong should be thinking about her career at two levels; at the first level, her own faithful service to the firm and her working group, and at the second level her professional leadership and long-term positioning in the profession and the employment market. Managing her own learning is a big part of that larger picture and will end up helping her firm and working group at the same time.

These three simple cases can help us link the trends articulated in this chapter to the kinds of problems faced by today's learners and learning providers. We could continue with more aspects of these questions, for example, policy issues facing governments and institutions. The greater point is, however, that the trends provide only a starting point for discussion about nowcasting conditions, the very short-term futures that we are looking toward as we engage in our present work.

CONCLUDING REMARKS

If there is a single cohering idea to the analysis offered above, it might be summarized as:

To be successful as distance educators, we must engage in ongoing review and analysis of emerging trends and issues. This understanding provides a context for making sense of our present activities, aims, and agendas, all of which will be judged based on emerging conditions in the near and not-so-near future.

Emerging trends are necessarily outside or beyond our current models and theories; they are the grist for the mill that future theories will use to better explain and guide our practice. Emerging trends provide a needed context for our present practice. Like any other kind of enterprise involving risk and investment, those who do their homework and understand the trends will be better positioned to make informed decisions in the present (Gladwell, 2010).

Critics may well contend that the analysis above is too conscious of markets and costs, and that it reduces distance education to only the business side of things. I have tried to balance the objective/business trends with more craft-like views of the learning experience and interests of open sharing and educational equity, which is where my own research is presently focused. I personally see great value in acknowledging multiple perspectives and assessing their relevance to present practice and to nowcasting the future. While sensitive to the U.S.-centric perspective offered in the chapter, I eagerly look forward to hearing perspectives coming from other parts of our global professional community.

COMPREHENSION AND APPLICATION QUESTIONS

1. Postmodern critics tell us it's the assumptions that we take for granted as common sense that most need interrogation and critique. As you read this chapter, what strongly held assumptions or beliefs do you see challenged? Are there any "commonsense" beliefs that you personally hold, that you feel uncomfortable examining closely? An example might be, Distance education is good because it makes education more accessible to learners. The question is, what kinds of learners benefit, and what kinds might be hurt by a given distance ed program? In short, how can we be more thoughtful and mindful as we think about distance education and trends affecting its practice?

2. Malcolm Gladwell (2010) challenges the myth that successful entrepreneurs are maverick deal-makers, willing to take unprecedented risks on a new idea or product. In fact, successful entrepreneurs are better at analyzing situations, estimating risk, and then minimizing their personal risk by using other people's resources

and money in their ventures. In short, they control the downside risk while maximizing the upside potential. Applying that way of thinking to distance education planning, what kinds of investments in distance education would make good sense for 2–3 years? What risks are presently too great? How would you go about explicitly defining and articulating the various risks associated with a program innovation?

3.   You are the Minister of Education for a progressive government in a small South American nation. Part of your job is to negotiate with nongovernmental organizations (NGOs) as they partner with you to improve educational infrastructure. A major priority for you and the NGOs is to leverage your limited resources to benefit larger numbers of children. One NGO officer challenges the idea of distance education: "We don't want to invest large amounts on technology; there's no use in getting Internet connectivity when 98% of the children can't access it." How would you respond to this need and this challenge to help your country move into the information age while benefiting more children and not just an elite privileged class of people?

RESOURCES FOR FURTHER EXPLORATION

George Siemens is an active trendsetter and interpreter relating to higher education. I keep a close eye on his blog, because it points me to valuable resources in and out of the field; see: http://www.elearnspace.org/blog/

The Horizon Project generates annual reports relating to emerging trends in distance education and emerging technologies. These are good benchmarks for gauging change over time; see http://www.nmc.org/horizon

Pat Parrish maintains a website at http://homes.comet.ucar.edu/~pparrish/. He and I have worked on a common research agenda exploring aesthetic principles of instructional design. Other innovators in this area include George Veletsianos, Luca Botturi, Aaron Doering, and Charlie Miller.

REFERENCES

Allen, I. E., & Seaman, J. (2010, January). *Learning on demand: Online learning in the United States, 2009*. Retrieved from http://www.sloan-c.org/publications/survey/learning_on_demand_sr2010

Arnett, J. J. (2000). Emerging adulthood: A theory of development from the late teens through the twenties. *American Psychologist, 55*(2), 469–480.

Balasubramanian, N., & Wilson, B. G. (2010). *Continuous improvement for K12 school systems: An assessment tool for educators*. HarnessData White Paper. Retrieved from http://ilearnllc.com/docs/HarnessData_Described.pdf

Buckingham, D. (2003). *Media education: Literacy, learning, and contemporary culture*. London, England: Polity.

Christensen, C. M., Horn, M. B., & Johnson, C. W. (2008). *Disrupting class: How disruptive innovation will change the way the world learns*. New York, NY: McGraw-Hill.

Crowe, E., & Rhodes, L. K. (2009, November). *Graduates from schools of education: Outcomes and impact*. Unpublished manuscript.

de Castell, S., & Jenson, J. (2004). Paying attention to attention: New outcomes for learning. *Educational Theory, 54*(4), 381–397.

Field, K. (2011, May 8). Faculty at for-profits allege pressure to keep students constantly enrolled. *Chronicle of Higher Education*. Retrieved from http://chronicle.com/article/Pawns-in-the-For-Profit/127424

Garrison, D. R., & Anderson, T. (2003). E-learning in the 21st century: A framework for research and practice. London, England: Routledge/Falmer.

Gladwell, M. (2010, January 18) The sure thing. *New Yorker*, pp. 24–29.

Hemphill, C., Nauer, K., Zelon, H., & Jacobs, T. (2009). *The new marketplace: How small-school reforms and school choice have reshaped New York City's high schools*. New York, NY: Center for New York City Affairs. Retrieved from http://www.newschool.edu/milano/nycaffairs/documents/TheNewMarketplace_Report.pdf

Jenkins, H., (with Purushotman, R., Clinton, K., Weigel, M., & Robison, A. J.) (2006, September). *Confronting the challenges of participatory culture: Media education for the 21st century*. Retrieved from http://www.newmedialiteracies.org/files/working/NMLWhitePaper.pdf

Johnson, A. G. (2005). *Privilege, power, and difference*. New York, NY: McGraw-Hill.

Johnson, L., Smith, R., Willis, H., Levine, A., & Haywood, K., (2011). *The 2011 Horizon report*. Austin, TX: New Media Consortium. Retrieved from http://wp.nmc.org/horizon2011/

Kelly, K. (1994). *Out of control: The new biology of machines, social systems, and the economic world*. Reading, MA: Addison-Wesley.

Miles, M., & Huberman, M. (1994). *Qualitative data analysis* (2nd ed.). Thousand Oaks, CA: SAGE.

Parrish, P., Wilson, B. G., & Dunlap, J. C. (2011). Learning experience as transaction: A framework for instructional design. *Educational Technology, 51*(2), 15–22.

Prensky, M. (2001). Digital natives, digital immigrants. *On the Horizon, 9*(5). Retrieved from http://www.marcprensky.com/writing/Prensky%20-%20Digital%20Natives,%20Digital%20Immigrants%20-%20Part1.pdf

Reese, D. D. (2010). Games to evoke and assess readiness to learn conceptual knowledge. In R. V. Eck (Ed.), *Gaming & cognition: Theories and perspectives from the learning sciences* (pp. 227–254). Hershey, PA: IGI Global.

Roam, D. (2010). *The back of the napkin (expanded edition): Solving problems and selling ideas with pictures*. New York, NY: Penguin.

Rossett, A. (2009). Beyond Kirkpatrick: A fresh look at analysis and evaluation [Slide presentation]. Retrieved from http://edweb.sdsu.edu/people/arossett/Rossett_analysis_eval_ASTDModel.pdf

Scrogan, L. (2010, February 13). *The Olympics in 3D—and a* caveat. Retrieved from http://bvsd.org/iteach/BlogCentral/default.aspx

Siemens, G. (2007, March 27). *Scholarship in an age of participation*. Retrieved from http://www.elearnspace.org/Articles/journal.htm

Slaney, M. (2011). Web-scale multimedia analysis: Does content matter? *Multimedia, 18*(2), 12–15.

Wilson, B. G. (2012). Constructivism in practical and historical context. In R. Reiser & J. Dempsey (Eds.), *Current trends in instructional design and technology* (3rd ed., pp. 45–52). Upper Saddle River, NJ: Pearson Prentice-Hall.

Wilson, B. G., & Parrish, P. (2011). Transformative learning experience: Aim higher, gain more. *Educational Technology, 51*(2), 10–15.

CHAPTER 4

OBSTACLES AND OPPORTUNITIES OF DISTANCE HIGHER EDUCATION IN INTERNATIONAL SETTINGS

Lya Visser

This chapter focuses on the role distance higher education can play in a world in which globalization and internationalization, both characterized by increased global interdependence and international competition, are flourishing, while academic solidarity is simultaneously weakening (IAU, 2010). I begin by examining globalization and internationalization as forces in today's economic and learning landscapes and then discuss the growing role of distance education within today's context, including the obstacles and benefits of distance education programs. The current movement toward commercialization of distance higher education is next highlighted. I conclude the chapter by discussing some factors surrounding globalization and internationalization in future distance higher education efforts.

Trends and Issues in Distance Education:
International Perspectives, Second Edition, pp. 55–70
Copyright © 2012 by Information Age Publishing
All rights of reproduction in any form reserved.

INTRODUCTION

For many individuals today, it has never been easier to communicate and to be aware of what is happening around the world, and there are currently more opportunities than ever before for interconnectedness. Much of this interconnectedness has resulted in positive outcomes: improved transport, increased trade, and more accessible communication technology, all results of today's interconnectedness levels, have doubtless benefited many countries, sectors of society, and individuals.

Unfortunately, there continue to be many people around the world who are still living short of the most basic levels of a decent existence. According to the World Bank (2010), extreme poverty (i.e., income of less than $1.25 a day) is still a reality for close to a billion people.

Although our sense of space, culture, and time may have narrowed through improved access to communication technology and increased mobility, this does not always mean that we understand each other better or are more aware of each other's situation. The information we receive about international affairs and the situation in the world is sometimes manipulated and is often superficial and limited. Such information distortions can contribute to significant misunderstandings. Stedman (2004), for example, mentions the case of an American businessman and guest speaker working in international trade who reported that he often asks his American audiences what percentage of the world population they believe the United States represents. His anecdotal survey revealed that many in his American audiences estimate that the United States makes up anywhere from 10% to 25% of the world's population, grossly overestimating the real figure (the United States actually makes up about 5% of the world population).

This informal example illustrates that connectedness may actually be an "imaginary" connectedness, influenced by concepts that have become buzzwords, including *our small planet*, *the world community*, *globalization*, and *internationalization*. In response to the terrible 2010 earthquake in Haiti, international assistance was apparently overwhelming. The United States, Europe, China, and myriad other countries offered help in the form of food, human resources, and shelter, and this response was a moment when we came together and witnessed concrete signs of global involvement and connectedness. Unfortunately, such moments are rare, and it more often seems that, on the contrary, we are often struggling with the idea that our world is increasingly diverse, and that many believe that their cultural identity is under attack, with differences between cultures and nations on the increase.

A CLOSER LOOK AT
INTERNATIONALIZATION AND GLOBALIZATION

Internationalization refers to relationships between and among countries, nations, and cultures. Individual countries approach internationalization in a manner that reflects their own history, culture, and context. The internationalization of higher education refers to institutional arrangements by governments, universities, organizations, and other education agents that involve the delivery of higher education in more than one country. Internationalization thus focuses on the process of incorporating a global, international, or intercultural dimension into the delivery of postsecondary education (Knight, 2004).

In contrast to internationalization, *globalization* is a process of interaction and integration of people, organizations, companies, and governments of different nations (Knight, 2004). Globalization is often driven by international trade. Held (1999) defines globalization as "the widening, deepening and speeding up of world-wide interconnectedness" (p. 2). Globalization refers to economic as well as cultural change, and it is in the area of communication, education, and information where the economic and cultural aspects meet (Castells, 2004).

Both internationalization and globalization have influenced higher education in important ways. Different nations and institutions bring varying capacities and different agendas to the global education landscape. Under the influence of globalization, competition has increased and has, in the last few decades, also influenced education in important ways. The risk of commercialization in traditional and distance education is real. Many new educational providers have arisen in recent years, while it seems that educational cooperation and academic solidarity have at the same time been weakened and undermined. Although one of the goals of internationalization of education is promoting a greater understanding of global and international issues, it can be shown that international students and staff remain subject to differing "realities." Nevertheless, internationalization should be seen as a positive force for the world's population, enabling increased partnerships between peoples, cultures, and religions on both micro- and macrolevels.

GLOBALIZATION AND INTERNATIONALIZATON

The International Association of Universities (IAU) recently published its third Global Survey Report, *Internationalization of Higher Education: Global Trends, Regional Perspectives* (2010). An impressive 745 institutions in 115 countries from all regions of the world responded to the survey, and many new and challenging insights regarding internationalization are offered in this report. Some 78% of the institutions surveyed mentioned internationalization in their strategic plan, while curiously, another 78% reveal that during the years 2006–2009, internationalization had substantially increased in perceived importance within their environment. The survey also revealed some important concerns regarding internationalization. Lack of funding was reported to be a significant barrier to advancing internationalization efforts. In the majority of the surveyed institutions, it was noted that the percentage of students who get the opportunity to enroll full time in higher education institutions remains low.

Another important concern voiced in the third Global Survey Report of the IAU (2010) relates to "brain drain," the loss of skills that a country or region experiences when skilled individuals either leave or do not return to their originating locale. When brain drain occurs, significant effects on the country's development and on higher education can be experienced. Brain drain can result from a number of causes. Living abroad for a number of years is often not easy for most individuals and may alienate students from their original surroundings. In addition, if after a number of years individuals have finally more or less settled abroad, they may be reluctant to move again, particularly as financial conditions may be attractive in an industrialized country. A U.S. survey of selected Canadian and American universities, for example, estimates that of the African PhDs trained in North America from 1986 to 1996, only 64% returned to Africa (Ndulu, 2003). Zeleza (2003) has pointed out that the study shows that rates of return vary considerably by age, discipline of study, and other factors. Younger graduates (20–29 years) are less likely to return home than their older counterparts (40–49); 36% of the former and 58% of the latter return home. Loss of its best and brightest students has had a negative effect on Africa's economic development (Bloom, Canning, & Chan, 2006).

Political instability in a student's home country may also impact the brain drain phenomenon. Before 2000, 43% of the Ghanaians who left the country to study did not return (Ndulu, 2003). A recent report of the International Organization for Migration (2010) on Ghana highlighted its relative peace, security, and political stability, finding a growing incidence of return or circular migration. Of the more than 1.1 million Ghanaians who left the country between 2000 and 2007, only 153,000 did not return.

Having briefly discussed internationalization and globalization, we next turn our attention to the growing role distance education is undertaking in many international contexts. As distance education is a modality that is not restricted by geographical distances, the approach can be a cost-effective method for opening doors and minds. As such, distance education therefore has the potential to influence today's international learning landscape in both positive and negative ways.

A GROWING ROLE FOR DISTANCE EDUCATION

Education and sustainable development go hand in hand. Education is a crucial means of building human capital, leading to societal development that meets the needs of today's generation without compromising the ability of future generations to meet theirs too (WCED, 1987). Today, both developing and industrialized countries recognize that global productivity and competitiveness are enhancing the caliber and resilience of the workforce (Jegede, 2001), hence, there is an increased interest in promoting citizen training and education. The number of international students at colleges and universities in the United States has increased from some 50,000 in 1959 to over 670,000 in 2008. These students contributed $15.5 billion to the U.S. economy (OpenDoors, 2009).

Looking solely at the costs of higher education mentioned, it can be understood that, for many countries, distance education offers an excellent opportunity for their citizens to have access to education. In addition to the cost factors, there are many other well-known advantages offered by distance education: flexibility, the ability to study at one's own pace, the opportunity to learn and earn and apply what is learned in the one's daily work situation while continuing studies. Ministries of education may consider distance education an important cost-saver: the approach makes use of fewer classrooms, requires fewer teachers, and in addition, the students remain within the country. Economies of scale may apply. Taking into consideration the pressure on developing countries to join the global information economy, distance education promises to offer a chance to train more people at a lower cost and in their own environment.

Although international distance education can be shown to be a financially sound approach, if such programs are to be successful, cultural sensitivity and awareness within such programs is essential. Exposing students to current events in countries around the world and opening a dialogue between and among students in different contexts will strengthen the role of distance education. For example, I have recently linked up 17 students in a graduate-level distance education course hosted by an American university with 28 students from an Egyptian university where the programs are taught in English. The students were divided into groups, each having equal representation from the U.S. university and the Egyptian university (i.e., seven Egyptian students and four or five American students per group). During a weeklong collaborative session, the students worked within their groups to participate in discussions on a variety of topics of mutual interest. Once the session was completed, the students were asked to complete a survey. (Of the 45 students who participated in the session, 28 answered the postdiscussion survey. In all, 42% of the respondents were American students, and 58% were Egyptian students.) The survey revealed that a large majority (85%) was of the opinion that the weeklong international discussion had been very useful, and 71% reported that the atmosphere among the participants was pleasant. A majority (58%) found that the discussions had increased their understanding of international educational challenges. Responding to whether such a discussion week should be repeated, 63% either agreed or strongly agreed. While these findings were yielded from a modest and relatively small-scale effort, they suggest that distance education students can be positively impacted by such "international" interactions, and that distance education can be used in discussing crucial challenges facing individuals today.

DISADVANTAGES AND BENEFITS OF DISTANCE HIGHER EDUCATION

The process of internationalization of higher education may bring many important benefits, but there are also important obstacles to be discussed. Distance education can have numerous advantages, such as increasing the opportunity for many to enroll in distance education, but there also exist important disadvantages of distance education for both developed and developing countries alike.

Disadvantages

Initially, establishing distance education programs is cost and capital intensive. Distance educators are generally required to have increased IT skills due to the nature of the technology involved such as the Internet and the wide variety of software programs used to deliver instruction. Learning materials must be well-designed and developed. Student support assumes a greater role, and motivational communication must be implemented along with the instruction. Groups of students often are no longer homogeneous, but may consist of students with different national and cultural backgrounds and differing linguistic abilities. Instructors have to work with students who have to get accustomed to being isolated from teachers and peers, have to be technology literate, and possess the ability to work independently.

The distance education approach does not "work" for all students. Some students may simply require close, in-person accompaniment as they study, and may also not be able to take responsibility for their own learning. Visser and Visser (2000), for example, showed that students in Hong Kong strongly needed an instructor who offered continuous guidance, leadership, and who was willing to take responsibility for students' learning. Distance education lacks the strong bond that the in-person classroom community can offer and that often facilitates the strong social cognitive interactive learning, seen as crucial by Vygotsky (1978). Those students who are not able to cope with the form of studying required within distance education are at risk of failing or noncompletion of courses.

There are other problems such as the impact of using technology in environments that have traditionally been well-served by teachers. Teachers may think that they are no longer recognized as the provider of knowledge but have become equipment monitors, causing alienation. The cohort model, enabling students to study with a class or group coordinator, is not widely used, although it, according to Schlosser and Burmeister (1999), has been very effective

Many students have difficulty with a pure online learning model as it lacks face-to-face contact among students and with the instructor. There is not much chance for effective and affective communication. Only a few programs and universities use a cohort model; most students enter and exit a program at different times, although they sometimes share classes. It is usually tougher for online learners to bond with other participants; this may be even more difficult when there is a great variety in cultural backgrounds.

As an instructor, I have witnessed that it can be more difficult for international students to communicate effectively than for nationals. One has to master the language of instruction very well to avoid the conversation flow being inhibited by imprecise or ambiguous use of language. The lack of face-to-face interaction and the impossibility to quickly correct or explain vague or faulty use of the language is an often-cited complaint. This can affect the learners' level of motivation and cause feelings of isolation.

In summary, some of the traditional obstacles to the success of distance education include high start-up cost of programs, insufficient instructors and/or student technology skills, lack of student motivation, weak time-management skills, underestimation of student responsibilities, lack of ability to work independently without face-to-face contact, and communication difficulties with the language of instruction

Benefits

Distance education and blended learning (i.e., mixing two or more methods of instruction or training) offer attractive opportunities to get more and/or better schooling. Distance higher education can be seen both as a product and a producer of the globalization of access to education. Distance education thus has the potential to alleviate many of the problems developing countries face, but in order to do so, must be employed both wisely and efficiently. Just buying predeveloped programs from industrialized countries may not necessarily be very effective; adaptation to the local context is important. Quality control also plays a crucial role in the effectiveness of distance education. Many countries, such as India, Pakistan, Brazil, South Africa, and Mexico have been successful in implementing quality distance higher education (Litto, this volume).

In the last few years, the United States and some countries within the European Union have been tightening visa and applied travel restrictions, making it more difficult for students from around the world to travel to institutions in these areas to complete a degree. To ensure that students worldwide can continue to earn degrees from renowned universities in these locales, educational institutions are increasing their distance education offerings.

In summary, some of the traditional benefits that are often mentioned are the ability to incorporate study around social and work patterns, the ability to study part time or full time and vary study load based on circumstances, the ability to prepare for upcoming classes without being rushed via a fixed schedule, the ability to develop lifelong learning habits and foster self-direction, and cost savings (i.e., studying "green").

Achieving success in distance education thus means overcoming the challenges this mode of learning may offer. It is the task of the instructor to assess the needs of the student. This is not always an easy task. Reflection is one of the keywords. Reflection on the content of the course, reflection on the learners, and reflection on the methods will lead to specific strategies that can reduce the interpersonal distance, nurture interaction, and enhance learning (Eastmond, 1994).

THE BUSINESS OF GLOBAL DISTANCE EDUCATION

The growth in interest in international distance education has also led to increased commercialization of education. *Commercialization* is defined as efforts within the university to make a profit from teaching, research, and other campus activities. There was a time that U.S. universities made extra money through their sports teams, but this is no longer the main method for alternative funding: today, much additional funding is secured through education and research (Bok, 2004). Reductions in government funding for higher education have also forced these universities to look for alternative sources of revenue. From 1999 to 2004, the number of students studying abroad increased by 61% (IAU, 2010). In 2005, five of the top eight host countries (Australia, New Zealand, United Kingdom, United States, and Canada) that "export" higher education together exported over $28 billion in commercial value through educational programs.

Although the majority of international higher education is still delivered in a face-to-face format, distance education programs continue to grow on a yearly basis. North America is projected to be the largest e-learning market for the next 5 years, while Asia, with a "breathtaking" 5-year compound annual growth rate of 33.5%, is projected to edge out Western Europe by 2014 to take second place (Nagel, 2010). There is therefore an important international competition among universities offering distance education to international students. As colleges and universities pursue market-oriented activities in search of added revenue, increased enrollments, and greater prestige and visibility for their "brand names," they are increasingly turning to the for-profit company model as a means to meet these goals. This is particularly evident as nonprofit colleges and universities create for-profit subsidiaries to deliver distance education (Bleak, 2002).

When I was recently working in Central America, I visited several local distance education institutions that, in addition to their normal programs, also offered use of classrooms and computer facilities for students enrolled in distance programs (mainly with American and British universities). When I asked the director of one such institution why students enrolled in foreign distance education programs and not in programs from a good regional university (such as the University of the West Indies), he replied that the brand name of the university was very important for students, although the cost was maybe tenfold. This ad hoc observation provides evidence regarding the growing importance of international distance education as a commercial enterprise and the financial cost many students are willing to forgo in order to achieve a degree from such institutions.

THE FUTURE OF INTERNATIONAL DISTANCE HIGHER EDUCATION

With the advantages international distance education provides, its future may be promising, but that future also largely depends on how prepared we are for the challenges and changes surrounding international distance education. I next briefly discuss some of those areas that will play a crucial role in the future of distance education.

Communication and Motivation

Communication is an often undervalued concept in distance education. Effective communication helps eliminate existing communication barriers. Communication processes are related to building relationships that are, in turn, the vehicles for growth (Rogers, 1962). Schrage (1990) suggests that to motivate, communications—including letters, e-mails, text messages, conversations, and the like—should serve to create a *shared experience* and not an *experience that is shared*. Tubbs and Moss (2006) state that communication is effective when the stimulus as initiated and intended by the sender/source corresponds closely to the stimulus as perceived and responded to by the receiver. In online education, effective communication is particularly important because students and instructors may rarely or never come to a physical campus. Communication will mostly be in writing, and therefore loses the benefit of voice cues or a wink or pat on the shoulder. The manner in which messages are constructed in such settings can in important ways increase the autonomy of learners and increase the awareness of learning as an active and social process. Therefore, a working awareness of potential communication barriers makes both students and facilitators more productive and more effective and affective communicators.

What will be necessary to face the future of international distance higher education with confidence is a thorough critical and analytical look at how communication processes between instructor and students, materials and students, and students and students take place, and whether such messages motivate and show empathy and are free from culturally biased language and content.

Technology-Enhanced Learning

There remains a significant divide between developing and industrialized (i.e., developed) countries as to the availability of technology and the readiness to use it effectively. Leary and Berge (2006), reviewing 150 distance education programs in sub-Saharan Africa, concluded that traditional, paper-based means of distance learning continues to be more reliable, sustainable, and widely used than online and web-based methods. Thus, preparing students to enroll and actively participate in distance higher education may require additional training and more substantive support.

Meredith and Burkle (2006) state that although e-learning has been an important topic within education and training for more than a decade, it is probably fair to say that the development of this type of learning is still evolving. Although distance education technology may increasingly become more challenging, there are also attempts at addressing the need for collaboration in providing affordable access. International distance higher education may therefore have to make more use of free course management systems such as the open-source and free software system Moodle. This type of software is both teacher and student friendly, and the accompanying international support and guidance groups have increased international cooperation in the field. Integration, sharing, understanding, and support should be the base of international collaboration.

In developing countries, Internet access may be unfeasibly costly as well as unreliable, and there remain many individuals with limited resources who are thus excluded. It appears that education providers are not yet making use of cheap and reliable technology such as cell phones in their distance education efforts. A better understanding of the "markets" and the target population present in the developing world will be necessary to improve the success of international distance higher education at-large.

Cultural Diversity

As has been touched upon above, cultural identity is an important concern in most regions of the world. Many instructors working in distance education, for example, support increased use of asynchronous discussions and problem-based learning. Transferring such approaches to other countries may be neither the best nor the easiest way (Asunka, 2008). Asunka reports about a qualitative case-study approach that examined the attitudes, experiences, and perceptions of undergraduate students in an online, collaborative learning course at a Ghanaian private university (2008). Data sources included surveys, student and instructor journal entries, e-mail records, individual interviews, and web-server logs. The study found that the students did not respond favorably to online constructivist teaching approaches such as asynchronous discussions and ill-structured project-based learning activities, and perceived collaborative online learning within their context as a complex, demanding, and time-consuming experience.

To achieve greater global participation and reach, providers of international distance education will have to work hard to increase the cultural awareness of educational designers and instructors. In another example, I recently asked students in one of their first online lessons in a course with international students to interview one another and post the interview along with a photo of the interviewee. This requirement caused a problem for a student who was assigned to interview her Saudi colleague, in whose environment, in some cases, photographs do not circulate. The interviewer found a beautiful solution—the interview was posted within a border of flowers.

Increased Competition

Globalization leads to increased competition. The focus on the economic aspects of education will almost certainly increase the commercialized aspects of education. One of the results of globalization is that of an emerging borderless education market. The increase of private operations within international distance education may decrease the quality of the programs and courses that are offered and, even in extreme cases, result in "diploma mills."

Commercial delivery of distance higher education will certainly increase. There is a tendency to think that offering learning materials to those countries that solicit assistance is an effective way of promoting learning. Learning, however, is change and is human development. Human development should focus on the capacity to constructively interact with a world in change (Visser, 2005) and on exploring diversity, not simply supplying ready-made pieces of content. It is likely that educational providers, aiming at making profit, may avoid seeing learning as a change process in favor of simply providing learning materials. This approach has in the past resulted in most distance education efforts settling for a vision of learning as learning via structured isolation.

It is clear that distance higher education must adapt to the increased demand, but must also position itself so that the global competition from large corporate and virtual universities does not end up dominating the educational landscape. Nunan (2005) also warns that there will be great pressures upon distance education providers to maintain parity of esteem between distance and face-to-face programs.

Blended Learning

Blended learning is on the rise in higher education. According to Bonk and Graham (2006), 93% of higher education instructors and administrators say they are using blended learning strategies somewhere in their institution, while 7 out of 10 decision makers expect more than 40% of their schools' courses to be blended by 2013. Not everyone agrees: Ferratt and Hall (2009) posit that most writing on distance learning, including blended learning and technology-enhanced learning, is dominated by a vision of extending education through the use of technology, but fails to reach beyond current technology limits. Although distance education has allowed more flexibility regarding when and where students engage in learning, its implementation is often based on this limited vision and has moved education backward through loss of the benefits of "being there" in the traditional classroom environment. The use of blended learning will likely increase, as it allows students to gradually move to online learning solutions. In addition, blended learning facilitates a wide variety of learning styles and thus may increase motivation and satisfaction. In international education, blended learning may remain difficult to implement, although I have seen that some distance education programs offer support services abroad by engaging an adjunct instructor to accompany the students, as well as to offer additional lectures supporting the course.

CONCLUSION

So-called e-learning/distance education is here to stay, but we should carefully consider whether it should stay in its current form. Technology is essential, but technology alone will not get us where we want to go with distance education. Face-to-face teaching and training also is not going away, but its role, too, may change. Both online teaching and face-to-face teaching will continue to play an important role in education, with the use of technology also increasing (Rosenberg, 2006).

The role of instructional design in international distance education is likely to increase, because as the requirement to more specifically detail learning needs increases, it will become increasingly important to design instruction that is relevant to achieving these learning goals.

Instructors will continue to play an important role in this process and therefore should be trained to be effective, affective, and efficient facilitators. Training of online instructors is nevertheless often deficient (less than half of my colleague instructors at two universities had any experience in studying via distance education or had been trained to support distance education students.)

In one example, some of the centers of the Open University in the U.K. require instructors to participate as a student in at least one online course to help them build an understanding of the online learning experience. Here again, the sage on the stage mentality of the traditional classroom should be substituted with a model more aligned with the distance education setting.

How can international distance learning contribute to improving our world? How can we help people to develop a passion for learning? How can we challenge those who think that distance education does not have the capacity to bring about change? How can we deal with today's complex problems, such as living together in peace on this small planet? One important contribution that could be made is a renewed focus on learning and facilitating. Globalization of distance higher education can play an important role in increasing the number of meaningful learning networks around the globe, forming a dynamic learning community that focuses on living together in harmony.

COMPREHENSION AND APPLICATION QUESTIONS

1. The complexity and the nature of the forces that are involved in globalization raise fundamental issues regarding education. Identify some of these issues and discuss their possible impact upon higher distance education.

2. What, if any, is the role information and communication technology (ICTs) can play in supporting education? More specifically, to what extent is ICT-enabled distance education better equipped than traditional models of distance education for addressing the particular needs of developing countries

3. At the end of this chapter, the author asks questions, including the following:

- How can international distance learning contribute to improving our world?
- How can we help people to develop a passion for learning?
- How can we challenge those who think that distance education does not have the capacity to bring about change?
- How can we deal with today's complex problems, such as living together in peace on this small planet?

What would your answers be to these questions? Discuss your thoughts and observations with others in your class or group.

RESOURCES FOR FURTHER EXPLORATION

Evans, T., & Nation, D. (2003). Globalization and the reinvention of distance education. In M. G. Moore (Ed.). *Handbook of distance education*. Mahwah, NJ: Erlbaum.

Rosenberg, M. J. (2006). *Beyond e-learning*. San Francisco, CA: Pfeiffer.

Spector, J. M. (2007). Finding your online voice. Mahwah, NJ: Erlbaum.

Visser, J., & Visser-Valfrey, M. (2008). Learners in a changing learning landscape. Dordrecht, The Netherlands: Springer.

REFERENCES

Asunka, S. (2008). Online learning in higher education in sub-Saharan Africa: Ghanaian university students' experiences and perceptions. *The International Review of Research in Open and Distance Learning, 9*(3).

Bleak, J. (2002). *Insulated or integrated: For-profit distance education in the non-profit university.* Retrieved from http://www.westga.edu/~distance/ojdla/summer52/bleak52.html.

Bloom, D., Canning, D., & Chan, K. (2006). L'enseignement supérieur et le développement économique en Afrique [Higher education and economic development in Africa]. *World Bank Human Development Sector, Africa Region.* Retrieved from http://siteresources.worldbank.org/EDUCATION/Resources/278200-1099079877269/547664-1099079956815/Enseignement_superieur_Afrique.pdf

Bok, D. (2004). *Universities in the marketplace: The commercialization of higher education.* Princeton, NJ: Princeton University Press.

Bonk, C. J., & Graham, C. R. (Eds.). (2006). *Handbook of blended learning: Global perspectives, local designs.* San Francisco, CA: Pfeiffer.

Castells, M. (2004). *End of millennium.* London, England: Blackwell.

Eastmond, N. (1994). Assessing needs, developing instruction, and evaluating results in distance education. In B. Willis (Ed.), *Distance education: Strategies and tools.* Englewood Cliffs, NJ: Educational Technology.

Ferratt, T., & Hall, S. (2009). Extending the vision of distance education to learning via virtually being there and beyond. *Communications of AIS, 25,* 425–435.

Held, D. (1999). *Global transformations: Politics, economics and culture.* Palo Alto, CA: Stanford University Press.

International Association of Universities (IAU). (2010). *Internationalization of higher education: Global trends, regional perspectives, 3rd Global Survey Report.* Paris, France: IAU.

International Organization for Migration (IOM). (2010). Views of the International Organization: National Stakeholders Roundtable Forum in 2010. Retrieved from www.iom.int/.../ghana/IOM-Ghana-Strategic-Plan-2011-2015.pdf

Jegede, O. J. (2001). Distance education in Hong Kong. In O. J. Jegede & G. Shive (Eds.), *Open and distance learning in Asia-Pacific region.* Hong Kong, China: Open University of Hong Kong Press.

Knight, J. (2004). Internationalization remodeled: Definition, approaches, and rationales. *Journal of Studies in International Education, 8*(1), 5–31.

Leary, J., & Berge, Z. L. (2006). Trends and challenges of e-learning in national and international agricultural development. *International Journal of Education and Development using ICT, 2*(2). Retrieved from http://ijedict.dec.uwi.edu/viewarticle.php?id=179&layout=html

Meredith, S., & Burkle, M., (2006). E-learning: Encouraging international perspectives. A Mexican-UK comparative case study analysis. *International Journal on E-Learning, 5*(4), 472.

Nagel, D. (2010). *The worldwide market for self-paced elearning products and services: 2009–2014 forecast and analysis.* Retrieved from http://campustechnology.com/Articles/2010/03/03/The-Future-of-E-Learning-Is-More-Growth.aspx?Page=2

Ndulu, B. (2003). *Human capital flight: Stratification, globalization and the challenges to tertiary education in Africa.* Washington, DC: World Bank. Retrieved from http://www.worldbank.org/afr/teia/pdfs/human_cap.pdf_

Nunan, T. (2005) Markets, distance education and Australian higher education. *International Review of Research in Distance and Open Learning, 6*(1). Retrieved from http://www.irrodl.org/content/v6.1/nunan.html

OpenDoors. (2009). *Report on international educational exchange.* Retrieved from http://opendoors.iienetwork.org/

Rogers, C. (1962). The interpersonal relationship: The core of guidance. *Harvard Educational Review, 32*(4), 416–429.

Rosenberg, M. J. (2006). *Beyond e-learning.* San Francisco, CA: Pfeiffer.

Schlosser, C., & Burmeister, M. (1999). Best of both worlds: The Nova ITDE model of distance education. *Tech Trends, 43*(5), 45–48.

Schrage, M. (1990). *Shared minds: The new technologies of collaboration.* New York, NY: Random House.

Stedman, C. (2004). *Advancing need for global studies.* Retrieved from http://www.educationworld.com/a_issues/chat/chat122.shtml

Tubbs, S., & Moss, S. (2006). *Human communication: Principles and contexts.* New York, NY: McGraw-Hill.

Visser, J. (2005). The long and short of distance education: Trends and issues from a planetary human development perspective. In Y. L. Visser, L. Visser, M. Simonson, & R. J. Amirault (Eds.), *Trends and issues in distance education: International perspectives* (1st ed.). Greenwich, CT: Information Age.

Visser, L., & Visser, Y. L. (2000). Perceived and actual student support needs in distance education. *Quarterly Review of Distance Education, 1*(2), 109–117.

Vygotsky, L. (1978). Interaction between learning and development and the prehistory of written language. In M. Cole, V. J. Steiner, S. Scribner, & E. Souberman (Eds.), *Mind in society.* Cambridge, MA: Harvard University Press.

World Bank. (2010). *Extreme poverty rates continue to fall.* Retrieved from http://data.worldbank.org/news/extreme-poverty-rates-continue-to-fall

World Commission on Environment and Development (WCED). (1987). *Our common future. The Brundtland report.* London, England: Oxford University Press.

Zeleza, P. T. (2003). *Rethinking Africa's globalization. Vol. I: The intellectual challenges.* Trenton, NJ: Africa World Press.

CHAPTER 5

DISTANCE LEARNING IN BRAZIL

A Case of the "Fabulous Invalid?"

Fredric Michael Litto

This chapter presents some significant issues and trends in the development of distance education in Brazil. Although pioneering work in distance education took place in the 1970s in Brazil, there was an unfortunate backlash in the 1980s, and it was only in the 1990s that new developments in distance education in primary and secondary education took off. The chapter discusses the constraints holding back the full development of distance education over a 2-decade timeframe. It also shows how perseverance and cooperation have resulted in a new and fresh approach to establish more and better institutions of distance education and at the same time has led to acceptance and appreciation of this mode of instruction in Brazil.

INTRODUCTION

I was brought up in New York City by parents who loved the theater, and often I heard them refer to the circuit of theatrical houses that make up Broadway as the "Fabulous Invalid." I later came to learn that this popular

Trends and Issues in Distance Education:
International Perspectives, Second Edition, pp. 71–86
Copyright © 2012 by Information Age Publishing

term referred to the fact that the specialty of these showplaces of entertainment was glitter, color, action, and celebrity—all the ingredients necessary for diversion and the expression of popular culture—while in truth this magnificent industry of artistic production was perpetually harried by problems of finance, management, and regulation. Though continually described as being in crisis and threatened with demise, it has always, like the phoenix, returned to its reputable past of grandeur.

When reflecting upon the current state of distance learning in Brazil, where I have spent the last 40 years of my life, I find it tempting to revert to the old oxymoron: a "fabulous invalid"—an apparent success belying congenital constraints and contingencies.

WHERE WE ARE WITH DISTANCE LEARNING IN BRAZIL

In this vast, continent-sized country with nearly 200 million inhabitants and the world's sixth largest economy, the good news about distance learning is that the numbers of practicing institutions and that of students grow apace. In its survey of both academic and corporate distance learning, the Brazilian Association of Distance Education (ABED, 2010) offered the following panorama of significant results about distance education in Brazil:

Enrollment Trends

- The country has 6.4 million postsecondary students (13% of the population between 18 and 24 years of age).
- Neighboring countries Argentina and Chile each have 30% of the same cohort group in higher learning; the United States, Canada, and the UK about 60%, while South Korea has about 85%.

Distance Education Institutions

- Over 160 institutions of higher education have been accredited by the Ministry of Education to offer distance learning courses at the undergraduate level since 2002.
- More than 200 corporate universities are offering courses online and through closed-circuit television to some 500,000 executives, employees, suppliers, and clients.
- "Novo Telecurso" (New TeleCourse) offers off-campus primary and secondary education reaching 500,000 adults each year through open-circuit television, DVDs, and printed material. In its third 10-

year cycle, it is fulfilling an important role in giving working adults a second chance at completing a basic education.

Off-Campus and Other Distance Education Students

- Around 780,000 university students are studying off-campus in courses authorized by the Ministry of Education (MoE) and a similar number of students in distance programs whose structure does not require Ministerial approval.
- In terms of demographic distribution, off–campus students are roughly equal in gender distribution, with the vast majority (92%) between the ages of 18 and 39 years.
- Just under half of off-campus students want to become teachers, while the other half study in other fields, principally business administration and social service.
- Two thirds of off-campus students are enrolled in private institutions, while one third are enrolled in public ones.
- The number of distance education students increased almost 1,200% from 2004 to 2008. In spite of this, they represent only about one sixth of the total number of postsecondary students.
- Distance education students graduating in 2007 performed better than their campus-based peers in 9 of the 13 domains of the nationally administered exams.

A Snapshot: Distance Education in 2008

To provide a "flavor" of distance education, consider that in 2008 there were

- some 5,300 centers of student support scattered throughout the country;
- almost 650 different undergraduate courses off-campus;
- 650,000 students enrolled in distance education courses. Enrollment was down over 100,000, because of the closing in 2009 of a large number of remote student support centers. The Ministry of Education considered these centers excessively precarious.

DISTANCE EDUCATION IN BRAZIL: GETTING STARTED

Before further exploring the full development of (and challenges to) distance learning in Brazil, it is useful to discuss the cultural context in which it operates. In a nutshell, Brazil's educational heritage, initially arising from Portugal, is characterized by 300 years of intellectual barrenness (1500–1808), followed by some 200 years in which schooling was permitted in few areas (e.g., mining, medicine, and law). In the mid-twentieth century, universities were established, but were often perceived of dangerous places where people were given to thinking and criticizing (Litto, 2008).

Hence, it may not be surprising that Brazil entered the twenty-first century showing evidence of having both a weak educational background and a rigid educational universe, in which, for example, home schooling is prohibited by law; the school day is limited to 4 hours for almost all learners enrolled in formal education; and most teaching institutions possess limited technological resources, laboratories, and libraries (Litto, 2002).

As Figure 5.1 shows, distance education in Brazil took off in the 1940s with correspondence courses in vocational subjects. The 1970s saw several initiatives that used television for primary and secondary education and for in-service teacher training (Litto, 2002). These initiatives were quite successful and caught the attention of the international community. During the 1980s, however, very few new programs were initiated, even though some 60% of the country's population was still living in rural areas, with limited access to education and likely to benefit greatly from such access to knowledge. Many professionals who had worked in the field left distance education for better opportunities elsewhere, and it was only in 1996 that a new law established reforms at all levels of education, including the possibility of offering academic programs in higher education through distance learning (Alves, 2009). Some 10 years elapsed before the Ministry of Education authorized a handful of institutions to establish modest distance learning programs. Although the Constitution grants autonomy to universities in their pedagogical and administrative mission (through Article 207 of the Federal Constitution), the Ministry of Education and the State Secretariats of Education are currently the only accrediting bodies in the country, and they maintain a tight rein on institutional activities (Litto, 2002).

THE STORY OF THE BRAZILIAN OPEN UNIVERSITY (UAB)

Getting Started (Somewhat Slowly)

One of the major developments in Brazilian distance education has been the establishment of an Open University. The realization of this achievement was not without challenge. Initial efforts got underway in the 1970s and carried on from there (de Azevedo, 2011; Mota, Chaves Filho, & Cassiano, 2006). As noted by de Moura Castro (n.d.), "in the

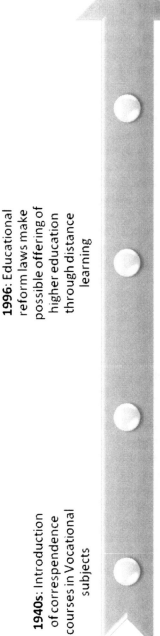

1940s: Introduction of correspondence courses in Vocational subjects

1970's: Television for primary, secondary and teacher training

1996: Educational reform laws make possible offering of higher education through distance learning

2002 onward: Higher education institutions begin offering programs through distance learning

Figure 5.1.   Key events in the development of distance education in Brazil.

early eighties, the success and visibility of the British Open University led several people to ask: why not have something similar in the country? After all, with seven million square kilometers of territory, there is no better place to deploy distance education" (p. 20). The long-awaited Brazilian Open University (UAB) was finally founded in 2006, after some legal wrangling (Mota, 2008). Brazil was the last country with over 100 million inhabitants to create an open university. (The delays in the establishment of the UAB may be attributed to challenges within and between three conservative bodies: the academic community, the National Congress, and the MoE.)

The UAB has been established as a consortium of some 90 public institutions, entirely supported and administered by the Brazilian MoE (Holzhacker & Prates, 2008). Its set-up was along the lines of the Center of Distance and Higher Education of the State of Rio de Janeiro (CEDERJ), which had proven to be very successful. Its focus is on offering optimized distance learning opportunities for those who do not have access to education in their own communities (UAB, 2011). Now that the UAB is underway, it is imperative that it focus on adequately fulfilling its mission; this is a matter of the greatest importance as it will affect the lives and the careers of millions of people.

Current Operations

While the primary goal of the UAB is the training of teachers for the public school system, a secondary goal is the introduction of higher education into cities and regions where little opportunity for higher education exists. In order to qualify for distance education through the UAB, a city or region must establish a learning/support center that includes a library; a computer lab; and labs for physics, chemistry and biology; and it must agree to offer face-to-face tutoring (UAB, 2010).

In 2011, the UAB had approximately 200,000 students. In the next 10 years, it is expected to triple the number of Brazilians enrolled in undergraduate courses (Congresso Nacional, n.d.). With the establishment and growth of this institution, it is hoped that the country will not only continue to make strides in its national and human development goal, but also in its international standing. In particular, there is an expectation that the UAB will help increase the nation's low international ranking of young adults enrolled in distance education, an important indicator of economic development (Mota, 2008).

At present, the UAB awards only undergraduate degrees. Admission to the UAB is based on passing an entrance exam similar in all respects to that required of candidates to on-campus study in the highly competitive admission system of Federal universities (UCAS, 2006). There remains some residual prejudice on the part of the general population against distance education (explored in more detail in another section of this chapter), but this is very likely to change with time, given the high quality of the courses offered and the positive attitude of the MoE.

DESCONFIANÇA, TERRITORIALIATY, AND DISTANCE LEARNING IN BRAZIL

Two unique issues impacting education at all levels and from all angles in Brazil are the challenges of territoriality and distrust. *Territoriality* is perpetuated by conflicting laws governing the "teaching systems" of Brazil's government systems at state and federal level. The jurisdiction of different distance education institutions has caused "territorial conflicts," particularly in secondary education and abbreviated baccalaureate education (i.e., the equivalent to the 2 or 3 years of community college studies). One open question is, If a student lives in State A and the course is offered by an institution in State B, will the certificate earned be recognized by the student's home state (State A)? Likewise, the MoE has not yet established the conditions, as required by law, regarding the authorization of institutions to offer postgraduate courses via distance modality. Such delays result in considerable losses for the country as a whole.

Distrust, referred to as *desconfiança* in Portuguese, appears endemic in the education system. This distrust is slowing down the continued and complete development of distance learning practice in Brazil. Both distrust and territoriality generate unique challenges, and they can combine to create evermore entrenched and complicated situations. Some illustrative examples follow:

- Matters of distrust manifest themselves in lengthy bureaucratic procedures for distance learning initiatives. Certification and authorization processes by the MoE are perhaps the most vulnerable points. Due to increased bureaucratic red tape,
  - o The MoE has not yet established the conditions, as required by law, authorizing institutions to offer postgraduate courses in the distance modality.
  - o It may take over 2 years for an institution to get approval to begin distance learning activities; this is too long a time span for academic activity in a field characterized by dynamic updating of ideas and increasing faculty mobility.

- Policies put in place to regulate distance learning have resulted in sometimes inflexible and illogical requirements put forth by the MoE. Some recent examples:

  o A high-cost private university offering online courses, whose students have personal computers with broadband access, was forced by the MoE to create regional study centers for student support, in compliance with existing policies (Ministerio da Educaçao, 2005). (The MoE requires that each center be furnished with 10 Internet-ready computers and a small library; several years of experience at the institution in question had shown that study centers would not be used by the students, because they already had personal computers and would only increase the cost for learners.)

  o No clarification has been given as to whether the certificate earned will be recognized in a student's home state if he or she lives in one state and takes a course offered by an institution in another state.

- Residual prejudice found in the general population against distance learning (prejudice along the lines of, "I don't know it, but I don't like it"). Such prejudice results from distrust and compares modern distance learning to the often overly simplified notion of correspondence technical courses of earlier decades (Aguilhar, 2010).

Brazil still suffers from regional differences; higher education institutions are located in only 40% of its municipal districts. In 2007, only 10% of the 18–24 year olds were enrolled in higher education. In that same year, the dropout rate was close to 50% (Holzhacker & Prates, 2008). Although there are centers of excellence in different parts of the country, these are effectively concentrated in certain locations (close to book publishers, scientific journal headquarters, and advanced research laboratories, among others). Further regional inequalities are the monopolization in the localization of materials of high academic quality in only specific locations. However, some of these regional differences are moderated through the access to materials made possible through distance learning; students from remote regions can have access to knowledge generated far away without leaving their homes.

In Brazil, the impact of distrust and territoriality, often manifested in policies of "supervision" of the distance learning activities in higher education, deserve to be revisited. Strategic supervision and oversight should focus on the progress and improvement of the institution, be responsive to student demand for distance education, and ensure that learners do not suffer the consequences of either territoriality or distrust in the quality of their academic experience.

ATTEMPTS AT BUILDING A
LATIN AMERICAN DISTANCE LEARNING COMMUNITY

While it may sound somewhat brusque, Brazilians do not consider themselves Latin Americans. They say they are "Brazilians," period. The reality is that for 500 years they have turned their backs on their neighbors in Latin America and looked instead to Europe and North America. Even today it seems there is not much communication among the people living in different Latin American countries. We know very little about our neighbors, and they know very little about us; this is, of course, a serious omission, because if we are to have a feeling of "community"—of belonging to the same region—we must truly know one another. Some years ago, writing about this lacuna, I wrote:

> Here in South America … we should have a greater sense of "regionalism." It is a good thing to think of ourselves as Brazilians; but besides being Brazilian, we must identify ourselves as Latin Americans…. Distance learning, mainly at the primary school, high school and undergraduate levels, is a way of achieving this defensive awareness. Using the Internet and collaborative learning activities, it would be possible to link Brazilian schools with schools in Argentina, Chile, Uruguay and Paraguay, to create this sense of regional community. (Litto, 1997, p. 2)

To date, there have been no significant projects applying distance learning to reinforce the Latin American identity. ABED has made efforts to involve colleagues and experts from other Latin American countries, including

- inviting distance learning educators from other countries as speakers in different events it organizes in Brazil; and
- sharing a variety of key resources, including the Association's constitution, the structure and code of ethics (as possible organizational models for a national learned society), and its online voting software system (for association elections, judging articles for publication, and judging submissions for its academic conferences).

ABED believes that other Latin American countries should consider establishing similar national associations in order to bring together distance education professionals in each of these countries. In reality, however, communication among educators in much of Latin America is limited.

Language barriers (also in the form of linguistic variations) may play a role. There is a highly interactive community of distance learning professionals in Brazil, with scientific meetings and a wide range of scholarly publications. While one would perhaps expect other countries in the region to have similar levels of professional communication and activity, such productivity is relatively isolated in most other Latin American countries.

OBSTACLES AND OPPORTUNITIES FOR
DISTANCE LEARNING IN BRAZIL

Obstacles to distance education are significant in almost any country in the world. Common obstacles include: lack of adequate funding (Holzhacker & Prates, 2008), difficulties in access to specific distance education formats, student support difficulties, and related issues with retention rates (Holzhacker & Prates, 2008). To be sure, Brazil is experiencing some of these challenges in different forms at different times during its distance education journey.

On the other hand, each country, and the particularities of its educational system, history, and culture, faces unique challenges with the adoption and effective implementation of distance learning. In the case of Brazil, some of the key unique obstacles deserving some consideration include

Governance and Strategic Issues

- The presence of a high level of regulation and red tape embedded in the overall system of governance, and applied to the educational system, present significant, systemic challenges. These challenges not only affect the potential of distance education in Brazil, but also the fundamental culture of education underlying it. They likely require a systemic-level overhaul, such as the design and implementation of a distance education framework with clear, well-formulated accompanying regulations striving to improve quality and student success.
- There is a need for strategic expansion of the public distance education system. Determining the specific attributes for a public distance education system to address critical needs throughout the country requires long-term strategic planning and coordi-

nated public policy, which is often difficult to accomplish at a national level. Basic education, training, and human development needs remain, especially in the least developed regions of Brazil.

- Addressing the issues of competitive entry requirements caused by the restriction of access to higher education through the administration of very competitive exams (UCAS, 2006). The number of students passing these exams may be limited and thus may prioritize, unintentionally, students of higher socioeconomic status and students who have had greater educational opportunities. In addressing this, the MoE and the university system are especially encouraged to look at approaches adopted by open universities worldwide, whose fundamental principle has, by and large, been to provide open admission to students. As stated by the British Open University (2011),

Nearly all of our undergraduate courses have no formal entry requirements.... We allow people who have missed out on education to fulfill their potential and achieve a university-level qualification ... it is the qualifications with which our students leave, rather than those with which they enter, that count. (para. 5)

- On average, Brazilians pay some 10 times more for access to broadband than do citizens in more developed countries. The resulting cost factors may affect access to distance education. Cost of broadband may be a function of several factors, including the sheer geographic area and population distribution, as well as the extent of market competition (Ricknäs, 2010). Such issues must be taken into consideration in the determination of the design and delivery of distance education courses so that a balance between effectiveness and access can be achieved.
- The Internet penetration rate as a percentage of population for Brazil is 36.2%, heavily concentrated around major urban areas. There was an Internet access growth rate of 1300% from 2000 to 2011. The resulting Internet access factors may affect access to distance education. When compared with other Latin American countries such as Argentina (49%) and Chile (50%), data for Brazil suggest room for improvement (Miniwatts Marketing Group, 2011). While Internet connectivity remains somewhat low and inconsistent, mobile connectivity in Brazil is very high. This presents opportunities for determining innovative mobile-blended strategies to offer effective distance education (Santos, 2011).

Student Issues

- There are tens of millions of functionally-illiterate Portuguese-speaking people worldwide. (This is likely to be the result of the fact that the majority of Portuguese-speaking people are located in relatively poor countries. Because of their living conditions, they are unlikely to have the access to quality instruction in English, the principal idiom of the web.) Available data suggests only *1.5%* of information on the Internet is in Portuguese (approximately 80% is in English). This drastically limits the utility of the web for learners whose preferred learning and information exchange language is Portuguese. (The amount of Portuguese web content is moot, at best. According to Ebbertz [2002], upon counting websites, 56.4% of sites were attributed to English and 1.5% to Portuguese. Aires and Santos [2002], using a search with connective words unique to Portuguese, concluded that Portuguese represented 0.99% of web content. The different methods of data collection do not permit definitive conclusions since site/server traffic may only indicate popularity; the use of "cookies" or "biometric signatures" such as "typing rhythms" are too new to be persuasive. Bialik (2010) refers to more recent statistics as "a murky business.")

- Although open educational resources (OER) have taken their rightful place on the worldwide stage, Brazilian institutions have shown relatively little desire to participate in the movement and make their academic resources electronically available to the public; only 10 universities have such programs in place (Santos, 2011). (The Ministry of Education's portals, "Public Domain" and "Portal do Professor" are generous examples of OER.)

Faculty Issues

- There is the question of faculty resistance to distance education. This is often related to issues with technology. The faculty often feel threatened and unable to propose alternatives that meet the needs of an increasingly dispersed population and respond to the needs of eager young adults seeking to use technology to become culturally and professionally competent. It is widely known that universities throughout the world resist change. (Eggins [2000] referred to the need for "confronting and overcoming cultural resistance … the ability of university managers to deliver successful change management is crucial to the acceptance of those strategies by employees." Citing Kanter's [1989], *When Giants Learn to Dance*, as identifying "in social and psychological terms the specific sources of such resistance. Among the behaviors that she enumerated were the loss of control linked to sudden, unprepared changes; loss of staff confidence; and fear of loss of status" [p. 63–81]. See also the report of the open meeting of faculty members of Brazil's leading public research institution, the University of São Paulo, called to dissuade the central administration from its idea of initiating distance learning activities [Garcia, 2009]. Despite this resistance, with the entry of a new rector in early 2010, the institution begrudgingly joined the ranks of dual mode universities with a single, online undergraduate program in science education, as if reluctantly accepting the fact that the function of the university is to prepare people for *their futures*, not for *our past*.)

• There is a gap in research that challenges faculty and other practitioners (as well as policymakers) seeking to identify and adopt best practices and lessons learned for distance education in Brazil. A review of the research on distance education conducted several years ago (Litto, Filatro, & André, 2005) revealed a lack of quantitative studies, resulting in inaccurate knowledge about the efficiency and efficacy of distance learning in the country. There is a need for establishing valid assessment and evaluation procedures. Such assessment and evaluation are crucial tools for instructional designers and instructors seeking to develop systematic, high-quality distance learning programs and courses. (For a description of benchmarking approaches used in the United States and Europe, see Barnett, 1994.)

Challenges will abound in all distance education efforts. Yet if we believe that in a democracy all citizens have the right to learn to the fullest extent of their aptitude, and if we believe it is better for as many members of society as possible to have the opportunity to interact with advanced knowledge, then we most certainly will have to invest in the future of distance learning—massively, and with the best possible quality (Daniel, Kanwar, & Uvalic-Trumbic, 2009).

CONCLUSION

There are important signs that distance education in Brazil is facing a promising future. To give just one example, between 2007 and 2008, the number of distance education students in undergraduate courses almost doubled to 761,000, which composes 13% of the total number of students in Brazilian undergraduate courses in 2008 (Boef, 2010). This, combined with the excellent results obtained in the National Student Performance Test of 2007, has contributed considerably to convincing instructors and students alike of the opportunity distance education offers. In fact, from my perspective, distance education is increasingly less on the defensive. Those who criticize distance education should now be on the defensive: the burden of proof is now on their side. It is up to them to show with measurable data the evidence that off-campus learning is neither effective nor democratic.

This is not to suggest that distance education is a solution to all the educational needs Brazil faces, but it will play an important role in meeting the needs for an educated workforce. In addition, the growth of distance education may enable Brazil to participate, as an equal partner, in the growing distance education "market" and lead to an increase in exchange students and faculty. Brazil has come a long way, and, as shown, concrete signs exist that distance education and distance higher education are here to stay, and that the obstacles we have confronted and are occasionally facing again are gradually turning into opportunities, not only for the happy few, but for the entire Brazilian population.

COMPREHENSION AND APPLICATION QUESTIONS

1. Some universities, especially more traditional ones, are considered to have a view of their educational mission as being almost "sacred," while some others are considered as having a view of their educational mission as one principally oriented by the "market." In your opinion, which of the two types of institution would be, or could be, best served by distance learning, and why?

2. Some institutions of higher education around the world employing distance learning are called "Open Universities." While some of these institutions follow a policy of requiring candidates for study to pass an initial entrance exam that measures academic preparedness, many others do not. What would be the strongest arguments in favor of requiring such an exam, and those in favor of not requiring it?

RESOURCES FOR FURTHER EXPLORATION

Litto, F. M., Filatro, A., & André, C. (2005). *Brazilian research on distance learning, 1999–2003: A state-of-the-art study*. Retrieved from http://www.abed.org.br/congresso2004/por/htm/180-TC-D4.htm

Researching Virtual Initiatives in Education. Retrieved from http://www
.virtualcampuses.eu/index.php/Main_Page
UNESCO Open Educational Resources Wiki. Retrieved from http://
oerwiki.iiep.unesco.org/index.php/Main_Page

REFERENCES

ABED. (2010). *CensoEAD.Br Analytic report of distance learning in Brazil* [Bilingual
ed.]. São Paulo, Brazil: ABED and Pearson Education Brazil.
Aguilhar, L. (2010, November 8). O dilema da educação a distância. *O Estado de S.
Paulo*. São Paulo, Brazil. Retrieved from http://economia.estadao.com.br/
noticias/sua%20carreira,o-dilema-da-educacao-a-distancia,42368,0.htm
Aires, R., & Santos, D. (2002). *Measuring the web in Portuguese*. Retrieved from
http://www.linguateca.pt/Diana/download/
posterAiresSantosEuroWeb2002.pdf
Alves, J. R. M. (2009). A história da EAD no Brasil. In F. M. Litto & M. Formiga
(Eds.), *Educação a Distância – O estado da arte* (pp. 9–13). São Paulo, Brazil:
Pearson Prentice Hall.
Barnett, R. (1994). *The limits to competency. Knowledge, higher education, and society*.
London, England: Society for Research into Higher Education.
Bialik, C. (2010). *Dot-complicated: Measuring traffic on the web*. Retrieved from http:/
/online.wsj.com/article/
SB10001424052748703983004575074103038050426.html
Boef, R. D. (2010). *Distance higher education in Brazil*. Retrieved from http://
www.nesobrazil.org/dutch-organizations/column/distance-higher-education-
in-brazil/
British Open University. (2011). The OU's mission. Retrieved July 31, 2011, from
http://www8.open.ac.uk/about/main/the-ou-explained/the-ous-mission
Congresso Nacional. (n.d.). *Plano nacional de educação*. Brasilia, Brazil.
Daniel, J., Kanwar, A., & Uvalic-Trumbic, S. (2009, March–April). Breaking higher
education's iron triangle: Access, cost, and quality. *Change, the Magazine of
Higher Learning*.
de Azevedo, J. C. (2011). Os primórdios do ensino superior a distância no Brasil.
In F. M. Litto & M. Formiga (Eds.), *Educação a distância: O estado da arte* (Vol. 2,
pp. 2–8). São Paulo, Brazil: Pearson Prentice Hall.
de Moura Castro, C. (n.d.). *Is education TV obsolete?* [Unpublished manuscript].
World Bank. Retrieved from http://info.worldbank.org/etools/docs/library/
235964/D3_TV_in_Education_WB.pdf
Ebbertz, M. (2002). *Distribution of languages on the Internet*. Retrieved from http://
www.netz-tipp.de/languages.html
Eggins, H. (2000). Costing technology-based education. In M. J. Finkelstein, C.
Francis, F. I. Jewett, & B. W. Scholz (Eds.), *Dollars, distance and online education.
The new economy of college teaching and learning* (pp. 63-81). Phoenix, AZ:
American Council on Education and Oryx Press.
Garcia, D. (2009). *Evento na USP prossegue série de debates sobre EàD* (p. 3). São
Paulo: Brazil: Informativo ADUSP [Association of Professors of the University
of São Paulo].

Holzhacker, D., & Prates, E. (2008). *Distance higher education in Brazil: A social inclusion perspective*. [Unpublished manuscript].

Litto, F. M. (1997). Soberania nacional e regional e educação a distância. *Galáxia da Educação a Distância, 2*(3), 2.

Litto, F. M. (2002). The hybridization of distance learning in Brazil: An approach imposed by culture. *The International Review of Research in Open and Distance Learning, 2*(2). Retrieved from http://www.irrodl.org/index.php/irrodl/article/view/65/133

Litto, F. M. (2008). Public policy and distance learning in Brazil. In T. Evans, M. Haughy, & D. Murphy (Eds.), *International handbook of distance education* (pp. 671–684). Bingley, England: Emerald Group.

Litto, F. M., Filatro, A., & André, C. (2005). *Brazilian research on distance learning, 1999–2003: A state-of-the-art study*. Retrieved from http://www.openpraxis.com/

Matkin, G. W. (1997). Indirect costs and the cost-effectiveness of promotion expenditures. *Using financial information in continuing education, accepted methods and new approaches*. Phoenix, AZ: Oryx.

Ministério da Educação (MEC). (2005). *Estabelece as diretrizes e bases da educação nacional*. (Law 9.394, Decree 5.622). Brasilia, Brazil.

Miniwatts Marketing Group. (2011). Latin American Internet usage statistics. *Internet World Stats: Usage and Population Statistics*. Retrieved from http://www.internetworldstats.com/stats10.htm

Mota, R. (2008). A Universidade Aberta do Brasil. In F. M. Litto & M. Formiga (Eds.), *Educação a distância: O estado da arte* (pp. 297–303). São Paulo, Brazil: Pearson Prentice Hall.

Mota, R., Chaves Filho, H., & Cassiano, W. (2006). Universidade Aberta do Brasil: Democratização do acesso à educação superior pela rede pública de educação a distância. In S. d. E. a. Distância (Ed.), *Desafios da educação a distância na formação de professores* (pp. 13–26). Brasília, Brazil: SEED-MEC.

Ricknäs, M. (2010). *Fast mobile broadband costs vary greatly worldwide*. Retrieved from http://www.networkworld.com/news/2010/041310-fast-mobile-broadband-costs-vary.html?hpg1=bn

Rumble, G. R., & Litto, F. M. (2005). Approaches to funding. In C. McIntosh & Z. Varoglu (Eds.), *Perspectives on distance education: Lifelong learning and distance higher education*. Paris, France: UNESCO.

Santos, A. I. (2011). The state of the art of OER in Brazil. *Open Educational Resources: State-of-the-Art, Challenges and Prospects for Development*. Moscow, Russia: ITE-UNESCO.

UAB. (2010). *Researching virtual initiatives in education*. Retrieved from http://www.virtualcampuses.eu/index.php/Open_University_of_Brazil

UAB. (2011). *O que é*. Retrieved May 11, 2011, from http://uab.capes.gov.br/index.php?option=com_content&view=article&id=6&Itemid=18

UCAS. (2006). *International qualifications for entry to university and college in 2007*. Cheltenham, England: Universities and Colleges Admissions Service.

CHAPTER 6

REFLECTIONS AND A CRITICAL REVIEW OF THE PERSPECTIVES ON GLOBAL TRENDS AND ISSUES IN DISTANCE EDUCATION

J. Michael Spector and Yusra Laila Visser

This chapter presents a series of critical reflections on the second edition of *Trends and Issues in Distance Education: International Perspectives,* focusing primarily on the chapters in Section I of the book. The chapter is introduced with some brief reflections on the book's thematic relevance and its potential significance to the field, identifying both its contributions and the areas it has left unaddressed. The remainder of the chapter focuses on analyzing Section I while considering the broader themes and goals of the book. Section I provides the perspectives of six authors (represented in five chapters) on global trends and issues in distance education. Each chapter takes a significantly different approach, such that themes in this section include the case for reconceptualizing distance learning, the need to define an international distance education research agenda, implications of short-term forecasting of the impact of commercial technologies on distance learning, the role of postsecondary distance education in the context of globalization, and the implications of concrete experiences of large-scale distance education efforts in Brazil. In critically reviewing the contributions, we reflect on the relevance and timeliness of the trends and issues covered in Section I,

Trends and Issues in Distance Education:
International Perspectives, Second Edition, pp. 87–94

critically analyze the perspectives represented, and respond to some of the key opinions expressed by the authors. We conclude the chapter with some brief reflections on the collective of chapters in Section I.

REFLECTIONS ON THE SECOND EDITION OF *TRENDS AND ISSUES IN DISTANCE EDUCATION: INTERNATIONAL PERSPECTIVES*

The first edition of *Trends and Issues in Distance Education: International Perspectives* appeared in 2005. Given the pace of instructional development and new learning technologies, it is appropriate for a second edition to appear now. Much has been learned in the intervening years with regard to what works best in various circumstances and how best to make effective use of new learning technologies. In this second edition, there are many valuable contributions about the use of new technologies to support distance education and about their implications for instructional design and technology practice. The book also reflects important contributions to the dialogue on the philosophical and empirical foundations of the field. What the book also reflects, however, is the lack of substantive analysis in the distance education field of what has been working (or not), and why (or why not), with regard to the use of *existing* and *older* technologies. This shortcoming is not all that surprising in the community of educational technologists, a community which is habitually optimistic about what new technologies can offer by way of support for learning and instruction. In our opinion, educational technologists have historically not been as serious about analyzing the evidence about the use of earlier technologies and building a cumulative body of research to guide progress (although it should be recognized there are important exceptions to this overgeneralization). That shortcoming aside, there is still much to offer practitioners and scholars in this new edition, which contains the contributions of many distinguished scholars, as did the first edition.

CONTEXTUALIZING SECTION I: "PERSPECTIVES ON GLOBAL TRENDS AND ISSUES IN DISTANCE EDUCATION"

The second edition of *Trends and Issues in Distance Education: International Perspectives* is divided into four sections, each with a specific theme assigned. The theme for Section I, which is the subject for reflection in this chapter, is "Perspectives on Global Trends and Issues in Distance Education." Each chapter in the section draws on the authors' expertise in bringing forward critical reflection on distance education themes of global significance.

The chapters of Section I focus on setting the stage for the 15 chapters in the remainder of the book. This section prepares the reader for a discussion and reflection on what current challenges and obstacles the international distance education community is facing. The chapters in this section are not only conceptual in nature, but also discuss research and application. The chapters in the remaining three sections bring forward significant trends, challenges, and case studies in key areas of distance education practice, including formal education (primary, secondary and postsecondary), as well as nonformal learning (such as workplace training). Through this approach, the book opens opportunities for cross-fertilization, or in simpler terms, for learning collaboratively in a global community. As such, the book offers useful and interesting learning and exploration opportunities for today's learners in the international and global distance education landscape.

REFLECTIONS ON SECTION I: "PERSPECTIVES ON GLOBAL TRENDS AND ISSUES IN DISTANCE EDUCATION"

The first chapter, "International Research: Responding to Global Needs," is by Deborah LaPointe and Jennifer Linder-VanBerschot. The authors of this chapter point out that distance education, a crucial element to meeting global human development goals, faces a variety of challenges, including issues of quality, the proclivity for using the traditional classroom model as the basis for the distance courses, and the absence of a unifying international research agenda for the distance education field. Building on that last point, the chapter begins by exploring the advancements in what we know about distance learning. The authors point out that some of these advances can be attributed to the proliferation of open-access journals, which have given a platform to distance education researchers living in regions of the world that were previously largely unrepresented in the literature. Exploring advances in international research on online and e-learning, LaPointe and Linder-VanBerschot report on recent findings on several key and complex issues, including the relationship between culture and distance education, the role of language (particularly in countries where a large number of languages are spoken), tutoring and mentoring, social software technologies for student engagement, and student retention rates (in which research results remain contradictory).

In the second section of the chapter, LaPointe and Linder-VanBerschot introduce the case for critically exploring the question, *Why has the field been unsuccessful in establishing an international research agenda?* They identify a variety of factors servings as barriers to such an agenda (e.g., the absence of clearly operationalized variables, the need for more action research and multivocal research, unique challenges in collecting and managing data, and minimal standards in the field). LaPointe and Linder-VanBerschot argue that the barriers to establishing a coherent distance education research agenda are reflective of the challenges in the broader discipline of education. However, from our perspective, it could also be argued that these barriers reflect specific issues directly evident in the field of distance education, thereby presenting an opportunity to reflect on the needs of the field. Examples of these barriers in distance education include difficulty in reaching the distance learner (for both instructional and research purposes); low standards, which present challenges in the certification of some distance education (an issue touched on by Wilson and Litto in subsequent chapters); and significant variation in the design, implementation, and measurement of distance education across settings.

Jan Visser's chapter has been somewhat playfully titled "Why Don't We Simply Call it 'Environmental Design for the Provision and Use of Distributed Learning Resources'?" We suppose the short answer to that long question is because "distance education" is, in our view, widely recognized as having a broad interpretation consistent with Jan Visser's alternative term, and there is an advantage to brevity in a great many circumstances. Jan Visser, however, argues that the common conception of distance education is increasingly outdated and out of sync with the needs of the twenty-first century learner. In arguing this perspective, he discusses in detail the issues around distance education's failure in responding to the education needs in developing countries, as well as the implications of the trend toward the commoditization of distance education. Jan Visser proceeds to make a strong argument for the role of autonomous learning and, more broadly, the importance of adopting a research-based approach to determining and validating the competencies today's learners should possess.

Building on the notion that equitable human development is crucial to addressing the increasingly complex challenges we face, Jan Visser takes a global perspective and calls for a transformative breakthrough that will cut across the boundaries between the many fields involved in technology-enhanced education. This is not an unfamiliar call to remake the world of distance education and educational technology. While Jan Visser presents a passionate and inspiring case, in our view, this call is not likely to be heeded. The world seems to be more comfortable with gradual change and graceful evolution with regard to things related to education, in spite of such calls for a more radical makeover. Jan Visser does acknowledge some of the shortcomings of previous efforts to make systemic and systemwide improvements in learning using new technologies; more detailed analysis of the data pertaining to current and past efforts of this nature would be a most welcome addition to the discipline.

In the third chapter, "Trends and Issues Facing Distance Education: A Nowcasting Exercise," Brent Wilson focuses on the notion of making shorter-term predictions with regard to trends and issues in distance education (i.e., within a 2- to 3-year time frame). With these *nowcasts* in mind, Wilson identifies several trends and issues he believes will apply to distance education within the next 2 to 3 years. They include a growing role of technology in facilitating the creation and sharing of knowledge and experience; an increase in the use of standardized assessment of student performance to evaluate distance education systems, teachers, and methodologies; a growing commercial viability of (distance) education; and increased systematic inquiry into learning *engagement* and *experience* by educational researchers.

By exploring economic issues relevant to distance education, Wilson sets the stage for a dialogue regarding the inherent labor-intensive nature of the craft of distance education, and, on the other hand, the technology supporting distance education, which in many cases is easily replicable and capable to large scale dissemination at relatively low cost. Ultimately, Wilson makes a strong argument in favor of the importance of recognizing the value of both craft *and* technology if distance education is to succeed. Further, his discussion on the measurement of learning progress and performance is key to the future of distance education—serious assessments that can and do provide the basis for meaningful, near real-time formative feedback are critical to the future of technology-enhanced education.

Wilson's discussion is a most refreshing blend of what is practical and affordable, what is highly desirable in light of new affordances, and a progressive view of learning and instruction. In our view, his chapter is an excellent representation of the quality of contributions to be found in this book, and it serves as a benchmark against which to gauge current critical thinking about distance education.

The next chapter, "Obstacles and Opportunities of Distance Higher Education in International Settings," by Lya Visser, explores the place of postsecondary distance education in an increasingly globalized, interdependent, and competitive international environment. In this context, Lya Visser distinguishes between *internationalization*, which refers to relationships between countries and cultures, and *globalization*, which involves interactions and integrations of people and organizations. Both are pertinent to distance education, as she rightfully recognizes. Like other contributors to this volume, Lya Visser recognizes the growing role distance education (particularly at the postsecondary level) will play globally, particularly as a result of the movement toward globalization and internationalization. She explores the obstacles and opportunities for distance learning in international settings. Among the obstacles mentioned are high start-up costs and insufficient numbers of skilled instructors and technology-literate students. Low student motivation and weak time-management skills are also identified. Further barriers include underestimation of student responsibilities, the inability of many students to work independently (without face-to-face contact), and communication difficulties due to the language of instruction and Internet resources. She also cites a number of benefits such as the ability to incorporate study around social and work time and place, and the possibility to study part or full time based on one's circumstances. Other benefits are lack of the pressure of a fixed schedule (not in all situations) and cost-saving due to less travel and lowered infrastructure requirements. Lya Visser sees the future as more bright than dim. Like several of the other contributors, she is realistic about the very real practical issues confronting the advancement of distance learning around the world.

Section I concludes with a chapter by Fredric Litto about distance learning in Brazil. This is consistent with the editors' desire for the volume to have a global perspective and aligned with Jan Visser's contribution in Section I. The title of Litto's chapter, "Distance Learning in Brazil: A Case of the 'Fabulous Invalid'?" is explained by referring to the example of the Broadway showplaces the author heard about while growing up in New York. They were referred to as the "fabulous invalid" as they specialized in creating an illusion of excesses, when all along these very showplaces were under great financial and management duress. Litto thus begins the chapter with the provocative question of whether the fabulous invalid is the most appropriate metaphor for the trajectory of distance education in Brazil.

Brazil is a large country with rich resources and a significant economy. Litto documents the history of distance learning, providing a context for the current situation. In telling the story of distance education in Brazil, he identifies issues that may help other countries avoid some of the same pitfalls. He identifies key obstacles to distance learning in Brazil, which include the high cost for broadband access and electricity (a challenge to developing countries elsewhere), the fact that Portuguese is not nearly as dominant on the Internet as English (an issue faced in all non–English speaking countries), and lack of support for open educational resources. Two additional issues raised are the presence of highly competitive entrance exams for postsecondary distance education (a practice not uncommon in developing countries) and the gap in empirical research on the Brazilian distance education experiences (hampering efforts to adopt best practices and lessons learned for distance education in Brazil). Litto also documents several experiences likely to be unique to the Brazilian experience, or certainly limited in their generalizability. He discusses the impact of the vestiges of the colonial era on the development of distance education, particularly in terms of the presence of complex bureaucratic processes and overregulation. Litto also explores the specific issues of territoriality and *desconfiança* (distrust), both of which present unique challenges for systemic distance education efforts in Brazil. Litto's chapter makes a strong case that the practical issues mentioned in Wilson's chapter are real constraints in the Brazilian context. These are pressing issues that need to be addressed if we wish to move technology-enhanced learning and instruction forward into the next generation.

CONCLUSION

The chapters in Section I reflect a series of diverse perspectives on globally significant trends and issues in distance education. Each of the authors has taken a unique approach in framing their chapter, ranging from LaPointe and Linder-VanBerschot's more conceptual literature-referenced approach to Litto's discussion of a country case study. This diversity in approaches gives the reader the opportunity to explore the broader theme through several different "lenses," each of which provides a unique vantage point for presenting perspectives on trends and issues in international distance education.

At first blush it might appear that there is a tendency toward contradicting perspectives among the chapters. For example, Lya Visser's cautionary comments about the possible dangers of commercialization of distance education are countered to some extent by Wilson's recognition of the role of commercial technologies in the future of e-learning. Upon more careful reflection and analysis, however, profound thematic interactions between the chapters are evident. Litto's discussion of the realities of implementing distance education in Brazil closely mirrors the concerns expressed in Jan Visser's chapter. Likewise, Wilson's framing question about providing traditionally underserved communities access to learning (and learning technologies) is explored in some manner in virtually every chapter in Section I. The need for more systematic research to inform distance education is echoed by LaPointe and Linder-VanBerschot, Jan Visser, and Litto.

Section I provides a framework for the chapters in the remaining sections in the book. Given the field's tendency to place all its faith in new technologies while failing to fully explore the potential of older technologies (a point also brought forward in Jan Visser's chapter), the section might have benefited from some treatment of specific data regarding what we know about the use of current and older technologies. That having been said, however, the chapters in Section I include many thoughtful and provocative contributions. The contributions in Section I should motivate the reader to explore the subsequent sections of the book; these sections provide the opportunity for more detailed exploration of trends and issues in distance education in specific contexts, including elementary and secondary education, higher education, and nonformal learning environments.

SECTION II

APPLIED DISTANCE EDUCATION INITIATIVES IN DIVERSE SETTINGS

Michael Simonson, Section Editor

INTRODUCTION

This section takes a global perspective on the application of distance education in widely differing settings. It examines the disparate and creative ways in which distance education is designed and implemented to meet human development needs in a wide variety of settings. The chapters in this section scan the globe, covering an array of countries, including Guyana, Portugal, Madagascar, Mozambique, the United States, and Zambia. These countries differ greatly in terms of human, economic, and technological development (e.g., market size, infrastructure, technological readiness, and political/economic stability). Thus, distance education in the United States or Portugal will appear substantially different from that of Madagascar or Zambia.

In the first chapter of this section, Tom Clark and Zane Berge present an analysis of the developments in *virtual schooling*, which is emerging as a prominent aspect of distance education in the United States. Virtual schooling is a relatively recent but increasingly important phenomenon. The authors of this chapter are leading educational researchers and practitioners who have written extensively on the growth of virtual public schools, and in this chapter they explore a variety of topics critical to the success of virtual schooling in the United Sates.

The second chapter, written by Jennifer Ho and Hetal Thukral, focuses on the role of distance education (in this case, interactive radio instruction) in meeting basic education needs of hard-to-reach and underserved audiences worldwide. This chapter spans a multitude of different countries and reports on the effectiveness of the interactive radio instruction (IRI) methodology. The choice of radio, a low-cost and widely available technology, has been especially important since access to education is denied due to barriers caused by infrastructure, telecommunications, or finance. IRI has been particularly used where trained teachers are in short supply, where teaching materials are not available, and with orphans and vulnerable children.

The next chapter, written by Pedro Reis, examines distance education in Portugal, with a particular emphasis on the growth of e-learning in that country. Reis reports on trends in the use of information and communication technologies and e-learning platforms, and discusses the impact of political and legal frameworks on both facilitating and challenging the growth of e-learning in Portugal. The chapter is concluded with a summary of the issues presenting potential barriers to e-learning in Portugal.

In the section's final chapter, Muriel Visser-Valfrey, Jan Visser, and Cynthia Moos revisit the rich history of distance education in Mozambique, a decades-long experiment in this East African country. While focusing on distance education for teacher training, the authors identify and discuss three key phases in the evolution of distance education in Mozambique over the last four decades. Within this framework, the chapter discusses lessons learned in terms of the successes and the obstacles faced with the implementation of teacher training distance education in this important country.

A careful reading of the four chapters in this section will reveal that the concept of distance education is practiced in a variety of ways that are successful because the educational systems are matched to the needs and expectations of the societies served. Virtual schooling in the United States, for example, takes on a different characteristic than interactive radio instruction for rural regions in sub-Saharan Africa. The independent adoption of e-learning by universities in Portugal is also qualitatively different than that from Mozambique's efforts at creating a national coordinating structure for distance education.

Finally, the reader should not only concentrate on differences in the approaches and locations described in these four chapters, but should also concentrate on the less obvious and potentially more important *similarities* these cases present. One exercise might be to produce two lists—one of similarities and another of differences—and then conclude by attempting to reconcile the two lists. It will also be informative to explore the outstanding credentials of the eight authors who have shared their expertise in the four chapters of this section. Enjoy!

CHAPTER 7

VIRTUAL SCHOOLS

The American Experience With International Implications

Tom Clark and Zane Berge

More educational organizations, especially in the United States and Canada, are providing online learning opportunities for students at the primary and secondary levels (i.e., servicing students between 5 and 18 years of age). As "virtual schools" grow both in numbers and in the scope of offerings made to meet their school district's purposes, school leaders are faced with issues and decisions that have implications for finance, policy, and practice within their school districts. The chapter's aim is to help school leaders find the most effective and efficient ways to serve their student needs through the opportunities afforded by online learning. To this end, this chapter reviews trends in virtual schooling in the United States, gives an overview of published standards designed to help assess quality in virtual teaching, and reviews the key considerations relevant to planning, building, and evaluating an online learning program.

Trends and Issues in Distance Education:
International Perspectives, Second Edition, pp. 97–111
Copyright © 2012 by Information Age Publishing
All rights of reproduction in any form reserved.

INTRODUCTION

In the future, the issues will be centered on how to use the innovation of online learning to solve the bigger problems in K–12 education: how to offer a world-class education for every student, how to improve teaching and course quality, how to move to performance- and competency-based models of learning, how to ensure every student is college-ready, and how to scale the delivery model for all students. (Patrick, 2008, p. 28)

Over the last decade, the number of virtual schools in the United States has increased dramatically. Additionally, access to full-time, online, and K–12 (kindergarten through 12th grade) learning opportunities has expanded, especially for students at the elementary and middle-school level. Watson (2008) found that 44 of the 50 states reported online learning opportunities for K–12 students. Of these 44 states, more than half reported K–8 (kindergarten through 8th grade) online learning options. It is interesting to consider that just 5 years ago, supplemental high school courses were the primary types of K–12 online learning opportunities (in terms of course enrollments). By comparison, in 2008, a total of 21 states reported full-time, public virtual schools, usually charter schools. (In the U.S. primary and secondary education system, a charter school is a publically funded school that is privately managed. Charter schools have specific accountability requirements, which are agreed upon when the school is established. Charter schools are not allowed to charge tuition. However, they are permitted to establish admission requirements.) Enrollments have grown rapidly as well; Picciano and Seaman (2009) estimated over one million enrollments in K–12 online courses in 2008, while Watson (2008) estimated 450,000 course enrollments in K–8 virtual schools alone (based on full-time enrollment numbers).

In this chapter, several key terms are used. A *virtual school* refers to any K–12 online learning program offered by an educational organization in which students can earn credit toward graduation or toward promotion to the next grade. *Online learning*, a related concept, refers to educational courses delivered either through the Internet or by using web-based methods either in real time (synchronously) or occurring without the constraints of time and location (asynchronously). In this chapter, the terms *virtual school* and *K–12 online learning program* are used synonymously.

CHARACTERISTICS AND PURPOSES OF VIRTUAL SCHOOLS

Virtual schools do not necessarily have a common set of attributes in terms of how they are set up. They typically have differing characteristics, all of which have implications for funding, policymaking, and practice. For instance, virtual schools may offer exclusively full-time learning opportunities, exclusively supplemental learning opportunities, or both supplemental *and* full-time learning. Likewise, they may use solely synchronous instructional methods, solely asynchronous instructional methods, or a combination of both of these methods. Virtual schools may be set up to serve students within a specific school or district, a region, statewide, nationally, or internationally. Schedules can vary too: They may use rolling enrollment or fixed calendar schedules. Online learning programs can also be classified based on the basis of operational control, such as state-led, university, charter, consortia, private, or district programs. Virtual schools can be developed locally, or they can be outsourced to various vendors.

Newman, Stein, and Trask (2003) propose four broad components of a virtual school: technology, curriculum, instruction, and administration. Essential aspects of these components include (a) an online learning management system (LMS), (b) course content and instructional services delivered via this LMS, and (c) administrative functions such as supervision and evaluation.

Virtual schools may serve many different purposes. According to Watson (2008), a virtual school can

- increase the range of courses/programs that any single school can offer students, including International Baccalaureate (IB) and advanced placement (AP), and college courses (particularly for small and rural schools);
- offer flexibility and improved use of time to students who have scheduling conflicts, are at-risk, are home schooled, have dropped out of school, are homebound, or face other unique circumstances (such as athletes);
- help meet the goal of teaching twenty-first century technology literacy skills across the curriculum; and
- provide qualified teachers in subject areas in which highly qualified teachers are lacking.

U.S. VIRTUAL SCHOOLS: GETTING STARTED

In addition to the purposes of virtual schools listed in the previous section, another key purpose of the virtual school is expanding school choice. Virtual schools have played an important role in expanding school choice, in part as a result of the passing of the federal No Child Left Behind Act (NCLB), in 2001. Under NCLB, K–12 online learning may be offered as a "Supplemental Educational Services" option or as an alternative public school option. The individual states are also promoting virtual schools as a choice. According to the U.S. Department of Education (2007), a total of 40 states, as well as the District of Columbia, permit charter schools, and many of these states permit virtual charter schools as an option. The characteristics of virtual charter schools vary from state to state. In Florida, the legislature mandated that online school be offered at grade kindergarten (K) through grade 12 by all public school districts. The virtual school was an option but often also almost a requirement.

In spite of the growing adoption of virtual schools by school districts throughout the United States, parents, educators, and policymakers often ask serious questions about virtual schools, such as

- Why should we consider a virtual school?
- What is the demand for such offerings?
- Are virtual schools worth the effort and costs involved?
- What impact do K–12 online learning programs have on student achievement?
- Should online learning programs be used as a supplement to in-person classes, or for full programs of study?
- What are the effective models of virtual schools, and how can they be sustained?

While these are valid issues worthy of discussion, the public dialogue tends to focus on specific preconceptions that people have regarding the implementation of K–12 online learning programs and their impact (Watson, 2007). The three misconceptions identified by Watson (2007), are explored below.

First Misconception: Online Learning is "Teacherless"

In reality, online learners in a public school program must be taught by a certified teacher. Good online teachers have regular interaction with their students, provide constructive feedback, and stay in touch with parents. Effective virtual schools provide training, mentoring, and monitoring to encourage such practices.

Second Misconception: Online Courses Are Easy

Many students and schools expect online courses to be easy. This misconception is one of the factors contributing to high initial dropout rates in online courses, as well as the "misassignment" of students to courses.

Online public school courses must be aligned to state standards, and many have challenging content. The sheer volume of work required for online classes, if not performed at a steady pace, can overwhelm students who lack the necessary time-management skills. Many students do better with external pacing and encouragement.

Third Misconception: Online Students Are Shortchanged On Socialization

This is especially a concern expressed about those studying at home in a full-time online program. However, these students often participate in extracurricular activities sponsored by their district of residence. The virtual school arranges field trips and social events, and parents form their own networks. It is impossible to conclusively prove or disprove such socialization concerns.

LEADERSHIP AND ADMINISTRATIVE CONCERNS WITH U.S. VIRTUAL SCHOOLS

Parents, students, and teachers have important questions when contemplating virtual schools. However, it is crucially important to discuss selected issues related to virtual schools from the management and administration perspective. Within the U.S. education system, the school system is broken down into local school districts. The superintendent is the chief administrative officer of a public school district, interfacing with other district-level administrators and managers of virtual schools. In this section, we focus on *district-level virtual schools* and explore what school leaders need to know, both with policy issues and with the practical issues involved in teaching and learning within their jurisdiction.

Financing the Local Virtual School: Costs and Funding

It is typical for school districts to use multiple online learning program providers that include postsecondary institutions, state-led virtual schools, independent providers, and their own online courses (Picciano & Seaman, 2009). Generally speaking, funding for virtual schools varies from state to state. There has been some money from grants and foundations, but mostly funding depends upon who is providing the courses. States have five primary options for funding virtual schools: (a) state appropriation, (b) a funding formula tied to full-time equivalent (FTE) public school funding, (c) course fees, (d) no state role, or (e) a combination approach (Anderson, Augenblick, De Cesare, & Conrad, 2006). Charter *virtual* schools are usually funded like any other charter school in the state. Similarly, district-level online virtual schools are usually funded by the public school financing provided to the district, often based on the number of students attending the district schools. Despite the perceptions of policymakers that virtual schools are less costly, the costs of different types of virtual schools vary, and overall, the costs are similar to those of brick-and-mortar schools. However, full-time virtual schools are more costly (Anderson et al., 2006).

Watson (2008) points out two important aspects of funding virtual schools in a state; whether state law allows students to choose online courses or not, and whether the state funding for virtual school students is at a level similar to traditional schools. The virtual schools showing the most growth in full-time programs are in states in which the money follows the student, and the student has a choice of a school in any district in the state. So essentially, state legislatures determine through their policies the funding, the growth rate, and what choices students and parents have within the state's virtual schools.

For any group of school district-level administrators considering virtual programs, a big set of financial issues surround the question of *where* virtual schooling will take place. District-level administrators may have questions such as, "Who will pay for computers and supporting technologies?"; "Who will maintain that technology?"; "Who will supervise online students, especially if virtual schooling takes place in the brick-and-mortar school?" Furthermore, these same administrators have to carefully consider issues related to curriculum design quality and teaching quality.

Standards and Quality Within the Virtual School

As virtual schools and online learning in K–12 have expanded, efforts have begun to develop standards for the field in the areas of online courses and teaching. Over the past 3 to 4 years, several organizations have distributed sets of standards based on best practices in K–12 online education. These standards can be used by districts to examine the quality of online courses and instruction, and the standards can be applied regardless of whether instructional the component is provided by a vendor or by the district itself.

Quality Online Courses

Several well-known organizations have published standards to help local educational agencies judge the quality of virtual schools. For example, in 2006, the National Educational Association (NEA, 2006) published the *Guide to Online High School Courses,* which addresses important issues when developing, managing, and participating in virtual schools.

The Southern Regional Education Board (SREB, 2006) published the *Standards for Quality Online Courses* to examine what a quality online course consists of and to outline specific standards for course content, instructional design, student assessment, technology, and course evaluation and management, stating,

> Several issues should be factored into setting appropriate standards for quality online courses. The courses must include rigorous content that is aligned with the state's academic standards and that enables teachers to adjust the scope and sequence of instruction to meet students' academic and learning needs. Ease of use is also important so students can focus on the content of the course and not be unnecessarily distracted by extraneous information or graphic displays. In keeping with what is known about the importance of interaction between students and their teacher and among students, the courses should provide as many options as possible to facilitate interaction. Assessments—both student self-assessments and teacher assessments of student progress—should be built into each course. (p. 2)

Subsequently, the North American Council for Online Learning (NACOL, 2010) published the *National Standards of Quality for Online Courses.* After conducting a comprehensive review of course standards, NACOL used the SREB *Standards for Quality Online Courses* (2006), added a standard for twenty-first century skills, and adapted these as the national standards.

Without reproducing the NACOL Standards here, the following are selected items to give the reader an idea of the scope of the standards:

1. Content

- The course goals and objectives are measurable and clearly state what the participants will know or be able to do at the end of the course.
- Information literacy and communication skills are incorporated and taught as an integral part of the curriculum.

2.   Instructional Design

- Course design reflects a clear understanding of student needs, and incorporates varied ways to learn and multiple levels of mastery of the curriculum.
- The course provides opportunities for students to engage in higher-order thinking, critical-reasoning activities and thinking in increasingly complex ways.

3.   Student Assessment

- Student evaluation strategies are consistent with course goals and objectives, representative of the scope of the course and clearly stated.
- Assessment strategies and tools make the student continuously aware of his/her progress in class and mastery of the content beyond letter grades.

4.   Technology

- The course makes maximum use of the capabilities of the online medium and makes resources available by alternative means; e.g., video, CDs, and podcasts.
- The course meets universal design principles, Section 508 standards and World Wide Web Consortium (W3C) guidelines to ensure access for all students.

5.   Course Evaluation and Management

- The results of peer review and student evaluations of courses are available.
- The teacher meets the professional teaching standard established by a state licensing agency, or the teacher has academic credentials in the field in which he or she is teaching and has been trained to teach online and to use the course.

6.   Twenty-First Century Skills

- The course intentionally emphasizes twenty-first century skills, including using twenty-first century skills in the core subjects, twenty-first century content, learning and thinking skills, information and communication technology (ICT) literacy, self-directed learning, global awareness

- The course includes twenty-first century assessments, as identified by the Partnership for 21st Century Skills.

Quality Teaching

There are some unique aspects to teaching online. The most unique may be that teachers and students may rarely or never see one another. This requires teaching and learning to be technologically mediated and places a heavy reliance on written communication. Another aspect is that courses are often delivered asynchronously, that is, with students and teachers in the course participating at different times and different locations from each other.

There are certainly conveniences afforded by anytime and anyplace teaching and learning, but it can present significant challenges for some students, especially those with poor time-management skills or who procrastinate. Students differ in terms of the rate at which they learn, the levels of instructional support they require, and the times in the curriculum in which they need differing levels of instructional support more during their competency-based learning (Patrick, 2008). Online learning is an option for providing such self-paced, student-centered instruction, particularly if learners can demonstrate effective self-regulatory skills. When considering the blending of virtual- and classroom-based instruction, online learning can also be used to support group-focused instruction that is *not* whole-class instruction. Examples of this include online collaboration and team-based learning activities. Teachers and students need strategies to help ensure active participation in a timely manner from each student (Rice & Dawley, 2007; Rice, Dawley, Gasell, & Florez, 2008; SREB, 2003).

As they did with the national standards for online courses, the North American Council for Online Learning conducted a comprehensive literature review for standards involving online teaching. The NACOL *National Standards for Quality Online Teaching* were published in 2008 and updated in 2010; NACOL's standards use the SREB *Standards for Quality Online Teaching* (2006), with minor revisions. As noted in the NACOL's (2010) publication, the organization also added two standards from the Ohio Department of Education's *Ohio Standards for the Teaching Profession* and the Electronic Classroom of Tomorrow's *Teacher Evaluation Rubric*.

The NACOL (2010) standards use a rubric with the following rating scale:

0: Absent—component is missing

1: Unsatisfactory—needs significant improvement

2: Somewhat satisfactory—needs targeted improvements

3: Satisfactory—discretionary improvement needed

4: Very satisfactory—no improvement needed

The 12 categories below have several items in each to score using the rubric above.

- The teacher meets the professional teaching standards established by a state-licensing agency, or the teacher has academic credentials in the field in which he or she is teaching.
- The teacher has the prerequisite technology skills to teach online.
- The teacher provides online leadership in a manner that promotes student success through regular feedback, prompt response, and clear expectations.
- The teacher models, guides, and encourages legal, ethical, safe, and healthy behavior related to technology use.
- The teacher has experienced online learning from the perspective of a student.
- The teacher understands and is responsive to students with special needs in the online classroom.
- The teacher demonstrates competencies in creating and implementing valid and reliable assessment instruments and procedures in online learning environments.
- The teacher develops and delivers assessments, projects, and assignments that meet standards-based learning goals and assess learning progress by measuring student achievement of learning goals.
- The teacher demonstrates competencies in using data and findings from assessments and other data sources to modify instructional methods and content and to guide student learning.
- The teacher demonstrates frequent and effective strategies enabling both the teacher and the students to complete self- and preassessments.
- The teacher collaborates with colleagues.
- The teacher arranges media and content to help students and teachers transfer knowledge most effectively in the online environment.

BUILDING A VIRTUAL SCHOOL FOR A
SCHOOL DISTRICT IN THE UNITED STATES

For-profit and nonprofit vendors provide the full range of solutions regarding virtual schools. District-level administrators making *build or buy* decisions can often buy the services needed while supplying internally those components of the virtual school they are capable of delivering at a given time—a learning management system (LMS), instructional content, or management. *LMS providers* make available the online learning platform in which courses are housed. *Instructional content providers* sell online learning objects or complete courses for those who do not want to build their own course content for their virtual schools. For school districts facing a shortage of qualified teachers, instructional content providers also offer the services of teachers who have been trained to teach online and certified in their content area. *Educational management* providers provide products and services for instructional supervision and other administrative functions.

A series of questions must often be addressed when deciding whether to build a component for a district virtual school or to outsource it to a vendor. For example, "Should we have a vendor provide the teachers, or should we provide them?"; "If we provide them, should we have existing teachers add an online course or two to their workload, hire new online teachers, or both?"; "What union and contract issues do these decisions raise, and who needs to be involved in decisions?"; "If we provide the teachers, how will they be trained?"

Planning the Virtual School Program

In *Virtual Schools: Planning for Success* (Berge & Clark, 2005), we presented a brief road map for decisions a local school should make in establishing a local online learning program. These decision steps also apply at the district level. In some cases, a decision must be made about whether or not to offer a virtual school; in other cases, the decision has already been made in favor of offering virtual schooling, and the question is how to best implement the virtual program. In either case, proactive districts will seek to determine how a K–12 online learning program can best be aligned with school improvement needs, desired outcomes, audiences, and curricula.

Before determining what to build and what to buy from vendors, we suggest that school district administrators create a *school district planning group*. This group should

- identify school district improvement needs. For example, a higher graduation rate or improved test scores;
- consider overall equity goals. For instance, are there student subgroups that are underserved or underperforming that might benefit from a virtual school option?
- identify desired student outcomes and target student audiences, such as students seeking to make up courses or to graduate early;
- identify appropriate curricula to meet needs. For example, core curriculum, advanced placement, and summer-school courses; and
- prioritize needs related to a virtual school.

Many school districts already have much of the needs-related information on hand from school improvement processes. After looking at needs, the planning group must consider virtual school options in more depth. It needs to build organizational knowledge of virtual schools, assess the readiness of key stakeholders for a virtual school option, and determine the cost/benefit of various options.

Implementing the Virtual School Program

Once the school is poised for implementation, the district needs to

- set virtual learning program goals and objectives;
- develop a communication plan and begin building a positive image and stakeholder support; and
- establish development teams as needed in key areas, to consider appropriate curriculum and instruction models, and to create development timelines.

Simultaneously, the district must consider partners and outsourcing arrangements for all or some virtual school components. In so doing, it should

- consider the district's capacity and willingness in terms of resources (funding, staffing, equipment, etc.) to build the components of a virtual school program;
- consider and select virtual learning providers and external partnerships to provide components the district will not be building initially; and
- build district technology, curricular, instructional, and administrative capacity as needed, based on build-or-buy decisions.

Evaluating the Virtual School Program

Evaluation is about determining *what is good* or *what works* about an educational program. Evaluators start with a set of clear questions, the answers to which are often the basis for stakeholder decisions about policy, practice, and legislation. Unfortunately, different stakeholders may have different definitions of what it means for a program to *be good* or *to work*.

In general, evaluation of online programs or courses follows the same principles as evaluation of other educational programs and courses. Early on, school districts should consider how they will know if they are meeting their mission and goals. This early planning will help the school districts avoid future surprises that could derail the program's success. School districts should consider evaluation strategies such as (a) instituting performance-measures at the beginning of the online learning program, (b) continually evaluating the program for improvement and accountability purposes, and (c) demonstrating and communicating the success of the program to district stakeholders.

SUMMARY

Virtual schools continue to grow in numbers and in the scope of offerings across the United States. They may be full-time or supplemental in nature and may serve all or some grade ranges. Virtual schools are operated by a variety of organizations.

Finance, policy, and practice around virtual schooling depend on the local school district's goals and purpose for the virtual school. Decisions about online programs should be informed by standards and quality considerations. In the past few years, several organizations have published standards to help school districts judge the quality of virtual school courses and teaching. Ultimately, it is the responsibility of the local school district to serve the educational needs of their students. In the case of the United States, school districts are evaluating cost, effectiveness, access, and efficiency. Taking these factors into consideration, a growing number of school districts and state legislatures are arriving at the conclusion that virtual schooling plays an integral role in serve student needs.

COMPREHENSION AND APPLICATION QUESTIONS

1. What implications does the U.S. virtual school experience have for schools in other parts of the world?

2. In the U.S. education system, the virtual school is most often considered a public school and thus is publically funded. Is this model appropriate for virtual schools in other countries?

3. Virtual schooling is often called a "disruptive technology." What is a disruptive technology? Do virtual schools fit the description of a disruptive technology? If so, why? If not, why not?

RESOURCES FOR FURTHER EXPLORATION

Means, B., Toyama, Y., Murphy, R., Bakia, M., & Jones, K. (2010). *Evaluation of evidence-based practices in online learning: A meta-analysis and review of online learning studies.* Washington, DC: U.S. Department of Education. Available at http://www.ed.gov/rschstat/eval/tech/evidence-based-ractices/
finalreport.pdf . Note: This document was revised in 2010 due to errors discovered in 2009 report.

Oliver, K., Kellogg, S., Townsend, L., & Brady, K. (2010). Needs of elementary and middle school teachers developing online courses for a virtual school. *Distance Education, 31*(1), 55–75. doi: 10.1080/01587911003725022

Picciano, A. G., & Seaman, J. (2010). *Class connections: High school reform and the role of online learning.* Babson College, CUNY: Babson Survey Research Group. Retrieved from http://www3.babson.edu/ESHIP/research-publications/upload/Class_connections.pdf

Watson, J., Gemin, B., Ryan, J., & Wicks, M. (2009). *Keeping pace with online learning 2009.* Evergreen, CO: Evergreen Education Group. Retrieved from http://www.kpk12.com/downloads/KeepingPace09-fullreport.pdf

ACKNOWLEDGMENT

This chapter was presented in an earlier form during a virtual summit meeting sponsored by the Fischler School of Education and Human Services at Nova Southeastern University. Sessions from this conference can be viewed at http://www.schoolofed.nova.edu/virtualschoolsummit/ or www.virtualschoolsummit.com

REFERENCES

Anderson, A., Augenblick, J., De Cesare, D., & Conrad, J. (October, 2006). *Bell-South 20/20 Vision for Education: Costs and Funding of Virtual Schools.* BellSouth. Retrieved from http://inacol.org/resources/docs/Costs&Funding.pdf

Berge, Z. L., & Clark, T. (Eds.). (2005). *Virtual schools: Planning for success.* New York, NY: Teachers College Press.

NACOL. (2010, February). National standards of quality for online courses. *North American Council for Online Learning.* Retrieved September from http://

inacol.org/resources/nationalstandards/
NACOL%20Standards%20Quality%20Online%20Courses%202007.pdf

National Education Association (NEA). (2006). *Guide to online high school courses.* Retrieved from http://www.nea.org/assets/docs/onlinecourses.pdf

Newman, A., Stein, M., & Trask, E. (2003, September). *What can virtual learning do for your school?* Boston, MA: Eduventures.

Patrick, S. (2008, Fall). Future issues in online learning. *Threshold Magazine,* 28–31. Retrieved from http://www.ciconline.org/thresholdfall08

Picciano, A. G., & Seaman, J. (2009, January). K–12 online learning: A 2008 follow-up of the survey of U.S. school district administrators. *The Sloan Consortium.* Retrieved from http://www.sloanconsortium.org/publications/survey/pdf/K–12_online_learning_2008.pdf

Rice, K., & Dawley, L. (2007, November 2). *Going virtual! The status of professional development for K–12 online teachers.* Retrieved from http://edtech.boisestate.edu/goingvirtual/goingvirtual1.pdf

Rice, K., Dawley, L., Gasell, C., & Florez, C. (2008, October). *Going virtual! Unique needs and challenges of K–12 online teachers.* Retrieved from http://www.inacol.org/resources/docs/goingvirtual.pdf

Southern Regional Education Board (SREB). (2003, April). *Essential principles of high-quality online teaching: Guidelines for evaluating K–12 online teachers.* Retrieved from http://www.sreb.org/programs/edtech/pubs/PDF/Essential_Principles.pdf

Southern Regional Education Board (SREB). (2006, November). Standards for quality online courses. *Southern Regional Educational Board.* Retrieved from http://www.sreb.org/programs/EdTech/pubs/2006Pubs/06T05_Standards_quality_online_courses.pdf

U.S. Department of Education. (2007). *The condition of education.* 2007 (NCES 2007-064). Retrieved from http://nces.ed.gov/pubs2007/2007064.pdf

Watson, J. (2008, Fall). Online learning: The national landscape. *Threshold Magazine,* 4–9. Retrieved from http://www.ciconline.org/thresholdfall08

CHAPTER 8

INTERACTIVE RADIO INSTRUCTION AS A DISTANCE EDUCATION APPROACH IN DEVELOPING COUNTRIES

Jennifer Ho and Hetal Thukral

This chapter provides an overview of interactive radio instruction (IRI), a distance education approach that has a strong track record of meeting the needs of hard-to-reach audiences across the globe for some 35 years. Since IRI is not part of the common distance education lexicon in places such as the United States, we begin the chapter with an overview of IRI's attributes in relation to distance education. Next, we discuss lessons learned for successfully leveraging IRI for a variety of purposes, included improving classroom quality, reaching out-of-school youth, and training in-service teachers. We contextualize the discussion with examples where appropriate. The chapter concludes with a discussion of a recent evaluation conducted on the impact of IRI on student learning and instructor performance in hard-to-reach educational settings.

Trends and Issues in Distance Education:
International Perspectives, Second Edition, pp. 113–124
Copyright © 2012 by Information Age Publishing
All rights of reproduction in any form reserved.

INTRODUCTION

Where trained teachers are in short supply, classrooms are in poor repair, and learners are required to travel long distances to school, distance learning is often looked to as a mechanism for reaching those facing significant challenges to being physically present at an institution of learning. In the world's most resource-poor countries, distance learning is an important mechanism for increasing access to quality education. Distance learning can be particularly appealing because it can bridge the constraints imposed by same-place, same-time classroom-based instruction.

Not all distance learning methodologies are equally useful in poorly resourced contexts. A disadvantage of some distance learning approaches is their heavy dependence on (often expensive) technologies that rely on the presence of a strong telecommunications and electricity infrastructure. For instance, while e-learning has taken off in the developed world, the effectiveness of e-learning in meeting the vast education needs in developing countries can face significant complications. Some of the factors limiting the potential effectiveness of e-learning include the absence of a reliable or comprehensive power grid, prohibitive or unreliable Internet connectivity, limited access to hardware and software, and a lack of locally relevant and curriculum-based instructional content. Other distance learning methods have been used effectively to increase access to education, but without necessarily keeping educational quality as a core consideration.

This chapter highlights interactive radio instruction (IRI), which is one method of distance education that has been shown to be particularly effective in reaching the most underserved and hard-to-reach audiences. IRI has been used for over 35 years, and during this time has shown to be an effective, low-cost, large-scale instructional methodology (Tan, 2005).

WHAT IS IRI?

Historically, the radio has been a popular technology for providing access to education in hard-to-reach areas. Radio has been leveraged for instruction in a variety of ways, with differing degrees of success. The main reason for selecting radio as the medium for instruction is that it is a particularly popular, easy to use technology. It is also relatively low cost, and almost universally available. In regions with little access to electricity or batteries, hand-cranked solar radios can be made available. In an analysis of media patterns in 17 sub-Saharan African countries, the African Media Development Initiative (2006) reports that, "Radio is the most accessible and the most consumed media in all of the countries" (p. 26) and that "radio dominates the mass media spectrum with state-controlled radio services still commanding the biggest audiences in most countries" (p. 13).

IRI is a unique, extensively tested, and systematically designed approach to the use of radio for educational purposes. Tan (2005) describes IRI as "a distance education system that combines radio broadcasts with active learning to improve educational quality and teaching practices" (p. 5). The IRI methodology was developed by researchers at Stanford University in the early 1970s, applying radio (a one-way communication technology) as a cost-effective tool for active two-way learning on the part of both teachers and students (Tilson, Jamison, Fryer, Godoy-Kain, & Imhoof, 1991).

While IRI is implemented in a multitude of different settings, this method has several common attributes:

- *Pedagogical Consistency*: IRI is carefully designed to achieve predetermined learning goals through the use of active learning strategies. The IRI design approach is iterative in nature (making extensive use of formative evaluation), and integrates key pedagogical principles including active learning, structured learning, recognition of prior knowledge, diversified learning activities, reinforcement of learning, and the use of engaging characters and stories. In addition, IRI has a defined teacher role (Tan, 2005).

- *Systematic Implementation*: School-focused IRI programs are typically broadcast (through local radio stations) on a regular schedule (usually 4 or 5 days per week), throughout the academic year. An IRI curriculum includes between 80 and 120 prerecorded radio programs, each 30 minutes in length (Ho & Thukral, 2009).

- *Contextualization*: The radio broadcasts are designed in collaboration with local specialists, aligned with national learning objectives, and focus on presenting examples that are contextualized to the local context (Dock & Helwig, 1999).

- *Multichannel Learning*: The curricular content is delivered to students by engaging multiple sensory channels (aurally, orally, physically, and at times, visually).

- *Interactivity*: IRI distinguishes itself from conventional radio instruction by focusing on *interactive* learning. Through the use of pauses and action prompts, both of which are crucial to creating an interactive, two-way learning experience with a one-way communication technology (Tan, 2005).

In addition, a common attribute of IRI is its dual focus on educational quality and teaching practices. The primary goal of IRI is to deliver a high-quality, effective learning experience rather than simply increasing access to instruction. The IRI broadcast replaces teacher-led instruction for that subject, thereby ensuring consistent, quality learning experiences even where teachers lack sufficient training (Tan, 2005).

In recognition of the deficiency in teacher training, IRI has a secondary goal of improving teaching practices. Tan (2005) notes that the teacher assumes an important mentoring role in IRI, using a teacher guide to facilitate the learning process. Through the modeling in the broadcasts and the content of the teacher guide, IRI strives to promote teachers' use of interactive, student-centered strategies.

IRI EXPERIENCE

What does IRI look like in practice? In this section we briefly describes how IRI is implemented in the classroom, how teachers participate in the process, and what goes into a radio broadcast script.

IRI in the Classroom

As previously mentioned, IRI programs are usually broadcast four or five times a week, with each broadcast lasting about 30 minutes. Prior to the broadcast, the teacher positions a radio in the classroom and elicits prior knowledge by reviewing content from previous IRI lessons with the students.

During the broadcast, students participate in structured learning activities, each of which are introduced and led by the radio characters. Timed pauses (built into the program recording) allow the learners to immediately engage with the instructional content being presented. Pauses are periods of time provided for the students to react verbally and physically to the questions posed by the radio characters, engage in a discussions, work in groups, or for the teacher to facilitate an activity as it has been set up by the radio characters (Tan, 2005). The purpose of the timed pauses is to use the radio, a one-way communication tool, to enable a two-way learning experience. It has been seen that the radio lessons are characterized by a high rate of student responses.

Following the radio broadcast, the teacher uses the IRI Teachers Guide to review what was learned. In addition, the teacher may choose to extend a particular learning activity based on student needs.

The IRI Script

The design and development of the radio scripts used in IRI is carefully conducted, using systematic instructional design principles and focusing on the contextualization of the content to ensure meaningful learning. Through the scripts, the radio characters interact with the students (and teacher) through timed pauses. The timed pauses are built into the learning activities and are a crucial element to making IRI an *interactive* learning experience. Below is a short excerpt from an IRI script second-grade instruction on addition, developed for the Radio Mathematics Project in Guyana.

Wise Man: Here is where Number Seeka lives.

Control: Musical bridge

Amar: (Whispering) Lana ... look at the Number Seeka ... he looks very serious!

Control: Instrumental music – "Happy Birthday" (:05)

Seeka: Mother ... happy birthday! (He kisses ... kisses ...)

Mother: Thank you, dear.

Seeka: Mother, I have a surprise for your birthday! Here are two red roses for you.

Mother: Thank you, dear

Seeka: And here are three yellow roses. You can make a bouquet with them.

Control: Musical bridge

Ray: [happy] Boys and girls listen.... The Number Seeka gave his mother two red roses ... and then he gave three yellow roses. Tell me, how many roses did he give his mother altogether?

Pause: :02

Amar & Lana: Five!

Leila: Yes! Two plus three is five. {/ex}

The IRI Teachers Guide

During the radio program broadcast, the broadcast "drives" the learning process while the teacher takes on a facilitative role. The IRI Teachers Guide is a print-based resource that provides information on the content to be covered during each day's lesson and is used by teachers to review what instructional content each broadcast will cover and to make any special classroom arrangements. Teachers use the Guide to plan and implement prebroadcast activities such as recalling prior learning and postbroadcast activities such as reinforcing what was learned. The Guide also helps minimize any perceived threatening role of IRI in the classroom, as it helps teachers anticipate what will be expected of them as facilitators of the IRI process.

The IRI Teachers Guide plays an important role in improving the quality of learning (by guiding the teacher in the adoption of sound instructional design principles) and teaching (by serving as a resource the teacher can use to learn the instructional content and strategies).

IRI AS A DISTANCE EDUCATION METHODOLOGY

IRI and Defining Distance Education

The world of distance education has become very heavily focused on applications of e-learning and, more recently, m-learning. IRI occupies a unique and different place in the distance education world. It is a methodology that predates the computer revolution, but whose demand has not waned over the years as more advanced technologies such as computers have assumed an increasingly important role in distance education (Bosch, 1997).

A logical question that often arises when IRI is introduced as a distance education methodology is, How does it qualify as distance education if the teacher and the students are in the same location, at the same time? In responding to this question, we will briefly look at IRI in the context of Moore and Kearsley's widely cited definition of distance education. Moore and Kearsley (2005) define distance education as "planned learning that normally occurs in a different place from teaching, requiring special course design and instruction techniques, communication through various technologies, and special organizational and administrative arrangements" (p. 2).

Dock and Helwig (1999) suggest that IRI can be described as

interactive lessons in which an external teaching element, delivered by a distant teacher through the medium of radio, ... is carefully integrated with classroom activities carried out by the classroom teacher and learners. Within this structure, the distant teacher carries the main weight of the teaching, and directs learning activities (such as exercises, answers to questions, songs, and practical tasks) that take place during carefully timed pauses in the audio script. The classroom teacher's role is often to facilitate the lesson, give individual assistance to learners, and provide follow-up support after the audio component is finished. (p. 7)

Immediately clear in this description are several of the components of Moore and Kearsley's (2005) definition, including planned learning and special instructional techniques (described earlier in this chapter). Key to Dock and Helwig's (1999) explanation is the presence of an external teaching element (the interactive scripts) and a distant teacher (the teacher recorded in the radio program) reaching the students through a technological medium. As was pointed out earlier, with IRI the radio broadcast replaces the in-class teacher-led instruction for that subject (Tan, 2005). This is consistent with Moore and Kearsley's (2005) focus on learning occurring in a different location from teaching. This also aligns with Perraton's (1982) definition of distance education as "an educational process in which a significant portion of the teaching is conducted by someone removed in space and/or time from the learner" (p. 4). With IRI, the decision to replace the in-class teacher for the duration of the broadcast is motivated largely by recognition of the lack of access to adequately trained teachers in the very areas in which IRI projects are often implemented. Dock and Helwig (1999) point out that the distant teacher carries the main teaching responsibility. In addition to addressing an immediate educational need, relieving the in-class teacher of the responsibility of teaching makes space for the teacher to build pedagogical skills and improve his or her own content knowledge.

The interactive scripts, delivered by radio, are the external teaching element by which the distant teacher interacts with the learner. These two components align with the specific instructional techniques and communication techniques, as outlined in the Moore and Kearsley (2005) definition. Finally, IRI projects are set up as special programs in partnership with local stakeholders so that the radio broadcasts are effectively integrated into the curriculum for the target audience, requiring the establishment of administrative and organizational approaches specialized to this distance education approach.

In considering IRI as a distance education approach, Siaciwena and Lubinda (2008) further point to the fact that IRI content is primarily managed and delivered through the radio program to learners (and teachers) sitting together in a classroom. In this sense, one might also point to IRI as a distance education method in that the content is primarily managed and delivered through the radio program to learners at a remote location. The remote delivery of the instructional content fulfills one of the most critical niches in education in developing countries; beyond a lack of adequately trained teachers, lack of access to quality instructional content is a major barrier to educational quality. Particularly in remote, poor, and hard-to-reach areas, IRI has been a more efficient method compared to textbooks, which are often already in short supply and expensive (as a result, most classes may have just a handful of textbooks that are often kept stored in the school to prevent loss or damage).

With the prominence of modern technology and its capability to narrow gaps in time and space, it is recognized that the objectives of distance education span wider than increasing the efficiency of content delivery. Populations of remote learners are oftentimes faced with more than issues of locality, and distance education has been looked to as a means of providing opportunities to those who can't attend school either because they are working, there is a shortage of qualified teachers (and thus schools), or because the system simply cannot provide the infrastructure necessary to make learning convenient and affordable (through provisions of buildings, books, and teacher salaries, for example). In observance of these needs, IRI seeks to increase the reach and flexibility that are hallmarks of distance education methods. As such, it is one of the approaches in international development education focused on guiding undertrained teachers, introducing active hands-on learning activities to students, or to ensure continuous delivery of quality curricula to remote or hard-to-reach populations.

The field of distance education is implicitly charged with developing instructional approaches more effective than, say, simple book delivery. Materials developed for distance education, as a result, bear the burden of engaging students in active and meaningful ways, integrating strategies that optimize the learning experience; something beyond simply reading textbooks, completing written exercises, or traditional chalk-and-talk methods (Perraton, 1982). This necessary level of engagement, or meaningful student-content interaction, poses one of the greatest challenges to distance education. IRI seeks to achieve this by building on research showing that effective programs tend to link broadcasts and print with some kind of face-to-face study (Perraton, 1982).

What Makes IRI Effective as a Distance Education Method?

Today, through IRI, radio continues to be used the world over to deliver curriculum-based active learning instruction in more than 25 countries. It has been evaluated extensively, and has been found to be a low-cost yet effective way of meeting priority educational objectives for many developing countries. Tan (2005) summarizes, "there is consistent and significant evidence that IRI can increase learning across subject matter, age, gender, and rural or urban location" (p. 5), with learning gains increasing with time. The effectiveness and apparent success of IRI is the result of several important factors.

- *Capitalizing on a readily available and simple communications technology (the radio)*: The radio is perhaps one of the few technologies still often used in both resource-rich and resource-lean countries. Frequently found in homes and places of work, the commonplace nature of the radio lends to the speed with which it has been adopted as an instructional tool since the earlier part of the twentieth century. In places where radio use is limited due to the price and/or scarcity of batteries, wind-up solar-powered crank radios can be used. With one crank these radios can perform for at least an hour.

- *Leveraging existing curriculum and print materials in the development of the radio programs*: Using national curriculum requirements and local learning resources, the radio broadcasts scaffold culturally appropriate learning content using interactive methodologies. As a result, the IRI programs are complementary, rather than supplementary, to the curriculum the teachers are implementing. Furthermore, by integrating into national curriculum requirements, IRI can be used to ensure that students are exposed to required instructional content on a consistent basis, even in classrooms where inadequate teacher preparation and/or a lack of resources would otherwise compromise student learning.

- *Focusing on improving teaching strategies*: In developing countries, IRI has played an important role in building teachers' professional skills while providing direct instruction to students. Radio broadcasts model pedagogical and classroom management techniques that teachers can practice as the instruction is being broadcast. During an IRI lesson, the teacher facilitates interaction between the students and the radio. Keeping the focus on student learning, teachers are simultaneously "walked through" various pedagogical and classroom-management techniques that they can later use on their own (Nambiar, 2010).

The Impact of IRI

The authors conducted a review of research to compile the available data on IRI and to draw conclusions on its impact on student learning and teacher outcomes. Based on data from 15 countries (37 total records), the review revealed that the impact of IRI varied significantly across subject area, country, and context of implementation. This variation suggests that several factors affect the degree to which exposure to IRI can improve student achievement. Some of the primary factors may include the availability of qualified local resources, the quality of implementation and monitoring of IRI programs, and the extent to which students actually listen to and participate in IRI programs (Ho & Thukral, 2009).

Results by Grade-Level

Analysis of extant research resulted in several notable trends. The data indicate the following findings by grade level (Ho & Thukral, 2009).

- First-grade level: IRI is most effective in improving student achievement scores in mathematics, local language literacy, and English.
- Second-grade level: Results were positive, but not as strong as the first-grade level.
- Third-grade level: Results in mathematics, local language literacy, and English were positive, though not as strong as the 1st-grade level. A positive impact on social studies was detected too.
- Fourth-grade level: There was a generally positive impact of IRI on student achievement in local language literacy, English, and social studies, although results varied by country and were less consistent with respect to mathematics.

Disaggregation of the Data

Given the preponderance of IRI in difficult learning situations, the data were further disaggregated based on several variables, including gender, geographic location, teacher training impact, and programs for special audiences. In summary, the disaggregation led to the following findings (Ho & Thukral, 2009):

- *Gender*: When comparing the impact of IRI on the learning gains of boys versus girls, the data suggest that when boys perform well, girls do too (and vice versa).
- *Geographic location*: In many developing countries, more remote students also tend to have poorer learning opportunities. With IRI,

rural students achieved on par with urban students in English and mathematics, although results on the impact in local language literacy were less conclusive. In one particular context (Pakistan), data were further disaggregated by urban, rural, and isolated schools. Findings suggest that IRI students in isolated schools achieved on par with their urban and rural peers.

- *Special audiences*: Among orphans and vulnerable children (OVC) who attended IRI centers and community schools (in Zambia), results were more modest. The performance of OVCs who attended IRI centers and community schools exceeded that of OVCs who attended non-IRI community schools, although their achievement levels were below those of IRI learners in formal schools. Among pre-primary learners, the data suggest that IRI has overall been an effective intervention for young learners in both urban and rural environments, as well as in informal learning centers (which often lacked trained teachers). IRI programs for preprimary students have focused on developing social, physical, and cognitive skills.

- *Teacher Training*: IRI has been a teacher training method using both a dual-audience approach and, at times, a direct training mechanism. Observational data showed that teachers not only gained a better understanding of pedagogical concepts conveyed through the IRI programs, but were also observed using active learning and student-centered techniques in their own classrooms (independent of the radio program).

In all, these data suggest that IRI can, and often does, boost student achievement. The magnitude of the boost varies across subject, grade level, and student population.

COMPREHENSION AND APPLICATION QUESTIONS

1. Look up the human development, technology, and infrastructure data for a low- or middle-income country (accessible through the OECD or UNESCO websites). Based on the data available on the country, how would you rate the feasibility and suitability of interactive radio instruction in comparison to other forms of distance education? With emphasis on the advantages and disadvantages of interactive radio instruction as compared to other forms?

2. IRI emphasizes the word *instruction* as opposed to *learning*. Would you suggest a name change from IRI to IRL? If so, why? If not, why not?

RESOURCES FOR FURTHER EXPLORATION

Ho, J., & Thukral, H. (2009). Tuned in to student success: Assessing the impact of interactive radio instruction for the hardest-to-reach. *Journal of Education for International Development, 4*(2), 1–16.

International Institute for Education Planning. (2004). *Adapting technology for school improvement: A global perspective*. Paris, France: UNESCO.

REFERENCES

African Media Development Initiative. (2006). Research Summary Report: African Media Development Initiative. *BBC World Service Trust*. Retrieved from http://downloads.bbc.co.uk/worldservice/trust/pdf/AMDI/AMDI_summary_Report.pdf

Bosch, A. (1997). Interactive radio instruction: Twenty-three years of improving educational quality. *Education and technology technical notes series, 2*(1). Washington, DC: World Bank.

Dock, A., & Helwig, J. (1999). Interactive radio instruction: Impact, sustainability, and future directions. *Education and Technology Technical Notes Series, 4*(1). Washington, DC: World Bank.

Glewwe, P., Maiga, E., & Zheng, H. (2007). *The contribution of education to economic growth in sub-Saharan Africa: A review of evidence*. Unpublished manuscript.

Ho, J., & Thukral, H. (2009). Tuned in to student success: Assessing the impact of interactive radio instruction for the hardest-to-reach. *Journal of Education for International Development, 4*(2), 1–16.

Moore, M., & Kearsley, G. (2005). *Distance education: A systems view* (2nd ed.). Belmont, CA: Wadsworth.

Nambiar, A. (2010). Interactive radio instruction (IRI) improves Indian student learning. *Educational Technology Debate*. Paris: UNESCO. Retrieved from https://edutechdebate.org/ict-tools-for-south-asia/interactive-radio-instruction-iri-improves-indian-student-learning

Perraton, H. (1982). *Alternative routes to formal education*. Washington, DC: World Bank.

Siaciwena, R., & Lubinda, F. (2008). The role of open and distance learning in the implementation of the right to education in Zambia. *International Review of Research in Open and Distance Learning, 9*(1).

Tan, J. (2005). *Improving educational quality through interactive radio instruction: A toolkit for policy makers and planners*. Africa region human development working paper series No. 52. Washington, DC: World Bank.

Tilson, T., Jamison, D. T., Fryer, M., Godoy-Kain, P., & Imhoof, M. (1991, March). *The cost effectiveness of interactive radio instruction for improving primary school instruction in Honduras, Bolivia and Lesotho*. Paper presented at the CIES Annual Conference, Pittsburgh, PA.

CHAPTER 9

E-LEARNING IN THE PORTUGUESE EDUCATIONAL CONTEXT

Pedro Reis

E-learning in Portugal has taken on an increasingly important role during the past decade. Starting with the Bologna Process in 1999, Portugal has followed practices outlined by the European Union and subsequently enacted its own national policies to help the country move toward broader European educational integration, including the recognition of knowledge and learning as valuable assets and the importance of a technology infrastructure to support learning. These movements to increase the use of e-learning in Portugal have been bolstered by a number of technological advances, including improved Internet penetration rates, open-source learning management systems, and ICTs. In this chapter, we briefly outline Portugal's experience with e-learning over the past decade and describe the increasing role of e-learning in both business and academic contexts.

Trends and Issues in Distance Education:
International Perspectives, Second Edition, pp. 125–136
Copyright © 2012 by Information Age Publishing

INTRODUCTION

The Bologna Process, a European educational reform process initiated in 1999 by 29 European countries, has strongly influenced recent changes to the basic laws of the Portuguese education system. The Bologna Process recognizes knowledge as a universal good, seeks to harmonize higher education, highlights the need to make education more attractive to society at large, and recognizes the need to adapt the process of teaching and learning to today's societal and technological realities. And because distance education promotes lifelong learning, mobility, and a European dimension of education, distance learning has been legally and formally selected as one of the modes of education under the Bologna Process. Indeed, e-learning has now been given a greater range of application than ever before: no longer limited to higher and continuing education, e-learning now assumes an important current role in both primary and secondary education efforts (European Commission, 2001).

E-LEARNING IN THE PORTUGUESE EDUCATION SYSTEM

An amendment to the Law of the Education System driven by the Bologna Process provided several opportunities for the development and use of e-learning within Portugal. The report *Reviews of National Policies for Education: Tertiary Education in Portugal* (OECD, 2006), for example, recommends that particular attention be paid to the availability of opportunities for formal and informal learning. This recommendation expects that new methods of teaching, learning, and training should be developed, which consider new media and appropriate formats and circumstances more favorable to learners. Building on this understanding, the importance of e-learning was formally and legally recognized by Portugal in 2005 (Paragraphs 1 and 2 of Article 8 [Distance Education] of Decree-Law No. 42/2005), establishing the equitable parallelism of the distance education and face-to-face teaching modalities. Thus, e-learning represents one of the best potentials in meeting three of the main "action lines" of the Bologna Process: promoting mobility, the European dimension of higher education, and lifelong learning.

Soon after this amendment, additional legal movements were made in Portugal that enhanced the role of distance learning within the country. In particular, distance education was established (Article 19 and Article 24, Law No. 49/2005, August 30, 2005, on the second amendment to the Law of Education and first amendment to the Law on Financing of Higher Education) as one of the special functions of education that

1. Can be considered an *alternative*, rather than just a *complementary*, form of mainstream education, accomplished through the use of multimedia and new information technologies.

2. Is particularly focused on adult education and the continuing training of professionals.

These legal enactments help ensure that financial, professional, familial, geographic, or health issues no longer hinder the ongoing teaching and learning process within Portugal. The net result is that each individual should now have the opportunity to learn according to his or her own availability and pace of learning (Gomes, 2006).

In spite of these legal advances, however, educational institutions still face several constraints that may obstruct the development of new educational approaches and technologies, including e-learning, but more positively, these financial, technological, and cultural constraints have been on the decline. Since January 2006, for example, all public primary and secondary education schools have broadband Internet connectivity. In addition, the Portuguese Technological Plan (Portuguese Ministry of Education, 2008) mobilized the agenda of the Portuguese society and sought to increase the percentage of participation in lifelong learning from 4.8% to 12.5% during the period covering 2004 to 2010 (cf. OECD, 2006).

The practices of Portuguese distance education undertaken in recent years were intended to address the temporal and geographical issues that face-to-face instruction is unlikely to address. For now, it remains essential that Portuguese distance education streamline access to learning resources, implement teaching strategies adjusted for more effective learning, make use of existing case studies, sustain cooperative relations, and facilitate learning using newer, more effective, and efficient information technologies and communication.

Roberto Carneiro (2003), the former Portuguese Minister of Education, argued that it was impossible to reclassify millions of people in Portugal without the implementation of more resourceful and versatile practices that capitalize on new technologies. Carneiro also insisted that there would be no reason to think that the world of education in Portugal, though resistant to change, could not be positively transformed by the use of these new technologies. Recent governmental initiatives, such as the Technological Plan and the creation of the Observatory for E-learning in Portugal, leave little doubt as to the importance of this type of education and training approach. Nevertheless, Portugal has several obvious inherent technological weaknesses in developing software systems to support education and training.

THE TECHNOLOGICAL PLAN FOR EDUCATION

The use of e-learning for educational delivery is now growing in Portugal, and it may be argued that the country at-large is beginning to accept this format for teaching and learning. It is now expected that the opportunities for e-learning will increase in all areas and in all institutions within Portugal. There are many indicators toward great growth potential of e-learning in Portugal that are currently being witnessed, particularly those that regard blended formats making use of ICT. To help ensure the success of this transformation, e-learning must remain focused on both quality and positive pedagogical outcomes. The evolution and convergence of communications technologies, especially in terms of broadband connectivity (both fixed and mobile), will certainly lead to new services, platforms, technologies, and methods for education; and further developments in the level of customization of e-learning environments based on these developments should be expected. And even though a teaching modality that was once viewed as ineffective now seems to many in Portugal as more attractive and efficient, it is necessary that Portugal continue to experiment, evaluate, and promote initiatives that demonstrate the fully realized pedagogical potential of e-learning.

E-LEARNING PLATFORMS

A study titled *Platforms for Distance Education in Portugal* (Delta Consulting Ltd. and the Higher Institute of Applied Psychology, 2007) examined a series of Portuguese institutions that make use of platforms for e-learning. The study showed that the e-learning platform most used by students in Portugal is Moodle (35%), followed by Blackboard (17%), and Teleformar.net (14%), with a level of user satisfaction exceeding 90%. An overwhelming majority of facilitators (72%) use Moodle as the working tool typically provided by the educational/training institution (see Figure 9.1).

Several reasons contribute to the success of Moodle (Modular Object-Oriented Dynamic Learning Environment) as the most frequently used platform by facilitators and trainees. As an open-source course management system (CMS), also known as learning management system (LMS) or virtual learning environment (VLE), Moodle has become very popular with educators worldwide as an online tool to create dynamic websites for students. This platform was developed in order to provide educators with tools to manage and enhance learning, improving and/or increasing the channels of knowledge mobilization; and the platform is available free of charge. Moodle allows the establishment of highly collaborative

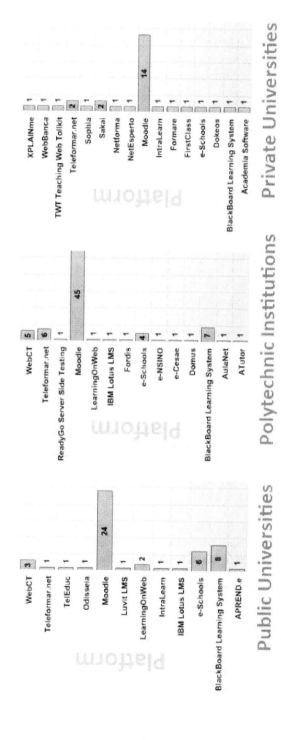

Figure 9.1. Distribution of platforms in Portugal, considering different sectors of Higher Education (adapted from Delta Consulting Ltd., 2007).

communities, but it also offers several tools for evaluation of students within the learning process.

Like Moodle, if e-learning platforms in general make it more possible to overcome issues that are raised by today's Portuguese society (such as, for example, the growing lack of "leisure" time), these tools can be used to support the fight against social exclusion. In fact, as e-learning platforms allow greater distribution of educational resources, a much wider range of individuals can have access to personal or professional enhancement than ever before.

The continuing need for additional and more effective learning opportunities requires constant improvement of the tools used to deliver such education. Nevertheless, current technological realities, such as the available bandwidth and the need for improvement of computers, must be taken into consideration. These technological realities can be seen as a disadvantage to this movement, since expertise is required of the agents involved, and they may also face technical barriers. On the other hand, as we argue, it can be viewed as an advantage, since it will compel the acquisition of knowledge in the area of new technologies, and it also works as a tool in combating the exclusion of many from the acquisition of new knowledge.

INFORMATION AND
COMMUNICATION TECHNOLOGY (ICT) IN PORTUGAL

According to Cardoso and Bidarra (2005), lifelong learning can be much enhanced by the development and spread of ICTs. ICTs have the potential to support new models of communication that tend to be more personalized, interactive, and global, thus extending the capacity of generating knowledge and human interaction. In the case of Portugal in the 1990s, an evolution in the quality of information technology took place, although this change was not sufficient in scope to meet today's convergence with the European Union (EU) (Sousa, 1997). Currently, Portugal is undergoing what is considered an ICT technological revolution, leading to the designation of Portuguese society as a "Knowledge Society." The use of computers and the Internet is an essential condition for nonexclusion in such a society, in which those who thrive and continue to be included in the knowledge society are the consumers of those goods (Castro, 2006).

Researchers have reported data that supports the contention that Portugal is moving toward a technologically focused existence. According to the publication of the National Statistics Institute (INE, 2008), for example, the percentage of Portuguese computer users aged 16 to 74 is 46%, while the percentage of Portuguese Internet users in the same age group is

40%. Among the Portuguese households that have Internet access, 77% have access through broadband (INE, 2008). At the corporate level, companies with more than 10 employees (with the exception of the financial sector) have a 90% Internet connection rate, with 76% possessing a broadband connection. For small businesses, 88% possess Internet connectivity. This threshold increases to 98% for medium-sized Portuguese businesses, and 100% for large companies. The findings of this study demonstrate the great efforts Portugal has made to converge with the EU in the implementation of a "digital culture" through the field of technology, including its pedagogical use.

EVOLUTION OF THE E-LEARNING MARKET

In 2000, following the recommendations of the Lisbon European Council to converge the educational systems with other training in Europe, the European Union announced the *eLearning: Designing Tomorrow's Education* initiative (Europa, 2003). The major objective of this initiative was to improve the quality of learning in order to facilitate access to resources and services, as well as to facilitate exchange of communication through the use of new multimedia technologies based on the Internet.

The effort of member states, especially Portugal, to implement the *eLearning: Designing Tomorrow's Education* initiative has shown significant progress. According to the Institute for Innovation in Training (INOFOR in Carneiro, 2003), in Portugal, e-learning is an educational model implemented by various types of public and private entities, the majority of which are located in the north of the country (see Figure 9.2).

In the first 5 years after the adoption of the initiative, there was a significant investment in the e-learning market in Portugal, as can be seen in Figure 9.2. According to studies in vocational training ("E-learning and Training in Europe" and "Feedback From Users on E-Learning," in Vieira, 2001), between 60% and 70% of the Portuguese training providers already offer or plan to implement an e-Learning system. Nevertheless, it should also be noted that, paradoxically, about 32% of teachers and trainers have indicated a low level of competence in preparing e-contents or pedagogical e-learning tools, and only 17% claim to have a level of competence of very good or excellent.

Portugal has also recently seen the emergence of so-called corporate universities, which were first developed to meet the need to provide ongoing training to corporate employees. Due to its reduced costs, e-learning has become the ideal solution for these organizations. The high levels of training and the success achieved by these organizations have served as an example for other companies and institutions (Leitão, 2004).

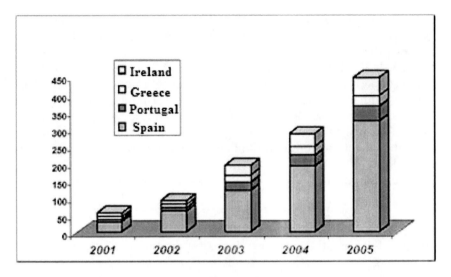

Figure 9.2.   Evolution of the e-learning market (million Euros) (adapted from S.P.I., 2003).

Primary and secondary schools, universities, and training centers, in both public and private sectors, also increasingly consider e-learning as an opportunity to overcome the training needs of employees and the other people they serve. However, it is important to note that these opportunities are not yet universally available. The equipping of institutions with adequate human and technological resources and increased training in ICT has been and will continue to be essential for the continuing success of e-learning (Lima, 2003).

In order to describe some important limitations of the current situation of e-learning in Portugal, it will be pertinent to mention the conclusions of two studies from two independent institutions examining the issue. The former is a study conducted by Paradigm Consulting, SA for the Portuguese Entrepreneurial Association (AEP). Summarized by Eiras (2001), the main conclusions of this study were as follows:

1. The main educational goal to be achieved by e-learning, i.e., developing the capacity for self-learning, was not identified in most Portuguese distance learning programs.
2. It is not current practice to give trainees the opportunity to configure and contribute to the distance learning systems in order to tailor the system to meet specific needs or to create greater interactivity.

3. It is often not possible to identify the intentions of created virtual communities and informal networks between former trainees.

4. The existence of face-to-face sessions is a standard practice, with subject-matter content primarily delivered in a face-to-face setting and only learner practice being conducted in the distance setting. This means, then, that b-learning (i.e., blended learning) is more prominent in Portugal than e-learning.

The second study was conducted by Markup for the Digital Society-Association for the Promotion of Knowledge Society and addressed to 831 respondents. The technique used for gathering information was an online survey distributed on Technology, Stock Exchange, and in the space of Economics on Sapo Portal, as well as through e-mail messages. The study's findings were as follows:

1. Some 20% of the respondents reported participation in an online course, and of the remaining 80% who never participated, the overwhelming majority (94%) reported interest in enrolling in an e-learning course. The reasons for this interest were reported as flexible hours (21%) and self-paced or self-learning (15%). The remaining 6% who reported no interest in e-learning most frequently reported (23%) the lack of confidence in e-learning content and in the educational results of the method.

2. Of the 20% of respondents who had participated in online training activities, the majority reported satisfaction with the activities provided through this format. In all, 47% reported satisfaction with the virtual classroom, 41% reported satisfaction with the library, 41% with the forum, 40% with messaging, 24% with chat, and 43% with online assessments.

3. The vast majority (97%) of respondents reported being comfortable with the LMS, with 95% reporting that they found the LMS intuitive. Only 18% reported technological difficulties with the LMS, and only 9% reported that they had missed some component of the system.

4. Regarding the quality of content, 44% felt very pleased with the ability to apply the knowledge acquired in the course. A significant number (41%) also reported feeling very satisfied with the appropriateness of the courses to meet the proposed objectives. A total of 59% reported satisfaction with web design, 52% with how content is structured, and 51% with the clarity of the language used.

5. With regard to teacher performance, 40% reported being very satisfied with the quality of the explanations provided, and 36% were satisfied with the rapidity of reply to requests. The percentage of those who reported that they did not ask for assistance from the facilitator was small (11%).

6. Overall, 40% of respondents reported that they were quite satisfied with the level of demand for the courses taken and, of all respondents, 84% reported that they wished to attend a course online over the next 6 months.

CONCLUDING COMMENTS

The systems that support the processes of teaching and learning at a distance are of great importance to the so-called Knowledge Society of Portugal. This opening of doors for basic or advanced training or education to a large number of people who can potentially see their academic qualifications or professional circumstances improved is essential. E-learning systems have a potentially wide range of application in Portugal, since these systems can be developed to support basic and secondary education, the university level, and the customized needs of companies and businesses.

Nevertheless, e-learning in Portugal still has a long way to go to reach maturity and consolidation within the nation's society. In this sense, e-learning presents challenges and interesting lines of research both in the educational and technological fields, both of which are enriched if there is a convergence of the interests of both fields in order to achieve greater educational outcomes.

The human factor in e-learning cannot be ignored, of course. The human factor is undoubtedly a key component of any organization wishing to develop an e-learning strategy. In the learning process, technological platforms and pedagogical models will not be an end in themselves, but will be the means to achieve the ultimate goal of this process, that is, to increase knowledge and personal development. Thus, it is important to note that there exist individuals at both ends of this spectrum who believe in the benefits of e-learning and who will ultimately assist e-learning in achieving its highest goals. Without their assistance, commitment, and devotion, the triumph of e-learning in Portugal will be impossible.

RESOURCES FOR FURTHER EXPLORATION

Hasan, A., & Laaser, W. (2010, July 10). Higher education distance learning in Portugal: State of the art and current policy issues. Retrieved from http://www.eurodl.org/?p=current&article=414

Hasan, A. et al. (2009). *Reforming distance learning higher education in Portugal*. Lisbon, Portugal: Ministry of Science, Technology and Higher Education.

Simonson, M., Smaldino, S., Albright, M., & Zvacek, S. (2012). *Teaching and learning at distance: Foundations of distance education* (5th ed.) Boston, MA: Allyn and Bacon.

COMPREHENSION AND APPLICATION QUESTIONS

1. What is the relationship between e-learning and the Knowledge Society in Portugal? What factors surrounding a Knowledge Society are best supported with e-learning approaches?

2. How has national legal actions impacted the growth of e-learning within the Portuguese context? Would e-learning have blossomed in Portugal if such legal actions had not been taken? Are further legal proclamations concerning e-learning in Portugal necessary?

3. How does Portugal's experience with e-learning differ or agree with other European countries? Will e-learning throughout Europe tend to converge across countries over time, or will e-learning remain at widely different levels across European countries?

AUTHOR NOTE

Note: An interview with Dr. Reis can be found at: http://vimeo.com/8100057

REFERENCES

Cardoso V., & Bidarra, J. (2005). Open and distance learning: Does IT (still) matter? *EURODL*. Retrieved from http://www.eurodl.org/materials/briefs/2007/Cardoso_Bidarra_PTA.htm

Carneiro, R. (2003). *Evolução do e-learning em Portugal*. Lisbon, Portugal: INOFOR.

Castro, C. S. C. (2006). *A influência das tecnologias de informação e comunicação (TIC) no desenvolvimento do currículo por competências*. Master's dissertation. Braga, Instituto de Educação e Psicologia, Universidade do Minho, Portugal.

Delta Consulting Ltd. and Higher Institute of Applied Psychology. (2007). *Estudo das plataformas de formação a distância em Portugal*. Lisbon, Portugal: DeltaConsultores Tecnologia e Recursos Integrados, Lda. Retrieved from http://opac.iefp.pt:8080/images/winlibimg.exe?key=&doc=44717&img=241

Eiras, R. (2001). *"E-learning" domina 20% da formação em Portugal*. Retrieved from http://janelanaweb.com/oldindex.html

Europa. (2003). *E-learning: Designing tomorrow's education*. Retrieved from http://europa.eu/legislation_summaries/education_training_youth/lifelong_learning/c11046_en.htm

European Commission. (2001). *The e-learning action plan*. Retrieved from http://eur-lex.europa.eu/LexUriServ/site/pt/com/2006/com2006_0077pt01.pdf

Gomes, M. J. (2006). E-learning e educação on-line: Contributos para os princípios de Bolonha. In *Actas do VII colóquio sobre questões curriculares - Globalização e (des) igualdades: Os desafios curriculares*. Braga, Portugal: Centro de Investigação em Educação Universidade do Minho.

INE. (2008). *Sociedade da informação e do conhecimento - 2007*. Retrieved from www.ine.pt

Leitao, P. (2004). *Plataformas de e-learning no ensino superior: Avaliação da situação actual*. Master's dissertation, Universidade do Minho, Portugal.

Lima, J., & Capitao, Z. (2003). *E-learning e e-conteúdos*. Lisbon, Portugal: Centro Atlântico.

Organization for Economic Cooperation and Development (OECD). (2006). *Country background report: Portugal. OECD thematic review of tertiary education*. Retrieved from http://www.oecd.org/dataoecd/23/1/37745972.pdf

Portuguese Ministry of Education. (2008). *Technological plan for education: The Portuguese framework for ICT in education*. Retrieved from http://resources.eun.org/insight/PTE_english%20version.pdf

S.P.I. (2003). *Empre-learning*. Retrieved from http://www.spi.pt/empre-learning/Downloads/empre-learning.pdf

Sousa, S. (1997). *Tecnologias de informação*. Lisbon, Portugal: FCA – Editora de Informática.

Vieira, L. (2001). *Relatório nacional elaborado em Portugal para o CEDEFOP, sobre a evolução das competências dos formadores nos dispositivos de formação aberta e a distância*. Retrieved from http://www.dltconsult.eu/index.php/projectos/cedefop

CHAPTER 10

THE DIFFICULT ROUTE TO DEVELOPING DISTANCE EDUCATION IN MOZAMBIQUE

Muriel Visser-Valfrey, Jan Visser, and Cynthia Moos

This chapter traces the history of distance education in Mozambique over the past four decades. Three distinct phases in the development of distance education in Mozambique, often focused on teacher training and skills development, are identified and discussed. The first of these, the pre-independence phase, catered to students of Portuguese origin, was limited in scope, and was seen to be largely irrelevant in terms of the development needs of the country at the time. The second phase, occurring shortly after Mozambique's independence from Portugal in 1975, saw the establishment of teacher training by distance education via a combination of printed, self-study materials, and radio. Important expertise in distance education was gained during this period, and learners participated enthusiastically in these distance programs, but nevertheless, a variety of internal and external educational challenges hampered the impact of the experience. The third and final stage, occurring in the past two decades, has witnessed a resurgence in the interest and use of distance education. A national institute for teacher upgrading via distance education has been created. Distance education is increasingly used in private and public higher education. Further, a national coordinating structure for distance learning has now been established. After describing this history, the chapter discusses key lessons from these three phases. The chapter concludes that a coherent vision of learning translated into workable strategies for implementation and practice in the field will be required to realize the full potential of distance education in the country.

Trends and Issues in Distance Education:
International Perspectives, Second Edition, pp. 137–154
Copyright © 2012 by Information Age Publishing
All rights of reproduction in any form reserved.

INTRODUCTION

Distance education has gained a modest place within Mozambique's educational system in the past four decades. There remains, however, potential for a much greater use of distance education within the country, particularly when one considers pressing problems that the country continues to face, including an educational system with high dropout rates and grade repetitions, huge human resource needs, and the challenges of a high incidence and prevalence of HIV and AIDS.

With this background in mind, this chapter describes in greater detail the developmental history of distance education in Mozambique. After a brief introduction to the country, a discussion of Mozambique's first post-independence distance education course (launched in 1983) is used as an illustrative case study. Key issues and emerging trends from this experience are highlighted, and the implications for subsequent use of distance education are discussed. Next, current developments, trends, and issues in distance education in Mozambique are presented. The chapter concludes with a series of discussion points that are aimed at helping realize the full potential of distance education in Mozambique.

A BRIEF BACKGROUND

Mozambique lies on the east coast of Africa. The country has a population of 22.4 million people and a surface area twice the size of California. It has a 2,400-kilometer (1,490 mile) coastline (see Figure 10.1) that not only plays an important role in both Mozambique's tourism and fishery industries but also positions the country as an important transport and trade link for Africa's landlocked interior countries. The recent history of Mozambique has been a turbulent one. Mozambique gained independence from Portugal in 1975 after some 500 years of colonial rule. Post-independence peace, however, was short-lived. By the end of the 1970s, the country was racked by a war that lasted more than a decade. Over one million people were killed, with many more displaced. Much of the country's infrastructure was irreparably damaged or destroyed.

When the war finally ended (October 1992), the country experienced peace for the first time in many years. A multiparty democracy was adopted, and the first democratic elections were held in 1994, followed by three subsequent election rounds. Peace brought with it tremendous opportunities for national development, but the challenges during this period were substantial, with many industries and services requiring ground-up redevelopment and with poverty levels being very high. More

Figure 10.1.   Map of Mozambique.

than 35 years after Mozambique's independence, much national progress has been made, but the challenges remain real. Although poverty rates in the past decade have dropped by 15%, they remain high and continue to affect more than half the population. And recent developments, including the spread of HIV and AIDS, have added to the complexity of the issues that the country continues to face Table 10.1 provides an overview of key statistics on Mozambique.

DISTANCE EDUCATION PRIOR TO 1975

Three distinct phases in the development of distance education in Mozambique can be identified: the pre-independence stage, the initial post-independence stage, and the period covering the last two decades. We progress in chronological order, examining each stage in terms of distance education, drawing out and discussing relevant trends and issues, and discussing key lessons learned from each.

Very little information remains about distance education in Mozambique prior to 1975. The information that does exist indicates that distance education prior to independence occurred primarily through Portuguese correspondence courses. One exception was the courses

Table 10.1.   Key Statistics on Mozambique

Mozambique Today	
Total population	22.4 million
Life expectancy	48 years
GNI per capita	U.S$440
People below poverty line	54%
Unemployment	18.7%
Primary level enrollment rate	80%
Female adult literac rate	62.1%
Male adult literacy rate	77.7%
HIV/AIDS adult prevalence	11.5%
People living with HIV/AIDS	1.4 million

Sources: World Bank, 2008; UNAIDS, 2010.

offered by the national railway company, the Portos e Caminhos de Ferro (C.F.M.), which were produced locally. These and other similar courses were discontinued when Mozambique attained independence in 1975.

During the pre-independence period, education, and distance education in particular, catered to the needs of individual students of Portuguese origin and thus reached only a minute percentage of the population. Distance education therefore possessed little relevance to the country's developmental needs and was of a sporadic nature (M. Visser, 1997).

Had there at that time been the political will and an accompanying policy to do so, there would have been room for a far more prominent role for distance education than actually occurred in Mozambique during this period. For example, distance education could have been made to serve settlers and local populations in remote locations, could have focused on combating illiteracy, and also could have provided nonformal education to the local population in vital areas, including agriculture and health. In contrast, other colonies, such as Rhodesia (which had been under British rule), were more forward thinking in this respect and developed correspondence courses targeted at the children of settlers (Inquai, 1994).

MOZAMBIQUE'S FIRST POST-INDEPENDENCE DISTANCE EDUCATION EXPERIENCE

The first independent government in 1975 marked the beginning of a new era in social and economic life in Mozambique. The exodus of the Portuguese meant that almost no qualified human resources remained within the country. To overcome this situation, the government embarked on an ambitious program to extend education to the Mozambican population through the formal education system. The government at that time chose to focus such efforts on infrastructure and teacher training, with the initial effort focusing on formal, contiguous education. Most activity in those early years could be seen to have been spearheaded by euphoria and a drive to do away with the scars of colonial times. Much later in time, when the complexity of the problems within the educational and other social sectors became clearer, the country became sufficiently challenged to examine more detailed and well-studied solutions to these issues.

Nevertheless, engagement in education rapidly paid off. At the primary levels, participation doubled in 6 years, reaching 1.3 million students by 1982. In secondary education, the number of enrollments grew fivefold over the same period (Candido, Menete, Martins, & Ahmed, 1986). To meet the growing demand for education, teachers were trained in crash courses, and communities were involved in new school construction. The main challenge, then, became the requirement to build a new education system with so few qualified and experienced staff.

These positive developments in education did not go uncontested. As a "communist stronghold," Mozambique was seen as a threat to its neighboring countries. From the end of the 1970s onward, with the support of the neighboring regimes in Rhodesia and South Africa, a civil war raged in Mozambique, which brought terrible destruction and loss of life. The war marred progress in all areas, including education, and posed a significant challenge to the ambitiously defined goals.

It was against this backdrop that Mozambique implemented its first distance education experience. The impulse was given during the 3rd Party Congress in 1977, which mandated that the possibilities of distance education should be seriously studied (Table 10.2). A small team of experts drawn from various areas of education was given the task to produce a feasibility study on the use of distance education in Mozambique (J. Visser & Buendia, 1980).

The study highlighted the potential benefits that distance education could bring the country. The study identified a number of possible appli-

Table 10.2.   1977 Government Directive on Distance Education

3rd Party Congress (1977)
"Priority should be given to the training of people at the grassroots, through courses for workers, through the implementation of evening classes and correspondence courses" (FRELIMO, 1977a, p. 137).
"By 1979 study the conditions for the establishment of a national centre for distance education that also uses radio broadcasting" (FRELIMO, 1977a, p. 100).

cations, including the use of distance education for extending the formal school system, particularly at sixth- and seventh-grade levels (where enrollments were severely limited because of lack of schools), but also to expand opportunities of formal secondary, higher, and technical education. Continuous upgrading of the workforce "in accordance with the economic and cultural development needs of the country" (J. Visser & Buendia, 1980, p. 6) was also a potential target, as was the training of primary school and adult literacy teachers and educators.

Focusing on teachers was in line with the pressing need for more and better-qualified teachers, and on the priority for expanding access to education to generate a highly skilled labor force. Over 10,000 new teachers with fourth-grade education and no professional qualification were recruited. Various arguments were presented to support the rationale for this choice:

- Teachers were part of a relatively well-organized system, facilitating logistic and academic support and monitoring.
- Many teachers had expressed interest in furthering their academic and professional qualifications.
- Investing in teachers made good sense because well-qualified teachers would influence the quality of education and the development of children and the country.
- Teachers could be active participants in the process of analyzing and improving this first experience.

An interesting characteristic of this first attempt to define distance education is that the feasibility study specifically identified distance education as an instrument/tool for advancing learning that had the potential to be integrated throughout the education system rather than as a subsystem in its own right.

As a result, Mozambique's first Department for Distance Education was created. The Department selected 20 staff members to be trained and become the first group of distance education specialists. Course participants were trained in three key areas: production of radio programs, drafting of written instructional materials, and planning and evaluation (Neeleman & Nhavoto, 2003). The course was developed around self-contained study materials and tutorials, and supplemented by radio programs. These radio programs were so popular that they attracted an audience not only among the target group of teachers but also among the general public (Flinck & Flinck, 1998). Tutor support was developed, with study groups that held weekly meetings and a monthly meeting with the tutor. Teachers who successfully completed the course would receive an academic qualification equivalent to six years of primary schooling and one year of professional teacher training, and would be paid in accordance with their new academic qualifications (Franque, 1993). Table 10.3 provides an overview of the profile of the first group of post-independence distance education students in Mozambique.

Starting in 1984 (while the civil war continued to escalate), an initial group of 1,224 teachers from six provinces enrolled. It is important here to highlight some characteristics of the context of this first experience:

- No significant prior country-level distance education experience or expertise;
- An emerging, but poorly defined, educational policy framework;
- A dispersed educational network with poor communication infrastructure;
- An escalating war and deteriorating security situation;
- Increasingly severe resource constraints.

In spite of careful preparation, the challenges to this first experience were numerous, and only 30% of the teachers were able to complete the course. Successive assessments/evaluations of this first distance education experience took place between 1986 and 1988, which attempted to develop a fair assessment of the experience's impact, progress, and potential (cf. Candido et al., 1986; Flinck & Flinck, 1988; Zalzman & Visser, 1986). The identified constraints of the experience were found to include

- Insufficient quality of materials due to hurried production and lack of experience. Some texts were also too difficult for students.
- Delays in the production of materials, forcing students to interrupt their studies for weeks and lowering the morale. Course completion ended up taking 4 years, rather than the planned 2 years.

Table 10.3.   Profile of Participants in First Distance Education Course

Mozambique's first distance education experience	
Total number of students	1,224
Female students:	46.6%
Students owning a radio:	53%
Average age:	30 years

Source: Candido et al. (1986)

- Poor-quality support from insufficiently prepared tutors who did not themselves receive adequate support.
- Difficulties in accessing the radio programs due to lack of radios and particularly batteries, and reception problems (compounded by acts of sabotage as a result of the war).
- Transportation difficulties due to the war and lack of resources, which affected the contact between tutors and students.
- Emphasis on the output of the course (i.e., the number of graduates) rather than on a careful monitoring of the course process itself.

Further, and although not specifically mentioned in any of the evaluation reports, an additional problem that affected the morale of teachers was that they never received the promised academic qualification award nor the promised related salary increase. In spite of this, there was generally a very positive appreciation of the pertinence and relevance of the experience and of the potential that distance education could be seen to offer.

Nevertheless, in 1987 and as a result of a combination of internal and external factors, the Ministry of Education discontinued this first distance education initiative. The Department of Distance Education was disbanded, and distance education was integrated into the recently established National Directorate for Teacher Training.

An unfortunate consequence of this decision was that the original vision of distance education as offering potential to broaden access and quality in all domains of the education system, a concern that had been so carefully hammered out in the original feasibility study, was lost and would remain so for many years to come. Nevertheless, this first distance education experience allowed Mozambique to gain valuable insights into the working of a distance education system, as well as the specific organizational and technical capacity requirements. The detailed analysis of this case pinpoints a number of key issues, including

- the inherent vulnerability of an innovation, especially in a weak policy context and/or in a context of poor educational management;
- the overriding importance of contextual factors in determining success or failure and ultimately the sustainability of an innovation; and
- the constant tension between the time needed to create true innovation and the political importance of demonstrating quick results.

DISTANCE EDUCATION IN MOZAMBIQUE TODAY

More than 20 years have passed since the abrupt end of Mozambique's first distance education experience, and the country has changed greatly since then. The death of Mozambique's first president in 1986 marked the beginning of political and economic changes, including a movement toward a more open society and a market-oriented economy. The introduction of successive programs of economic austerity under the auspices of the International Monetary Fund (IMF) improved Mozambique's chances of receiving financing and investments to rebuild its severely damaged economy, but also brought more hardship to the poor as well as changed attitudes among the leadership in important social and economic sectors.

With respect to distance education, progress has been mixed. The lengthy period of stagnation from 1987 ended only in 1996 when the Institute for Teacher Upgrading (IAP) launched a new course for teacher upgrading. This experience and a patchwork of other initiatives in a broad range of size, scope, and vision, are briefly reviewed below.

Teacher Upgrading

It is in teacher training that distance education has continued to leave its most important mark. Delivered entirely in print form and with considerable support from tutors, thousands of teachers have been able to obtain professional qualifications and upgrade their academic level since IAP launched its first course in 1996. The level of the instructional modules is better adapted to the student profile than was the case in 1983, and topics of contemporary relevance were included, including HIV and AIDS. The courses have been criticized, however, for promoting rote learning and for doing little to change stifling teaching practices.

Providing Access to Upper Primary Education

Until 2003, distance education remained limited to teacher training. That year the vision and commitment of officers from the provincial education office in Gaza and of a local nongovernmental organization (NGO) known as UDEBA, resulted in the launching of an experimental distance education experience in formal primary schooling. Faced with tremendous problems in providing access to upper primary education (grades 6 and 7) for children living in severely underpopulated areas, a program that uses mandatory school books together with specially prepared study guides and supplementary materials (including experimental radio programs) was developed. The program permitted groups of up to 20 children to meet daily in school facilities not used in the afternoon, and to study under the supervision of a teacher or an adult from the community, as well as having weekly sessions with a teacher. The program proved to be hugely popular (Zalzman, Dowdall, Hofisso, & Cabral, 2003).

Establishment of a National Coordinating Structure for Distance Education

The year 2001 was the first year since 1980 that the debate around distance education resurfaced at the senior governmental level. Discussions surrounding the establishment of the new Ministry of Higher Education and the related proposal to use distance means for higher education resulted in the conclusion that distance education should be used for systemwide educational improvement (Neeleman & Nhavoto, 2003).

At that time, a decision was made to examine the possibility of integrating distance education at all levels and in all areas of education. In this context, the Mozambican Government launched and supported a project for developing a Mozambique Distance Learning Network (MDLN). The vision was that MLDN would result in the production of distance education programs "designed by the academic staff of higher education institutions ... and delivered through a network of distance learning centers located throughout the country" (Moore & Pereira, 2007, p. 3).

It is too early to make decisive comments about the success of this initiative, but some important steps have been taken that have the potential of redirecting the course of distance education. Following recommendations by the revised commission, a National Institute for Distance Education (INED) was created in 2006. The Institute's purpose is to provide advice and resources at different levels and for diverse purposes to distance education initiatives around the country; to oversee the chain of provincial distance education centers; and to facilitate cooperation between domestic and foreign distance education institutions. It is envisioned that pilot projects will be rolled out in the areas of secondary school teacher training, access to secondary education, and preparatory education for students who are planning to enter higher education.

Higher Education Through Distance Education

In 2007, the Eduardo Mondlane University launched a 4-year program to develop distance education. The program included training of staff, the provision of equipment to the university's distance education centers, the design of a 3-year pilot project in business management delivered entirely at a distance, and the launching of a doctoral program in multimedia in education that should "promote study and research taking advantage from [sic] the direct experience participants have in designing, deploying and managing distance education" (Ramos & Tajú, 2007, n.p.). Other higher-education institutions, as well as the Police Academy, have followed suit with pilot programs (Franque, 2008).

And Finally, a Selection of Smaller Initiatives

We conclude this section by briefly referring to other relevant experiences that have occurred over the years under examination in this period:

- Between 1986 and 1994, the Ministry of Agriculture ran a successful distance education course for extension workers, covering topics from livestock management and crop rotation to environmental issues and gender. Due to lack of funding, the project was ended (M. Visser, 1999).
- In the mid-1990s, radio programs were used to upgrade the level of adult literacy teachers. The experience did not expand beyond the pilot phase (M. Visser, 1999).
- In the 1990s, a worthwhile private sector initiative in financial management and accounting was put in place by one of Mozambique's largest banks and produced 3,000 graduates (Baule & Nacala, 2008).
- In the northern province of Niassa, collaboration between the Catholic Church and a local NGO resulted in a program that allowed secondary school students to complete degrees at a distance (Neeleman & Nhavoto, 2003).

EMERGING TRENDS OR A PATCHWORK OF EXPERIENCES?

Some 40 years after distance education emerged in the Mozambican landscape, we can discern a clear will to develop distance education through the use of information and communication technologies (ICT). As a matter of fact, ICT has been for Mozambique "a cross-cutting issue with potential to be effective in various poverty alleviation programs" (Greenberg, 2006, p. 6). The development of distance education provides obvious opportunities to harness such potential.

Throughout its recent history, Mozambique has embraced distance education. Many of the initiatives have been characterized by the enormous personal commitment of the people involved and constituted significant innovations at the time they were launched. However, these experiences were each set in specific contexts and have so far failed to consistently live up to the expectation to become an integral part of Mozambican educational policy and practice. It is unfortunate that statistics on distance education in Mozambique have only been sporadically maintained, and that therefore any discussion of trends within distance education must almost entirely be based upon anecdotal observations rather than on empirically verifiable data and careful monitoring. The three suggested emerging trends below should therefore be viewed as a mere first step in identifying the greater direction of distance education in Mozambique:

1. Distance education courses have become successively more ambitious in scope, particularly in terms of enrollments, and have achieved greater success rates through organizational improvement and stronger student support.
2. Distance education experiences have gradually diversified into various areas of formal and nonformal education.
3. Distance education has established itself as a legitimate modality within the domain of teacher training. In terms of the professional prospects, distance education has achieved parity with the regular teacher education courses and has established itself as a valued and desirable means of continued education for teachers.

PUTTING TOGETHER THE PIECES: WHAT ARE THE ISSUES TODAY?

It is important to recognize the success of Mozambique's distance education experience, particularly considering the adverse internal and external circumstances under which most of these successes have occurred. However, lessons and issues that continue to affect distance education today also need to be identified, as these may continue to hamper ongoing distance education efforts.

Issues From 1987 That Remain Relevant Today

The analysis of the first post-independence distance education course identified three main issues that remain pertinent and relevant today: the vulnerability of innovations, the overriding importance of contextual factors in determining the success and failure of distance education initiatives, and the constant tension between the drive for results and the need to allow time for innovation.

Additional Issues

Additional issues have since emerged, which will be summarized in this section.

Issue 4: Each Experience is the First One

With each successive distance education experience, very little is done to recognize and learn from preceding experiences. There may be some recall of what happened, some of those who participated in the earlier experience may contribute to inform the design of the new course, and a cursory attempt may be made to collect (surviving) modules from the previous course. However, there is rarely a systematic attempt to truly learn from the lessons, to critically assess strengths and weaknesses, and to build in safeguards to avoid the stumbling blocks of the past. As a result, successive experiences are almost as vulnerable to the same deficiencies as preceding experiences.

Issue 5: The Problem of "Institutional Amnesia"

Many countries, including Mozambique, have a very poor institutional memory. Archives are only sporadically kept, and those that are kept are easily lost. Distance education is often especially vulnerable, because many of the experiences that begin as pilot projects are not subsequently scaled up in size and scope. The consequence is that already-scarce resources are often squandered by reinventing the wheel with more "pilot" projects that cannot build on prior experiences.

Issue 6: So Few Staff for So Many Needs

Setting up a distance education course/initiative goes hand in hand with extensive and specialized training of staff in areas such as management, supervision, instructional design, and quality control. In resource-constrained settings, it is primarily newly trained people who are highly solicited for other jobs that offer better perspectives. The lack of continuity of specialized staff is related to well-documented problems, including low government salaries, lack of opportunities for formal training, and poor prospects for career progression.

A quick overview of training initiatives over the past three decades within the context of distance education in Mozambique illustrates this problem. In the case of the 1983 distance education course, 20 staff received specialized training from a Brazilian institution. When this distance education experience was subsequently cut short, the staff was relocated to other departments of the Ministry of Education. In the early 1990s, when the new distance education course for teachers was launched, only a handful of the original collaborators could be identified, and none were recruited into the newly created Institute for Teacher Upgrading. To solve the problem of lack of technical staff, a new, even larger, group of people received training, again from a Brazilian institution, and with financing from another donor. Of that group, very few remain at the Institute for Teacher Upgrading today.

The drain of scarce resources to other areas of activity exacerbates the problem of institutional amnesia, since recollections of previous work encompasses both what is physically recorded and what is learned and held in memory of those who participated. With each successive reshuffling of staff, the institution and the distance education community as a whole become weaker and less resistant to the whims of politicians and other decision makers.

There is some evidence within the Mozambican context that there is recognition of these problems. Recent evaluations have recommended associating the training of senior and part-time tutors, and others involved in the implementation of the pilot projects, with the development of a professional association for distance education cadres. This should allow distance education staff to exchange information through their own Web sites; develop online resources, such as newsletters or journals; and hold national and provincial conferences. Also, "in association with the Directorate of Accreditation, Research and Evaluation, members of the MDLN's professional associations should be encouraged to develop personal research agendas related to distance education" (Moore & Pereira, 2007, p. 19).

Issue 7: The Elusive Promise

For many people, the opportunity to participate in a course, attain a degree, or carry on studying, carries with it the promise of personal growth, professional advancement, and/or enhanced social status. However, in an increasingly competitive society in which dropout rates at all levels of the system are substantial, the chances that a degree will result in a better life are small, and so the inherent promise of (distance) education more often than not fails to bear fruit. It thus remains to be seen whether the hopeful participants in the distance education course for upper primary education in Gaza province (mentioned above) will have significantly better chances of a better life for themselves than their friends who were not able to go to school.

The teacher-upgrading course that is documented in this chapter is an exception to this phenomenon. Teachers who successfully complete the course receive a formal qualification and are entitled to be scaled in at a different salary level. This has enhanced and given greater legitimacy to distance education in Mozambique, and has been an incentive for those who participate in the course to stay on track and complete their degree.

In fact, in a substantial number of cases, students outpace the rhythm of the course in their enthusiasm to complete the modules (M. Visser, 1999). Nonetheless, concern remains that distance education as a field of study is not fully recognized—that there is a "lack of status" for "those engaged in distance education" (Moore & Pereira, 2007, p. 19)—and that insufficient steps have been taken to address this.

Issue 8: The Perpetuation of Mediocrity; Or An Opportunity to Innovate?

Unfortunately, distance education courses often end up replicating the mediocrity of existing face-to-face courses, with the only difference being the modality of delivery and some minor changes to the content. The drive for the attainment of a degree makes it all the more likely that distance education courses are marketed with the purpose of satisfying (or pretending to satisfy) this need, focusing on formal output rather than substantive content. The opportunity to radically and dramatically review the very fundamentals of what it means to learn, to redefine the learning experience as a life-long activity, and to equip learners with skills (such as creativity, critical thinking, the art of asking questions) that will serve them throughout their life is easily forgotten or relegated to a back shelf in this process.

Issue 9: Double-Checking Some Assumptions

Considering the importance that has been given to ICT in Mozambique, it is difficult to imagine following a distance education course without using a computer (ICTS and Higher Education in Africa, 2009). It is therefore crucial to ensure that study centers are well-equipped and accessible to students. A related key point relates to the distribution of learning materials and the collection of assignments. Two options can be raised: online communication technology (which requires Internet access) or televised programs through VSAT technology. The former implies an individualized nature of the learning, and the latter supposes a classroom and a more social environment. To quote Moore and Pereira, "the consensus seems to be moving in the direction of online communication technology" (2007, p. 17). Consequently, it is crucial to determine where (and when) Internet access is available in order to make sure that the envisioned pilot projects can be launched and produce the kind of impact that is envisioned.

CONCLUDING REMARKS

This chapter has provided a chronology of distance education in Mozambique. The analysis has shown that much has been achieved, but also that much remains to be done. At a basic level, what seems to be lacking is a clear and unambiguous answer to the question, "What do we (i.e., the government, social sectors, and society at large) expect from education, and what kind of learning environment do we wish to create?" It is the clear and unambiguous answer to this question that needs to guide every aspect of the planning and implementation process in education, as well as the decision on how distance education can play a part. What appears to be lacking for now is coherence between the vision of learning, the strategy for achieving it, and the practice in the field. There is no doubt that such coherence is very difficult to attain, but as long as compromises continue to be made at the different levels, the sustainability of distance education initiatives and the vision that is behind them will probably continue to be elusive.

COMPREHENSION AND APPLICATION QUESTIONS

1. This chapter about the ups and downs in the history of distance education in Mozambique calls attention to the importance of working within a propitious policy environment. Suppose you are a consultant assigned to work in a developing country where distance education has remained underdeveloped. You have been asked to provide advice to the Ministry of Education regarding the development of a policy framework for stimulating a more rational growth of distance education. What principal policy elements would you suggest? (To make the exercise even more realistic, choose a particular developing country, and search online for relevant indicators regarding its educational development.)

2. The following application question is best dealt with in the context of a small group discussion among students who collectively studied this chapter. One of the conclusions of this chapter is that first and foremost "a clear and unambiguous answer" must be found to the question of what we should "expect from education and what kind of learning environment ... we wish to create." Discuss with your colleagues what your answer to that fundamental question would be, and how the development of distance education could benefit from your answer.

3. Institutional amnesia (mentioned in the chapter as Issue 5 under "additional issues") is a feature not limited to developing countries like Mozambique. From your experience, or knowledge of the history of your own society, could you think of examples of institutional amnesia and the impact it has had on the efficiency and effectiveness of the development of innovation?

RESOURCES FOR FURTHER EXPLORATION

Distance education in Africa south of the Sahara. Retrieved from http://library
.stanford.edu/depts/ssrg/africa/africaneducation/african-distance
-learning.html

Perraton, H. (Ed.) (2006). *Open and distance learning in the developing world* (2nd
ed.). London, England: Routledge.

Perraton, H. (2010, September). Teacher education: The role of open and distance learning. Vancouver, BC, Canada: *Commonwealth of Learning*. Retrieved
from http://www.col.org/PublicationDocuments/
pub_TeacherEd_Role_ODL.pdf

Visser, J. (2007). Learning in a global society. In M. G. Moore (Ed.), *Handbook of
distance education* (2nd ed., pp. 635–648). Mahwah, NJ: Erlbaum. A long version of this chapter is available online at http://www.learndev.org/dl/
DEhdbk2ndEd.pdf

REFERENCES

Baúle, Z., & Nakala, L. (2008, May 22–23). *Country presentation Mozambique*.
Regional Meeting of Focal Points in Africa and the Mediterranean, Lilongwe,
Malawi.

Candido, A., Menete, A., Martins, Z., & Ahmed, Z. (1986). *Relatório de avaliação da
primeira experiência de ensino à distância em Moçambique para a formação em exercí-
cio de professores do ensino primário*. Maputo, Mozambique: MINED/INDE.

Flinck, R., & Flinck, A. W. (1998). *Establishing a new distance education in Mozambique*. Maputo, Mozambique: Ministry of Education/Institute for Teacher
Upgrading.

Franque, A. (1993). *Distance education in Mozambique: Feasibility and sustainability*.
Master's dissertation, Institute of Education, University of London, England.

Franque, A. (2008, April 11–12). Country report to Advocacy Workshop on Distance Education and Open Learning, Mauritius.

FRELIMO. (1977a). *Relatório do comité central ao terceiro congresso*. Maputo, Mozambique.

FRELIMO. (1977b). *Directivas económicas e sociais ao terceiro congresso*. Maputo,
Mozambique.

Greenberg, A. (2006). *A country ICT survey for Mozambique*. Retrieved from http://
www2.sida.se/sida/jsp/sida.jsp?d=118&a=2742&searchWords=greenberg

ICTS and Higher Education in Africa. (2009, December). *Mozambique*. Retrieved
from http://www.cet.uct.ac.za/files/file/mozambique.pdf

Inquai, S. (1994). The development of distance education up to 1970. In *Course 2:
Development of distance education*. London, England: IEC.

Moore, M., & Pereira, L. F. (2007). *Evaluation of the Mozambique distance learning
network*. Retrieved from http://www.mined.gov.mz/img/documentos/
20090302020347.pdf

Neeleman, W., & Nhavoto, A. (2003). Educação à distância em Moçambique. *Brazilian Review of Open and Distance Education, 2*(2).

Ramos, F., & Tajú, G. (2007). *International cooperation helps develop higher education through distance education in Mozambique.* Maputo, Mozambique: University of Aveiro and University Eduardo Mondlane.

UNAIDS. (2010). *Mozambique country report.* Retrieved from http://www.unaids.org/en/dataanalysis/monitoringcountryprogress/2010progressreportssubmittedbycountries/mozambique_2010_country_progress_report_en.pdf

World Bank. (2008). *Mozambique at a glance.* Retrieved from http://siteresources.worldbank.org/DATASTATISTICS/Resources/GNIPC.pdf

Visser, M. (1997, June). *Distance education in Mozambique.* Paper presented at the 18th World Conference of the International Council for Distance Education. Pennsylvania State University, University Park.

Visser, M. (1999). *Helping learners to learn: An assessment of support to teachers studying via distance education in Mozambique.* Unpublished master's dissertation. International Extension College, University of London, England.

Visser, J., & Buendia, M. (1980). *Ensino a distância: Uma primeira abordagem.* Maputo, Mozambique: Ministério da Educação e Cultura.

Zalzman, A., Dowdall, L., Hofisso, N., & Cabral, Z. (2003). *Avaliaçao intermédia do projecto UDEBA Gaza.* Netherlands Embassy, Maputo, Mozambique.

Zalzman, A., & Visser, J. (1986). *Development prospects of the distance education system in Mozambique.* Maputo, Mozambique: INDE.

SECTION III

DISTANCE EDUCATION IN UNIVERSITY AND OTHER FORMALIZED HIGHER EDUCATION SETTINGS

Ray J. Amirault

INTRODUCTION

Section III presents six chapters that focus on distance education in university and higher education settings. The coverage provided in these chapters is both wide and diverse. Ray Amirault begins the section by discussing from a historical vantage point the potential for e-learning to permanently alter the traditional university educational model that has been in place for nearly 1,000 years. Anglin, Morrison, and Maddrell, focusing on distance learning research, review the current state of the literature and pinpoint gaps in today's body of distance education research. Andrea Hope approaches the topic from a structural perspective, focusing on transnational distance education, the impact of massification, the quality of online degree programs, and student enrollment trends in Asian higher education distance providers. Torres Kompen, Edirisingtha, and Monguet take an applied look at how personal learning environments can be used to support learning in higher education distance education settings. Ng and Kong describe the critical importance of student support systems in higher education distance education programs. Finally, Minnaar, approaching the topic from a psychologically based view, reports on the critical need for addressing student metacognition in order to help ensure the success of higher education distance education efforts.

Section III, then, represents a wide range of entries designed to help broaden and enrich the reader's understanding of international distance education within the university and higher education settings. As in the rest of the volume, a rich set of comprehension and application questions, suggested resources for further study, and bibliographic references rounds out each chapter. I hope you enjoy this investigation into distance learning in the university and higher education settings!

CHAPTER 11

WILL E-LEARNING PERMANENTLY ALTER THE FUNDAMENTAL EDUCATIONAL MODEL OF THE INSTITUTION WE CALL "THE UNIVERSITY"?

Ray J. Amirault

The university has been considered the ultimate educational experience by much of the world for some 800 years. From its establishment as a degree-awarding institution in thirteenth century France, Italy, and England, the university has demonstrated a remarkable durability in its educational method and model, which from that time has weathered all types of political, curricular, and technological challenges. The e-learning movement, however, an event enabled by the confluence of the computer and telecommunications revolutions of the twentieth century, brought with it a series of capabilities that may bring into question some of the basic assumptions always present in the traditional university education model. In this brief chapter, we examine the possible impact of e-learning on the educational model of the university through the lens of seven "irreducible characteristics" that have traditionally described university education. We then consider what e-learning technology may mean for the future of the university's model of education.

Trends and Issues in Distance Education:
International Perspectives, Second Edition, pp. 157–171
Copyright © 2012 by Information Age Publishing

E-LEARNING REVOLUTION AS A
HISTORIC CHANGE POINT IN UNIVERSITY HISTORY

The university can be rightly viewed as a medieval organization operating in a twenty-first century world. In the purest sense, the institution represents the intellectual achievement of a collection of thirteenth century European educators who sought to move formalized medieval education beyond the rote memorization learning paradigm so prevalent within the High Medieval Period (Carruthers, 2008). The educational innovation established by these individuals was ultimately so successful that the university was to quickly find its model of learning exported to virtually every part of Europe and eventually, the world (Rudolph, 1990; Rüegg, 2003b). The modern university has certainly moved beyond such medieval instructional approaches as the scholastic method and has long since enlarged upon the originally prescribed curricular sequence of the trivium and quadrivium (cf. Daileader, 2001; Leff, 1992; North, 1992), but the institution's eight-century track record has demonstrated a robust underlying model adept at meeting a wide variety of educational challenges throughout its history (Radding & Clark, 1992). The university can therefore not only be rightly considered only a medieval educational concept but also a truly resilient model of teaching and learning.

The adaptations the university undertook in order to maintain its viability across these eight centuries were often profound in nature. In some cases, the university was forced to adapt to societal changes when its original international model of learning was subordinated to national goals, for example, during the nationalistic period of Europe in the Late Medieval Period (Hastings, 1997). In other cases, the university was forced to adapt to technological innovations that threatened to change the manner in which instructional content was delivered, as when moveable type printing was introduced into Europe (Sedlar, 1994), or when public loan libraries became readily available (Stockwell, 2001). Perhaps most challenging of all were the issues surrounding curricular adaptation, in which the university over time worked through and eventually exhausted key topical disputations, for example, the long-standing debate over "universals,"[1] which periodically threatened to drive the classroom into intellectual and academic stagnation (Radding & Clark, 1992). The university's history can therefore be envisioned as one that required repeated adaptation for the institution to survive (Amirault & Visser, 2009).

In spite of eight centuries of societal, technological, and curricular changes, however, the university has managed, remarkably, to keep its essential model of education intact (Haskins, 1957). This underlying model, which we will describe shortly, can rightly be considered one of the key factors behind the institution's long-term durability. Interestingly, the presence of an unchanged, underlying educational "model" gives rise to two ostensibly contradictory explanations for the university's long life: one, the institution's ability to change and adapt to new social, political, and technological realities; and two, the ability to make such changes while retaining an essential model of education. As a result, today's university is in many respects different from its thirteenth century incarnation, but as we shall also see, the similarities in its underlying structures are sufficiently durable to allow Haskins, an acclaimed historian of his day, to dub today's university "the lineal descendant" of the medieval variant (1957).

Among the numerous critical change events undertaken during the university's extended lifespan, perhaps none was more significant than the emergence of the e-learning revolution[2] in the late twentieth century. This technological revolution, precipitated by the confluence of break-through digital computer technology with advances in electronic telecommunications, brought with it deep and sustained changes in how communication around the world would thenceforth be conducted. By the emergence of the twenty-first century, this basic change in communication technology began to force a wholesale rethinking of how universities might conduct their educational work (Laurillard, 2002). The result is that, in 2011, many students now earn university credit for courses that they complete wholly online and at their own pace, and later graduate with university degrees without ever having set foot on a university campus (Parsad & Lewis, 2008).

This deep shift in educational metaphor has caused most universities to rethink the methodological approaches they have always used to deliver instruction. Such changes in the educational paradigm have also raised an important, additional question. If the e-learning revolution significantly alters how students are educated, what are the ultimate ramifications for the traditional university educational model? Will the advent of e-learning permanently alter the essential educational model of the institution we call "the university?

WHAT IS "THE UNIVERSITY?"

In attempting to answer this question, it is necessary to first establish what we mean by the term *university*. For purposes of this chapter, we choose to build a definition of the university[3] based on the essential characteristics of the institution's educational model. By this we mean that, in spite of the university's long and variegated history, there are certain basic descriptive characteristics of the traditional university that have remained largely invariant, regardless of historical timeframe and cultural context (cf. Norton, 1909). We contend that, when we understand the university in terms of what we might refer to as these "irreducible" characteristics, we are then capable of examining the broader question of e-learning's impact on the institution.

Briefly stated, it can be argued that the "traditional" university[4] model of education has historically included the following characteristics:

1. Relocation of students and faculty to a single geographic location;
2. Delivery of instructional content via face-to-face modality;
3. Direct, and often personal, interactions between students and faculty;
4. Application of a fixed curricula based on a hierarchical view of knowledge;
5. Dissemination and control of knowledge by faculty;
6. Development of school reputations based on faculty expertise;
7. Certification of students via universally recognized, transportable "degrees" or titles.[5]

Before we look at the impact e-learning may be having on each of these historical characteristics of the university, it is helpful to briefly establish the extent to which e-learning has permeated the university context.

ACCEPTANCE OF E-LEARNING WITHIN THE UNIVERSITY

E-learning can be said to have commenced in the late twentieth century, the period in which the requisite technologies for the approach became both available and relatively affordable. *Distance learning* was not, of course, a new concept—distance programs making use of written correspondence via postal mail had been in place for at least a century by this point in time (Wheeler, 2005)—but the computer and network-mediated approach of e-learning was a revolutionary mechanism by which to deliver instruction. Institutional adoption of the approach began in a somewhat incremental and sporadic manner, but the modality was eventually implemented in a variety of university programs, and by the start of the twenty-first century, data collected on the approach[6] provided strong evidence of its acceptance and likely durability as an instructional delivery method.

THE IMPACT OF E-LEARNING ON
UNIVERSITY EDUCATIONAL PROCESSES

While the available data make obvious the deep penetration of e-learning within many major universities, a different question altogether regards the specific impact this shift in modality is having upon the greater institutional educational model. If we, however, view the university through the lens of the previously described irreducible characteristics, we may frame some specific observations regarding e-learning's impact on each characteristic, and then by extension, the institution at large.

RELOCATION REQUIREMENTS AND FACE-TO-FACE INSTRUCTION: A SHIFT IN THE LOCUS OF INSTRUCTION

Perhaps the most fundamental characteristic of e-learning—and the one most likely to be the reason why learners choose the e-learning option—is the removal of the physical relocation requirement for learners and instructors. This single factor surrounding e-learning immediately carries with it a series of interlocked, cascading implications for the university classroom setting (cf. Gürüz, 2008). First, the traditional student migration patterns witnessed through eight centuries of university history (de Ridder-Symoens, 1992) have largely been eliminated in the e-learning context. Similarly, the traditional face-to-face delivery of instructional content is increasingly being replaced by the use of distance-based technologies such as digital electronic documents, e-mail, blogs, and podcasts. This change in relocation requirements, coupled with the use of distance-based, technology-enabled instructional approaches, means that the locus of instruction, long centered on student interaction with instructors in a physical classroom, has shifted toward digitally disseminated content materials. Because the distance setting requires that learners be able to independently study and learn from materials while separated from an instructor, the result is a change in the locus of instruction (Dewan & Dewan, 2010). These three fundamental changes (i.e., relocation requirements, instructional modality, and the locus of instruction) have deeply affected the university's traditional approach to educating students.

FACULTY/STUDENT RELATIONSHIPS: AN ALTERED REALITY

The e-learning revolution has similarly brought changes to the nature of the interaction between learner and instructor. The many intimate interactions mediated by presence in the traditional classroom are significantly altered in the online setting, with the majority of interaction accomplished through technology-mediated means. Although there are doubtless many benefits to technology-enabled communication, the elimination of direct, physical interaction between student and teacher means that many of the subtleties of human communication within these processes are reduced, and the opportunity for extended, personal interaction (either formal or informal) are greatly diminished. Compounding this effect is the increased use in many universities of non-full-time adjuncts to teach online courses (Bettinger & Long, 2006), which further reduces opportunity for the development of meaningful relationships between learners and full-time faculty members. When it is remembered that universities from their earliest days have attracted students with the promise to study directly under the guidance of specific teachers (Clanchy, 1999), the impact of such a paradigmatic shift can hardly be overlooked. Technology's inexorable march promises ever more lifelike and intimate communication via digital means, including real-time, high-definition multimedia (cf. Christou, Tiopanis, Tsekeridou, & Rousos, 2008), but this fundamental change in the nature of student/faculty interaction may portend significant future long-term ramifications for university educational processes.

A FIXED CURRICULUM WITH A HIERARCHICAL VIEW OF KNOWLEDGE: A CONSTANT FOR THE TWENTY-FIRST CENTURY UNIVERSITY

In terms of university online curricula, the hierarchical view of knowledge, manifested in a fixed curriculum of courses arranged in ascending order of complexity, remains unchanged. The view that knowledge can be categorized and hierarchically ordered originated in antiquity and was transmitted to the medieval university (Amirault & Branson, 2006; Leff, 1992; Lohr, 2003). This view of knowledge was subsequently carried through to present times, including the e-learning movement. As the e-learning revolution took shape, for example, many online university curricula were developed by direct conversion of existing face-to-face courses, passing this hierarchical knowledge schema directly into the online variants (Morrison & Anglin, 2009). Even with the eventual understanding that such direct "course conversions" were not always likely to succeed if the unique and varied characteristics of the online world were not taken into consideration during course design, online university programs continued to follow the original knowledge schema of the face-to-face curriculum, if for no other reason than that state and accrediting requirements made any deviations potentially problematic for the institution. It can even be argued that conversion of courses to an online format actually reinforces the hierarchical view of knowledge, due to the emphasis on lockstep sequences of courses organized in ascending order of complexity. For the foreseeable future, the view that knowledge can be hierarchically organized and dispensed through a fixed curriculum seems sure to continue to dominate both e-learning and face-to-face variants of university curricula.

DISSEMINATION AND CONTROL OF KNOWLEDGE: A PROCESS
FUNDAMENTALLY ALTERED BY TODAY'S TECHNOLOGY

The dissemination of content knowledge, long a key to the academic "power" wielded by faculty, has been significantly affected by the technology revolution. Once serving as the unchallenged "gatekeepers" of knowledge (cf. Altbach, 1987), faculty now increasingly find that the e-learning world, with its vast and diverse storehouses of information, is providing learners with content stores that rival and often surpass those of the traditional classroom.

This seismic increase in the quantity and availability of information (Lyman & Varian, 2003) potentially generates a variety of changes for the university educational model. An obvious potential benefit afforded by these immense knowledge warehouses is that instructors now have the ability to select from an almost limitless array of online informational content for use as either primary or secondary source material. But this free and unfettered access to online content also potentially induces a change in how students may view the instructor's role within the broader context of a university education. This is particularly true in the perceived credibility of instructor-provided information in contrast to the massive and growing compilations of online content. (Some instructors are seeing this change occur right before their very eyes in today's traditional classrooms, where students may increasingly seek to "verify" information provided in class by conducting online searches during lectures to validate, or sometimes challenge, the statements of instructors.) Printed textbooks, too, long the staple of the university classroom, are also increasingly affected by such technology-enabled affordances, with many printed textbooks either supplemented, or in some cases wholly replaced, with digital content. As the twenty-first century moves on, the increasing "commoditization" of information via the mechanisms afforded by a worldwide archive of generalist and specialist content will continue to challenge the ancient traditions of knowledge dissemination within the university, and the institution will increasingly find it difficult to maintain its traditional status as the exclusive source of specialized-domain information.

UNIVERSITY REPUTATIONS:
STILL IMPORTANT, BUT FOR ENTIRELY DIFFERENT REASONS

The commoditization of knowledge will likely impact university reputations in the twenty-first century. With the increasing availability of publicly accessible knowledge sources, the status and reputation of individual universities will no longer be established and maintained simply by knowledge control and dissemination, but on the ability to review, critique, and validate information. This fundamental shift in issues surrounding content essentially creates a second level of knowledge, a kind of metaknowledge, where the perceived value of instruction moves more toward the review and critiquing of information.[8] In such an environment, such content metaknowledge could conceivably become a key determinant in how the reputations of individual universities in the twenty-first century are built. Thus, the reputation of individual institutions, always historically established by the presence of premier faculty, is maintained as such in the e-learning world, but via a different mechanism.

The e-learning movement, however, also has the potential to negatively impact university reputations. There seems little doubt that universities in general will respond to market forces and increase the number of online offerings simply for financial reasons (Levis, 2005), whether simply to increase revenues or, in some cases, to struggle to maintain basic financial solvency in an increasingly economically competitive environment. These financial pressures may result in a downward movement in educational quality at the course and program level, due to the difficulties inherent in online course development and the specialized skill requirements for creating online instructional content materials. Thus, universities will increasingly become engaged in balancing the opposing forces of quality and quantity in the online setting, and institutional reputations may be potentially negatively affected through this process.

CERTIFICATION OF STUDENTS VIA "DEGREES": AN UNCHANGED PRACTICE FOR THE ONLINE UNIVERSITY

Finally, what impact has the emergence of e-learning had on the system of student academic certification via awarding of "degrees?" This key historical facet of the university appears to be left unchanged in the e-learning world. The fact that most online learners enroll for the express purpose of earning a degree, the continuing importance such degrees enjoy among organizations around the world (Bates, 2005, p. 38), and the additional reality that no other educational institution is currently poised to take over such a certifying function, it remains likely that today's university degree award system will continue for the foreseeable future. The degree and title awarding system as a universally recognized certifying function is perhaps one of the most durable of all university characteristics, but it is an ironic twist that this key factor still present in today's university is a *medieval* concept.

SUMMARY OF THE IMPACT OF E-LEARNING ON THE ESSENTIAL CHARACTERISTICS OF THE UNIVERSITY'S EDUCATIONAL MODEL

We can summarize our brief comments regarding the impact of e-learning on the "irreducible characteristics" of the university as follows:

1. Student and faculty relocation: *fully changed*
2. Face-to-face instructional content delivery: *fully changed*
3. Student-teacher relationship: *partially changed*
4. Fixed curricula based on a hierarchical view of knowledge: *unchanged*
5. Faculty as the dispensers, or "gatekeepers," of knowledge: *increasingly changed*
6. School reputations based on faculty expertise: *unchanged*
7. Awarding of universally recognized and accepted transportable "degrees" or titles: *unchanged*

CONCLUDING COMMENTS

In this brief chapter, we have argued that the historic concept of *the university* can be understood via a series of irreducible characteristics that have since the thirteenth century described the institution's essential model of education. Among these characteristics, perhaps the most fundamental is the notion that faculty and students from widely disparate geographical areas physically relocate and assemble to study and to learn together, and that direct, interpersonal faculty/student interactions play a key role, not only in the development of a university's culture and reputation but also in the educational experience offered students.

The emergence of Web-based e-learning in the late twentieth century has directly challenged this fundamental, historic assumption of university education through the mechanism of computer-mediated communication and learning. By viewing the traditional university educational model in terms of some "irreducible characteristics," we can more precisely examine to what extent each characteristic is affected by this large-scale technological change and then, by extension, "the university" at-large.

Of the seven proposed irreducible characteristics of the essential university educational model, we find that four are either fully or partially changed, and three largely unchanged. The greatest areas of change are found to be in the elimination of relocation requirements, the method of instructional delivery, faculty control and dissemination of content, and the nature of faculty/student interchange. Remaining either largely or fully unchanged are the use of a fixed, hierarchically organized curriculum; the congruence of school reputations with faculty expertise; and the use of degree and/or title awarding as an accrediting function.

How then do we move on to answer the more general, underlying question as to whether e-learning will permanently alter the essential educational model of the university? Do the changed characteristics outweigh the unchanged characteristics? Or the opposite?

It is possible to reenvision the answer to our question by returning to the institutional history of the university. As any historical account of the institution across eight centuries will attest, the university has been an entity both changing, and changed by, seismic world changes. The university would not have been able to continue for such an extended period of time without finding deep within itself the capability and willingness to meet in turn each historical challenge, and the result has been that the institution has managed to maintain its status as a ultimate educational body over this entire period. In that sense, the question can be answered, not by questioning *whether or not* the institution's educational model will be permanently changed by e-learning, but rather by recognizing that the institution will once again be required to adapt and change in order to ensure its continued success within a new historical reality. Germane to this question is the extent to which the university wishes to lead and control this change process, or rather to passively have change thrust upon it. The decisions that the university makes during today's revolution in computer and communications technology will dictate whether or not the institution's 800-year-old educational model will see a ninth century of continued use and success.

COMPREHENSION AND APPLICATION QUESTIONS

1. To what extent should the original educational goals of the thirteenth century university dictate its present function? What were these original goals? Are such educational goals "timeless," or should they be subject to the demands of modern life if the institution is to maintain ongoing relevancy?

2. Does the technology revolution that precipitated the e-learning movement represent a truly unique historical challenge to the university, or is e-learning simply one more in the long list of challenges faced by the institution over the centuries? What are the arguments for both positions?

3. How can the university best respond to the changes precipitated by e-learning if it is to remain the world's premier educational institution? Should the university seek to control e-learning technology

in order to make e-learning serve specified educational functions, or should the university let the continuously emerging capabilities of today's technology-centric world drive educational methods? Asked another way, should the university be a *leader* or a *follower* when it comes to e-learning technology? What are the advantages and disadvantages of each approach?

RESOURCES FOR FURTHER EXPLORATION

On the History of the University

Rashdall's (1895) classic work, *The Universities of Europe in the Middle Ages*, is a standard piece for study, although the text will be difficult to locate in printed format (some of the work, however, is available online in various locations). A recent four-volume set by Cambridge University Press (de Ridder-Symoens, 2003–2010), *The History of the University in Europe,* edited by Rüegg and de Ridder-Symoens may well become the new standard by which others are measured due to its quality of research and writing. The set is available in both paperback and hardback formats, and can be purchased per volume.

On University Medieval Themes

A truly fascinating set of audio lectures that cover university origins, instructional methods, and curricular content, are those by Philip Daileader of The College of William and Mary, published in audio CD-ROM format by The Teaching Company. Daileader's lectures on *The Early Middle Ages* (2004) and again on *The High Middle Ages* (2001) cover origins, philosophy, and early scholars; and his third set on *The Late Middle Ages* (2007) contains information on the university's alignment with nationalism during the Hussite Rebellion.

On The Growth of E-learning in the University Context

The Sloan Consortium (Allen & Seaman, 2008) has an extended series of data compilations that provides significant and meaningful detail for study. Most of Sloan's summarized data are freely available from their website.

NOTES

1.   The debate over "universals," a problem raised as far back as Boethius (sixth century), Porphyry (third century), and even Plato (fourth century

B.C.), concerned whether the existence of true archetypes of all common representations actually exist or whether these were simply naming conventions created by man to simplify cognition. For example, if the subject is *triangle*, does a perfect, universal archetype of a triangle exist from which all triangles (i.e., "the particulars") are based, or is the word *triangle* simply a man-made naming convention to conveniently categorize all triangles as a class of objects? The question is not as simple as a cursory pass of the subject might seem to imply, and the issue was debated within the university for centuries.

2.   E-learning emerged at the culmination of a series of technological advances in the late twentieth century (Amirault & Visser, 2010). Commencing with the development of the ENIAC digital computer in 1946, and quickly followed by the invention of the transistor in 1947 and the first working model of the integrated circuit in 1958, the resulting "personal computer" became a powerful, yet small and affordable, device increasingly present in homes around the world. The development of high-speed networks and the TCP/IP protocol by the early 1970s made possible the eventual linkage of these computers into a worldwide "Internet" (Clark, 2003). The development of the World Wide Web in the very early 1990s made the operational aspect of the Internet simple for anyone, regardless of technical background. The development of web-based software systems specifically for educational purposes—particularly learning management systems, but also a wide variety of knowledge repositories of text, audio, and video data—eventually enabled the birth of "e-learning" by the late twentieth century.

3.   Defining the term *university* has been a long-standing challenge. Newman (1891) attempted to lay out a parochial description of university education in a series of lectures entitled *The Idea of a University,* in which he described the university as "a place of teaching universal knowledge." Rashdall's (1895) critically acclaimed work on the history of the university offered a more historical view of the institution, emphasizing the university's historical development over time. Another historically oriented view was offered more recently by Rüegg (2003a). Alexander (2002) chose a slightly different view that described the university through the lens of its relationship to government, its objectives, and its role in society. A fixed definition remains elusive.

4.   Note that these "irreducible characteristics" are said to broadly apply to what we refer to as the "traditional" university model. There are notable exceptions to this description, primarily the Open University movement of the twentieth century (Chang, 1982; Tunstall, 1978). In spite of its success, the Open University movement represents but one important, although influential, vein in the broader history of the university from medieval times.

5.   "Transportable" means that other universities and institutions recognize a degree or title awarded by any recognized university. Transportable degrees and/or titles played a key role in establishing the medieval university by providing the mechanism by which a graduate of one institution

could teach at another. Today, transportable degrees continue to serve this academic "cross-seeding" function, but also serve as criteria for nonuniversity employment.

6. One such detailed review of online learning was conducted by the Sloan Consortium (Allen & Seaman, 2007) in the early years of the 21st century. Sloan reported that by 2006, about 3.5 million U.S. students were enrolled at least part time in an online course, doubling the previously recorded rate in 2002. Further, Sloan found that between 2002 and 2006, online enrollments were found to be increasing at a compound annual rate of between approximately 18% and 25%, with more than two thirds of all U.S. higher education institutions in 2006 offering some form of online learning, mostly fully online programs. A later review found that by 2008, approximately 11,200 higher education institutions within the United States offered fully online programs, with open enrollment rates growing at rates that were so large as to be "unsustainable," and no less than 3.9 million students taking at least one online course (Allen & Seaman, 2008)

7. In such an environment, many online university programs can be seen to attempt to address two contradictory forces: the learner's desire to study selected topics at a given choice in time and the requirement to move learners through a hierarchical course sequence.

8. Such metaknowledge has the added "bonus" for universities in that it exists as specialized knowledge sourced in the expertise of individual faculty members and is therefore resistant to commoditization.

REFERENCES

Alexander, K. (2002). The object of the university: Motives and motivation. In F. K. Alexander & K. Alexander (Eds.), *The university: International expectations* (pp. 3–20). Montreal, Quebec, Canada: McGill-Queens University Press.

Allen, I. E., & Seaman, J. (2007). *Online nation: Five years of growing on online learning*. Needham, MA: Sloan Consortium.

Allen, I. E., & Seaman, J. (2008). *Staying the course: Online education in the United States, 2008*. Needham, MA: Sloan Consortium.

Altbach, P. G. (1987). *The knowledge context: Comparative perspectives on the distribution of knowledge*. Albany: State University of New York Press.

Amirault, R. J., & Branson, R. K. (2006). Educators and expertise: A brief history of theories and models. In K. A. Ericsson, N. Charness, P. J. Feltovich, & R. R. Hoffman (Eds.), *The Cambridge handbook of expertise and expert performance* (pp. 69–86). New York, NY: Cambridge University Press.

Amirault, R. J., & Visser, Y. L. (2009). The university in periods of technological change: A historically grounded perspective. *The Journal of Computing in Higher Education, 21*(1).

Amirault, R. J., & Visser, Y. L. (2010). The impact of e-learning programs on the internationalization of the university. In F. Columbus (Ed.), *Higher education: Teaching, internationalization, and student issues*. Hauppauge, NY: Nova Science.

Bates, A. W. (2005). The impact of technology on the organization of distance education. *Technology, e-learning and distance education*. London, England: Routledge.

Bettinger, E. P., & Long, B. T. (2006). The increasing use of adjunct instructors at public institutions: Are we hurting students? In R. G. Ehrenberg (Ed.), *What's happening to public higher education?: The shifting financial burden*. Baltimore, MD: Johns Hopkins University Press.

Carruthers, M. J. (2008). *The book of memory: A study of memory in medieval culture* (2nd ed.). Cambridge, England: Cambridge University Press.

Chang, T. M. (Ed.). (1982). *Distance learning: On the design of an open university*. Dordrecht, The Netherlands: Kluwer.

Christou, J. T., Tiopanis, T., Tsekeridou, S., & Rousos, K. (2008). Grid-based interactive virtual scientific experiments for distributed virtual communities. In S. Salerno, M. Gaeta, P. Ritrovato, N. Capuano, F. Orciuoli, S. Miranda, & A. Pierri (Eds.), *The learning grid handbook: Concepts, technologies and applications* (pp. 199–218). Amsterdam, The Netherlands: IOS.

Clanchy, M. T. (1999). *Abelard: A medieval life*. Oxford, England: Blackwell.

Clark, M. P. (2003). *Data networks, IP, and the Internet: Protocols, design, and operation*. Hoboken, NJ: Wiley.

Daileader, P. (2001). *The first universities. The high middle ages* [audio CD]. Chantilly, VA: The Teaching Company.

Daileader, P. (2004). *The Carolingian renaissance. The early middle ages* [audio CD]. Chantilly, VA: The Teaching Company.

Daileader, P. (2007). *Renaissance humanism, Part 1. The late middle ages* [audio CD]. Chantilly, VA: The Teaching Company.

de Ridder-Symoens, H. (1992). Mobility. In W. Rüegg (Ed.), *A history of the university in Europe* (Vol. 1, pp. 280–304). Cambridge, MA: Cambridge University Press.

de Ridder-Symoens, H. (Ed.). (2003–2010). *A history of the university in Europe* (Vols. 1–4). Cambridge, MA: Cambridge University Press.

Dewan, S., & Dewan, D. (2010). Distance education teacher as a leader: Learning from the Path Goal Leadership Theory. *MERLOT Journal of Online Learning and Teaching, 6*(3).

Gürüz, K. (2008). *Higher education and international student mobility in the global knowledge economy*. Albany: State University of New York Press.

Haskins, C. H. (1957). *The rise of universities*. Ithaca, NY: Cornell University Press.

Hastings, A. (1997). *The construction of nationhood: Ethnicity, religion, and nationalism*. Cambridge, England: Cambridge University Press.

Laurillard, D. (2002). *Rethinking university teaching: A conversational framework for the effective use of learning technologies*. London, England: Routledge.

Leff, G. (1992). The trivium and the three philosophies. In W. Rüegg (Ed.), *A history of the universities of Europe* (Vol. I). Cambridge, England: Cambridge University Press.

Levis, K. (2005). What e-learning has taught us. In R. Paton, G. Peters, J. Storey, & S. Taylor (Eds.), *Handbook of corporate university development: Managing strategic learning initiatives in public and private domains* (pp. 157–168). Aldershot, England: Gowe.

Lohr, C. H. (2003). The ancent philosophical legacy and its transmission to the middle ages. In J. J. E. Gracia & T. B. Noone (Eds.), *A companion to philosophy in the middle ages* (pp. 15–22). Oxford, England: Blackwell.

Lyman, P., & Varian, H. R. (2003). *How much information?: 2003.* Retrieved October 10, 2010, from http://www2.sims.berkeley.edu/research/projects/how-much-info-2003/internet.htm

Morrison, G. R., & Anglin, G. (2009). An instructional design approach for effective shovelware: Modifying materials for distance education. In A. Orellana, T. L. Hudgins, & M. R. Simonson (Eds.), *The perfect online course: Best practices for designing and teaching.* Greenwich, CT: Information Age.

Newman, J. H. (1891). *The idea of a university.* London, England: Longmans, Green.

Norton, A. O. (1909). *Readings in the history of education: Medieval universities.* Cambridge, MA: Harvard University.

North, J. (1992). The quadrivium. In W. Rüegg (Ed.), *A history of the university in Europe* (Vol. 1, pp. 337–359). Cambridge, England: Cambridge University Press.

Parsad, B., & Lewis, L. (2008). Distance education at degree-granting postsecondary institutions: 2006–07. Washington, DC: National Center for Education Statistics.

Radding, C. M., & Clark, W. W. (1992). *Medieval architecture, medieval learning.* New Haven, CT: Yale University Press.

Rashdall, H. (1895). *The universities of Europe in the middle ages.* Oxford, England: Clarendon.

Rudolph, F. (1990). *The American college and university: A history.* Athens, GA: University of Georgia Press.

Rüegg, W. (2003a). Themes. In W. Rüegg (Ed.), *A history of the university in Europe* (Vol. 1, pp. 3–34). Cambridge, England: Cambridge University Press.

Rüegg, W. (2003b). Themes. In W. Rüegg (Ed.), *A history of the university in Europe* (Vol. 2, pp. 3–42). Cambridge, England: Cambridge University Press.

Sedlar, J. W. (1994). *East central Europe in the middle ages: 1000–1500.* Seattle: University of Washington Press.

Stockwell, F. (2001). *A history of information storage and retrieval.* Jefferson, NC: McFarland.

Tunstall, J. (1978). *The open university opens.* London, England: Cox and Wyman.

Wheeler, S. (2005). British distance education: A proud tradition. In Y. L. Visser, L. Visser, M. Simonson, & R. Amirault (Eds.), *Trends and issues in distance education: International perspectives* (1st ed.). Greenwich, CT: Information Age.

CHAPTER 12

DISTANCE EDUCATION

Practice Before Research or Research Before Practice?

Gary J. Anglin, Gary R. Morrison, and Jennifer Maddrell

In this chapter, results and implications of selected reviews and analyses of the distance education literature are summarized and discussed. An updated analysis of the literature as reflected in two distance learning journals is also presented. The role of theory in distance education research is discussed and a taxonomy for determining if distance education research leads to theory development, or testing of theory, is described. Areas for future research are then discussed. A classification framework is introduced that will help distance education researchers identify broad areas of distance education research, including areas that are underrepresented in the literature. Two final conclusions are drawn. First, distance education practice has outpaced both the distance education theory and research. Second, there is a significant need for distance education theory and distance learning research that either tests theories or that leads to the development of new theories.

Trends and Issues in Distance Education:
International Perspectives, Second Edition, pp. 173–188
Copyright © 2012 by Information Age Publishing
173

INTRODUCTION

During the past 20 years, we have observed the extraordinary expansion and development of distance education institutions, programs, and courses across the globe, particularly in higher education. For example, in the fall of 2008, there were some 3,090,000 active students enrolled at open universities in China (China, 2010). In another example, Anadolu University of Turkey, the national provider of distance education (open education) by Turkish statute, saw enrollment in open education programs growing from approximately 30,000 in 1982–1983 to over 1.5 million students today (University, 2010). Similarly, in India, the Indira Ghandhi National Open University reports a student enrollment of 1.5 million students coming from India and 35 other countries (Cener, 2010). The United States, too, witnessed a compound annual growth rate for students enrolled in at least one higher education course over the last six years of 19% (Allen & Seaman, 2010). Overall, two thirds of degree-granting postsecondary institutions for the period covering 2006–2007 offered distance education courses (Parsad & Lewis, 2008). International distance education programs and course offerings in higher education have therefore certainly continued to expand; but has the study of distance education kept pace with distance education practice?

In this chapter, we first discuss definitions of distance education and proceed to present a brief summary of recent selected reviews and analyses of the distance education literature, including our own updated analysis of the literature. We next discuss the need for theory-based research in the study of distance education. We conclude by suggesting a framework for planning future research studies in distance education, as well as identify areas for future research.

RECENT ANALYSES AND REVIEWS OF THE DISTANCE EDUCATION LITERATURE DEFINING DISTANCE EDUCATION

There are many perspectives on how to define distance education (Keegan, 1996). Since the publication of Keegan's third edition of *Foundations of Distance Education*, both course delivery and the technology for delivering courses have evolved. Currently, course content is delivered using several approaches including "traditional" (i.e., no Internet technology), "web facilitated" (posting of course information), "blended/hybrid" (i.e., both online and face-to-face), and "online" (exclusively) (Allen & Seaman, 2010, p. 4). Given the various delivery approaches, some courses may be labeled as "distance education classes" when in reality, they are not. Schlosser and Simonson (2002) define distance education as "institution-based, formal education where the learning group is separated, and where interactive telecommunications systems are used to connect learners, resources, and instructors" (p. 1). In this chapter, we will adopt the definition provided by Schlosser and Simonson, as this definition allows for a broader range of distance education delivery methods. More detailed discussions of the various distance learning and education definitions can be found in other sources (cf. Anglin & Morrison, 2000; Keegan, 1996; Simonson, Smaldino, Zvacek, & Albright, 2009).

SELECTED ANALYSES AND REVIEWS OF THE DISTANCE EDUCATION LITERATURE

A summary of results from recent analyses and reviews of the distance education literature will be discussed. We have attempted to be illustrative, but not exhaustive, when discussing the reviews, given the page limitations for this chapter. There are other good reviews that we could not include in this chapter due to length constraints.

In an analysis of the distance education research, Anglin and Morrison (2000) identified the types of articles appearing in two well-known distance education journals, *The American Journal of Distance Education* (1987–1999) and *Distance Education* (1991–1999). The articles were classified using the categories of *primary research, conceptual/theory, review, evaluation, lessons learned, how-to,* and *other* (Anglin & Morrison, 2000). Based on their summary and analysis, Anglin and Morrison concluded that many articles reviewed were participant reaction surveys, lacked a theory base, failed to distinguish between delivery technologies vs. instructional technologies, and that only a very few sustained programs of research currently exist.

Lee, Driscoll, and Nelson (2004) conducted a content analysis of the distance education literature included in four journals from 1997 to 2002. The four journals incorporated in the content analysis include *The American Journal of Distance Education, The Journal of Distance Education, Distance Education,* and *Open Learning.* Based on the classifications systems used by Anglin and Morrison (2000), Berge and Mrozowski (2001), Klein (2002), and Koble and Bunker (1997), Lee et al. developed a new method for classifying research studies including the categories *theoretical inquiry, experimental research, case study, evaluation research, developmental research, survey research,* and *combination of inquiries.*

For the 383 articles considered across the four journals included, Lee et al. identified 78 theoretical inquiry articles, 47 experimental research articles, 138 case studies, 23 evaluation research studies, 48 developmental research studies, 48 survey research studies, and 23 combination of inquiry studies. More case studies were reported than any other category. However, Lee et al. (2004) noted that in 2002, the number of experimental studies (12) was one less than the number case studies (13). As a result of the content analysis of the distance education literature as reflected in the four included journals, Lee et al. concluded that there were a very limited number of studies based on theory, and that a number of studies did not address validity, reliability, sample size, and random assignment issues.

An extensive meta-analysis of the empirical distance education literature was presented by Bernard et al. (2004) comparing distance education with classroom instruction in publications between 1985 and 2002 (inclusive). The meta-analysis found 232 studies that met their inclusion criteria. The meta-analytic review of the literature included three outcome measures: "independent achievement, attitude, and retention" (Bernard et al., 2004, p. 379).

General results reported based on analysis of the data were that "DE works extremely well sometimes and extremely poorly other times ... methodological weakness was considered an important deterrent to offering clear recommendations ... more than half (55.73) of the codable features were missing," and that it is "difficult to draw firm conclusions to what works and does not work in regard to DE" (Bernard et al., 2004, p. 405). One exception concerned the two outcome variables, *achievement* and *attitude*, for synchronous and asynchronous distance education. From the perspective of quality, Bernard et al. (2004) concluded that, overall, the comparative distance education literature on these two variables was low in quality.

Bernard, Abrami, Lou, and Borokhovski (2004) also evaluated methodologies used in the 232 studies included in their meta-analysis of the literature. Consistent with earlier reviews and analyses of the distance education literature (Anglin & Morrison, 2000; Berge & Mrozowski, 2001; Koble & Bunker, 1997; Lee et al., 2004), Bernard et al. concluded that for 232 studies evaluated for methodology, "we concur with those commentators who have judged, non-empirically, that this literature is of poor quality" (p. 186). In commenting on the research methodologies analyzed, Bernard et al. suggest that research designs could be improved by improving experimental controls, criterion measures, equivalence of treatments and delivery, and course duration. The investigators also suggest (after Clark, 2000) that in future studies, it may be more productive when judging the effectiveness of strategies to compare across distance education classes rather than between traditional classes and distance education classes.

In a recent review of the literature, Zawacki-Richter, Baecker, and Vogt (2009) conducted an analysis of the distance education literature (2000–2008) in the areas of research, methods, and authorship patterns in five journals, including *Open Learning*, *Distance Education*, *The American Journal of Distance Education*, *The Journal of Distance Education*, and *The International Review of Research in Open and Distance Learning*. A classification system resulting from an earlier Delphi study conducted by Zawacki-Richter (2009) was used in the analysis of these five journals. The categories of research areas included "*macro level: distance education systems and theories*," "*meso level: management, organization, and technology*," and "*micro level: teaching and learning in distance education*," along with 15 subcategories (Zawacki-Richter et al., 2009, p. 23). In addition to classifying the studies according to research areas, studies were also classified by research method as *quantitative*, *qualitative*, or *mixed-method* (Zawacki-Richter et al., 2009). Based on the results of their review, Zawacki-Richter et al. (2009) concluded that the distance education research is not balanced across the categories of *macro*, *meso*, and *micro*. In particular, much of the research reported in the five journals had a focus on the "micro level" of "teaching and learning in distance education." Issues concerning such topics as policy, cost effectiveness and delivery technology, equity, and the cultural implications for distance education were clearly underrepresented in the journals included in the analysis. For example, there was only one study identified concerning "globalization of education and cross-cultural aspects" of distance education (Zawacki-Richter et al., 2009, p. 31).

We identified one review of the literature that focused on online learning (Means, Toyama, Murphy, Bakia, & Jones, 2009). In this meta-analysis study, Means et al. (2009) evaluated and compared face-to-face instruction with classroom instruction. The 46 studies included in the meta-analysis examined the effect of online-only or blended approaches (online and face-to-face), included random-assignment or controlled quasi-experimental designs, and included (as a requirement) objective measures of student learning. A narrative review was conducted for comparative studies not meeting the criteria for inclusion in the meta-analysis. Selected findings identified by Means et al. based on the results of their meta-analytic review found that

- few rigorous research studies of the effectiveness of online learning for K–12 students have been published;
- students who took all or part of their class online performed better, on average, than those taking the same course through traditional face-to-face instruction;
- instruction combining online and face-to-face elements had a larger advantage relative to purely face-to-face instruction than did purely online instruction; and

- the effectiveness of online learning approaches ranges broadly across different content and learner types (pp. xiv–xv).

Findings reported in the narrative review also stated that

- blended and purely online learning conditions implemented within a single study generally result in similar student learning;
- elements such a video or online quizzes do not appear to influence the amount that students learn in online classes;
- online learning can be enhanced by giving learners control of their interactions with media and promoting learner reflection; and
- providing guidance for learning for groups of students appears less successful than does using such mechanisms with individual learners.

Means et al. offer the caution that, while the results of the review yield positive effects for learning online, the conditions in the online treatments varied from the face-to-face instruction in areas, including "time spent, curriculum and pedagogy" (p. xvii).

ANGLIN AND MORRISON (2000) UPDATED

Anglin and Morrison (2000) presented an analysis and discussion of the distance education research literature in *The American Journal of Distance Education (AJDE)* (1987–1999) and in *Distance Education (DE)* (1991–1999). The purpose of our updated analysis is to provide a discussion of recent research areas and methods on distance education, including two additional journals not included in our earlier analysis.

Method

We selected the two distance education journals, *The American Journal of Distance Education* and *Distance Education,* which were included in an earlier analysis of the distance education literature conducted by Anglin and Morrison (2000). For our updated analysis, we selected two additional journals, the *Quarterly Review of Distance Education (QRDE)* and the *Journal of Distance Education (JDE)*. All articles published in the four journals from 2003 to 2008 (inclusive) were included in our classification of studies and analysis. The classification system used included seven categories: *descriptive, literature review, experimental, conceptual/theoretical, lessons learned, how-*

to, evaluation, and *other*. For each article, we determined if a learning measure was included. The studies were classified and coded as *learning measure not present, objective measure of learning present*, or *self-report of learning present*. Each article in the four journals was classified using one of the seven categories. The author(s) name, publication date, article type, and learning measure code were recorded in a database. For articles difficult to classify, a final classification was completed by consensus of the authors. One article was omitted from the learning measure classification, as it was not possible to determine if a specific learning measure was present. It was also possible to classify some studies using more than one classification term. We classified each study in one category based on the primary focus of the study. The number of articles included was 74 for *AJDE*, 109 for *DE*, 152 for *QRDE*, and 61 for *JDE*.

Results

A summary of the results, including the number of studies by category type, is included in Table 12.1. Some 60% of the studies across the four journals included were classified as being *descriptive*. The remaining studies were classified as literature *reviews* (3%), *experimental* (7%), *conceptual/ theoretical* (10%), *lessons learned* (7%), *how-to* (1%), *other* (9%), and *evaluation* (1%).

Similar to the results reported by Anglin and Morrison (2002), many of the descriptive studies reported the results of participant surveys. All four journals analyzed included a high number of *descriptive* studies ranging from 53% (*QRDE*) to 79% (*JDE*). The number of *literature reviews* identified across the four journals was relatively small, ranging from one to seven. Five reviews were identified for the *AJDE*, and seven for the *QRDE*. There were relatively few *experimental* studies reported across the four journals, ranging from 2% (*QRDE*) to 15% (*AJDE*). For *lessons learned*, the frequency of articles appearing ranged from 3% (*AJDE*) to 9% (*JDE*). Five (1%) articles were classified as *how-to* across the four journals. For the "catchall" category of *other*, the number or articles ranged from 1 to 21 (1% to 19%). A total of four (1%) *evaluation* studies were identified.

Given that we assume the primary purpose of distance education programs is student learning, we also identified the number of studies that included a "measure" of student learning. The results of the summary for learning measures included are provided in Table 12.2. In 84% (333) of the studies, a learning measure was not present. Only 11% (43) of the studies included an objective measure of learning, and 5% (19) incorporated a self-report of learning.

Table 12.1. Number of Articles Included in AJDE, DE, QRDE, & JDE by Type of Article

	AJDE N	AJDE Percent	DE N	DE Percent	QRDE N	QRDE Percent	JDE N	JDE Percent	Mean	Percent Total
Descriptive	49	66%	64	59%	81	53%	48	79%	–	61%
Lit Review	5	7%	1	1%		5%	0	0%	–	3%
Experimental	11	15%	2	2%	14	9%	1	2%	–	7%
Conceptual/theoretical	6	8%	11	10%	20	13%	2	3%	–	10%
Lessons learned	2	3%	8	7%	14	9%	5	8%	–	7%
How-to	0	0%	1	1%	4	3%	0	0%	–	1%
Other	1	1%	21	19%	10	7%	4	7%	–	9%
Evaluation	0	0%	1	1%	2	1%	1	2%	–	1%
Total	74		109		152		61		396	100%

**Table 12.2.   Total Learning Measures
Reported Across AJDE, DE, QRDE, & JDE**

Learning Measure Present	Total	Percent
Not Present	333	84%
Objective Measure of Learning Present	43	11%
Self-report of learning	19	5%
Total	395	–

Note: AJDE—*American Journal of Distance Education,* DE—*Distance Education,*   QRDE—
Quarterly Review of Distance Education, JDE—*Journal of Distance Education*

Note: Not able to determine "learning measure present" for one study.

CONCLUSIONS

Based on the results of our current analysis of the distance education literature, we draw many of the same conclusions that we did in our earlier
analysis (Anglin & Morrison, 2000). We conclude that the research conducted in the four journals has contributed to our understanding of the
distance education process in higher education. It is easy to find fault with
much of the research in the social and behavioral sciences given that there
are many variables to consider and control. While progress has been
made, we suggest that there is much room for improvement in distance
education research.

First, over half of the articles identified reported the results of descriptive research. In almost all cases, the results of the descriptive research we
identified are usually not generalizable to other contexts and settings. At
best, results from such studies will have limited usefulness to individuals
working in a similar context to the one identified in the study.

Second, the results in many studies are dependent upon surveys of distance education students and participants. Very few studies measured
actual learning. In our analysis, we determined that only 43 of the 395
analyzed studies included some objective measure of learning. Given that
the purpose of distance education is student learning, we think it is critical that future studies objectively measure student learning to determine
the effectiveness of an intervention.

We did not code studies as *theory based* or not; however, based on our reading of the studies, we also conclude that much of the distance research as
reflected across the four journals that we analyzed is not based on any type
of distance education theory. Mayer (2008) considers these studies as a pure
applied research approach on a dead-end street with limited application.
Consistent with the results of our earlier analyses of the distance education
literature (Anglin & Morrison, 2000), we conclude that few sustained

research programs are evidenced in the literature. We also did not specifically code for programs of research, but a review of the author list and article titles across the four journals analyzed in the database revealed that the literature is still quite fragmented. We believe that three critical concerns for future distance education research that should be pursued are *theory development*, *theory confirmation*, and *learning assessment*.

GENERAL SUMMARY: RECENT ANALYSES AND REVIEWS

In this section, we provide a summary of results from recent analyses and reviews of the distance education literature, including an update of our own earlier analysis. While progress has been made in distance education research, there remains much to be improved, and overall, the distance education research literature is relatively poor in quality (Anglin & Morrison, 2002; Bernard et al., 2004; Lee et al., 2004). Significant problems with methodological issues in this body of research have been identified. It is often difficult, too, to identify effectiveness based on the empirical literature (Bernard et al., 2004). The focus of distance education research is primarily technical (Zawacki-Richter et al., 2009). Much of the research lacks a theory base (Lee et al., 2004). There are few studies that examine issues in the areas of distance education policy, equity, and global culture. Finally, while one major focus of distance education is improvement of student learning, few studies include objective measures of learning. There is much that needs to be improved in distance education research in the future. Next, we will discuss the issue of theory and distance education.

DISTANCE EDUCATION THEORY AND RESEARCH

In this section, we will first define the concept *theory* and discuss theory-based research in distance education. Second, we will discuss a taxonomy we believe can be used by investigators in conceptualizing initial research projects and by reviewers evaluating existing distance education research literature.

A number of individuals (Anglin & Morrison, 2000; Garrison, 2000; Lee, et al., 2004; Moore & Kearsley, 1996; Saba, 2000) discuss the lack of theory-based research in distance education. Theory is defined in the *Concise Oxford English Dictionary* (2004) as "a supposition or a system of ideas intended to explain something, especially one based on general principles independent of the thing to be explained" (p. 1495). Garrison (2000) provides a definition of theory stating, "theory is a coherent and systematic ordering of ideas, concepts, and models with the purpose of constructing meaning to explain, interpret and shape practice" (p. 3).

More than three decades ago, Dubin (1978) discussed issues concerning theory-building in applied research areas. Dubin described the intent of his book to be that of addressing four issues: the "source of hypotheses"; "requirements for a theoretical model that will generate testable hypotheses"; "the nature of the test of an hypotheses"; and the nature of the "feedback from the "empirical test of an hypothesis to the theoretical model generating it" (p. 1). Dubin then describes the components of a theory including "units," "laws of interaction," "boundaries," "system states," "propositions," "empirical indicator," and "hypotheses" (pp. 7–8). Since the publication of Dubin's book, many other approaches have been developed and accepted as valid methods for conducting inquiry in applied areas, including phenomenological, grounded theory, ethnography, case study, mixed method, critical theory, and discourse analysis (Creswell, 1998; Dooley, 2002).

Although many investigators use a variety of methods to examine issues in distance education, not every case of research is designed to either test an existing theory or contribute to the development of a new theory. Such studies will not contribute to the development of new theories or shape or inform general practice. We suggest that there is a need for primary researchers, reviewers, and critics of the research literature to conduct research studies and literature analyses that either test existing theories and/or contribute to the development of new theories.

Colquitt and Zapata-Phelan (2007) developed a taxonomy for determining if an empirical research study contributes to either theory development or theory testing in applied fields. There are two dimensions in Cloquitt and Zapata-Phelan's taxonomy, including "Building New Theory" and "Testing Existing New Theory" (p. 1283). There are five levels for each dimension. Using both dimensions of the taxonomy, it is possible to classify studies as either "high theoretical contribution" or "low theoretical contribution" (p. 1283). For example, an investigation rated as low (level 1) on the "testing theory dimension" would be described as "is inductive or grounds predictions with logical speculation." A study rated as high (level 5) on the testing theory dimension is described as "grounds predictions with existing theory" (p. 1283). A study rated low (level 1) on the building new theory dimension would be described as "attempts to replicate previously demonstrated effects" and studies rated high (level 5) would "introduce a new construct (or significantly reconceptualized an existing one)" (p. 1283). The taxonomy developed by Cloquitt and Zapata-Phelan was initially designed for empirical studies. However, we believe with some adaptation that it would be useful for evaluating studies incorporating other methodologies.

Based on the results of our reviews or earlier reviews and our own updated review, we conclude that there is clearly as lack of theory-based research in distance education. We think that the taxonomy provided by Colquitt and Zapata-Phelan (2007) could help investigators and reviewers both in planning original research studies and conducting analyses of the literature. The focus of future distance education investigations should be on testing existing distance education theories and developing new theory.

DISTANCE EDUCATION RESEARCH: A FRAMEWORK AND SUGGESTIONS FOR THE FUTURE

We have already analyzed distance education research and discussed the need for theory-based research. We have also established that much of the distance education research literature is segmented and is not theory based. What then are, and should be, the important areas of research in distance education? In a Delphi study, Zawacki-Richter (2009) identified significant research categories (levels) in distance education, as well as areas of needed research in each category. One result of the Zawacki-Richter study was the development of a classification system for distance education research on three levels: "macro level: Distance education systems and theories"; "meso: management, organization, and technology"; and "micro: teaching and learning in distance education" (p. 3). Using the three levels identified by Zawacki-Richter, Zawacki-Richter, Backer, and Vogt (2009) conducted an analysis of the distance education as reflected in five well-known distance education journals, and concluded (p. 21) that much of the distance education research has been conducted at the "micro" level, with an emphasis on "instructional design and individual learning processes" as discussed earlier in this chapter. Few studies focused on the "meso" and "macro" levels. If used by researchers when identifying topics, questions, and planning future studies, we think that the classification system developed by Zawacki-Richter could lead to more unified research programs of research at all three levels.

Our first recommendation is that more research is clearly needed at both the "meso" and "macro" levels in all areas identified by Zawacki-Richter (2009). Anglin and Morrison (2002) suggested areas of research that were lacking in the distance education literature, including globalization and cultural diversity, access and equity, and policy issues (i.e., "meso" and "macro" levels). However, in the ensuing 8-year period, few studies have addressed such issues. Other areas for future study include motivation in distance education, student characteristics for success, the costs and benefits of distance education programs, delivery technology, and the implications of Web 2.0 (Bernard et al., 2004). In the first edition of this book,

LaPointe (2005) stated that, "despite the fact distance education has been on the educational scene since the 1800s, the field has not made research a central focus of its practice" (p. 75). We hope that in the future, there is a specific focus on studies at all levels that lead either to theory testing or theory development.

GENERAL SUMMARY

In this chapter, we first summarized the results of selected earlier analyses and reviews of the distance education literature and included an update of an earlier analysis that we conducted. It was concluded that the existing literature has contributed to our understanding of distance education, but that overall, the distance education research is poor in quality. We then discussed the issues concerning theory in distance education. A taxonomy was introduced that we believe will help both individuals planning theory-based research studies and those evaluating the research literature from the perspective of theory. It was suggested that future distance education research should have the purpose of either testing existing theories and/or contributing to the development of new theories. We then presented a framework that could be used to plan future distance education studies and assist in identifying areas of needed research, particularly areas that are underrepresented in the literature. Finally, we identified areas for future distance education research. It is clear that distance education practice has outpaced both the distance education theory and research, and given the rapid changes in technology, this condition could become a relatively permanent trend. We believe that even given the current state of affairs, there is a significant need for distance education theory and distance education research that either tests theories or leads to the development of new theories.

COMPREHENSION AND APPLICATION QUESTIONS

1. It is important to define a concept before using it in distance education research. There are many definitions of distance education provided by various writers. What do you think are the important differences between the various definitions? What is your definition of distance education? What is your definition of distance learning? How does one's definition of distance education affect the research questions that will be identified?

2. There are a number of perspectives or viewpoints that are touted as "theories" of distance learning. What criteria would you use to

determine if a perspective or viewpoint is actually a theory? Using your criteria, do the existing viewpoints and perspectives meet your criteria for a valid theory? Do the perspectives meet Dubin's (1978) criteria for a valid theory?

3. It is apparent that distance education programs are being distributed on a global level, yet little research has been conducted on the implications of cultural differences on distance learning policy and design. Discuss the reasons that you think much of the research on distance learning has an instructional design focus, while few focus on the implications of cultural factors.

RESOURCES FOR FURTHER EXPLORATION

American Distance Education Consortium (http://www.adec.edu/), Lincoln, Nebraska. Consortium of 65 state and land grant colleges in the United States. The consortium provides an extensive database including many areas including accessibility, international cooperation, resources, and standards.

International Center for Distance Learning (http://icdl.open.ac.uk/), Literature Data Base, The Open University, Milton Keynes, England. The database includes over 12,000 references to various type of literature concerning distance education.

Moore, M. G. (Ed.). (2007). *Handbook of distance education* (2nd ed.). New York, NY: Routledge. This book provides an extensive collection of chapters on all facets of distance education. Both current practice and future research needs are discussed.

United States Distance Learning Association (http://www.usdla.org/), Boston, MA. This organization provides training, conferences, and research reports to those interested in distance education.

REFERENCES

Allen, E., & Seaman, J. (2010). *Learning on demand: Online education in the United States, 2009*. Wellesley, MA: Babson Survey Research Group; Newburyport, MA: Sloan Consortium.

Anglin, G. J., & Morrison, G. R. (2000). An analysis of distance education research: Implications for the instructional technologist. *Quarterly Review of Distance Education, 1*, 189–194.

Anglin, G. J., & Morrison, G. R. (2002). Evaluation and research in distance education: Implications for research. In C. Vrasidas & G. V. Glass (Eds.), *Distance education and distributed learning* (pp. 157–180). Greenwich, CT: Information Age.

Berge, Z. L., & Mrozowski, S. (2001). Review of research in distance education, 1990–1999. *The American Journal of Distance Education, 3*, 5–19.

Bernard, R. M., Abrami, P. C., Lou, Y., & Borokhovski, E. (2004). A methodological morass? How we can improve quantitative research in distance education. *Distance Education, 25*(2), 175–198.

Bernard, R. M., Abrami, P. C., Lou, Y., Borokhovski, E., Wade, A., Wozney, J., ... Huang, B. (2004). How does distance education compare with classroom instruction? A meta-analysis of the empirical literature. *Review of Educational Research, 74*(3), 379–439.

Cener, I. R. R. (2010). *IGNOU: A brief profile.* Retrieved May 20, 2010 from http://www.ignouranchi.in/ignoubrief.htm

China, T. O. U. O. (2010). *General information.* Retrieved from http://en.crtvu.edu.cn/about/general-information

Clark, R. E. (2000). Evaluating distance education: Strategies and cautions. *Quarterly Review of Distance Education, 1,* 3–16.

Colquitt, J. A., & Zapata-Phelan, C. P. (2007). Trends in theory building and theory testing: A five decade study of the academy of management journal. *Academy of Management Journal, 50*(6), 1281–1303.

Concise Oxford English Dictionary. (2004) *Theory* (11th ed.). New York, NY: Oxford University Press.

Creswell, J. W. (1998). *Qualitative inquiry and research design: Choosing among five traditions.* Thousand Oaks, CA: Sage.

Dooley, L. M. (2002). Case study research and theory building. *Advanced in Developing Human Resources, 4*(3), 335–354. doi: 10.1177/1523422302043007

Dubin, R. (1978). *Theory building* (Rev. ed.). New York, NY: Free Press.

Garrison, R. (2000). Theoretical challenges for distance education in the 21st century: A shift from structural to transactional issues. *The International Review of Research in Open and Distance Learning, 10*(6). Retrieved from http://www.irrodl.org/index.php/irrodl/article/view/2/333

Keegan, D. (1996). *Foundations of distance education* (3rd ed.). New York, NY: Routledge.

Klein, J. D. (2002). Empirical research on performance improvement. *Performance Improvement Quarterly, 15*(1), 99–110.

Koble, M., & Bunker, E. (1997). Trends in research and practice: An examination of *The American Journal of Distance Education* 1987 to 1995. *The American Journal of Distance Education, 11*(2), 19–38.

LaPointe, D. K. (2005). Distance education international research: What the world needs now. In Y. L. Visser, L. Visser, M. Simonson, & R. Amirault (Eds.), *Trends and issues in distance education: International perspectives* (1st ed., pp. 67–69). Greenwich, CT: Information Age.

Lee, Y., Driscoll, M. P., & Nelson, D. W. (2004). The past, present, and future of research in distance education: Results of a content analysis. *The American Journal of Distance Education, 18*(4), 225–241.

Mayer, R. E. (2008). Applying the science of learning: Evidence-based principles for the design of multimedia instruction. *American Psychologist, 63*(8), 760–769.

Means, B., Toyama, Y., Murphy, R., Bakia, M., & Jones, K. (2009). *Evaluation of evidence-based practices in online learning: A meta-analysis and review of online learning studies*. Washington, DC: Department of Education, Office of Planning, Evaluation, and Policy Development.

Moore, M., & Kearsley, G. (1996). *Distance education: A systems view*. New York, NY: Wadsworth.

Parsad, B., & Lewis, L. (2008). *Distance education at degree-granting postsecondary institutions: 2006–2007* (NCES 2009-044). Washington, DC: U.S. Department of Education, National Center for Education Statistics, Institute of Education Sciences.

Saba, F. (2000). Research in distance education: A status report. *The International Review of Research in Open and Distance Learning, 1*(1). Retrieved from http://www.irrodl.org/index.php/irrodl/article/view/4

Schlosser, L. A., & Simonson, M. (2002). *Distance education: Definition and glossary of terms*: Bloomington, IN: Association for Educational Communications and Technology.

Simonson, M., Smaldino, S., Zvacek, S., & Albright, M. (2009). *Teaching and learning at a distance: Foundations of distance education*. Boston, MA: Allyn and Bacon.

University, A. (2010). About. Retrieved May 20, 2010, from Yunusemre Kampusü https://www.anadolu.edu.tr/en/

Zawacki-Richter, O. (2009). Research areas in distance education: A Delphi study. *The International Review of Research in Open and Distance Learning, 10*(3). Retrieved from http://www.irrodl.org/index.php/irrodl/article/view/674

Zawacki-Richter, O., Baecker, E. M., & Vogt, S. (2009). Review of distance education research (2000–2008): Analysis of research areas, methods, and authorship patterns. *International Review of Research in Open and Distance Learning, 10*(6), 21–50. Retrieved from http://www.irrodl.org/index.php/irrodl/article/view/741/1433

CHAPTER 13

THE GLOBALIZATION OF THE HIGHER EDUCATION ENTERPRISE

Issues in the Delivery of Transnational Education in 2011

Andrea Hope

The reality faced by higher education institutions today is one that is shaped by an increasingly integrated world economy, the rise of new information and communications technologies (ICTs), the emergence of an international knowledge network, and the role of the English language. In order to prepare students for engagement in such a globalized world, higher education institutions have intensified their efforts to internationalize their programs. The last decade has seen a veritable explosion in the numbers of programs and institutions that are operating internationally. To date, the promise of global dominance by dedicated e-learning providers has not been realized, although cross-border e-learning continues to grow in potential for new kinds of pedagogy and access. Concerns about quality underpin much of the debate about transnational education, as increased demand for access to higher education has fostered the emergence of diploma mills and accreditation mills; that is, bogus providers and accrediting bodies who seek to evade the scrutiny of national and international quality assurance agencies. One of

Trends and Issues in Distance Education:
International Perspectives, Second Edition, pp. 189–206
Copyright © 2012 by Information Age Publishing
189

the most significant new developments in transnational education in the past 10 years has been the establishment of overseas branch campuses in the Gulf States and in the economic powerhouses of the Far East by prestigious universities from the English-speaking world to satisfy the needs of an emerging affluent middle class. This chapter argues that the higher education sector needs to be informed and vigilant about the risks and benefits of transnational education and the need for appropriate policies and regulations to guide and monitor future developments.

GLOBALIZATION OF HIGHER EDUCATION

The reality faced by higher education institutions today is shaped "by an increasingly integrated world economy, new Information and Communications Technologies (ICTs), the emergence of an international knowledge network, the role of the English language and other forces" beyond anyone's control (Altbach, Reisberg, & Rumbley, 2009, p. iv). In order to prepare students for engagement in such a globalized world, which is characterized by Knight (2006a, p. 18) as the increasing "flow of people, culture, ideas, values, knowledge, technology and economy across borders," higher education institutions have intensified their efforts to internationalize their programs. At the simplest level, this may involve the introduction of an international or intercultural dimension into programs of study and extracurricular activities provided to home students in the form of international exchanges of academic staff and students, as well as the recruitment of international students to study on campus. It may also extend to the establishment of international cooperation and development projects and networks, international agreements for the delivery of programs across national borders, joint and double degree programs, twinning partnerships, and even the establishment of branch campuses in overseas locations.

At the beginning of the second decade of the twenty-first century, having an international profile enhances the competitiveness and prestige of an institution, and in a world where global rankings provide the key to opening lucrative new markets and ventures, the pressure on institutions to demonstrate credentials as international players through the creation of strategic alliances has created a scramble to secure reputable international partners. Olds (2009) has described this as the move from "the promiscuous acquisition of hundreds, if not thousands, of Memoranda of Understanding" to the creation of more focused, intense, and "deep" mutually beneficial relationships.

The last decade saw a veritable explosion in the number of international programs and institutions. While there is a lack of accurate data on all aspects of cross-border education, especially the movement of education programs and providers (Adelman, 2009; Knight, 2007; McBurnie & Ziguras, 2009; Naidoo, 2009), the trend away from students moving across borders to students moving across programs and providers has been clearly observed. UNESCO (as cited in Altbach et al., 2009) estimates that in 2007, there were approximately 2.8 million students studying outside their home country. An Australian survey conducted by IDP in 2002 (Bohm, Davis, Meares, & Pearce, 2002) predicted that this number would rise to 7 million by 2025. However, the most recent IDP study (Banks, Olsen, & Pearce, 2007) forecasts that global demand for international education will grow from 2.173 million in 2005 to 3.720 million in 2025. Although the numbers of students seeking education abroad continues to grow in absolute terms (the latest IDP forecast represents a 71% growth over a 20-year period), student mobility is being outpaced by program and provider mobility as greater emphasis is placed on delivering academic courses and programs to students in their own country. Predictions from the UK government in 2004 suggested that demand for UK transnational education will grow at an annual rate of just over 9%, from 190,000 student places in 2003 to 350,000 in 2010 and 800,000 by 2020 (Bohm et al., 2004). The study notes that "this is significantly greater than the growth for the base scenario forecasts for international students onshore in the UK which is expected to be about 4.7% per annum" (Bohm et al., 2004, p. 9). This trend is a wake-up call for countries such as the United States, United Kingdom, and Australia that traditionally have aggressively pursued the recruitment of overseas students. Marginson (2007, p. 6) predicts the end of the "cash cow" of incoming students to Australia as a result of "demographics, development, competition and the financial tsunami," forcing higher education institutions to adopt a "wider internationalization agenda where there is balance in overseas activity between recruitment, partnerships, research and capacity building."

IMPACT OF THE MASSIFICATION OF HIGHER EDUCATION

In its 2005 survey of higher education, *The Economist* magazine (Woolridge, 2005) identified four major and interrelated forces that are fuelling the drive for internationalization: the massification (i.e., the democratization) of higher education; the rise of the knowledge economy; globalization itself; the "the death of distance"; and competition from new providers.

The scale of the massification of higher education in the developed world may be demonstrated by noting that the proportion of adults with higher education qualifications in the OECD countries nearly doubled between 1975 and 2000 (from 22% to 41%). Altbach et al. (2009) explain the inevitable "logic" of massification, which includes greater social mobility for a growing segment of the population, new patterns of funding higher education and increasingly diversified systems that encompass public, and private providers operating in both for-profit and not-for profit mode. As rich countries still struggle to digest this growth in student enrollment, countries in the developing world are making efforts to catch up. In 2006, five countries (China, the United States, India, Russia, and Japan) accounted for 53.1 million students, more than half of the total number of students in the world (Knight, 2006a). Some 25 million of those students were in China, representing an age participation rate (APR) of 22%, while the 13 million enrollments in India accounted for a 12% APR. It is estimated that perhaps one third of the world's 140 million postsecondary students are enrolled in Indian and Chinese institutions of higher education (Altbach, 2009).

In a globalized world economy characterized in all sectors by the "cross-border matching of supply and demand" (Zha Qiang, 2003, p. 248), emerging nations such as India and China actively seek international partners who are willing to provide transnational programs to supplement local supply in areas of greatest demand. Students, for their part, will enroll in transnational programs because of a lack of opportunity to enroll in top domestic programs, as foreign institutions are seen to have more prestige than local ones, and because it is cheaper and more convenient than studying abroad (McBurnie & Ziguras, 2009). Access can take many forms, including branch campuses, franchised foreign academic programs or degrees, offshore programs delivered by distance learning and/or face-to-face by visiting overseas faculty, or independent institutions based on foreign academic models.

One of the traditional roles of higher education systems has been to prepare the next generation of leaders. Institutions in a massified system may espouse a broader vision of opening the pathways to leadership by ensuring that a wider spectrum of society has the opportunity to succeed in a globalized world, empowered by rapid advances in ICTs and characterized by interdependence, diversity, and rapid change. In this environment, knowledge is replacing physical resources as the main driver of economic growth. Universities are among the most important engines of the knowledge economy, producing the "brain workers" who will be able to find, analyze, and synthesize information to advance knowledge and solve emerging problems. At the forefront of the drive to produce excellent knowledge workers and future leaders are the world institutions that form the super-league of global universities that appear in world rankings of universities, such as the Times Higher Education's *QS World University Rankings* (QS World University, 2010) and the Shanghai Jiao Tong University's *Academic Ranking of World Universities* (Academic Ranking of World Universities, 2010).

Massification has ensured that there is still a large and lucrative market (estimated by the World Bank to be in the range of $300 billion) to be spent on "demand absorbing programs" (Altbach & Knight, 2007, p. 294) that provide access to students who would not otherwise attend a postsecondary institution. It is perhaps inevitable that the less prestigious end of the higher education system offers most of the demand-absorbing programs in the international arena. Altbach (2008) has decried the "irrational exuberance" and "bubble mentality" of institutions seeking to penetrate the "large, growing and basically unregulated" marketplace of the "Wild East" (particularly China and India), stating that

> In this market, some sellers are prestigious universities ... but many are subprime institutions, sleazy recruiters, degree packagers, low-end private institutions seeking to stave off bankruptcy through the export market and even a few respectable universities forced by government funding cuts to raise cash elsewhere. (p. 24)

THE ROLE OF ONLINE LEARNING

Given the rapid development of ICTs and the apparently insatiable demand of the knowledge economy for computer-literate problem solvers and information workers in every sphere of life, some commentators in the late 1990s predicted the demise of traditional universities and the inexorable rise of online learning. In 1998, the consulting firm of Coopers and Lybrand issued a white paper in which they described the Internet and new technology as creating a "massive, structural change in the higher education industry" (Coopers & Lybrand, 1998). Coopers and Lybrand suggested that "Instructional software could easily substitute for campus-based instruction, or at least be a substantial part of the delivery system."

To date however, with few notable exceptions, the promise of global dominance by dedicated e-learning providers has not been realized. In 2005, the OECD confirmed that "cross-border e-learning has not displaced existing institutions, but continues to grow with open potential for new kinds of pedagogy and access." It noted that conventional universities still predominate, but face "formidable increase in volume, innovation and impact from commercial providers and from corporate universities" (OECD, 2005, p. 67). Many of these providers are active in e-learning, with one of the most successful being the University of Phoenix, which offers no-frills, accredited, online programs in high-demand areas.

There have, however, been many notable e-learning disasters. A few, generally prestigious, universities shot too high, aiming for the most able and affluent 2% of the potential student population, but found insufficient demand and revenues to offset high start-up expenses. In 2003, Columbia University and its partners in a consortium of elite education and cultural institutions closed their for-profit online portal *Fathom*, having invested $25 million just three years earlier. Its CEO reported that there were "still too many barriers to for-profit, online learning, even with an Ivy League cachet to it" (Angelo, 2003). In 2004, the much vaunted U.K.-based *eUniversities Worldwide Limited* shut down. The venture had been launched by the Secretary of State for Education in 2000 with a budget of £62 million to provide the technological and marketing resources for UK universities to deliver their distance learning programs to a worldwide audience. By the time it failed because of lack of demand, it had used up almost half of the budget (Perraton, 2005, p. 156). As recently as 2009, the University of Illinois scaled down its *Global Campus* initiative, which it had hoped would attract 70,000 new students, in the face of "unspectacular enrollment and punishing recession." What was planned to become a separately accredited entity with its own programs will now become a support-focused distance education portal for campus-based initiatives. The Global Campus Initiative's $9 million budget was subsequently reduced to $1.75 million (Parry, 2009).

It is undeniable that, in the world's most developed economies, the presence of ICTs has expanded exponentially and touched virtually all dimensions of the higher education enterprise (Altbach et al., 2009). International academic research and collaboration is facilitated by e-mail and online social networking sites; electronic journals provide ready access to research findings for academics whose institutions may not boast well-stocked research libraries; and the open educational resources movement has gained momentum and is providing free access to course materials and even whole programs of study not locally available to students or educators.

In developing countries, however, the costs and difficulties of reliance on ICT in terms of hardware, software, technical support, training, and continual upgrades are huge, and the digital divide continues to widen for the world's poorest countries. Nevertheless, the world's fastest growing emerging markets, including the so called BRIC countries (Brazil, Russia, India, and China), which currently account for more than a quarter of the world's land area and more than 40% of the world's population (Goldman Sachs, 2010), continue to attract the interest of educational entrepreneurs in the major higher education exporting countries.

That the potential of ICTs to revolutionize global higher education has not yet been fully realized is reflected in the January 2010 announcement from Bill Gates (Gates, 2010, p. 12) that the Gates Foundation is keen to support online learning, noting that "so far, technology has hardly changed formal education at all. But a lot of people, including me, think this is the next place where the Internet will surprise people in how it can improve things—especially in combination with face-to-face learning."

While many of the new providers in the e-learning market are driven by the profit motive, the fledgling University of the People (http://www.uopeople.org/) bills itself as the world's first global, tuition-free university. Backed by the UN and funded by the Israeli entrepreneur Shai Reshef, the University of the People opened its first virtual courses in Business Administration and Computer Science in September 2009. The University of the People aims to offer educational opportunities for the world's poorest countries by providing free online materials and social networking tools via the Moodle e-learning platform. Students are allocated to collaborative peer learning groups of 15–20 learners, and learning support is provided by a volunteer community of university professors, graduate students, retired academics, and computer specialists. Classes commenced at the University of the People on September 10, 2009. In March 2010, Reshef reported that over 300 students from 69 countries were enrolled (Reshef, 2010).

The major issue facing the University of the People, however, is accreditation. The University of the People is not yet authorized to award degrees, either in California (where it is based), or in other U.S. states, nor in any of the countries where its students are located. In our 2005 chapter, we discussed the issue of accreditation, and in particular, the problems of accrediting online institutions in the United States, which led to the demise of the U.S. Open University initiative. It is interesting to note that the debate about accreditation criteria for distance learning institutions continues. The vice president for international initiatives at the American Council on Education confirmed that the University of the People's chances of gaining accreditation may be hampered by their unconventional model, stating that "[The accreditation agency] would have to do a lot of bending and rethinking to have regional accreditation fit this model" (Green, as cited in Kolowich, 2010).

DEGREE MILLS AND BOGUS ACCREDITORS

Concerns about quality have continued to underpin much of the debate about transnational education. In 2005, UNESCO/OECD published "Guidelines for Quality Provision in Cross-Border Higher Education." In the foreword, Sir John Daniel, CEO of the Commonwealth of Learning, noted that cross-border education cannot help developing countries unless it is "acceptable, affordable, relevant and of acceptable quality" (Daniel, 2008, p. xiii).

The stance of the accreditation community toward the University of the People may be influenced by the recent research undertaken by the U.S. Council for Higher Education Accreditation (CHEA) to explore the challenges and problems of "degree mills" or bogus providers of higher education, particularly as these operations affect the growing internationalization of higher education. Degree mills offer credentials based on little study or engagement in higher education activity. The CHEA study, published in 2009, found that they are "easy to start, difficult to eliminate and, at least to date, relatively immune to regulation" (CHEA/ UNESCO, 2009, p. 1). This view is echoed by the Head of International affairs of the U.K. Quality Assurance Agency, who states that "even potentially strong national laws will do little to stop online diploma mills" (Campbell, as cited in Lederman, 2010), and suggests that Internet service providers (ISPs) and domain name sellers need to be engaged in the fight to eliminate the unscrupulous individuals who exploit the demand for higher education credentials and that inevitably accompanies the worldwide growth of higher education. The CHEA report finds that "the Internet gives them an instant platform to launch bogus institutions which students often cannot readily distinguish from the online learning opportunities offered by legitimate institutions" (CHEA/UNESCO, 2009, p. 1).

A 2010 report, "Diploma and Accreditation Mills: Exposing Academic Abuse," published by Verifile, a U.K.-based background-checking company, which runs a global database of bogus and/or unaccredited providers, reveals that there are 810 institutions operating in the United States and 459 in Europe, of which 271 operate out of the UK. The report suggests that the diploma mill operators are banking on the prestige of the U.K. and U.S. higher education systems and exploiting potential students from outside these countries wishing to improve their prospects by obtaining a degree from a U.K. or U.S. university (Cohen & Winch, 2010). Cohen and Winch reiterate the concerns of the accreditation bodies about the ease with which anyone can "set up a web-site and claim to be located anywhere in the world, using a few misleading photographs and a virtual address" (p. 11). Regions with lax regulatory regimes and large populations of students with little access to higher education are particularly vulnerable. The Caribbean, for example, is believed to be home to some 89 diploma mills (Daniel & Uvalic-Trumbic, 2009).

The continued rise in the number of diploma mills worldwide is accompanied by the emergence of "accreditation mills" (Altbach & Knight, 2007, p. 301). Like higher education itself, the accreditation process is also becoming internationalized and commercialized. Bona fide

U.S. national and regional accreditors provide or sell their services in more than 65 countries. Unfortunately, there has also been a growth in nonrecognized, illegitimate accreditation mills that sell accreditation without any independent oversight.

It is estimated that in the United States alone, degree mills award as many as 200,000 credentials a year, and that the federal government alone spends roughly $300 million a year on employee raises for those who get jobs or seek promotions using fraudulent degrees or certificates (Lederman, 2010). Newly proposed legislation announced in January 2010 seeks to cement definitions of diploma mills and accreditation mills in federal law, bar federal agencies from using degrees from diploma mills for the purposes of appointment or promotion to jobs that rely on the individual's educational credentials, and give the Federal Trade Commission more authority to define and crack down on deceptive practices by dubious institutions.

HIGHER EDUCATION AS A GLOBAL SERVICE INDUSTRY

Despite the threat to national reputations posed by the poor quality of provision, the lack of effective regulation in the receiving countries to prevent bogus providers and accreditors, and evidence of early failures of global consortia and other e-learning initiatives, governments continue to treat higher education as an "urban/national/global services industry" (Olds & Robertson, 2009). Driven by the need to generate revenue (often because of a reduction in government funding for national provision), higher education institutions, notably in the United Kingdom and Australia, have been encouraged to take part in more transnational initiatives. Export figures for education services are widely cited. In the UK in 2007, for example, education exports were worth £28 billion, a figure greater than for either automobiles or financial services. In Australia in 2007, education was the country's third largest export, after coal and iron ore and its largest service export item, worth AU$13.7 billion (Vincent-Lancrin, 2009). In New Zealand in 2009, education ranked above wine exports in its contribution to the national economy (Olds & Robertson, 2009). In January 2010, the then UK Prime Minister, Gordon Brown, announced a "new ambition for Britain" to double the value of higher education exports by using a four-pronged strategy: firmer regulations for incoming students to prevent immigration fraud; building on the UK's reputation for the rigor and quality of exams and qualifications; developing international partnerships in order to "take knowledge and share it with the billions of people who understand that education is the key to survival and success;" and by using distance education to harness the use of IT and online learning across the world (Olds, 2010).

DEVELOPMENT OF TRANSNATIONAL EDUCATION IN ASIA

In their review for the OECD of trends and future scenarios in program and institutional mobility, McBurnie and Ziguras (2009) suggest that, while the push and pull factors for the growth of transnational education that we have already identified will ensure its continued growth (i.e., the use of foreign provision by importing countries to absorb unmet demand, the search for financial and reputational gain on the part of exporting countries, and the lack of domestic places, allied with a search for the prestige of an overseas qualification at lower cost on the part of students), a new phenomenon is emerging in the richer developing countries. The researchers have observed that within the last decade, a number of net importers of education (particularly in Asia and the Middle East) have now put strategies in place and have declared their ambition to become net education exporters, primarily by establishing themselves as regional educational hubs that attract international students from their region and beyond.

The trajectory of transnational education in Hong Kong, Singapore, and Malaysia since the 1980s clearly reveals that the outward mobility of students that accompanied rapid economic development early in that period was accompanied by concerted local higher education capacity building. By the late 1990s, this led to a slowing of outward student mobility and increased inward program mobility, as foreign providers acted in capacity-building and demand-absorbing roles in partnership with the new local providers. Eventually, domestic providers are able to meet local demand. As domestic providers become more competitive, governments become more concerned with quality than quantity, and more stringent quality-assurance requirements are enforced, squeezing out the lower-status transnational programs. When domestic capacity and quality is sufficiently established, governments are positioned to take the first steps toward establishing themselves as educational hubs. In the case of Singapore, Malaysia, the United Arab Emirates, and Qatar, a major plank in this strategy has been to invite prestigious foreign universities to set up international branch campuses. These international branch campuses can be described (Altbach, 2010) as

An off-shore entity of a higher education institution operated by the institution through a joint venture in which the institution is a partner in the name of the foreign institution. Upon successful completion of the course program, which is fully undertaken at the unit abroad, students are awarded a degree from the foreign institution. (p. 2)

BRANCH CAMPUSES AND REGIONAL EDUCATION HUBS

The growth of branch campuses has been perhaps the single most significant new development in the internationalization of higher education in the past 10 years. Becker (2010) reports that since September 2006, the number of international branch campuses in the world has increased by 43% to 162. Institutions for the United States continue to dominate, with 78 campuses, followed by Australia (14 campuses), the United Kingdom (13 campuses), and France and India (11 campuses each). In Singapore, Qatar, and the UAE, the branch campuses form part of prestigious educational clusters. In 2009, Dubai Knowledge Village constituted the world's largest cluster of branch campuses with 15 foreign universities. It aims to have 30 foreign universities by 2015. Qatar's Education City is host to mostly U.S. institutions. Through its Global Schoolhouse program, Singapore aims to increase the number of international students studying there from a reported 80,000 in 2006 (Gribble & McBurnie, 2007) to 150,000 by 2015. Malaysia plans to open the Kuala Lumpur Education City (KLEC) in 2012.

In the case of all of these clusters, the hosts are seeking to be the preeminent business hubs for their regions and need to develop attractive clusters of specialized services to support the knowledge-intensive aspects of multinationals' operations. In Singapore's case, it also hopes to attract top international graduates to remain in the country as skilled immigrants. The KLEC Development Web site   (www.klec.com.my) clearly sets out the vision of the Malaysian government, one that mirrors the aspirations of other countries in the region:

KLEC's main target markets will be China, the Middle East as well as India and South East Asia. Although it is estimated that the majority of students and places are for the local market, the main growth in student recruitment will come from the regional markets. In line with the government's aim of attracting international students to Malaysia, KLEC will in fact play a major role in achieving that goal. But it is not only about attracting regional and international students, but also providing more opportunities to the local students to allow them to have access to world-class education, especially for their undergraduate education. As for postgraduate education, with the participation of the top universities, this will attract a huge number of the local faculty and graduates to undertake postgraduate education and this will benefit and promote the government's drive for more Masters and PhDs in both local public and private universities.

The reality of branch campuses, like so many ventures in transnational education, has not always lived up to its promise. George Mason University opened its campus in Qatar in 2005, but pulled out in May 2009 without having graduated a single student (Lewin, 2009). Each of the hubs have experienced the withdrawal of high-profile providers, either through failure to meet unrealistic student enrollment targets, failure to meet hosts' expectations for nature or quality of programs, or because of disagreements with funding sponsors.

Altbach (2010) casts doubts on the long-term sustainability of international branch campuses, citing difficulties in persuading professors from the home university to teach at the branch campus, particularly in the longer term; limited branch office curriculum offerings (generally, subjects that attract large enrollments, require limited infrastructure, and are relatively inexpensive to teach); a hollowing out of the faculty role (e.g., stripping out research); difficulties in establishing a student body (a particular issue for the most prestigious universities with high admissions criteria); and, as many have found to their peril, attracting sufficient numbers of students as competition from domestic and international providers across the region continues to increase.

EMERGENCE OF CHINA AND INDIA

One of the key triggers of the continuing demand for transnational education in Asia that the educational hubs in Malaysia, Singapore, and the UAE are seeking to satisfy is the emergence of an affluent middle class with income sufficient to pay tuition fees, and a large cohort of university-age young people who cannot find places within the domestic system. Two countries in the region, India and China, already satisfy these criteria. In 2008, for example, China and India were the top two exporters of students. Approximately 200,000 Indians and 892,000 Chinese were studying abroad (Agarwal, 2008, p. 83). Meanwhile, over 1,000 overseas programs are currently offered in China, notably from the United States, the UK, and Australia, via joint degree or other collaborative arrangements, including two full-fledged branch campuses. China also aggressively seeks to attract students from outside its borders. In 2007, China hosted 200,000 international students, 75% of whom came from other Asian countries. India, with South Asia's largest academic system, hosts students and conducts exchanges with Sri Lanka, Nepal, Bangladesh, and Bhutan. Political differences have so far prevented collaboration with Pakistan. Indian institutions have a presence in the education hubs in Singapore and the UAE, and the Indira Gandhi National Open University (IGNOU) has for many years offered programs through distance education to the Indian diaspora in the Middle East. In 2003, China, concerned about the quality of some of the international programs offered within its borders, passed legislation regulating foreign educational collaboration. The Indian government is still in the process of implementing similar rules. Altbach (2009) reports that

> The role of independent branch campuses, ownership of institutions, the role of the private and the for-profit sectors, quality assurance for foreign institutions, the role of franchised overseas degree programs, and other complex issues have proved controversial.... They seek to maintain control over foreign institutions and programs on their territories while welcoming international involvement. (p. 189)

CONCLUSION

In 2005, we identified issues of quality, equity, access, and recognition as significant issues arising from the rise of transnational education, as governments in developing countries sought a cost-effective means to provide mass education at minimal cost (Hope, 2005, p. 24). Just 5 years later, despite a global economic meltdown in 2008–2009, transnational education ventures continue to grow and develop in new ways, but the issues of quality, equity, access, and recognition remain. The traditional prominence of the large education exporting nations, such as the United States, the United Kingdom and Australia, is now being challenged by the newly emerging Asian economic superpowers. In this new market, it is the prestigious "Ivy League" institutions of the traditional provider countries that can boast high-ranking status in international university league tables that can be seen to have been most successful. These institutions have seized the opportunity to attract emerging affluent local and regional middle classes to enroll in their programs at branch campuses within regional education hubs intended to replicate the student experience in the home institutions. Meanwhile, demand-absorbing programs in popular subject areas are thriving in the newly emerging markets, where host governments, desperate to meet demand, impose few regulatory requirements. Inevitably, in these jurisdictions, the poor quality of some of the provision continues to challenge the credibility of transnational programs, and the scourge of degree and accreditation mills has been seriously unaddressed by the international accreditation community. Unfortunately, the losers in all of this new development continue to be the least privileged members of society in the host nations with the least developed domestic provision. These underprivileged individuals are hampered by lack of access to technology and cannot afford the tuition fees charged by the transnational providers operating within their country. Ventures like the University of the People seek to address these needs, but their graduates will be denied recognition for their achievements if the institution is unable to overcome the barriers to accreditation currently being experienced.

Vincent-Lancrin (2009) proposes three future scenarios for the sustainable development of transnational education:

1. The sustained diversification of internationalization of all types, supported by national quality assurance and painstaking recognition protocols.

2. Convergence toward a liberal model of education in which higher education becomes a service industry based on commercial trade. Large numbers of new providers, including private companies in partnership with traditional universities, seek out the lucrative markets. University rankings will exert increasing influence on consumer choice, and less-competitive programs will disappear.

3. The triumph of the former emerging economies. Countries that were previous net education importers, who have developed their own higher education systems competitive in terms of quality and price, and have mature, robust quality assurance systems, will become net education exporters. Assuming that English continues to be at the centre of the global knowledge system, driven by the weight of the Anglo-American block in the world economy, the cultural industries and the Internet itself, India's competitive advantage of being an English speaking nation may lead to it becoming the world's leading educational export country.

Our analysis of developments in transnational education over the 5 years since our last review indicates that these scenarios are already emerging in parallel on today's world stage. We would therefore echo Knight (2007, p. 16) in concluding that the higher education sector needs to be informed and vigilant about the risks and benefits of transnational education, as well as the need for the implementation of appropriate policies and regulations to guide and monitor future transnational educational developments.

COMPREHENSION AND APPLICATION QUESTIONS

1. In a globalized knowledge economy, the desire for access to higher education increases, but the "digital divide" between developed

and developing nations continues to widen. What are the major factors influencing access to international higher education in developing countries?

2. What are the major factors that influence higher education institutions in the United States, the United Kingdom, and Australia to participate in transnational education?

3. Account for the rise of the international branch campus phenomenon in the Gulf States and the Far East. What are likely to be the major stumbling blocks to their long-term sustainability?

RESOURCES FOR FURTHER EXPLORATION

Altbach, P., Reisberg, L. & Rumbley, L. (2009). *Trends in global higher education: Tracking an academic revolution.* Report prepared for the UNESCO World Conference on Higher Education. *The New Dynamics of Higher Education and Research for Societal Change and Development.* Paris, France. Retrieved from http://unesdoc.unesco.org/images/0018/001832/183219e.pdf

OECD. (2009). *Educational research and innovation higher education to 2030 –Vol.2 Globalisation,* 63–88. OECD Publishing. Retrieved from http://browse .oecdbookshop.org/oecd/pdfs/browseit/9609041E.PDF

REFERENCES

Academic Ranking of World Universities (2009). *Academic Ranking of World Universities - 2009.* Retrieved from http://www.arwu.org/ARWU2009.jsp

Adelman, C. (2009). The spaces between numbers: Getting international data on higher education straight. *Report for Institute for Higher Education Policy.* Retrieved from http://www.ihep.org/assets/files/publications/s-z/ (Report)_The_Spaces_Between_Numbers-Getting_International_Data_on_Higher_Education_Straight.pdf

Agarwal, P. (2008). India in the context of international student circulation: Status and prospects. In H. de Wit, P. Agarwal, M. Elmahady Said, M. T. Sehoole, & M. Sirozi (Eds.), *The dynamics of international student circulation in a global context* (pp. 83–112). Rotterdam, The Netherlands: Sense.

Altbach, P. (2008, February 14). The "global market" bubble. *Times Higher Education.*

Altbach, P. (2009). The giants awake: The present and future of higher education systems in China and India. *Educational Research and Innovation Higher Education to 2030 –Vol. 2. Globalisation,* 179–201. Paris, France: OECD. Retrieved from http://browse.oecdbookshop.org/oecd/pdfs/browseit/9609041E.PDF

Altbach, P. (2010, Winter). Why branch campuses may be unsustainable. *International Higher Education,* 58. Boston, MA: CIHE.

Altbach, P. & Knight J. (2007). The internationalization of higher education: Motivations and realities. *Journal of Studies in International Education, 11,* 290–305.

Altbach, P., Reisberg, L., & Rumbley, L. (2009). Trends in global higher education: Tracking an academic revolution. Report prepared for the UNESCO World Conference on Higher Education, *The New Dynamics of Higher Education and Research for Societal Change and Development.* Paris, France. Retrieved from http://unesdoc.unesco.org/images/0018/001832/183219e.pdf

Angelo, J. M. (2003, February). It's hard to "fathom," but Columbia University, which poured $25 million into its commercial online venture Fathom.com, will pull the plug on April 1. *University Business.* Retrieved from http://www.universitybusiness.com

Banks, M., Olsen, A., & Pearce, D. (2007). *Global student mobility: An Australian perspective five years on.* Report for IDP Education Australia.

Becker, R. F. J. (2010). International branch campuses: Markets and strategies. *Report of the Observatory on Borderless Education.* Retrieved from www.obhe.ac.uk

Bohm, A., Davis, D., Meares, D., & Pearce, D. (2002). *Global student mobility 2025: Forecasts of the global demand for international higher education.* Report for IDP Education Australia.

Bohm, A., Follari, M., Hewett, A., Jones, S., Kemp, N., Meares, D., … Van Cauter, K. (2004). *Vision 2020: Forecasting international student mobility—A UK perspective.* London, England: British Council. Retrieved from http://www.britishcouncil.org/eumd_-_vision_2020.pdf

CHEA/UNESCO. (2009). *Toward effective practice: Discouraging degree mills in higher education.* Retrieved from http://www.chea.org/pdf/degree_mills_effective_practice.pdf

Cohen, E., & Winch, R. (2010) Diploma and accreditation mills: Exposing academic credential abuse. *Verifile.* Retrieved from http://www.accredibase.com/upload/documents/accredibase_report_20_jan_2010.pdf

Coopers & Lybrand. (1998). The transformation of higher education in the digital age. *Report based on the Learning Partnership Roundtable.* Aspen Institute, MD, July 1997. Reproduced in H-Net Discussion Networks - H-MMEDIA. Retrieved from http://h-net.msu.edu/

Daniel, J. (2008). Preface. In S. Marshall, E. Brandon, M. Thomas, A. Kanwar, & T. Lyngra (Eds.), *Foreign providers in the Caribbean: Pillagers or preceptors?* Vancouver, BC: Commonwealth of Learning.

Daniel, J., & Uvalic-Trumbic, S. (2009, January 26–29). *Combating degree mills.* Presented at the CHEA 2009 Annual Conference and International Seminar, Washington, DC. Retrieved from http://www.chea.org/pdf/2009_IS_Combating_Degree_Mills_Daniels.pdf

Gates, B. (2010) *Annual letter to the Bill and Melinda Gates Foundation.* Retrieved from http://www.gatesfoundation.org/annual-letter/2010/documents/2010-bill-gates-annual-letter.pdf

Goldman Sachs. (2010, May 20) Is this the "BRICs decade? *BRICs Monthly Issue, 10*(3). Retrieved from http://www2.goldmansachs.com/ideas/brics/brics-decade-doc.pdf

Gribble, C., & McBurnie, G. (2007, Summer). Problems within Singapore's global schoolhouse. *International Higher Education, 48*.

Hope, A. (2005). Quality, accreditation and recognition: Issues in the delivery of transnational education. In Y. L. Visser, L. Visser, M. Simonson, & R. Amirault (Eds.), *Trends and issues in distance education: International perspectives* (1st ed., pp. 23–34). Greenwich, CT: Information Age.

Knight, J. (2006a). *Higher education crossing borders: A guide to the implications of the general agreement on trade in services (GATS) for cross-border education.* COL/ UNESCO. Retrieved from http://unesdoc.unesco.org/images/0014/001473/ 147363e.pdf

Knight, J. (2006b). *Internationalization of higher education: New directions, new challenges.* The 2005 IAU Global Survey Report. Paris, France: International Association of Universities.

Knight, J. (2007). *Implications of crossborder education and GATS for the knowledge enterprise.* Paris, France: UNESCO. Retrieved from http://unesdoc.unesco.org/ images/0015/001593/159389e.pdf

Kolowich, S. (2010, February 22) Tuition-free, on-line education? Try the University of the People. *Inside Higher Ed.* Retrieved from http://www.insidehighered.com/

Lederman, D. (2010, January 29). Taking aim at diploma mills. *Inside Higher Ed.* Retrieved from http://insidehighered.com

Lewin, T. (2009, February 28). George Mason University, among first with an Emirates branch, is pulling out. *New York Times.*

Marginson, S. (2007, October 16). The global positioning of Australian higher education: Where to from here? *University of Melbourne, Faculty of Education, Dean's Lecture Series.* Retrieved from http://www.edfac.unimelb.edu.au/news/ lectures/pdf/simon.pdf

McBurnie, G., & Ziguras, C. (2009). Trends and future scenarios in programme and institution mobility across borders. *Educational Research and Innovation Higher Education to 2030 –Vol. 2 Globalisation,* 89–107. OECD Publishing. Retrieved from http://browse.oecdbookshop.org/oecd/pdfs/browseit/9609041E.PDF

Naidoo, V. (2009). Transnational education: A stock take of current activity. *Journal of Studies in International Education, 13*(3), 310–330.

Olds, K. (2009, November 5). From rhetoric to reality: Unpacking the numbers and practices of global higher education. *Global Higher Ed.* Retrieved from http://globalhighered.wordpress.com/2009/11/05/from-rhetoric-to-reality/

Olds, K. (2010, January 15). Is a UK funding crisis an effective mechanism to spur on the "education as a global growth industry" development agenda? *Global Higher Ed.* Retrieved from http://globalhighered.wordpress.com/2010/01/15/ is-a-uk-funding-crisis-needed/

Olds, K., & Robertson, S. (2009, Nov. 25). Taking note of export earnings. *Global Higher Ed.* Retrieved from http://globalhighered.wordpress.com/2009/11/25/ taking-note-of-export-earnings/

Organization for Economic Cooperation and Development (OECD). (2005). *E-learning in tertiary education: Where do we stand?* Paris, France: OECD. Retrieved from www.oecd.org/dataoecd/55/25/35961132.pdf

Parry, M. (2009, May 19). U. of Illinois weighs more humble version of "global campus." *The Chronicle of Higher Education*. Wired Campus blogpost. Retrieved from http://chronicle.com/blogs/

Perraton, H. (2005). Counting the cost. In A. Hope & P. Guiton (Eds.), *Strategies for sustainable open and distance learning*. London, England: Routledge.

QS Top Universities. (2010). *World university rankings 2010*. Retrieved from http://www.topuniversities.com/university-rankings/world-university-rankings/home

Reshef, S. (2010). Educating the many. *Educause Quarterly, 33*(1).

Vincent-Lancrin, S. (2009). Cross-border higher education: Trends and perspectives. In *Educational research and innovation higher education to 2030—Vol. 2, Globalisation* (pp. 63–88). Paris, France: OECD.

Wooldridge, A. (2005, September 8). The brains business. *The Economist*. Retrieved from http://www.economist.com/surveys/displaystory.cfm?story_id=4339960

Zha Qiang. (2003). Internationalization of higher education: Toward a conceptual framework. *Policy Futures in Education, 1*(2), 248–268.

CHAPTER 14

DISTANCE EDUCATION SUPPORT SYSTEMS

Challenges and Opportunities

Wai-Kong Ng and Sow-Lai Kong

Distance education support (DES) is a critical factor in the success of students in a distance education program. Because students in distance education institutions are normally not physically present on a university campus, they are often not accorded the full range of DES support that could be used to sustain their involvement in academic pursuits. In this chapter, we present evidence from six core areas of student support based on the experience of some select Asian distance education providers and discuss issues surrounding each support area. These DES areas include face-to-face tutorials, telephone tutoring/e-mail, regional learning centers, course materials, tutor-marked assignments, and learning management systems. We discuss these areas in the context of a technology-rich learning setting where DES services are increasingly being mediated by technology and further consider how DES services may evolve in the future. It is certain that the impact of emerging technologies will redraw the landscape of DES services in the immediate future, and therefore institutions implementing DES systems will be required to make critical decisions on selecting and maintaining DES systems, while at the same time eliminating redundant supports.

Trends and Issues in Distance Education:
International Perspectives, Second Edition, pp. 207–222
Copyright © 2012 by Information Age Publishing
All rights of reproduction in any form reserved.

INTRODUCTION

Distance education can broadly be described as educational or instructional programming delivered to students in one or several remote locations, either via synchronous or asynchronous mode (Southern Association of Colleges and Schools, 2000). Keegan (1990) identified some key elements of distance education, including *separation of teacher and learner, use of media to link teacher and learner, two-way exchange of communication*; and *learners as individuals rather than groups*. Newer technologies attempt at narrowing the gap between distance teachers and learners, theoretically making possible "conversation in context" (Sharples, 2005). As distance learners are widely dispersed and physically separated from the institution as well as their peers, they must be served with better methods and technological supports for presentation, management, and evaluation of course processes. Simultaneously, there are trends in traditional institutions transitioning into distance education as a result of the general demand for distance education. A survey report, "Class Differences: Online Education in the United States, 2010," stated that 5.6 million students were enrolled in at least one online course in fall 2009 in more than 2,500 colleges and universities (Allen & Seaman, 2010). This represents an increase of nearly one million students over the number reported the previous year, with more than two thirds of all educational institutions now offering online classes. This statistic implies that ever greater numbers of students are taking advantage of the convenience of distance learning to further their education without adherence to strict schedules and transportation logistics (Fairfax, 2010). This growing diversity of learner population demands a rethinking of how learner services and support should be developed to meet learner needs in a wide variety of educational environments (Garland & Grace, 1993; Newman & Peile, 2002; Tait, 2000). Adult learners generally turn to distance education because of its "anyplace/anytime" nature, thus allowing a balance between the demands of family, work, and school (Kemp, 2002). Transcending time and geography, distance education can provide greater access and flexibility for those who cannot attend on-campus classes (Paul & Brindley, 1996). Distance learners generally also decide where and when to learn; how quickly or slowly to complete a program; or when to take a break from learning, hence meeting their individual needs (Holmberg, 1995).

THE ROLE OF
DISTANCE EDUCATION SUPPORT IN DISTANCE LEARNING

The key to sustaining distance learners' interest and motivation to continue in a distance learning program thus appears to be learner services and support, which enables learners to remain in "contact" with the institution. These support services appear in a variety of distance education institutions. For example, there is Student Support Services (SSS) at the University of Wisconsin System Administration (UWSA Board of Regents, 2000). Then there is academic, administrative, and informative support before, during, and after a learning program (cf. IGNOU, 2009). Similarly, with far-flung locations, institutions such as the Universitas Terbuka Indonesia (Open University of Indonesia), student learning support services have been developed alone or in partnerships (Zuhairi, Adnan, & Thaib, 2007). Unsurprisingly, in most distance education institutions, the main mode of support to learners in a program is scheduled tutorial support, not unlike those conducted by traditional institutions. The Annual Survey of Courses of the Open University (UK) revealed that various forms of tutorial support are the most strongly and frequently requested items by the students (Burt, 1997).

With advances in technology of delivery, it has become clear that a substantive amount of distance education support (DES) will be borne by computer-based technology. Fearn (2009) reported that the technology to support instruction in institutions had blossomed to create different facets of instruction and learning opportunities. Students thus now have a broad range of opportunities of distance education institutions from which to choose. As a matter of principle, the Southern Association of Colleges and Schools (2000) concurs that distance education institutions should provide adequate access to a range of student services appropriate to support the programs, including admissions, financial aid, academic advising, delivery of course materials, and placement and counseling. In addition, the institution provides an adequate means for resolving student complaints (Southern Association of Colleges and Schools, 2000).

Distance education providers are hence aware of the need to support their students in their pursuit of education and are increasingly implementing online-based support, in addition to using regional or city centers to serve neighborhood students. Wallace (1996), in analyzing demographics and motivation of distance learners, contended that reducing barriers to success in distance education hinged on DES and DES policies, as well as teaching resources and fees. While DES is appreciated as an "assurance," as well as a determinant, for students who remain enrolled in a distance education program, it must be pointed out that even the traditional universities are also transitioning into distance education. For example, the first distance education program was launched in 1971 in a public university in Malaysia. Then, in 1999, a new private university, the Open University Malaysia, was established to "coordinate the DE programs of the 11 public universities" (Wikibooks, 2010). Increasing participation in distance education is made possible with the integration of technology into teaching and learning, chief among which are Internet technologies, portable iPods and MP3s, and social networking systems and communities that have grown by leaps and bounds. With so many organizations now operating in distance learning, either as hybrid entities or pure open and distance learning (ODL) players, it is imperative that institutions provide proper DES to ensure that their students continue on until program completion, as well as to help guarantee enrollment numbers. Student retention and course completion are both considered to be influenced by the quality of DES (Nitsch, 2003).

THE CONSTITUENTS OF DISTANCE EDUCATION SUPPORT

An institution that has played an important role in the development of DES standards is the University of Wisconsin System Administration (UWSA). The UWSA educates more than 170,000 students on 26 campuses and also conducts distance education programs. In September 2000, the UWSA Board of Regents issued the "Standards for Academic and Student Support Services in Distance Education Credit Course, Degree and Certificate Programs" (UWSA Board of Regents, 2000, pp. 1–4), which describes five categories in which DES should be considered. These categories are

   (a) Curriculum and Instruction (Academic rigor and quality instruction; courses are current; use of appropriate technology; training of faculty; faculty support services; interactions between faculty and students.)
   (b) .Evaluation and Assessment (Meeting expectations of students; evaluation of effectiveness of distance education; course evaluation including student satisfaction.)
   (c) Library and Learning Resources (Student access and effective use of resources; institution monitors usages.)
   (d) Student Services (Access to student related services like admissions, financial aid, course materials, and placement and counseling; help desks, etc.)
   (e) Facilities and Finances (Appropriate equipment, facilities, technical expertise, etc. available and sustainable over a period of time; faculty has access to instructional design support to ensure quality of student learning experiences; institution has long-range planning, budgeting, etc.)

Careful reflection on these standards allows us to make a series of inferences regarding DES. First, it is incumbent upon the distance education institution to provide quality instruction for students, including scheduled lectures, lecture notes, self-instructional materials, and accompanying technologies. Next, the evaluations provided by distance students on their instructional experiences should be carefully examined and reviewed for purposes of gaining insight on current DES efforts, particularly in light of the difficulty of obtaining such information from widely dispersed learners. Next, the costs of maintaining and supporting widely dispersed, physical library services, a key source of DES support, but which often are too great for distance education providers to bear, may be made more reasonable via use of shared electronic "virtual" libraries. Finally, student services are increasingly being viewed as compulsory administrative support services for both current and future students. Strategies of such support before, during, and after their learning program are included as part of IGNOU (2009), although some practitioners may disagree with the need for "support before entering the program," and considering this as part of registration and/or marketing efforts. In summary, this range of implied and/or required supports could better be viewed in this chapter as a range of services that are currently practiced by many DE institutions, with the standards understood as *policies*, and the DES as *strategies*.

DES can usually be represented by at least six core areas of support: face-to-face tutorials; remote tutoring (e.g., telephone tutoring/e-mail, etc.); regional learning centers; course materials; tutor-marked assignments; and learning management systems. A detailed description of DES based on these strategies is necessary. We thus need to strategize the proposed standards into actions, or services, as these can better be observed, measured, and evaluated. We now turn to review evidence of the need for and an appreciation of these six core areas of DES using the experience of specific Asian distance education providers as a context for discussion.

Face-to-Face Tutorials

To meet part of the USWA Standards for Curriculum and Instruction, many distance education institutions design the majority of their instruction in print and electronic format, and then supplement that content with face-to-face sessions. Face-to-face sessions are deemed to be the major effort component in delivering curriculum and instruction to students, and are intended to assist students in overcoming learning difficulties as well as facilitate interaction between students and tutors (Mason, 2002). This is truer of undergraduate courses than for postgraduate courses. It would thus appear that younger students still feel a need for a physical presence at tutorials, lectures, or even just for the sake of meeting up with fellow students. For smaller distance education institutions in concentrated population centers, the facility for face-to-face sessions can easily be met; but what of mega-universities like IGNOU in India and UTI of Indonesia with widely dispersed student populations? UTI, for example, offers courses over the world's largest archipelago of 17,000 islands and has significant logistical issues to serve some 400,000 students. UTI students' needs for tutorials have been met by regional offices, over 1,700 tutorial locations, and over 600 examination locations. A variety of tutorial methods have been implemented, including face-to-face, correspondence, broadcast, and online formats. It also engages an external network with the state universities across the archipelago for curriculum, course material, and test item development, as well as for the provision of qualified tutors. Thus, for mega-distance education institutions such as IGNOU and UTI, the course materials are strongly supported with scheduled satellite-based broadcast television sessions and taped sessions. This function is available to "regional learning centers" (RLCs) and tutorial centers possessing the necessary viewing and recording/playback facilities.

One common practice for face-to-face sessions is making attendance optional. Most distance education and hybrid distance education institutions in Malaysia attest to the declining frequency of tutorial attendance over any given semester. Ng and Kong (2009), for example, reported that over five sessions in a semester, tutorial attendance declined from nearly 100% in the first tutorial to only 35% by the fifth and last tutorial. Does it then make sense to maintain redundant, face-to-face sessions, or can institutions move to abort face-to-face sessions? Surveys at Universiti Putra Malaysia (Daing & Abu Daud, 1997) and Wawasan Open University (Ng & Kong, 2009) confirmed that, on a 5-point Likert scale, most students consider face-to-face sessions very important, with mean scores of 4.5 to 4.7.

As the costs of conducting face-to-face sessions increase, and as the avenues for increased and improved access via Internet technology become a reality, Web-based technologies are beginning to take over physical meeting requirements. Some institutions have begun launching Web-based video conferencing sessions either through dedicated leased lines or public lines, for example, Wawasan Open University (Ng & Kong, 2008) and Massey University of New Zealand (Thompson & Hills, 2005). This frees the regional centers to focus more on marketing and student recruitment, and also maintaining walk-in student counseling services. Similarly, courses and sessions at postgraduate levels have migrated onto the online platform quite quickly at Wawasan Open University. However, a note of caution is required here. In a comparison study on course success among students taking a similar course either through face-to-face or teleclass modes, students attending the face-to-face course performed significantly better than the teleclass cohorts (Deka & McMurry, 2006). The researchers surmised that the higher attainment has much to do with successful contact with the course instructors at Missouri Western State University, while the low-contact teleclass students had to increase the effort and time to maintain communication with the instructor. One ramification of this study is that, for the sake of equity and fairness to all students, institutions should consider using a single delivery modality for instruction so as not to create unhealthy advantages or disadvantages among students.

Telephone Tutoring/E-Mail

This aspect of DES can be viewed from a variety of perspectives and fulfills part of the USWA standards required for delivery of curriculum and instruction. Depending on the history of DES at a given institution, telephone tutoring can be either a stand-alone DES support method or a supplement to an existing face-to-face tutoring system. The same can be said of e-mail-based DES. E-mail, being an asynchronous technology, provides a ready platform for more individualized DES, particularly at the level of student-academic discourse. The telephone has become increasingly less popular, both because of the nature of the technology itself and the economic cost associated with that system. We must remember that follow-up telephone tutoring is only an adjunct to the traditional face-to-face tutorial method, but nevertheless requires scheduling of tutors and students, which involves costs as well. With asynchronous technologies such as e-mail and discussion board forums, and synchronous technologies like "chat," now universally available, there are indications that more and more tutor-student interactions will occur via the Internet as opposed to via telephone. The four-semester study by Ng and Kong (2009) confirmed that the means of the statements on telephone tutoring/e-mail are all less than 4 (on a 5-point scale) and thus appear to indicate that the respondents neither agree nor disagree with the statements. Compared to the other areas of concern, this would imply that, in one of the statements, the use of telephone (either fixed-line or mobile) with an average mean of about 3.6, had not been largely viewed as a useful or helpful DES strategy, while the means for availability of the tutors in e-mail support lie around means of 3.9 and 4.0, effectively suggesting that DES through e-mail has been viewed more positively.

The question of the usefulness of mobile technology for DES is also important. Nurhizam (2004) of Open University Malaysia (OUM) discussed the possibility of Short Messaging System (SMS) as a supplementary learning tool, for example, multiple-choice questions with feedback, pre- and post-self-test, quizzes and assignment notification, crucial assignment reminders, access to examination and test marks, fact of the week.

Currently, various course conductors at OUM have used SMS to send brief facts concerning specific course content to students on a scheduled basis and advise students to retain these SMS messages as course notes for their reference. The larger question would seem to be, however, that with the presence of Web-based learning management systems, forums, chats, and even Facebook interactions, does the small-screened SMS-capable mobile phone make an important difference in student support, apart from the obvious capability to disseminate time-sensitive information? For both tutoring and e-mail/telephone assist, it is evident that such sessions are structured to enable the students to keep pace with traditionally scheduled course delivery and evaluation strategies. Thus it would also seem peculiar that, while most distance education institutions claim that the students can progress at an individualized pace, in reality, most courses are conducted and delivered in a lockstep, semester-scheduled manner. Perhaps we could more accurately claim that self-pacing is practiced if the student is allowed to complete courses over a non-semester-based schedule.

Regional Learning Centers (RLC)

While most distance education institutions claim that they can do with less physical presence as a means to control costs, the setting up of regional learning centers (RLCs) inevitably often becomes a necessity, if for no other reason than a reminder to the populace around these centers that the distance education institution is reaching out to them. RLCs and libraries are thus fulfilling parts of the UWSA Standards for Library and Learning resources, as well as for Student Services and Facilities. As cost becomes an imperative, we can see that the RLC becomes more restricted to marketing and student recruitment as the RLC staff actively pursues students. Increasingly, tutorial rooms are being rented from local educational institutes, and, for larger distance education institutions, tutors are brought in from these institutes. Managing costs is critical, and molding Web-based technologies to take over face-to-face methods appears to be the way forward.

In the Ng and Kong (2009) study, the RLC personnel were seen to be of great assistance in receiving student assignments and responding to student queries. However, the standard setup of a physical library at RLC is not really that significant, as most students go online to the e-library of the distance institution. Also, with student chat and forums actively established, physical libraries are slowly being phased out, with cost being the overriding motivation for this move. For example, Wawasan Open University (Ng & Kong, 2008) has embarked on an electronic online assignment submission (OAS) system, and thus the need for RLC personnel to accept hard-copy assignments diminishes as more students become comfortable with the online submission system. We see that, as the distance education institution grows in student population and geographical reach, more RLCs will be set up in association with local partners, and the focus of the RLSs will be mainly that of marketing and student recruitment, with most other DES directed through the Internet to the main campus.

Course Materials

Without doubt, course materials are what greatly distinguish the distance education institution from the traditional university. Self-learning course materials are the main DES mechanism, as they are generally designed and executed through rigorous testing and trial processes. Most distance education institutions can claim proprietorship of their self-learning materials, as such materials have usually been designed with a standard format unique to that institution, developed in collaboration with the academic staff, instructional designers, editors, and increasingly, digital-format designers. Course materials thus represent the realization of the standards for Curriculum and Instruction as well as Facilities of UWSA Board of Regents (2000). In general, for distance education environments, students are more dependent on self-instructional modules (SIM) with activities and self-tests, as well as Web links and supplementary course materials, through learning management systems. Interactions with course materials through reflective thinking (Wikieducator, 2008), regular practice with the activities, and redirected access to other learning resources are also important for student success in the course (Field, 2008). The efficacy of SIMs can only be confirmed through feedback from the students. In Wawasan Open University, Ng and Kong (2009) confirmed that the SIMs were well-received and appreciated by the students. Over a four-semester study, the overall acceptance of SIM materials ranged from means of 3.8 to 4.0 on a 5-point Likert scale. Among the items positively checked by the students were "The contents of the course materials were appropriate and relevant"; "The course materials helped me to become an independent learner"; "The activities in the course materials provided me opportunities to reflect and relate what I have learnt to my work and daily routines"; and "The self-tests and other in-text activities helped me confirm what I have learnt and understood of the course materials." SIMs often become the identity of the distance education institution, and traditional institutions with distance programs are scrambling to make concerted efforts to similarly brand their SIMs and inculcate distance education sense among their instructors. However, with emerging digital technologies, most distance education institutions are vying for space in the virtual environment, and SIMs or course materials are beginning to pressure technological limitations. It would make no sense, for example, to digitally display printed SIMs on the course Web site. As digital materials are ephemeral, however, and with most students wanting to keep a permanent copy of SIMs, many institutions, including Wawasan Open University, are starting to digitize their SIM content in interactive format on CD-ROMs. The reduced cost and portability of CD-ROMs, coupled with the ability to store and print content from the disk, make them a strong DES option. Another option is to have digital SIM content available on dedicated servers, with on-demand downloading.

Tutor-Marked Assignments

As part of a holistic evaluation of student performance in a course, tutor-marked assignments (TMA) are regularly featured in distance instruction. This provides a means for the course facilitator to monitor the progress made by students in the course over a semester, fulfilling UWSA's standards for Assessment and Evaluation. Depending on the institution and the geographical dispersion of students, it is becoming clear that the traditional printed assignments have migrated to e-submissions over the Internet. This also carries a slight advantage for on-time submission of assignments, as the management of such submissions becomes more focused, and tutors assigned to mark such assignments have a central monitoring system, as well as standardized marking formats across courses. Technological aids also make plagiarizing more difficult. Our own experience with the e-submission of assignments indicates that only a short training on the mechanics of e-submission are required for students to use e-submission for their courses. Once the current and continuing cohorts are tuned to the e-submission of TMA, new incoming students must be "captured" during their orientation sessions for similar training. Hence, TMA as a DES can be better described as the motivating factor to assist students in managing their progress over the duration of the course conduct. Increasingly, there are cries for changing the loading or contribution of TMA toward the final grade. Most distance education courses currently consider TMA as contributing to about 40%–60% of the course grades. There are pleas for either increasing or lowering that contribution, and such demands are mostly based on the nature of the courses.

Learning Management Systems

For online presence with Web-based learning management systems (LMS) such as Blackboard, Web City, and Moodle, there appears to be a "standardized mode of presentation" for managing learning materials for student access and practice. Most LMS interfaces are based on a three-pane screen format, with features such as resources, trial tests, and even chats and forums, accessed via hyperlink. Thus, LMS represents a means to meet a cluster of UWSA standards, such as curriculum and Instruction, Evaluation and Assessment, Library and Learning Resources, and Facilities. Newer distance education institutions have slight advantages in getting their LMS up and running compared to more established distance education institutions that have a steep learning curve in migrating their printed materials to an online format. Increasingly, we see students organizing online forums and chats, sharing concerns that may extend beyond their own "e-tutorial" groups. Course facilitators are advised to monitor such proceedings, as these may provide evidence relating to deficiencies in current course materials. Also, for the sake of transparency, all information from course facilitators needs to be available to all students, not just specific individuals within the class. Distance education institutions thus need to expand the amount of content they make available via Web-based LMS systems. Careful planning and adequate resourcing and staffing are necessary to ensure the long-term viability of LMS as a DES support. Wawasan Open University (Ng and Kong, 2009) confirmed that most students considered LMS presentations and discussions during a four-semester period useful, with mean scores of 3.8 to 3.9 on a 5-point Likert scale. In terms of assessment and evaluation, a number of distance education institutions have mandated that assessments also be built into the LMS, and these tests contribute to a small percentage of the final course grades. However, other distance education institutions have provided tests only for practice use, as they are unable to verify the actual taker of the online assessment. Perhaps when more effective security and identity recognition technologies are available, these can be built into the LMS, perhaps using a secured virtual private network as opposed to a public network, and the LMS approach for assessment and evaluation can be expanded.

DISCUSSION

Are these described DES services providing adequate support to students? Financial issues are one of the UWSA standards for consideration, and certainly most distance education institutions have mechanisms for student financial support, fees deferment, and sponsorships/scholarships to attract potential students. But are there other DES services that could be established beyond these approaches, and what will be the emerging financial trends for DES in the future?

Increasingly, costs of operations, plus competition from traditional universities that have moved into the distance education arena, will be a major impetus for distance education-only institutions to evolve from their current mode of operation. While most distance education institutions have chosen blended instructional delivery, many institutions are still trapped with printed DES materials and conducting classes through satellite television, because both approaches are seen as cost-effective. Ease of use, familiarity with lecture-like presentations, lack of ICT infrastructures, and student entry costs are usually used as justifications for delaying the move into the digital environment. Simultaneously, within the same student populace, we are seeing demands by students for digital materials and virtual 24/7 Internet experiences. This has created a dilemma for distance education institutions concerning which methodologies to adopt, and ultimately, most institutions adopt hybrid analog and digital systems with unfortunate levels of course delivery and content redundancy. Cost of presentation thus grows while trying to please all varieties of student demands and needs. Within various Asian nations, there are disparate efforts to employ Web technologies, as broadband is still not widespread and remains costly. Wireless telephony has therefore been given prominence in this setting, but this situation may serve as the trigger for wireless broadband efforts in many nations. Such a move would provide distance education institutions a pathway toward Web-based instruction.

Contemporaneously, academic staff are also forced to become highly versatile in as many delivery and interaction modes as possible, consuming much time that might have been concentrated on quality course-content design. Staffing projections can move into disarray as workload increases with additional technologies. The focal point of distance education excellence falls flatly on content, and how students can best learn from the delivery of, and interaction with, this content. Other DES systems, such as tutor support, counseling, ease of assignment submissions, and timely feedback, supplement the gamut of student satisfaction with the institution. Tait and Mills (2003) provide a comprehensive and very useful source of information on developing and delivering learner support services. However, the challenge to many DES implementations lies in its frequent use of redundant strategies, which significantly add to operating costs. Distance education institutions have to make important decisions soon as to how many avenues of DES they can comfortably maintain while ensuring the quality of materials and the satisfaction of their students.

CONCLUSION

DES is a varied and dynamic service that involves many departments and staff of a distance education institution. The overall aim of DES is to manage student expectations within a distance education course. For the distance education operator, quality assurance of DES is of utmost importance. Standards are set for the DES; delivery of DES is strategized so that the standards are consistently met, and consequently student confidence in the distance education program is maintained. DES also has implications on student retention. It is foreseeable that with technology-enabled means, we can enroll more staff to engage in regular and continuous advising of students, fostering a sense of community and belonging for all distance students. Staff presence in a digital environment can assure students that their needs are being met by assisting students with their learning and responding to them as individuals. We foresee a gradual devolvement in DES from more personal contact to more digital contact over time as technology improves. This shift will increase in scope as a greater percentage of the world's learners are provided with broadband access or similar facilities.

COMPREHENSION AND APPLICATION QUESTIONS

1. The chapter contends that different persons/staffs may provide academic, administrative, and informative support to distance students. Develop a list of these individuals (up to eight such persons).

2. In your opinion, who among these 8 persons identified rank among the top three in DES by students? Support your choice with examples.

3. This chapter discusses a variety of strategies to provide maximum DES for students, with Curriculum and Instruction strategies rated as being most important. Choose from among the remaining strategies ones that you consider redundant and could be removed to reduce costs while still maintaining the quality of DES. Provide a rationale for your choice.

RESOURCES FOR FURTHER EXPLORATION

For a further look into the presentations of DES through web-based technologies, it will be useful to consult the website of the University of Victoria Distance Education Services:

University of Victoria Distance Education Services. (2010). Distance education services resources: Hints, tips and instructions—stored in convenient blog form. http://blog.uvcs.uvic.ca/desresources/
Similarly, a short write-up on the possibilities of DES can be glimpsed from this Knowledge Series of the Commonwealth of Learning, Canada:
Robertshaw, M. (2000). Support groups in distance education. Commonwealth of Learning Knowledge Series. http://www.col.org/SiteCollectionDocuments/KS2000%20supportgroups.pdf

REFERENCES

Allen, I. E., & Seaman, J. (Eds.). (2010). Class differences: Online education in the United States, 2010. *Babson Survey Research Group & The Sloan Consortium.* Retrieved from http://sloanconsortium.org/sites/default/files/class_differences.pdf

Burt, G. (1997). *Face to face with distance education.* In A. Tait & R. Mills (Eds.), *Rethinking learner support in distance education: Change and continuity in an international context* (p. 92). London, England: RoutledgeFalmer.

Daing Z. I., & Abu Daud, S. (1997, November 11–14). *Assuring quality learning support for teachers' distance education program.* Paper presented at the 11th Annual Conference of Distance and Open Learning, Putra World Trade Centre, Kuala Lumpur, Malaysia. Retrieved from http://elib.unitar.edu.my/staff-publications/daing/For.pdf

Deka, T. S., & McMurry, P. (2006). Student success in face-to-face and distance teleclass environments: A matter of contact? *International Review of Research in Open and Distance Learning, 7*(1), 1–16.

Fairfax, B. J. (2010). Distance education gains popularity. *Online-Education.net.* Retrieved from http://www.online-education.net/articles/general/distance-education.html

Fearn, H. (2009, June 18). Coming to a screen near you. *Times Higher Education.* Retrieved from http://www.timeshighereducation.co.uk/story.asp?sectioncode=26&storycode=406903&c=1

Field, M. (2008). *Top 10 tips for distance learning success.* Retrieved from http://www.topuniversities.com/news/article/top_10_tips_for_distance_learning_success/

Garland, P. H., & Grace, T. W. (1993). *New perspectives for student affairs professionals: Evolving realities, responsibilities and roles.* ASHE-ERIC Higher Education report No. 7 Washington, DC: The George Washington University School of Education and Human Development.

Holmberg, B. (1995). *Theory and practice of distance education* (2nd ed.). London, England: Routledge.

IGNOU. (2009). *Section IV: Student support services in distance education.* Retrieved from http://www.ignou.ac.in/institute/handbook1/section%204.pdf

Keegan, D. (1990). *Foundations of distance education.* London, England: Routledge.

Kemp, W. C. (2002). Persistence of adult learners in distance education. *The American Journal of Distance Education, 16*(2), 65–81.

Mason, R. (2002). Online learning and supporting students: New possibilities. In A. Tait & R. Mills (Eds.), *Rethinking learner support in distance education: Change and continuity in an international context* (pp. 90–101). Oxon, England: RoutledgeFalmer.

Newman, P., & Peile, E. (2002, July 27). Valuing learners' experience and supporting further growth: Educational models to help experienced adult learners in medicine. *British Medical Journal, 325*, 200–202.

Ng, W. K., & Kong, S. L. (2008). Training of distance education tutors at Wawasan Open University: One semester later. *Quarterly Review of Distance Education, 9*(1), 85–96.

Ng, W. K., & Kong S. L. (2009). Student feedback on tutor and academic support of Wawasan Open University: A four semester study. *Quarterly Review of Distance Education, 10*(4), 363–379.

Nitsch, W. B. (2003). *Examination of factors leading to retention in online graduate education.* Unpublished paper presented in partial fulfillment of the requirements of ED 7212 Administration and Leadership of Distance Education Programs. Retrieved from http://www.decadeconsulting.com/decade/papers/StudentRetention.pdf

Nurhizam, S. (2004, November 27–30). *The use of short messaging systems (SMS) as a supplementary learning tool in Open University Malaysia (OUM).* Paper presented at the 18th Annual Conference Association of Asian Open Universities (AAOU), Shanghai, China. Retrieved from http://asiapacific-odl2.oum.edu.my/C33/F156.doc

Paul, R., & Brindley, J. (1996). Lessons from distance education for the university of the future. In R. Mills & A. Tait (Eds.), *Supporting the learner in open and distance learning* (pp. 43–55). London, England: Pitman.

Sharples, M. (2005), *Learning as conversation: Transforming education in the mobile age.* Retrieved from http://www.fil.hu/mobil/2005/Sharples_final.pdf

Southern Association of Colleges and Schools. (2000). Distance education: Definition and principles. *The Commission on Colleges, Southern Association of Colleges and Schools.* Retrieved from http://www.nova.edu/ocean/disted/sacs_distance.pdf

Tait, A. (2000). *Planning student support for open and distance learning.* Retrieved from http://www.c3l.uni-oldenburg.de/cde/support/readings/tait00.pdf

Tait, A., & Mills, R. (Eds.). (2003). *Rethinking learner support in distance education: Change and continuity in an international context.* London, England: RoutledgeFalmer.

Thompson, J., & Hills, J. (2005, December 4–7). *Online learning support services for distance education students: Responding to and maintaining the momentum.* Paper presented at ASCILITE 2005: Balance, Fidelity, Mobility: Maintaining the Momentum, The Queensland University of Technology, Brisbane, Australia. Retrieved January 2010, from http://www.ascilite.org.au/conferences/brisbane05/blogs/proceedings/76_Thompson.pdf

UWSA Board of Regents. (2000). *Distance education standards for academic and student support services: Guidelines for distance education credit program array and approval.* Retrieved from http://www.uwsa.edu/acss/acis/destandards.pdf

Wallace, L. (1996). Changes in the demographics and motivation of distance education students. *Journal of Distance Education, 11*(1), 1–31.

Wikibooks. (2010). *Megauniversity/Malaysia*. Retrieved from http://en.wikibooks.org/wiki/Megauniversity/Malaysia

Wikieducator. (2008). *Principles of ODL*. Retrieved from http://www.wikieducator.org/images/0/0f/Principles_of_ODL.pdf

Zuhairi, A., Adnan, I., & Thaib, D. (2007, October). Provision of student learning support services in a large-scale distance education system at Universitas Terbuka Indonesia. *Turkish Online Journal of Distance Education, 8*(4).

CHAPTER 15

PERSONAL LEARNING ENVIRONMENTS IN DISTANCE EDUCATION

**Ricardo Torres Kompen,
Palitha Edirisingha, and Josep M. Monguet**

Personal learning environments (PLEs) entered the educational discourse in the early twenty-first century with the aim of shifting the focus of technology-supported learning from the instructor-designed virtual learning environments (VLEs) toward a more learner-designed and learner-customized environment through the use of no-cost, Web 2.0-based Internet tools. In this chapter, we propose that PLEs can be conceptualized and developed either as pre-built programs, similar to a commercially available VLE, and managed by a central authority such as a university computer services department or as learner-built and learner-customized systems that make use of a variety of Web 2.0 technologies that learners manipulate to construct unique PLEs. In this second conceptualization, each resultant PLE would emerge from a combination of the learners' specific learning needs, competence in working with Web 2.0 technologies, and other personal preferences. The PLE would be used by the learner to organize and share information as well as to manage learning. The chapter describes how a group of university students in Spain used this second approach to develop their own PLEs to support both their formal academic and informal learning. We outline the methodology that was used to help these students develop and use their own PLEs over a 2-year period. We provide an analysis of empirical

Trends and Issues in Distance Education:
International Perspectives, Second Edition, pp. 223–237
Copyright © 2012 by Information Age Publishing
All rights of reproduction in any form reserved.

data of students' use of their PLEs and the resultant learning outcomes achieved through the PLE development process. We conclude with suggestions for developing learner-created PLEs for academic learning and for the application of PLEs in distance learning contexts.

INTRODUCTION

According to the Joint Information Systems Committee (JISC, 2007), the first use of the concept of a Personal Learning Environment (PLE) was in an unpublished paper by Olivier and Liber (2001). Other sources establish 2004 as the year in which the PLE emerged as a concept. Wikipedia, for example, claims that the first recorded use of the term *Personal Learning Environments* was in the 2004 The Personal Learning Environments Session at JISC/CETIS Conference (History of Personal Learning Environments, n.d).

A PLE can be described as an environment that enables learners to organize and carry out learning activities in an autonomous fashion using a collection of tools assembled by learners to support the management of their learning process. A computer-based PLE also provides the ability to connect and interact with other participants in the learning activities, including peers and instructors. The capitalized term "Personal Learning Environment" usually refers to a computer desktop-based PLE, developed with web-based tools and applications.

The majority of e-learning approaches in distance education are based on Virtual Learning Environments (VLEs), computer software systems that help manage an online learning setting (e.g., Blackboard, WebCT, Moodle, Sakai, and PebblePad). There is, however, a growing trend toward e-learning environments that are based on the notion of the more learner-centric PLEs. Some organizations working with PLEs include the Manchester PLE Project (Hedtek, 2010) and the SAPO Campus (University of Aveiro, 2010). Downes (2010) argues that many recent developments in educational technology have centered on the concept of the personal learning environment, rather than the more traditional VLE-based approach.

The growing interest in PLEs has a number of drivers. The policy and pedagogical discourses surrounding "personalization" of learning and learning environments (DFES, 2005) is a primary driver, with the idea being that learning technologies should help learners manage their own learning (including the content, the mode of delivery and the access) according to their own preferences. Personalization of learning, it is argued, provides the learner with greater flexibility and options for learning. In a PLE, it is the learner, not the teacher, who is in the center of the learning process.

A second driver for interest in PLEs is the emergence and widespread use of a new generation of Internet-based tools and technologies, generally known as Web 2.0 tools. The term *Web 2.0*, coined by Tim O'Reilly, captures a "trend toward greater creativity, information sharing and collaboration amongst internet users" (The Economist, 2008). As Mason and Rennie (2008) noted, podcasts, wikis, blogs, social networking sites, social bookmarking tools, and many other Web 2.0 tools enable greater participation by users with limited technical know-how to create and share content and to communicate with others.

A further reason for the enthusiasm for PLEs is a dissatisfaction with VLEs by both teachers and learners. VLEs are commonly viewed as institutionally owned and managed, serving the needs of the institution rather than the learner (cf. EDUCAUSE, 2006). According to Downes (2010), PLEs are increasingly seen as a replacement for the VLE-based approach.

The view that current higher education learners are increasingly familiar with computers and the Internet is a further reason for the interest in PLEs, because it is believed that these learners are now more capable of manipulating Web 2.0 technologies than previous generations of computer users. New terms have been coined to refer to this generation, all emphasizing their technological savvy. For example, the terms *net gen* learners, *millennials* (Oblinger & Oblinger, 2005), and *digital natives* (Prensky, 2001) are all used to refer to the current generation of learners.

A FRAMEWORK FOR BUILDING A WEB 2.0-BASED PLE

Our framework for building PLEs is based on the idea that a PLE is best conceived as a *concept* rather than as a particular software application. However, it is helpful for the learners to choose one application as a "hub" (a central component) for the PLE to act as the foundation for the remainder of the tools to connect. The advantages of this approach are that users can easily access their collection of Web 2.0 tools from one single point, manage a variety of logins and passwords, and share data between the applications that make up the PLE. The PLE hub will allow the learner to gradually build upon it, thus creating a dynamic set of learning tools.

A diversity of tools and applications has been proposed by different commentators as foundations or hubs for building PLEs. In our framework (Torres Kompen, Edirisingha, & Mobbs, 2009), we considered four different approaches to building a PLE with Web 2.0 tools according to the choice of hub:

1. A Wiki-based PLE (e.g., Google Sites)
2. A social network-based PLE (e.g., Facebook)
3. A social aggregator-based PLE (e.g., Netvibes)
4. A browser-based PLE (e.g., Flock)

The choice of hub was guided by the evidence of the popularity of these tools among higher education students or by the availability of APIs (Application Programming Interfaces) to other Web 2.0 applications, such as RSS feeds (Really Simple Syndication, a mechanism for publishing frequently updated Web content), calendars, virtual storage, search engines, and such. Below we describe the four approaches that compose our framework, highlighting the advantages and disadvantages of each.

Wiki-Based PLEs: Google Sites

The intrinsic connectivity of the various Google services means that Google sites could be expanded to create a PLE. A user with a Gmail account, for example, has access to Google Sites and numerous other Google applications that could be used to construct a unique PLE. As just one example, Google Docs, a Google system that allows the storage and online editing and sharing of documents, can easily be integrated into a PLE to allow users to create, share, and collaborate with files of many types. The disadvantage of such an approach for a PLE is that the connectivity is limited to Google applications, and any external, non-Google application would not be as tightly integrated into the PLE, perhaps accessed only by external links.

Social-Network Based PLEs: Facebook

A social networking application (e.g., Facebook) could also be used as a hub for a PLE. Facebook was developed with college students as its main target, so it makes an obvious choice for a PLE platform. The advantage of using a system like Facebook as the basis for a PLE is that the users, many of whom are digital natives, are already a captive audience. MacLeod (2007, para. 4) noted that "Facebook is well on its way to becoming the ideal tool for the creation of ... PLEs."

Facebook's popularity means that there are many applications associated with Facebook that enable the users to connect their Facebook pages to other Web 2.0 tools using APIs. In this manner, blogs may be accessed through RSS feeds. Some commercial VLEs are now developing extensions for Facebook. (Blackboard, for example, allows users to access the system from Facebook using the Blackboard Learn application or through an intermediate application such as CourseFeed). Facebook also provides applications to access other systems, such as Google Docs, Twitter, delicious, Flickr, Picasa, wikis, SlideShare, Gmail, and others.

Social Aggregator-Based PLE: Netvibes

Netvibes is an "aggregator" system that allows users to connect a variety of Web 2.0 tools and to access these tools from one site. Netvibes has a wider range of supporting tools compared to Google Sites and adds a "social" element by providing connections, or "widgets," to Facebook, delicious, Flickr, and other applications. Users are required to create an account and set up a start page, adding the necessary widgets to establish connectivity with other Web 2.0 tools.

Browser-Based PLE: Flock

Flock[1] is a Firefox-based browser (with a new version based on Google's Chromium system) that offers full integration with a number of social networking sites as well as with blogging tools. Flock also collects information from feeds; allows users to share text, pictures, and videos; and provides integration with social bookmarking and photo storage services. Flock works as a one-stop access portal to a variety of applications, but the program requires installation on a local computer using administrator privileges. This also means that the Flock profile is stored on that particular computer, making the system inaccessible from other machines.

PILOT STUDY

To study the use of PLEs, we conducted a pilot study at the Escuela Superior de Estudios Internacionales (ESEI) in Barcelona, Spain, between September 2008 and May 2009. A total of 33 students from a second-year business management undergraduate program participated in the study. The objective of the pilot study was to apply in practice our conceptual framework of creating PLEs using the four approaches previously described (i.e., wiki-based, social network-based, social aggregator-based, and browser-based PLEs). In the study, we guided participants in the development of their own PLEs and then gathered empirical evidence on the students' development of, and engagement with, their PLEs.

The pilot study was divided into four phases. The first phase was conducted during the first of the three trimesters of the academic year 2008–2009. The three remaining phases were carried out in the following two trimesters. The second year of the study built on the lessons learned during the pilot study and also comprised three trimesters within the 2009–2010 academic year.

Students who participated in the pilot studied in a face-to-face setting. However, the activities involving Web 2.0 and PLEs were designed as "e-tivities" (cf. Salmon, 2002), and some activities were carried out at a distance using free video conference software (e.g., WiZiQ and Skype). Thus, the results and lessons learned in this mixed-format pilot study should be easily adaptable to a distance learning context.

First Phase: Introducing Web 2.0 Tools

The first phase of the pilot study was carried out over a period of 12 weeks. The Web 2.0 concept was presented and discussed with participants, and Twitter (a microblogging application system) was introduced. Although adoption of the Twitter tool was at first slow, after a 3-week period, 90% of the students were using Twitter for both academic and social purposes. Usage of Twitter varied during the trimester, with peak usage occurring around exams and school events. Approximately 20% of the class began to use Twitter as their main channel of communications with the teacher and the class.

Participants were encouraged to explore other Web 2.0 tools in addition to Twitter. Some of the students were already using a variety of Web 2.0 tools and were keen to share their knowledge and experience of those tools with their peers. Participants also wanted to research available options and additional tools to meet their academic and social needs. The instructor (first author of this chapter) guided students by suggesting certain applications as a starting point, but participants were free to choose any applications they felt most appropriate for their needs. In one example, a student researched the potential of the Clipperz program as a solution to the problem of managing a large number of usernames and passwords. In another example, one participant explored the use of Flickr for sharing images, which in turn motivated another participant to explore a second image-management program, Google Picasa, giving the class the opportunity to explore two different approaches to image sharing and to discuss the advantages and disadvantages of both. Other tools discussed were FriendFeed, Jooce, RSS feeds, Blip.fm, last.fm, MOG, and Blogger. Some of these tools were eventually used during class activities or class e-tivities.

At the end of this trimester, students were asked to reflect on how they used Web 2.0 tools and to illustrate this by drawing a diagram that visually depicted the connections among the different Web 2.0 tools that they used and/or had intended to use. This activity was repeated during the second phase of the study (see next section) before introducing the concept of PLEs to the class. (An interesting moment during this experience was when, after formally introducing the concept of PLEs, participants realized they had already built a PLE of their own.)

Second Phase: Web 2.0 Diagrams

At the beginning of the 2008–2009 trimester, participants continued the process of drawing diagrams of their PLEs started at the end of the first trimester. Participants were encouraged to consider their own learning objectives and to explore additional tools and applications to meet those objectives and to develop an understanding of the tools with which they were unfamiliar.

Students were told that the involvement in the study was optional and not assessed as part of their course. In all, 10 participants dropped out of the study. The number of participants in the PLE experiment cohort was reduced to 21 (three students from the original group transferred to another school, and one exchange student joined the class). Out of these, six participants submitted very simple diagrams, while eight participants showed in greater detail the links between their selected tools as they tested the possibilities of linking these tools together.

The PLEs that the participants designed (represented by the diagrams they produced) covered a wide range of the previously described approaches. Eight participants, for example, proposed a platform or web service that would allow access to a set of tools, with the majority of these pointing out that a safe, single log-in is needed as part of the service. One participant called his diagram his "personal page of everything." This diagram matched the "browser-based PLE approach."

The "start-page/aggregator-based PLE" approach was proposed by a student who described her PLE as "a centralized platform allowing the access to user-selected Web 2.0 applications through a single password from one site." This participant continued on to actually search for such a tool and subsequently discovered and set up an account for the Pageflakes tool.

Another participant also referenced the "aggregator page approach," but was using the Google application iGoogle. This format actually matched our Wiki-based PLE approach: the method employed primarily Google applications, but the idea of using a wiki for a single user was not even considered by participants, probably because students already had two wikis being used for collaborative projects.

An additional fifth approach was proposed by one of the participants, one that had not been considered in our initial framework. This approach involved the use of a virtual desktop application (i.e., Jooce, a tool that went offline shortly after the study and is no longer available) that allows users to manage multiple computer desktops from a single account, allowing the user to share desktops and files, as well as providing access to multiple working spaces.

Third Phase: Introducing the Notion of PLEs and the Four Approaches

During the third phase of the study, the PLE concept was introduced and explained to participants, including a description of the proposed four PLE approaches. Students compared their own Web 2.0 diagrams with our proposed four approaches. They were asked to "build" or structure their PLEs based on the diagrams they had drawn (or should be drawn) on one of the four approaches, or a combination of both. The fifth approach (using a virtual desktop) was also presented and discussed with participants. The participant who proposed this fifth approach later decided not to use Jooce as a hub, deciding rather to explore alternatives, which the participant later presented as a short paper at a conference (Jaroszyńska, Torres Kompen, & Edirisingha, 2010).

At the end of the third phase, 17 participants had built or developed their PLEs, out of the original 33 participants who began with the pilot phase (first phase). Four students dropped out of the study due to a perceived lack of usefulness. As previously mentioned, 10 participants did not participate beyond the first phase.

Fourth Phase: Essays and Interviews

In the fourth and final phase of the study, participants wrote an essay describing their PLE experience and took part in personal interviews, some face-to-face and others by e-mail.

We next report the themes that emerged from these essays and interviews under three categories: evidence of PLEs as organization and management tools, evidence of strengthening social interactions, and evidence of learning and developing skills. Participants' critical comments and suggestions for improving the use of PLEs are also included.

SUMMARY OF RESULTS

PLEs as Organization and Management Tools

Most participants reported a sense of chaos and confusion about the sheer number of Web 2.0 tools available and identified the need for some type of organizational framework for the PLE. The four PLE approaches provided participants such a framework. Most students came up with their own methods for managing their Web 2.0 applications and tools. Flock was repeatedly mentioned as a tool for centralizing the applications and offering a one-stop access to all tools as well as a method for addressing issues with multiple logins and passwords.

Some advantages identified in using Web 2.0 tools as a PLE included the ability to organize and manage existing content, the opportunity to integrate newly discovered tools with those already in use, and the filtering of information (as their PLEs helped them choose relevant information). One participant reported, "[a PLE] is an easy way to manage and organize all the information I get from online sources, and also offline ones."

PLEs to Strengthen Social Interactions

For participants, the social element was one of the most important aspects of using Web 2.0 tools. The PLEs that participants developed helped them to carry out collaborative activities. The class activities constituted a collaborative approach to learning, using a wiki, a blog, microblogging, and social bookmarking. Students reported that this approach increased the learning opportunities and the availability of useful resources. Participants pointed out that the network of peers they were developing through PLEs would continue as a growing network of colleagues and professional contacts. A surprising observation was that none of the participants considered Facebook as an option for building or managing a PLE.

Other benefits of using PLEs included the ability to discuss ideas with peers and teachers outside the classroom; collaborating, sharing, and creating knowledge; and continuing such actions on an ongoing, continuous basis. One participant reported, "What I like the most about all these Web 2.0 tools is the ability to get inspiration, knowledge and to be able to interact with other people."

Learning and Developing Skills

Most students reported as highlights of participating in the study the new tools they learned and the skills they acquired. Although some participants were already familiar with Web 2.0 applications, most had not considered how these tools could be used for learning. As expected, many participants were Facebook users prior to the beginning of the study, but none had used Twitter or delicious. They had been using blogs as a source of information (e.g., for entertainment, news, and specific interests), but very few knew about RSS feeds or how to use them. Although the use of Wikipedia was widespread among the class, participants reported that either they did not use wikis or believed that Wikipedia and "wiki" were one and the same.

For this group of participants, PLEs made the learning process more dynamic and interesting. PLEs helped participants transform the information provided in the class and from course textbooks into personal knowledge. PLEs served as a platform for discussions reflecting on the concepts covered in class and a tool to search for additional information. Participants highlighted that their PLEs were valuable in both formal learning context and outside the school, where, in one participant's words, "a lot of learning happens." Another participant reported, "[The PLE] has changed my personal learning process."

Recommendations for the Use of PLEs

Participants were asked to provide suggestions on how to improve the study and improve the use of PLEs. A common theme that emerged was the confusion created by the diversity of tools and available applications, identifying a need for guidance and support at the beginning of the study.

Some participants complained about the large amount of initial time investment required for learning how to use Web 2.0 tools. Some students had trouble understanding how such tools could be used to support their learning. This finding was correlated to participants' current skill and experience with online applications. Context, support, and flexibility were all mentioned as important to participants and were identified as items to be considered when implementing these tools and applications in a learning environment. The social element played a large role in terms of communication and collaboration in this study. The PLE was not seen as an isolated collection of tools but as a means of keeping in touch with other participants and with the instructor, both in and outside school during study weeks and holidays, regardless of whether learning was accomplished at a distance or not. A "network" effect was also observed, with peer guidance and word of mouth being central to the adoption of some tools by some of the participants.

Attwell (2009, as cited in Wild, Mödritscher, & Sigurdarson, 2008) noted that "establishing a learning environment, that is, a network of people, artifacts, and tools (consciously or unconsciously) involved in learning activities, is part of the learning outcomes, not an instructional condition" (p. 2). This was also one of the main lessons learned from the pilot study: the most important outcome was not the PLE itself, but the learning process related to the building and development of the PLE. Muldoon (2008) emphasizes this point: "However, it is highly unlikely that simply knowing about the tools for lifelong learning will deliver learner and learning transformation. Learners need to learn with those Web 2.0 tools during their exposure to formal education" (p. 7).

PLEs in Distance Education

PLEs have a great potential to contribute to distance learning. The diversity of tools that make up a PLE allows for flexibility across a broad range of contexts and learners. Web 2.0-based PLEs have several specific advantages in the context of distance learning. Because of the very nature of Web 2.0 applications, the same considerations that apply to the use of multimedia in distance education also apply in this case. As noted by Garcia Aretio (2001), these techniques result in an increase in the retention of the information, since the interactivity of the material works as a reinforcement of the content and helps the student get the message. In a PLE, reflection could take form in several ways, including blog posts, microblogging, collaborating on a wiki, and more. Motivation may also be increased, because the student is actively involved in the learning process. Instead of being a receiver of information, the student becomes the protagonist of the learning experience: the Web 2.0 approach puts an emphasis on user-created content. The multiple channels of communication permit students to start and participate in dialogues and to ask and answer questions. The result is an increase in participation and control over the learning process.

In such an environment, the systems being used provide access to a large pool of additional information that can be used to support and complement the material being covered. Although students may start at the same point using a common source of content, the learning process may then become divergent between learners, the PLEs being personalized according to the interests and learning styles of each learner.

Adult learners enrolled in distance learning courses seldom have a homogeneous profile. It is not unusual to find within the same course different age groups, motivations, academic level, and personal circumstances. It makes sense to try and personalize the learning experience as much as possible. PLEs provide an excellent tool to meet this requirement. Although learners have access to the same content (hence ensuring that the quality of the material is constant and homogeneous for every participant), the actual processing of the information can be managed by learners using a unique set of their own tools, allowing learners to tailor the learning process to their own needs and circumstances. As noted by Attwell (2007), PLEs recognize that

> Learning is discontinuous ... [and] will take place in different contexts and situations and will not be provided by a single learning provider.... Personal learning environments can bring together learning from multiple contexts, including from home, from school, and from work, and can support formal learning activities provided by different educational institutions. (p. 2)

A MODEL FOR
IMPLEMENTING WEB 2.0-BASED PLES IN DISTANCE EDUCATION

Based on the PELICANS (Personal E-Learning in Communites And Networking Spaces, University of Leicester, U.K.) pilot, we can offer the following guidelines for using PLEs in distance education:

1. Suggest that students explore and propose Web 2.0 options with a focus on communicating, collaborating, and sharing with other members of the group, rather than the tools themselves. Students need to be encouraged to consider their individual needs and interests, to list these, and then attempt to find (and share) solutions for them. (For example, in our pilot study, one participant's need for managing and organizing his ever-growing list of IDs and passwords led him to try several options, which motivated him to try Clipperz, which he subsequently shared with the class.)
    Tip 1: Design online activities (e-tivities) to help participants practice with the tools and applications that are being explored; try to create e-tivities that use two or more of the tools, and are focused around relevant subject topics.
2. Start by creating a small community in which students feel safe and are not afraid to try applications and make mistakes. Once these networks are established, explore connections between them, between the tools themselves, and with other networks.

Tip 2: A small community is easier to manage, so consider tools that allow the group to create a closed, "safe" environment, such as Ning.

3. Once the networks are established, encourage the students to share information and interesting resources and links within their networks. New channels of communication might thus be discovered. (For example, it is one thing to talk about Impressionism, but is quite another to post pictures of your favorite Impressionist paintings and share your comments on these works with others.)

Tip 3: Take advantage of applications that allow users to share resources, such as delicious and Twine. Common interests will help create bonds within the group.

4. Do not limit information to what students find, but share original contributions, either individual or in groups. These contributions can be focused on content, but can also include comments and suggestions about the tools and applications currently being used.

Tip 4: Encourage and reward participation; emphasize the importance of sharing personal experiences and knowledge that could be of interest to the whole community.

5. Be flexible with students as they build their own PLEs. The steps described here should not be considered sequential in nature and will probably change based on each student's background and experience. We have found that it is useful to provide advice about "container" tools (i.e., the PLE hubs), so participants can explore different options or develop their own ideas about connecting and managing the applications that make up their PLE.

Tip 5: Flexibility and freedom are important. PLEs are, after all, personal. Let the students explore their own path.

COMPREHENSION AND APPLICATION QUESTIONS

1. Have you tried to construct your own PLE? If so, what is your PLE like? Does it rely mostly on online tools, or does it have a strong "real world" component?

2. How can your experience using Web 2.0 tools help enhance your (or your peers') learning experience in a distance education context? What strategies and approaches might help to enrich your learning using Web 2.0 tools?

3. Do you think that the learning process outcome can be affected (either positively or negatively) by the choice of PLE and/or tools?

Why? What steps could be taken in order to take advantage of the benefits of PLEs or to solve the problems of using a PLE?

ACKNOWLEDGMENTS

The work reported in this chapter was carried out under the PELICANS research project (Personal E-Learning in Communites And Networking Spaces, University of Leicester, UK), in collaboration with the Universitat Politècnica de Catalunya, the i2Cat Foundation, and Citilab, Catalonia, Spain. We also want to thank all the students that participated in the study, as well as the Escuela Superior de Estudios Internacionales, ESEI, for their trust and support.

NOTE

1. Flock is shown as an example of the social browsers category and was used both in the pilot study and the proposed framework; nevertheless, readers should be aware that the application is no longer supported by their creators and will be slowly phased out, with no replacement planned. There are of course other examples of social browsers, such as Rockmelt, and we encourage readers to explore these.

RESOURCES FOR FURTHER EXPLORATION

Attwell G. (2006). *Personal learning environment: A position paper.* Retrieved from http://www.knownet.com/writing/weblogs/Graham_Attwell/entries/6521819364 . A good starting point, it gives an overview of PLEs and analyzes different aspects, such as context, concepts, and applications of PLEs.
Proceedings from The PLE Conference 2010. Retrieved from http://pleconference.citilab.eu . The first face-to-face conference about personal learning environments, the proceedings show a variety of approaches to developing, managing, and applying PLEs to learning.
The Horizon Report. The 2009 edition shows the "Personal Web" as one of the emerging trends for the midterm horizon. http://wp.nmc.org/horizon2009/chapters/personal-web/

REFERENCES

Attwell, G. (2007). The personal learning environments: The future of elearning? *eLearning Papers, 2*(1).

Attwell, G. (2009). Barriers to personal learning environments. Retrieved from http://www.pontydysgu.org/2009/01/barriers-to-personal-learning-environments

DFES. (2005). Harnessing technology: Transforming learning and children's services. *Department for Education and Skills, UK.* Retrieved from http://www.dcsf.gov.uk/publications/e-strategy/docs/estrategy.pdf

Downes, S. (2010, January 10). *Pedagogical foundations for personal learning.* Keynote address at the "Learning Futures Festival," the Annual E-Learning Conference at the University of Leicester, England.

Economist. (2008, May 3). Innovation: Home invention. *The Economist,* 98.

EDUCAUSE. (2006). Learner-centered concepts. *EDUCAUSE.* Retrieved March 2009, from http://www.educause.edu/content.asp?page_id=940&bhcp=1

García Aretio, L. (2001). *La educación a distancia. De la teoría a la práctica* (p. 328). Barcelona, Spain: Ariel.

Hedtek. (2010). *The Manchester personal learning environment.* Retrieved from http://hedtek.com/current-projects

History of Personal Learning Environments. (n.d.). *Wikipedia.* Retrieved from http://en.wikipedia.org/wiki/History_of_personal_learning_environments

Jaroszynska, A., Torres Kompen, R., & Edirisingha, P. (2010). Using virtual desktops for developing personal learning environments: A learner's perspective. *The PLE Conference.* Retrieved from http://pleconference.citilab.eu

JISC. (2007). *A report on the JISC CETIS PLE project.* Retrieved from http://wiki.cetis.ac.uk/Ple

Mason, R., & Rennie, F. (2008). *E-learning and social networking handbook: Resources for higher education.* London, England: Routledge.

MacLeod, I. H. (2007). Facebook as PLE: I have seen the future! *MachIanations.* Retrieved from http://machianations.blogspot.com/2007/05/facebook-as-ple-i-have-seen-future.html

Muldoon, N. (2008, June 16–19) *Self-direction and lifelong learning in the information age: Can PLEs help?* Proceedings of the 5th International Lifelong Learning Conference, Yeppoon, Queensland, Australia.

Oblinger, D., & Oblinger, J. (2005). *Educating the net-generation* [EDUCAUSE e-book]. Retrieved from http://www.educause.edu/content.asp?PAGE_ID=5989&bhcp=1

Prensky, M. (2001). Digital natives, digital immigrants. *On the Horizon, 9*(5).

Salmon, G. (2002). *E-tivities: The key to active online learning.* London, England: Routledge.

Torres Kompen, R., Edirisingha, P., & Mobbs, R. (2009). Putting the pieces together: Conceptual frameworks for building PLEs with Web 2.0 tools. In *Distance and e-learning in transition.* Wiley-ISTE.

University of Aveiro. (2010). [Blog in Portuguese] Retrieved from http://labs.sapo.pt/ua/

Wild, F., Mödritscher, F., & Sigurdarson, S. (2008, July 9). *eLearning papers.* Retrieved from www.elearningpapers.eu

CHAPTER 16

METACOGNITION IN DISTANCE LEARNING

The Nelson-Narens Framework

Ansie Minnaar

The purpose of this chapter is to describe the role of metacognition in distance education and more specifically, metacognition's role in online learning as described in the Nelson and Narens framework. We define metacognition and present the current understanding of the concept as it appears in the literature. We proceed to examine the rationale for the importance of metacognitive strategies in distance and online learning. We discuss the implications of using the Nelson and Narens framework for metacognition in online learning. We conclude by developing a series of recommendations for both the implementation and further research of metacognition as it pertains to online learning.

> *Every morning in Africa, a gazelle wakes up.*
> *It knows it must run faster than the fastest lion or it will be killed.*
> *Every morning a lion wakes up.*
> *It knows it must outrun the slowest gazelle or it will starve to death.*
> *It doesn't matter whether you are a lion or a gazelle.*
> *When the sun comes up, you better start running.*

> —African proverb (Friedman, 2005, p. 114)

Trends and Issues in Distance Education:
International Perspectives, Second Edition, pp. 239–253
Copyright © 2012 by Information Age Publishing
All rights of reproduction in any form reserved.

METACOGNITION IN THE ONLINE LEARNING SETTING

The African proverb of the lion and the gazelle illustrates the increasing global competitiveness of education in global economics. This increasing global competitiveness in global education is motivated by many factors. Open and distance learning (ODL), for example, contributes to the massification of learning in higher education. Online learning as a part of ODL has the potential to reach the largest number of students ever before realized. Global technological advancement, too, has made online learning more feasible within developed countries. Governments are making large investments in mass education, of which online learning is the preferred choice in ODL. In developing countries, distance education in higher education is increasingly more appealing because of reducing costs.

ODL and online learning systems are therefore implemented for a variety of reasons across different institutions and contexts. The underlying, primary reason for developing such systems, however, is to expand educational access to postsecondary education. Online learning in higher education, regardless of its many advantages, is not without its own set of specialized issues. Of those, many researchers have focused on the metacognition of online learners as one of the keys to successful online learning experiences.

WHAT IS METACOGNITION?

Metacognition is one of the buzzwords in education, but exactly what is metacognition? Metacognition is defined as "thinking about thinking" (Livingston, 2003) and therefore falls into the category of higher-order thinking. Simple activities, such as planning how to approach a learning task, monitoring one's own understanding of a subject, or evaluating the progress of task completion are all essentially metacognitive operations.

Metacognition relates to acquired knowledge about cognitive processes, including knowledge of personal variables, task variables, and strategy variables. Metacognition is also related to the regulation of the sequential processes used for controlling cognitive activities and ensuring that cognitive goals are reached. What is the difference between *cognitive* and *metacognitive* strategies in learning? *Cognitive strategies* are used to help an individual achieve a particular goal, while *metacognitive strategies* are used to ensure that this goal is reached. Metacognitive experiences usually immediately precede or follow a cognitive activity. Metacognitive experiences often occur when cognition fails, and one realizes that a task has not been understood.

Metacognition has a dual role in that it forms a representation of cognitively based monitoring processes, but also exerts control over cognition, based on the representation of cognition. Metacognition has many facets that make it difficult to distinguish between *monitoring* (which includes metacognitive *knowledge* and *experiences*) and *control* (which includes the metacognitive *skills*). *Metacognitive knowledge* includes those aspects that we derive from long-term memory, such as ideas, beliefs, theories, personal traits, tasks, strategies, goals, and the validity of facts. Conversely, *metacognitive experiences* include those aspects that are intangible, such as feelings, judgments, estimations of time, and effort. *Metacognitive skills* include conscious, deliberate activities as well as the use of strategies, effort and time allocation, planning, checking, regulating, and evaluating outcomes (Efklides, 2006; Georghiades, 2004). Wang and Palincsar (1989, as cited in White, 1999) also argue that metacognition includes students' ability to organize knowledge, to recognize when they do not understand, and when to seek assistance.

Despite the problems of conceptualizing metacognition and its related processes, metacognition is generally accepted to be a *framework* of cognition. Metacognition operates at both the *meta* level and at the *object* level. The *meta* level is informed by the object world through monitoring, and according to Nelson and Narens (1996, as cited in Efklides, 2006), modifies the object world by means of the control function. Cognitive processes at the objective level include the basic operations traditionally subsumed under information processing, including encoding, rehearsing, and retrieving information (Nelson & Narens, 1996, as cited in Koriat, 2007). The metalevel is assumed to oversee object-level operations by monitoring and returning signals to regulate them in a top-down manner. Note that the object level has no control or access over the metalevel (for example, the study of new material, which involves a variety of basic object-level operations such as processing, comprehension of knowledge, and rehearsing of facts). Similarly, metacognitive processes are engaged in planning how to study, devising and implementing learning strategies monitoring the success at the objective level and modifying strategies as needed. Monitoring the degree of comprehension during study of new material and making decisions whether to repeat before proceeding is an example of a metacognitive process (Efklides, 2006; Koriat, 2007; McMahon & Luca, 2005).

METACOGNITION IN OPEN AND DISTANCE LEARNING ENVIRONMENTS

The Development of Online Courses

The unique nature of the online learning setting increases the need for a shift from teacher-centered to student-centered approaches. Some researchers in the open and distance learning literature (cf. Palloff & Pratt, 2001, as cited in Boyer, Maher, & Kirkman, 2006) have hypothesized that online learning environments do not necessarily provide for introspection, discourse, critical thinking, constructivism, and interaction. There is a growing literature base, however, illustrating how these metacognitive-related outcomes can be supported using technology-based tools within online course management systems, such as Blackboard, WebCT, eCollege, Moodle, or Sakai (Menchaca & Bekele, 2008).

The online learning setting demands additional support for these online tools if it is to move beyond the simple transfer of information to the development of deep, significant learning. Addressing the individuality of each learner is a key aspect in the facilitation of a student-centered approach, including learners' own metacognitive awareness and an understanding of how they best think and learn, and should be promoted via the implementation of interactive learning in the online environment. A student's most effective metacognitive strategy is to provide knowledge of cognitive processes, strategies, experiences, or practice by using both cognitive and metacognitive strategies while simultaneously evaluating the outcomes (Livingston, 2003).

Unfortunately, with the pressures higher education institutions face to transfer into the online format, many instructors may simply transfer their traditional, content-based face-to-face course materials to an e-format that can be accessed by students through Internet technology. Such direct translation of materials may result in a scenario in which there is little or no opportunity for the online learner to experience deeper learning, including interaction, dialogue, and reflection on the learning content, all of which are learning strategies that are indispensable to learner development (Sandi-Urena, Cooper, & Stevens, 2010). With online learning now increasingly becoming a common method for both graduate and undergraduate education (and even being seen at the grade school level), these issues have grown in importance.

Salmon's Five-Stage Framework

A five-stage framework for understanding the manner in which students engage in online courses has been proposed by Salmon (2000, as cited in Wallace, 2003). Salmon's five stages include access and motivation, online socialization, information exchange, knowledge construction, and development of the student (Wallace 2003). Salmon's five-stage framework can be used to inform the design of online courses in a manner that helps support student metacognitive processes. For example,

1. *Access and motivation*: Learners should explore their online course shell as well as all related online tools and supplemental web resources.

2. *Online socialization*: Learners should organize themselves into groups to share tips and advice as well as to facilitate other collaborative activities.

3. *Information exchange*: Learners should work in group-based assignments (e.g., learners might collaboratively conduct a literature search and then develop a literature review for the subject).

4. *Knowledge construction*: Learners should together review educational theories and examine ideas and implications.

5. *Development of self*: Learners should individually work on their own proposals within their focus area and outline the research project to finish in the given period.

An ad-hoc rule of thumb is that developing and implementing a high-quality online course that takes these factors into account might take about 10 months. The production time per course could be broken down into phases: an initial planning phase, in which time frames could vary but are estimated at about a month; a second phase of analysis and design, lasting some 2 to 3 months; a third phase for development, lasting about 3 months; and finally, an implementation phase, which includes a trial run, testing, and refinement, taking some 3 months. The estimate here adds up to at least 10 months per course, but it is often the case that this process takes longer than the estimate here.

Practical Aspects of Online Courses Supporting Metacognition

One key to a successful online learning experience is to implement a clear online course structure so that both learner and instructor expectations are clear. In online learning, a great deal of the contextual information that traditionally passed through nonformal means within a physical classroom is lost. Students in an online course, for example, cannot rely on body language, tone of voice, or other clues to clearly understand all expectations of an instructor. This can be compensated for by developing a structured format for the online course to clarify expectations.

Discussion forums should also ideally form part of an online course and should be accompanied by a description of the course and perhaps some type of "welcome" message. The welcome message can be considered an important component of an online course because it is this message that enables the instructor to establish expectations, set the tone, and communicate important initial information about the course to learners. The welcome message, as well as the majority of written communication from an instructor in an online course, should be written in a friendly tone and should guide the student through the course.

An important issue for faculty members designing new online courses is their role as teachers. Such concerns may involve questions such as, "What do I do when I am teaching online?" (Wallace, 2003). Obvious tasks for the online teacher include designing the course material, interacting with students and giving feedback, and assessing students' assignments. What is not so obvious is how these tasks should be carried out. Class discussions, small-group discussions, lectures, and the manner in which students' work will be assessed are particularly problematic issues for online teachers. One thing that stands out in online teaching is the unexpectedly large amount of time it can take to facilitate the discussions and lectures, a factor that can be overwhelming for first-time online instructors.

Social Presence

Social presence is a vital affective learning factor that can influence online learning. According to Tu and Yen (2007), social presence is the degree of feeling, perception of, and reaction to being connected to another intellectual entity through computer-mediated communication. Dimensions of social presence can include online communication, interactivity, and privacy. Polhemus, Sing, and Swan (2001, as cited in Tu & Yen, 2007) found that a high degree of social presence can facilitate both the initiation and maintenance of learner interaction. In contrast, a lack of social presence might lead to a high level of frustration and a lower level of effective learning.

Gunawardena and Zittle (1997, as cited in Tu & Yen, 2007) state that social presence is an effective predictor of the satisfaction that students experience in an online course. Social presence is the sense of being with another, of being together, or the degree to which someone is perceived as a real person in mediated communication. Social presence is, however, a temporary phenomenon that fluctuates over time. Trust plays an important part in social presence and is crucial to online learning, because humans naturally hesitate to share information before a trusting relationship has been established. The lecturer using an online learning model should therefore apply a model of open conversation with all participants in the course, featuring timely feedback on issues or questions or assignments, all of which can help to establish trust.

Garrison (as cited in Wallace, 2003) refers to social presence as "cognitive presence." Garrison defines this as a measure of students' engagement in inquiry. Garrison used a four-phase model of inquiry that includes triggering events, exploration, integration, and resolution. In terms of Garrison's model, students must actively participate in online classes in which discussions are valued, thus creating social presence by the nature and content of their participation. Social presence seems to be an important element of both satisfaction and learning, and establishing social presence is important at the start of online courses. Students in online courses value discussions with both their instructors and their peers. However, the correlation between how much students contribute to online discussions and their performance still remains to be formally established.

Online Student Metacognitive Support

Bonk (2000, as cited in Wallace, 2007, pp. 240–280) has developed a typology of learning assistance that categorizes the types of support online teachers should provide to support metacognition, including

- acknowledging social and cognitive aspects of learners through discussions and responses (including activities such as task definition, goal setting, planning, and ongoing study);
- questioning the learners through reflection and prompting;
- implementing direct instruction, facilitated by a step-by-step method, guiding and mentoring the online student;
- modeling of examples to aid in clarity;
- providing constructive and timely feedback or praise;
- cognitive task structuring aimed at learners progressing to higher levels of thinking, including ongoing self-monitoring of learning;
- providing cognitive explanations by a content facilitator concerned with students' understanding using models of interaction that define and explain constructs;
- pushing exploration by being an adviser-counselor, informing students about self-development and self-regulation of learning;
- fostering reflection or self-awareness by being a researcher concerned with relevance and course delivery and by developing students as self-reflecting practitioners;
- encouraging articulation or dialogue, and fostering this with
  o discourse, social presence, and communities of practice;
  o interaction and discussion between students;

    o addressing of learner problems through collaborative, group projects;

    o scaffolding with general advice and suggestions; and

   • providing management guidance in the form of metacognitive strategies.

This description provides evidence that the online instructor cannot simply upload a PDF file online and have much reason to believe that instruction will be successful. Although there is evidence that traditional courses cannot simply be "copied" into an online format to make a successful learning experience (Li & Akins, 2005), it is true, however, that what has been learned about face-to-face pedagogy can and should be used to inform online learning pedagogy. The current online medium is less rich than the traditional face-to-face setting, and so the selective adaptation of effective pedagogical strategies from face-to-face teaching is needed (Li & Atkins, 2005). The metacognitive framework, as described by Nelson and Narens (1990, as cited in Vovides, Snachez-Alonso, Mitropoulou, & Nickmans, 2007) can be used to inform, in a cost-effective manner, this process of transition into the online learning format.

Knowing and Thinking

One recent area being explored in cognition is the process of *knowing* vs. the concept of *thinking*. This research area involves perception, emotion, and action, and includes the entire process of life. Knowing that we are born to learn is at the core of a learning self-identity. What we learn in one sitting is of little importance. Practice makes perfect, and it is not solely the amount of time spent doing something that counts but rather the enjoyment gained from the process. A key to learning success is the establishment of the appropriate duration required for achievement. Quick fixes will not work here, as the learning effort may be lost under shortened time frames. By viewing the learning process as one that happens slowly and over time, failure in learning can be reduced. Self-development proceeds from the identification and development of a person's interest, through ongoing refinement, and deepens and extends to something that is interesting to the learner (Kolb & Kolb, 2009).

The Nelson and Narens Framework for Metacognition (1990)

The Nelson and Narens framework (Nelson & Narens, 1990) describes learning as a cyclical, interactive process between the cognitive processes, which takes place at the objective level (including information processing operations), and the processes at the metalevel (i.e., the overseeing operations; see Figure 16.1). When students are faced with new information, they engage in metacognitive monitoring by implementing strategies that will allow them to encode, rehearse, and retrieve what they consider to be important. At the metalevel, students adjust what they believe they should be learning from that information. The assumption is that a self-regulated student will continue to study and repeat a particular content item if his or her perceived degree of learning is below the desired degree. Self-regulated students are able to apply metacognitive control through self-reflection to assess their learning progress and adjust the processing of information to meet their goals (Vovides et al., 2007).

By the early twenty-first century, we have moved beyond the understanding that "online learning" is little more than creating a few Power-Point slides and posting the slideshow online. Taking our understanding of learner metacognition and applying it to the online learning setting, we should rather be creating online learning content that allows desired learning outcomes to be matched with metadata that facilitates more powerful and robust online course management systems. Additional features, such as intelligent learning mentors and tutors, can further extend the attractiveness and usefulness of such course management systems.

According to the Nelson and Narens framework, we assume that self-regulated students will continue to study content in greater detail if their perceived degree of learning is below their desired degree of performance. The assumption here is that self-regulated students are able to apply metacognitive control through self-reflection to assess progress in learning, and that learners will make adjustments as they proceed in order to achieve their goals (Narens, Graf, & Nelson, 1996). Reviewing Figure 16.1, we see under the object level the strategies students apply when learning new content. The monitoring of feedback outputs from task preparation, ongoing study, and retrieval can have a direct effect on performance, such as self-pacing study or retrieval.

Implications of Using the Nelson-Narens Framework

Figure 16.1 shows the proposed online learning design using a metacognitive approach that integrates the metalevel and the object level according to the framework by Nelson and Narens (1990, as cited in Vovides et al., 2007). The object level features identification of the strategies students apply as they learn new content. If students do not possess these skills, they will require additional training in the development and use of learning strategies. There are a number of methods for accomplishing this approach. Communities of practice, for example, can help

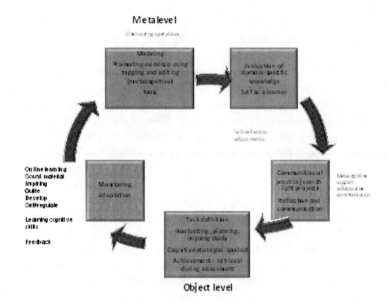

Figure 16.1.   Adapted metacognitive framework for designing e-learning courses from Nelson-Narens Framework (1990).

enable students to engage in reflective learning as they learn domain-specific content. Modeling and prompting, too, can assist students in engaging in self-evaluation of their learning. Finally, students can monitor and adapt their own strategies at will to improve their learning outcomes.

Implications for the Learning Process in General

Although most individuals engage in metacognitive regulation when confronted with an effortful cognitive task, some tasks are more metacognitive in nature than others. The good news is that learners can develop effective methods for regulating their cognitive activities. By using the Nelson and Narens metacognitive framework, learners can become more strategic, self-reliant, flexible, and productive in their learning endeavors.

Metacognition can enable online learners to benefit from instruction and encourage them to maintain their use of cognitive strategies. To simply provide knowledge without experience, or vice versa, does not seem to be sufficient for the development of metacognitive control in the learning environment. The impact of metacognitive experiences on self-regulation of learning is important, but more research in this regard is needed. The role of personal characteristics, the task, the context, and the influence of others in the metacognitive experience are of particular importance for further research (Efklides, 2006; Livingston, 2003)

Implications for Online Learning

The online learning environment can comprise many components, including the World Wide Web, e-mail, asynchronous discussion forums, and synchronous discussion forums (e.g., online chat room, video conferencing, online games, and others), to name but only a few. Four characteristics of the online learning environment, however, feature prominently in academic online learning when it comes to metacognition.

Flexible Time and Space

First, flexible time and space have given rise to the most significant revolution of online learning in modern ODL environments. Online learners can perform tasks at any time or place (assuming Internet access). Online learning environments thus differ greatly from the traditional face-to-face method in a classroom situation, which is typically based on a scheduled set of meetings within a specific time frame. Online learners are provided greater flexibility and freedom in the online setting; but are all learners actually ready for this self-monitored learning freedom? Are learners able to subject their learning to self-control and self-monitoring? Are they able to concentrate on their learning tasks and manage these effectively on their own? All these questions may challenge online students as they seek to control their strategies and metacognitive skills, including awareness, self-evaluation, self-monitoring, self-control, and time management (Tsai, 2009).

Indirect Social Action

Second, the indirect social interaction in the absence of the face-to-face interaction of the traditional classroom is an oft-criticized feature of online learning. This isolation in online learning can be a major frustration for learners. This situation challenges learners to implement new strategies for cooperating and negotiating with others via the Internet. Learners also need to understand the change in the role of the lecturer and to acquire new attitudes toward interacting with various online social support systems.

Abundant Information Availability

Third, learners should develop strategies for effectively dealing with the abundant information resources available via the Internet. Online learners can easily and quickly access information, but a greater problem is how to evaluate, integrate, and judge the information provided on the Internet. Learners therefore are required to become skillful online content manipulators who employ meaningful information searching strategies and maintain the will to locate online information to help ensure the success of their online learning experience. Metacognitive skills, such as monitoring and evaluation, as well as self-evaluation of goal achievement, are important.

Dynamic Characteristic of Internet Technologies

The learning dynamics of Internet technology used to create a learning platform for interaction between students and teachers is rapidly changing. Rapid technological change means that learners and instructors must understand the nature of Internet technology, its meaningful application to situations, and understand the various approaches that may be used online if they are to be successful at facilitating online learning experiences. Beyond that, online students need to develop and employ problem-solving skills to assess their progress, as well as to know when to request assistance when they encounter frustrations arising from the course management systems (Tsai, 2009).

There are numerous approaches that can be used to help students achieve the ability to self-evaluate their learning. Modeling and prompting, for example, can provide learners with the ability to implement their own strategies to improve their learning outcomes. "Stop-and-think triggers" also offer learners the time to meaningfully respond at critical points in their online learning experience. Such triggers can also be implemented as "feedback loops" to assist learners in toggling between, and adapting to, their set of developed cognitive strategies. Properly implemented, the course management system can help learners to become self-regulated students. Prompts and cues can be implemented to encourage students to think about their learning processes. Availability and reliability of technology, standards for course design, and instructor training can all be used to support instruction in the online setting (Vovides et al., 2007).

RECOMMENDATIONS

After reflecting on the content provided in this chapter, we are able to make a few recommendations for addressing metacognition in the learning setting. These recommendations are especially relevant for teaching and learning in the online setting.

First, to assist students in their metacognitive development, online programs should integrate multiple tools for different contexts, promote a positive attitude to technology, incorporate a social and situated learning environment, include some level of face-to-face interaction, and involve academic members to assist participants in developing appropriate skills, including the implementation of training and administrative support (McCracken, 2008; Ryan, 2008).

Second, the multitude of challenges faced by universities demand dedicated efforts that will promote program cohesion and develop a common strategic view for the advancement of open and distance learning. Student and staff support is critical to overall quality when providing significant and fruitful ODL and online learning practice. These efforts can assist students in applying metacognitive efforts as they move through a program.

Third, higher educational academics who are making the shift to online learning should be attentive to providing students with a theory-based, clear methodological pedagogy approach in such courses. In this chapter, we have presented one such pedagogical framework for online learning, the Nelson and Narens (1990) framework. There are other frameworks available, such as the Flavell, Bandura, and Zimmermann framework (Schunk, 2008), which could guide online learning using a metacognitive approach.

Fourth, online lecturers should ensure that assessments are clearly reflected in course processes. Metacognition, self-regulation, and self-regulated learning should be linked to students' learning achievements. Online lecturers should not assume that the achievements of students who use more self-regulated strategies will be greater than those of students who use fewer self-regulated strategies. Additional research is required to enlarge our understanding of metacognition, self-regulation, and self-regulated learning to ensure effective teaching strategies (Waters & Schneider, 2010).

Fifth, it should be established whether potential online students are ready to participate in the online environment. It is clear that, for a metacognitive framework for online learning to be effective, students should be oriented to this new modality to help ensure the success of the learning experience. Adequate support structures should be provided during courses. Technical support, too, is of critical importance.

Finally, and most importantly, mentoring programs must be made available to online students to provide them the opportunity to interact with mentors who can provide guidance throughout the duration of the online program.

SUMMARY

In this chapter, we have explored the critical role of metacognition in distance education and specifically, in the online learning setting. We have focused on the role of metacognition as described in the framework by Nelson and Narens (1990). The chapter has also reflected on what meta-cognition entails and what we currently understand about the concept of metacognition. We have explored the current rationales for addressing metacognition in learning and teaching. We concluded by making some basic recommendations for future research on metacognition.

COMPREHENSION AND APPLICATION QUESTIONS

Scenario: You are required to implement the first online postgraduate course at your university. Think about this new venture and answer the following questions:

1. Identify the specific course and give a short description of the outcomes for the course.
2. How would you decide which pedagogy to use to guide your initiative? Identify a suitable pedagogy for your course. Give reasons for your choice.
3. Describe in point form how you would use this pedagogy to guide the development of the postgraduate course content.
4. Describe how you would ensure student satisfaction in an online postgraduate course.
5. Give examples of how you would ensure social presence in your online postgraduate course.

RESOURCES FOR FURTHER EXPLORATION

Waters, H. S., & Schneider, W. (2010). *Metacognition, strategy use, and instruction*. New York, NY: Guilford.

Rudestam, K. E., & Schoenholtz-Read, J. (2010). *Handbook of online learning*. Los Angeles, CA: Sage.

Bramble, W. J., & Panda, S. (2008). *Economics of distance and online learning*. New York, NY: Routledge.

REFERENCES

Boyer, N. R., Maher, P. A., & Kirkman, S. (2006). Transformative learning in online settings: The use of self-direction, metacognition, and collaborative learning. *Journal of Transformative education* 4(4), 335–361.

Efklides, A. (2006). Metacognition and effect: What can metacognitive experiences tell us about the learning process. *Educational Research Review, 1,* 3–14.

Friedman, T. (2005). *The world is flat*. New York, NY: Farrar, Straus & Giroux.

Georghiades, P. (2004). From the general to the situated: Three decades of metacognition. *International Journal of Science Education, 26*(3), 365–383.

Kolb, A. Y., & Kolb, D. A. (2009). The learning way: Metacognitive aspects of experiential learning. *Simulation and Gaming, 40*(3), 297–327.

Koriat, A. (2007). Metacognition and consciousness. In P. Zelazo, M. Moscovitch, & E. Thompson (Eds.), *The Cambridge handbook of consciousness.* Cambridge, England: Cambridge University Press.

Li, Q., & Akins, M. (2005). Sixteen myths about online teaching and learning in higher education: Do not believe everything you hear. *TechTrends, 49*(4), 51–60.

Livingston, J. A. (2003). *Metacognition: An overview.* New York: State University of New York.

McCracken, H. (2008). Best practices in supporting persistence of distance education students through integrated web-based systems. *Journal College Student Retention, 10*(1), 65–91.

McMahon, M., & Luca, J. (2005, June 27–July 2). *Design explorations for an online environment to promote metacognitive processing through negotiated assessment.* Presented at the Ed-Media 2005, World Conference on Educational Multimedia, Hypermedia & Telecommunications, Montreal, Canada.

Menchaca, M. P., & Bekele, T. A. (2008). Student and instructor identified success factors in distance education. *Distance Education, 29*(3), 231–252.

Narens, L., Graf, A., & Nelson, T. (1996). Metacognitive aspects of implicit/explicit memory. In L. M. Reder (Ed.), *Implicit memory and metacognition.* New York, NY: Erlbaum.

Ryan, P. (2008). A small experiment in online learning. *South African Journal of Higher Education, 22*(4), 877–888.

Sandi-Urena, S., Cooper, M. M., & Stevens, R. H. (2010). Enhancement of metacognition use and awareness by means of a collaborative intervention. *International Journal of Science Education* (iFirst), 1–18.

Schunk, D. H. (2008). Meta-cognition, self-regulation and self-regulated learning: Research recommendations. *Educational Psychology Review, 20,* 463–467.

Tsai, M-J. (2009). The model of strategic e-learning: Understanding and evaluating student e-learning from metacognitive perspectives. *Educational Technology & Society, 12*(10), 34–48.

Tu, C. -H., & Yen, C-J. (2007). A study of multi-dimensional online social presence. In L. W. Cooke (Ed.), *Frontiers in higher education.* New York, NY: Nova Science.

Vovides, Y., Snachez-Alonso, S., Mitropoulou, V., & Nickmans, G. (2007). The use of e-learning course management systems to support learning strategies and to improve self-regulated learning. *Educational Research Review, 2,* 64–74.

Wallace, R. M. (2003). Online learning in higher education: A review of research on interactions among teachers and students. *Education, Communication & Information, 3*(2), 240–280.

Waters, H. S., & Schneider, W. (2010). *Metacognition, strategy use, and instruction.* New York, NY: Guilford.

White, C. J. (1999, November). The metacognitive knowledge of distance students. *Open Learning,* 37–46.

SECTION IV

DISTANCE EDUCATION IN THE WORKPLACE AND IN NONFORMAL SETTINGS

Lya Visser, Section Editor

INTRODUCTION

The five chapters of Section IV all focus on using distance education in either training or in challenging circumstances. In the first chapter, Ai Ping Teoh discusses a study about the use of distance education in an international corporate environment. In the next chapter, Mike Crudden, whose daily focus is on the reduction of aircraft accidents and incidents, looks at how distance education is increasingly used in the aeronautic world to train or retrain aviation personnel. In their chapter, Evgeny Patarakin and Lya Visser describe the use of wikis in extramural activities as well as in government and business environments in Russia. Barbara Zeus shows in her chapter how distance education could play an important role in the lives of refugees and also brings up that in reality there are many challenging and often limiting conditions, making it difficult for prospective students to enroll in distance education. In the last chapter in this section, Anita Wilson argues how offering distance education to prisoners could help inmates to focus on life after incarceration. Here also, we see that practical problems often make studying via distance education difficult, if not impossible.

Section IV offers a wide variety of uses and/or possible uses of distance education in a variety of circumstances. All five chapters aim at enriching your appreciation and understanding of distance education and its numerous opportunities and challenges.

CHAPTER 17

E-LEARNING AT THE WORKPLACE

The Case of a Manufacturing Company in Malaysia

Ai Ping Teoh

As Malaysia progresses into a new era of an information and communication technologies-driven and knowledge-based society, effective and timely training of the workforce is critical in enhancing productivity and performance. This case presents several aspects of e-learning at the workplace of a manufacturing firm in Malaysia. The study was undertaken by conducting a cross-sectional analysis on the use of online learning resources and the activities and patterns of interaction in the online environment. Interview sessions with management and participants of a selected e-learning program were also carried out to obtain further information on the experience of the virtual delivery of training at the workplace. Motivational issues and challenges faced by both management and participants in the e-course are also discussed.

Trends and Issues in Distance Education:
International Perspectives, Second Edition, pp. 257–271
Copyright © 2012 by Information Age Publishing
All rights of reproduction in any form reserved.

INTRODUCTION

Lifelong learning has become one of the fundamental transformation pillars for human capital development in sustaining and developing the competitiveness of nations. This is particularly the case in Malaysia as it embarks on a significant shift into a new era of information and communication technologies (ICT)-driven and knowledge-based society. Being one of the key determinants of human capital, effective and timely training of the workforce is critical to enhance the productivity and performance in realizing the country's agenda. Recognizing the importance of a skilled and well-educated workforce, many companies are discovering innovative ways to manage knowledge resources and provide continuous training to its workforce using ICT.

This case investigated several aspects of e-learning at the workplace of a manufacturing firm in Malaysia. The company requested to remain anonymous; I will call it Progress. Findings resulting from this study will contribute to discovering the uniqueness of the learning expectations, needs, and behaviors of adult learners in the context of e-learning at the workplace in Malaysia.

E-LEARNING IN MALAYSIA

Malaysia, located in Southeastern Asia, is a country with an open economy and stable socioeconomic development. It has a population of almost 26 million, with 63.6% in the age group of 15–64 and with a median age of 24.9 years (Central Intelligence Agency, 2009). Malaysia has three major ethnic groups: Malay, Chinese, and Indians. Bahasa Malaysia is the official language.

In most Asian countries such as Malaysia, e-learning is still in its early stages. In order to ensure the achievement of e-learning in Malaysia, the government has taken a number of initiatives, incorporated in the Ninth Malaysia Plan, that is, the second phase of the Malaysia Vision 2020, aiming to make Malaysia a fully developed country by the year 2020, where the use of Internet leads to growth in e-learning. There are about 15.9 million Internet users in Malaysia, approximately 61% of the population (Malaysian Communications and Multimedia Commission, 2009).

Over the past few years, the number of e-learning programs implemented in corporate training has increased dramatically, and e-learning has become a major form of training and development within modern organizations such as a variety of corporations, health service providers, and national institutions.

BACKGROUND AND DESIGN OF THE STUDY

Progress is a manufacturing firm with headquarters in Malaysia. The company has operations in Malaysia, China, Indonesia, and Vietnam, with a total of about 4,800 employees. Management of the company believes that education and development of its employees is crucial if one wants to attract and retain talent in the company. In this case study, an online training course conducted in Progress was selected to be examined within the context of e-learning at the workplace. This course, "SK201 Effective Problem Solving Techniques and Decision Making Skills" was delivered in English to middle-level managers in four different countries—Malaysia, China, Indonesia, and Vietnam—via a web-based learning management platform from July 2009 to December 2009. The purpose of the training was to equip middle managers with skills in problem solving and decision making. It was one of the first pilot online training programs launched by Progress.

This study was undertaken using both primary and secondary data. A cross-sectional analysis on the learning activities and experience of the trainees was done in December 2009. To better understand the motivation for and experience with e-learning in the workplace, qualitative data were acquired and analyzed via interview sessions with the management (including the learning and development manager) and participants in the e-learning program. Content analysis was conducted on the logs of the online activities of the participants. To measure the interaction of learners with the online content during the training, two indicators were developed: time and frequency of assessing online resources, and dimensions of interaction with online learning resources (including the online forums).

THE COMPANY AND ITS INITIATIVES TOWARD E-LEARNING

Interview sessions revealed that for the past 15 years, the company has been delivering face-to-face continuing education and training classes to all levels of employees. The content was based on a biannual training needs analysis. These training programs have various purposes such as the orientation of new employees, technical compliance training, professional competency, soft-skills training, and continuing education. Although management found these classes expensive, they see them as an investment in a valuable resource that will ultimately help the company grow.

Management noted several limitations in the approach used. For example, participating employees must be away from their work to attend classes, and based on employees' feedback, most of the training programs were conducted in an intensive/condensed mode. Lack of time to understand the material resulted in a low retention level. Recruitment and retention of competent employees have been important challenges. Management also observed increased training costs due to repetition of the training of the same subject matter to employees across sites in a number of countries. An increase in spending on training in the traditional manner would be unavoidable as the company was expanding its operations to more international markets.

Based on these observations, in 2009, Progress started to explore the use of an online platform to deliver training courses. This decision was also influenced by a strategic review of the training and development function in delivering learning solutions. It wanted to share best practices and encourage a culture of lifelong learning among its employees. As the company invested in e-learning within its training and development framework, there were several considerations about the impact, such as providing effective and efficient training via the online platform. Management also intended to focus on knowledge management and believed that through employees' participation in e-learning, individual competency could actually be turned into the company's property and develop its competitiveness.

When e-learning was introduced in Progress, a consultant was engaged to carefully consider the needs and input of all stakeholders: the key administrators, the learning and development (L&D) department, the information technology services personnel, and the employees. Representatives of the stakeholders participated in the planning, analysis, evaluation, design, and implementation of the online learning management system (LMS). Moodle, an open-source course management system was selected. It has good editing ability, which is GUI-based and has a strong monitoring function via a statistical reporting feature and log functions. The key concern has been how well the LMS is able to support the realization of the company's training objectives within its culture. While management adopts a long-term view of the investment, the impact on competitiveness and the development of a learning and knowledge-sharing culture is of great significance. Nevertheless, return on investment as well as the use and effectiveness of e-learning in training are areas of concern.

The delivery model of a typical training course conducted via e-learning involved three main components: the online learning management system LifeLearn, facilitator(s)/trainer(s), and learners/participants. While the basic system features, functions, and access are configured in LifeLearn by the L&D and IT support staff, the content of the training course is designed by the facilitator(s). For the first pilot e-learning courses, delivery of the training was mainly based on resources/functions put in LifeLearn, as discussed in the following sections.

LEARNING RESOURCES IN THE ONLINE LEARNING MANAGEMENT SYSTEM

Progress used LifeLearn (Moodle based), among which the common functions available are static course materials such as uploaded files, text pages, web pages, links, and directories, as well as interactive materials such as online quizzes, asynchronous forum boards, and synchronous chats.

As seen in Figure 17.1, on the main page of a typical training course in LifeLearn, the left panel shows a shortcut to the activities and the administration-related functions (only available to the facilitator and the administrator). In the right panel, learners view the latest course news. The essence of the online resources designed for the course was contained in the main window of the page, that is, the Topic outline.

In the upper part of the Topic outline, learners were able to access the Online Forums, which serve specific purposes such as Announcements from the facilitator, Public Forum, and Group Discussion forum. There was also an online real-time Chatroom available for synchronous interaction, and a Guide to Using LifeLearn. The facilitator welcomed the learners via a posted Welcome Letter. In the lower part of the section, learners were able to access the Course Overview information, Supplementary Materials, and other activities to assist their learning. Common resources within each of the six training modules for a 6-month skills training course in this case included a folder that contained presentation files and documents such as cases for discussions (as shown in Figure 17.2), hyperlinks to relevant external websites, online quizzes, and other online activities. Most of the online resources were made available at the start of the training course, but the facilitator constantly posted additional resources and initiated/replied to forum discussions during the training.

In order to track the use of each resource by the participants, online resources (OR) in LifeLearn were grouped into several categories:

1. OR1: Static pages (e.g., Welcome Letter from Facilitator, Course Overview Information, and User's Guide)
2. OR2: Folders of course content (e.g., attachment files including reading materials, case studies, presentation files, etc.)
3. OR3: Hyperlinks to external websites (e.g., educational and related websites that were related to the training content)

Figure 17.1.   Screen capture of the main section of a sample course in LifeLearn.

262

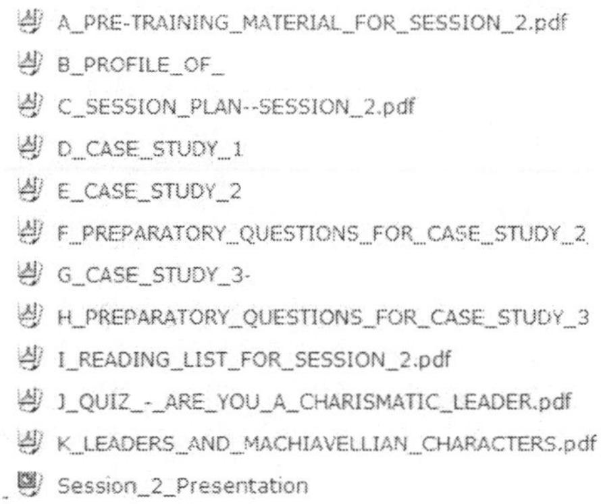

A_PRE-TRAINING_MATERIAL_FOR_SESSION_2.pdf

B_PROFILE_OF_

C_SESSION_PLAN--SESSION_2.pdf

D_CASE_STUDY_1

E_CASE_STUDY_2

F_PREPARATORY_QUESTIONS_FOR_CASE_STUDY_2

G_CASE_STUDY_3-

H_PREPARATORY_QUESTIONS_FOR_CASE_STUDY_3

I_READING_LIST_FOR_SESSION_2.pdf

J_QUIZ_-_ARE_YOU_A_CHARISMATIC_LEADER.pdf

K_LEADERS_AND_MACHIAVELLIAN_CHARACTERS.pdf

Session_2_Presentation

Figure 17.2.   . Screen capture of materials uploaded in the folder of a training module in LifeLearn.

4.   OR4: Online Discussion Forums (asynchronous)
5.   OR5: Online real-time Chat Room (synchronous)
6.   OR6: Online quizzes

LEARNING ACTIVITIES AND INTERACTION PATTERNS

Some 50 learners participated in the research. A total of 20 came from Malaysia, 15 from China, 10 from Indonesia, and 5 from Vietnam; and 61% were male. The average age was 38, and all were middle-level managers from various departments.

Online Learning Activities

Participation rate in LifeLearn was 100%, and the average time spent online was 61 hours over a period of six months. It was compulsory to log in and fulfill the minimum of 48 hours participation. Learners needed to achieve a score of at least 90% for all the online assessment/quizzes in each module.

Level and Patterns of Online Activities in LifeLearn

The frequency of interaction with the online content was measured by the number of times the participant accessed the online resources during the training, over the total number of participants, and was 52 times. In terms of the pattern of activity, the frequency of participants going online was somewhat evenly distributed throughout the period of the training but a decrease in activities toward the end of the training duration was observed, as shown in Figure 3. Part of the reason may be the weeklong public holiday in November.

As seen in Figure 17.3, learners' activities seemed to reach a peak in the second month of the course, but were the lowest toward the end of the program. Peaks were observed to occur about every 3 to 4 weeks.

Face-to-face interview sessions were conducted with learners in Malaysia and by Skype calls with learners in China, Vietnam, and Indonesia. The interviews used a loosely structured, open-ended format to ascertain the rationale of their actions in LifeLearn and their viewpoints on the e-learning. Of the 10 learners interviewed, 4 were from Malaysia, 2 were from China, 2 were from Indonesia, and 2 were from Vietnam. All learners interviewed indicated that at the beginning of the course they were rather skeptical about the use and effectiveness of the system. Before the start of the training, learners were given briefing sessions on the online platform LifeLearn and were made aware of the support system available via the L&D department and the information technology (IT) services helpdesk. Learners from Malaysia, China, and Vietnam were swiftly adapting to the system. The Indonesian participants needed more time. The latter indicated that they followed the suggested learning schedule very closely, while learners from China expressed that they exercised some flexibility with regard to their learning schedule and generally accessed the supplementary materials and discussion questions for each module at the start of the first week and spent the subsequent 1.5 to 2 weeks learning the key concepts and working through the module. Meanwhile, they had also started exchanges with peers and the facilitator in the forums and progressively interacted more as they concluded their module by attempting the compulsory online quizzes. The level of activities was higher in the first 3 months as the facilitator had planned and conducted online chat sessions with the learners.

Learners' Interaction With the Online Resources in LifeLearn

Figure 17.4 shows the distribution of use by learners of the various types of online resources available in LifeLearn for the course, as analyzed from the log files of the system.

Based on data analyzed from the activity log of the training course, learners accessed Online Discussions Forums the most (51%), followed by Online Real-Time Chat Room (20%) and Online Quizzes (16%). The least accessed resources were Static Pages (2%) and Hyperlink to external web-

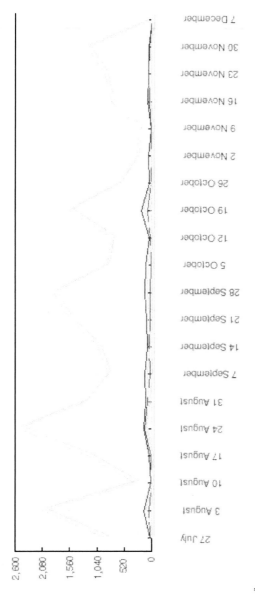

Figure 17.3. Level and patterns of activities of a training course in LifeLearn.

265

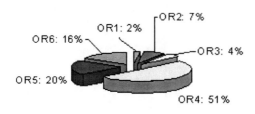
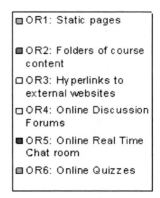

Figure 17.4.   Distribution of access to the various online resources of a training course in LifeLearn.

sites (4%). Learners preferred online resources that have evaluation and feedback capability, that is, allow for interaction between learner and peers/facilitator/content. Learners' access to the Online Forums is one of the indications of their interaction with the online content as the exchanges preserved in online discussion forums are an important learning resource in the online learning environment and also served as one of the contributors to the knowledge management system in the company. In the Online Chat sessions, held at predetermined times and on predetermined topics, learners, peers, and facilitators communicated in real time to discuss course content matters. Online Quizzes were a means for learners' self-evaluation and served as one of the tools for the facilitator to assess the learning process. Despite Online Quizzes being a compulsory component of the training course, participants appeared to have spent less time on this activity than on the Online Forums and Chat.

The aspects of interaction with online resources can be viewed in terms of the various dimensions of interaction, such as social, procedural, expository, explanatory, and cognitive (Oliver & McLoughlin, 1997). Similar dimensions were adopted in analyzing the forum exchanges at a later stage of the study. As observed from the data reported above, online resources that allowed interaction at expository, explanatory, and cognitive dimensions were accessed the most.

To understand the observations in more depth, feedback was obtained from the same group of participants via interviews. The Malaysian learners accessed Online Forums more than the learners from China, who spent most time with the Online Quizzes. Learners from Indonesia mentioned that they were reserved in voicing and responding individually to discussions from their peers from other countries. Malaysian learners were keen to try the Online Quizzes, but indicated that they were less concerned with the final score than their peers from other countries. Online Quizzes were prepared by the facilitator and included different types of questions. Each time the learners accessed the quizzes, questions would be extracted from the question bank and presented to the learners. Upon completion of the test, learners were informed about their score and got the answers to all attempted questions. Their score was recorded by the facilitator and submitted to the L&D Department at the end of the training course.

Dimension and Depth of Learners' Participation in the Online Forum Discussions

Further analysis was done by examining participation in the Online Forums. It was observed that in the first 2 months of the training, the facilitator initiated most of the discussions (53%), while when the course was progressing, the learners started most of the discussions (55%). It was also found that initiators of the online discussions were mostly female learners from China (40%), whereas female learners from Vietnam (2%) were not active in starting discussions in the online environment. Most of the discussions in the forums (63%) have progressed to at least four ensuring replies (threads).

In addition, discussions in the Online Forums were transcribed by categorizing the exchanges into the dimensions of interaction mentioned above. Figure 17.5 shows the dimension and depth of interaction in the Online Forum discussions in LifeLearn for SK201.

Learners' interaction was mostly at the Expository and Explanatory dimensions (32%) followed by the Cognitive dimension (25%). Exchanges on Procedural-related matters accounted for only 2%, while the Social dimension was about 9%. From the findings, it appeared that learners appreciated the online platform for subject matter-related discussions at a slightly higher level of dimension of interaction. These included demonstration of knowledge/facts with elaborated explanation based on peers and facilitator's responses, as well as providing constructive feedback and detailed commentary on course content via critical thinking. It was also noted that the majority of the learners involved at these dimensions were from Malaysia and China. Discussions related to Procedural dimensions on course-related requirements and administrative issues were the least dominant. Chinese learners were the most dynamic in discussions on Procedural-related matters, while learners from Indonesia appeared to be active in initiating Social exchanges.

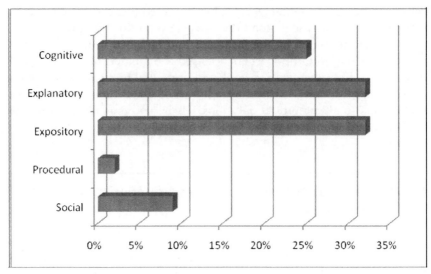

Figure 17.5.   . Dimension and depth of interactions in the online forum discussions in LifeLearn.

Based on feedback obtained during the interviews, learners from China voiced that following China's rapid social development, they considered continuing-education programs and retraining as essential in order to gain personal prestige in the workplace and improve their socioeconomic standing. Learners from Indonesia indicated that the LMS, next to acting as a platform for learning materials, also enabled them to establish friendships with their counterparts in other countries within the same organization. Even though most of the interviewees agreed that web-based learning offered a difference and allowed bridging the distance between learners and facilitators, they also acknowledged that online learning in Asia is still very "teacher centered." They noted that the facilitator planned the learning tasks and followed up with directives or instructions, which was particularly visible at the beginning of the training course. Meanwhile, Malaysian learners showed some independent thinking in articulating their views on the discussion topics and conveyed that they are intrinsically motivated in enrolling for training courses offered by the company despite the training being in an online format with which they may not have been too familiar. Learners also shared that they seldom challenged the facilitator directly, even in an online environment.

LEARNERS' FEEDBACK AND MANAGEMENT VIEWPOINT

The interview sessions were concluded by gauging the learners' overall satisfaction with the online training course as well as by seeking suggestions for improvement. By and large, the learners have rated a mean of 4.1 out of 5 in terms of overall satisfaction of the online learning course.

Learners did not mention major problems in following the suggested learning process in the online platform, that is, read the resources, do case analysis, discuss, and test understanding via the Online Quizzes. In fact, those interviewed voiced that online training had indeed been convenient to them and enabled them to work at their own pace and level of understanding. They added that a web-based course fit into their busy work schedule better than regularly scheduled classes. Female learners with families mentioned that they welcomed more online training as it eliminated the need for them to make up for missed work as a result of attending face-to-face training during working hours. With e-learning, they were able to learn at a more suitable time, for example, at night when they are home and finished with household chores.

In all, 9 out of 10 learners interviewed were of the opinion that Life-Learn worked for them, and that they were now better equipped to solve problems and to make effective decisions. Only one learner interviewed indicated that he found that face-to-face training was better, as he was unable to adapt to the virtual way of learning. Among the barriers he faced were challenges in learning without the physical presence of an instructor and dealing with written communication. The interviewees also indicated that they would prefer to have more opportunities to interact physically with the facilitator for certain types of training courses such as technical training. They suggested that the L&D Department should work together with the facilitator(s) in developing audio and video training materials for the online platform and to organize some video-conferencing sessions. Learners also pointed out that the case studies used in online training should be more directly relevant to their work by presenting cases that were compiled from their actual work scenarios.

From the management point of view, online delivery of training courses helped the company both directly and indirectly, even though the outcomes and the return on investment of such training courses need to be further investigated. The employees learned valuable skills more quickly, retained the knowledge, and were available throughout the working day. The L&D department was able to track the training needs and progress of knowledge/skills development of its employees. Management added that for corporate e-learning to be successful, all stakeholders should be included in the strategic decisions and be involved in the learning process.

CONCLUSIONS

Continuing education for employees is viewed as one of several ways of attracting and retaining human capital in a company by helping employees with personal and professional growth. The practical aspects of what trainees have learned can be directly applied to their work and result in more efficiency and in increased productivity for the company. The discussed case brought forward the experience and challenges facing Progress with regard to its delivery of online training courses, representing the transition period for Asian adult learners to shift from a traditional learning approach to a new web-based learning environment at the workplace.

The breadth and depth of the online resources and the capabilities, features, and adequacy functions of the LMSs in delivering e-learning courses at the workplace need to be further examined. The selection and delivery of online content should take into consideration practical guidelines such as interactivity, ease of navigation, motivational value, and its effectiveness. In addition, the influence of regional and national culture cannot be neglected in developing an effective online learning setting to deliver e-learning across several corporate sites. All these issues should be addressed to enhance the efficacy of the online learning environment at the workplace.

COMPREHENSION AND APPLICATION QUESTIONS

1. Identify suitable online resources to enhance the online learning environment in the company Progress. Justify your answers.
2. Discuss the influence of national culture to the learners' activities in the online learning environment. Elaborate on your answers.
3. Suggest suitable strategies to enhance the delivery of online training courses. Explain your suggestions.

RESOURCES FOR FURTHER EXPLORATION

Hofstede, G. (1986). Cultural differences in teaching and learning. *International Journal of Intercultural Relations, 10,* 301–320.

Moore, M. G. (1989). Three types of interaction. *The American Journal of Distance Education, 3*(2), 1–7.

Palaiologou, N. (2009). Needs for developing culturally oriented supportive learning with the aid of information and communication technologies. *Pedagogy, Culture & Society, 17*(2), 189–200.

Picciano, A. G. (2002). Beyond student perceptions: Issues of interaction, presences and performance in an online course. *Journal of Asynchronous Learning Networks, 6*(1) 21–40.

Sadler-Smith, E., & Smith, P. J. (2004). Strategies for accommodating individuals' styles and preferences in flexible learning programs. *British Journal of Educational Technology, 35*(4), 395–412.

Strother, J. B. (2002). An assessment of effectiveness of e-learning in corporate training programs. *International Review of Research in Open and Distance Learning, 3*(1).

Tapanes, M. A., Smith, G. G., & White, J. A. (2009). Cultural diversity in online learning: A study of the perceived effects of dissonance in levels of individualism/collectivism and tolerance of ambiguity. *The Internet and Higher Education, 12*(1), 26–34.

Woo, Y., & Reeves, T. C. (2007). Meaningful interaction in web-based learning: A social constructivist interpretation. *The Internet and Higher Education, 10*(1), 15–25.

Zhu, C., Valcke, M., & Schellens, T. (2009). A cross-cultural study of online collaborative learning. *Multicultural Education & Technology Journal, 3*(1), 33–46.

REFERENCES

Central Intelligence Agency. (2009). *The world factbook: Malaysia.* Retrieved from https://www.cia.gov/library/publications/the-world-factbook/geos/my.html

Internet World Statistics. (2009). *Internet in Asia: 2009 top 10 countries.* Retrieved from http://www.internetworldstats.com/stats3.htm

Malaysian Communications and Multimedia Commission. (2009). *Statistics and records.* Retrieved from http://www.skmm.gov.my/

Oliver, R., & McLoughlin, C. (1997). Interactions in audio-graphics and learning environments. *The American Journal of Distance Education, 11*(1) 34–54.

CHAPTER 18

DISTANCE LEARNING IN AVIATION

Applications and Impacts on a Global Industry

Michael Crudden

The incorporation of distance education methods into the training efforts of the aviation industry is a natural progression of the use of technology for the field. Technological development has spurred the continued growth of aviation and at the same time, has supported safety through providing effective training solutions. These training solutions have been found to be as necessary to the industry as the technology enabling growth. The access to technology-intensive training has largely been the domain of large organizations with information technology resources and the ability to finance and support tools like flight simulators. As access to technology has proliferated on the consumer level, smaller companies and individuals in the industry have since gained access to electronic-based methods that had previously not been available as practical solutions. Through these methods, additional innovations have been made, affecting how aviation is practiced. The applications of these methods are also supporting a wide-reaching industry change such as the redesign of airspace used by millions of passengers every year. The acceptance and increased application of distance education methods in aviation make it a likely permanent feature of future training.

Trends and Issues in Distance Education:
International Perspectives, Second Edition, pp. 273–283
Copyright © 2012 by Information Age Publishing
All rights of reproduction in any form reserved.

INTRODUCTION

The challenges that the aviation industry has been confronted with since its inception have been many, and few industries are subject to similar consequences of failure. The growing demand for air transportation, coupled with the essential need for safety assurance, has made training a primary focus. Performance is essential; a lack of performance has a strong potential to compromise safety.

Today's aviation system has many layers of control designed to isolate any individual failure in order to prevent small issues from causing catastrophic events. The current safety posture of the industry has been a century in the making, the result of hard-learned lessons. Those lessons have promoted the improvement of learning industry-wide, and the industry continues to learn to develop new approaches.

In 1903, there was a single powered airplane, the Wright Flyer, and it carried one person. Fast forward to 2007, when it was estimated that airlines around the world operated 29.5 million flights, the highest number ever recorded (OAG, 2007). Civil aviation authorities around the world have recognized the growth of air travel, and many predict the trend to continue. The Directorate General of Civil Aviation for India reported a 19.6% year over year increase in passenger enplanements between 2009 and 2010 aboard domestic scheduled carriers (DGCA, 2010). Similar growth is forecasted for China, 11.6% annually until 2020 (MacCorkle & Wong, 2009). In response, governments have begun adapting their entire systems of flying to accommodate this foreseen growth. Meeting the need will come down to performance, highlighting the requirement for effective and responsive training.

PROFILES OF TRAINING NEEDS

Meeting the learning needs of the aviation industry as a whole is a continually evolving challenge. The requirements vary; some learners are engaged as professionals, employed by airlines or by other aviation interests, while others participate in flying for business or recreational purposes. Regardless of how people interface with aviation, there exists a need for each participant to accomplish a minimum amount of training. Even commercial airline passengers receive a safety briefing prior to every flight. The safety-sensitive nature of the aviation environment requires all involved to, at a minimum, be aware of the extent to which their presence can affect safety.

The first training event for a participant of any specialization is an initial course, broad in its coverage of topics. Later, recurrent training events are focused on the participants becoming current on new operating requirements and the latest changes to practice. This basic structure applies to most roles within aviation. Within this structure, there are minimum training requirements established by the national civil aviation authorities, performance standards for which proficiency must be developed, and changes to the operating environment that must be trained for.

For those working toward their first pilot's license, their experience will encompass all of the subjects necessary to safely operate an aircraft: aerodynamics, rules of the air, and certification requirements. Ground classroom training will cover knowledge areas, and later, concurrent flight lessons will allow the aviator to develop skills and work toward correlation with knowledge. For an airline pilot, an initial course is called for when changing roles, from first officer to captain, or aircraft types at their airline. Maintenance personnel must also receive training for the specific aircraft on which they will work.

EVOLUTION OF TECHNOLOGY IN TRAINING

As the aviation industry was establishing itself as a bona fide field, the need for effective training was decided early. The United States airmail service, established in 1925, was one of the first public exposures to aviation, and the sentiment of that first exposure became largely negative. The early establishment of contract airmail routes was embroiled in scandal; commercial airlines were accused of fraud and collusion. As a result, President Franklin D. Roosevelt ordered the Army Air Corps to assume control from the private airlines and operate the service.

The number of airplane accidents and incidents skyrocketed during this period. The incompatibility of military aviation of the time with the civil needs was clear. Military pilots had been trained for wartime, largely to fly in favorable weather conditions, based on the ability to visualize the earth's horizon. Flying for commerce was an entirely different flying environment, driven by a schedule and economic need. This led to pilots and aircraft attempting to fly in conditions of poor weather or nighttime, for which they were neither qualified or equipped. The pilots were not trained, and the aircraft were not capable of supporting the mission. With the American public looking on, the industry made training a permanent priority.

In 1929, General James "Jimmy" Doolittle flew the first flight that was conducted entirely by reference to instruments and not the visual references outside the aircraft (Daso, 2003). This demonstration served as the basis for aircraft to operate safely in limited visibility, and while the technical capability was demonstrated, flight crews of the time remained unable to operate the equipment. Training was needed in order to introduce the flight crews to this new capability and to the new technology that would be used to accomplish the feat (Glines, 1980).

The technology that enabled instrument flight also resulted in a solution for delivering training to pilots away from the native aircraft. The Link Trainer was one of the first flight simulators and was able to reproduce a representation of the interaction between aircraft flight control inputs and the aircraft instrumentation through vacuum components and mechanical linkage. The United States Army Air Corps became interested in the trainer following the accidents associated with the air mail service and placed orders for the devices to be used in pilot training. This established simulator technology as a viable technology for training pilots, affirmed later in World War II when the military ordered 10,000 of the devices to support the training command (DeAngelo, 2000).

Flight simulation today has achieved a virtual level of fidelity, is used by airlines from Dubai to Denver, and its use has expanded beyond use only by pilots. Maintenance personnel are trained on aircraft systems, using the simulator to understand the interactions of aircraft systems, and to train troubleshooting techniques. Maintenance personnel also operate the aircraft on the ground to perform engine runs and test systems. These personnel need to be trained to respond to emergency situations such as fire, and the simulator provides a tool to accomplish that.

RETHINKING STANDARD PRACTICES

The capabilities of distance education brought cause to rethink the practices used to train personnel in aviation. The classroom has been the standard setting for knowledge delivery and the airplane the standard setting for skill development. The prevalence of the technologies has resulted in those standard practices being modified to present the best possible learning experience to industry members, utilizing distance learning in ways that best suit their organization and the needs of employees. The result has been a learning environment flexible to the needs of an industry, and at the same time formed the basis for other innovations beyond learning.

Few argue against the benefits of flight simulation in aviation; however, one limitation of the technology is that the users must travel from their base to the simulator facility to enjoy the benefits. This is distance learning in a way; a synthetic reproduction of flight away from the actual setting. In an industry in which personnel are moving around the world nearly constantly, the need to bring them all to a centralized location is a challenge. When a training issue is identified, it can take months to deliver that training to a crewmember. Because of the clear benefits of the tool, aviation professionals have been traveling to training centers on a routine basis for decades, accepting this as a necessary concession to take advantage of the advanced training potential of the device.

One idea that has emerged is the delivery of training via contemporary distance education that has traditionally been conducted in the simulator. While current technology does not provide a practical means to deliver the full flight simulation experience through a distance method, the technology does allow for a partial representation that behaves like the simulator. By providing this capability, personnel can manipulate the aircraft system controls, and the software will behave as the simulator, and the aircraft itself, would. This has application to both flight and maintenance personnel in learning the systems and operating procedures of an aircraft. An added benefit of this practice is the ability to free-play with the application—to explore the aircraft following the completion of the structured learning requirements. Because of the near constant use of the flight simulators, time is often the constraint in conducting training. With a remote application, the limitation becomes the amount of time the audience wishes to invest in the learning. Most companies have enabled their delivery systems to allow staff to access the resource at any time, during and outside of schedule training periods.

With this delivery of simulator-like interaction, the need for a motion system as part of a full flight simulator, an icon of professional aviation training, is being reconsidered. Recent studies have suggested that the motion components, some of the most expensive and complex parts of a simulator, may not be necessary to provide adequate fidelity. Researchers are investigating if the use of other sensory inputs, such as vision, sound, and tactile inputs can be applied to flight simulation to create an illusion of motion adequate for flight training (Cohen-Bürki et al., 2003). Currently nonmotion simulators, called Flight Training Devices, are used in the training of systems and procedures for crewmembers. The outcome of this research may result in the expanded use of these tools and of personal computer-based system simulators.

While some developments are at a hypothetical stage, others have resulted in the adaptation of established flying practices to take advantage of the technology. The written technical resource available to pilots in flight has been paper-based aircraft manuals, at times a very cumbersome technical document to use. As courseware has been developed to teach the contents of the manual to company personnel, in some instances the courseware has been developed to the point that it has become a more comprehensive and practical technical resource, replacing the aircraft manual as the onboard reference. What was limited to static text is evolving to an interactive tool applied to monitoring normal aircraft systems operations and managing abnormal aircraft conditions with the support of stronger situational awareness.

The tool used to make the electronic content available to the crewmembers on the aircraft is the electronic flight bag, or EFB (Daly, 2009). There are different devices that deliver this capability; for some organizations it is a common laptop computer issued to each crewmember. Some carriers have opted for more elaborate systems connected directly to the aircraft's systems. Some devices are able to detect abnormalities and immediately display on the related courseware as a reference for the crew. At the same time, the technology is allowing crewmembers to access the latest safety-related information, no longer being limited to the time constraints of paper-based delivery. For flight-related publications, any time saved is a benefit to safety, preventing the use of dated or inaccurate information. They are learning more and in more detail, faster and more accurately than in previous practice.

In building a training prescription for personnel, the basis has largely been driven by regulatory requirements established by the relevant authority and broad-brush topics selected by training program developers. Much of these requirements are somewhat generic subjects and time requirements, designed to ensure that personnel receive a core amount of content. Normally this training is delivered on an annual cycle.

Distance education has enabled the ability to deliver training that goes beyond minimum requirements and identifies needs in real or short time and facilitates the rapid delivery of training content to address those needs. There are a series of programs that serve as inputs to developing the learning content, which include safety information reporting and data-centric training programs. Voluntary safety programs come in several forms, one of which allows employees to report potential safety issues to the program confidentially. Another consists of using aircraft flight data recording obtained during revenue flight operations to monitor for undesired conditions, such as the aircraft being too high or too fast when on approach. When reports or flight data indicate a concern, training program managers are able to develop a training solution and scale the delivery to an individual or to personnel who are assigned to a particular aircraft fleet or to the entire company if necessary. It also removes, to some extent, the need to disrupt operations to bring the personnel into the training center to accomplish the training. Data-centered training programs, through an analysis of personnel performance, can also indicate a need for additional focused learning. The results can be aggregated into profiles, and that information sent to training program managers for consideration in calling for additional training or revision of the current program to address indicated areas of performance declines (FAA, 2006).

APPLICATIONS TO A DIVERSE SEGMENT

The process of obtaining training in general aviation has remained much the same during the period of massive technology proliferation of the past three decades. While it has not changed substantially, the benefit has been an improvement in the training experience through new electronic resources available to pilots around the world. This access has extended also to the flight instructors and small flight school training providers, who in the past did not have access to the volumes of information and research nor the resources to build multimedia courseware. Many of these resources have been incorporated into existing training practices and are generating innovations in aviation training.

One of these innovations is cue-based training, that is, training that teaches situational awareness to flight crews through learning references by which to identify areas of poor weather before continuing flight into the conditions. Wiggins and O'Hare (2003) conducted a study of cue-based training and its effect on decision making using computer-based training. The risk associated with an actual in-flight study of the subject made such observations unsafe to conduct. The research focused on pilots flying in deteriorating weather conditions, long known to be a factor in aircraft accidents, and the ability of flight crews to identify the condition and respond (FSF, 2009). Results indicate that the cue-based training did have a positive effect on the ability of pilots to identify poor weather conditions and avoid them. This is especially of concern in southeast Alaska, where aircraft often operate at lower altitudes in quickly rising terrain. The ability to deliver this type of simulation through personal computers addresses two issues: first, the ability to physically access a high fidelity resource for pilots based in isolated areas, and second, improving the ability for the crewmembers to more quickly identify deteriorating conditions and respond favorably.

Industry organizations have reached out to their members through distance education in an effort to improve the state of safety in their respective industry segment. The general aviation accident rate tends to be one of the highest, which can in part be attributed to the past quality and currency of the training resources available. There has been a dramatic digital divide between the organizations with training resources capable of developing and delivering distance learning and the individual airplane pilot, typically having access to much more limited resources in comparison. The content developed by the Air Safety Foundation of the Aircraft Owners and Pilots Association was recently recognized by the United States Distance Learning Association as representing some of the best practices in distance education. With unrestricted access available to the public via the Internet, this is one indication of the improvement in content that is being made available to aviators.

The availability of high quality distance learning resources for primary and advanced initial training for pilot certificates and ratings are increasing. Initial offerings consisted of videocassettes; however, once distributed, the content was infrequently updated. This has evolved into interactive courseware available via the Internet, constantly being updated by the vendors and serving the learning needs of a traditionally underserved segment of the industry.

Distance methods are also impacting air traffic management and the redesign of airspace around the world. The Federal Aviation Administration (FAA) in the United States and Eurocontrol, with its 12 member states including Belgium, The Netherlands, Luxembourg, and Germany are in the process of redesigning how air traffic is managed. The FAA NextGen program and the Eurocontrol program Single European Sky Air Traffic Management Research (SESAR) are developing new equipment and procedures to optimize the flow of air traffic to eliminate delays for aircraft. The FAA operates over 500 air traffic control facilities of various types where over 14,000 air traffic control specialists work; and EUROCONTROL, with its central facility located at Maastricht (The Netherlands), houses just under 700 air traffic control professionals. Each organization has it challenges: the FAA in the number of facilities and personnel, and EUROCONTROL in its coordination with the dozens of different air traffic facilities in the multiple countries it must coordinate with. In such an effort, distance education methods allow for personnel to be trained on changes quickly, and promote coordination among the air traffic controllers and managers between facilities and countries.

In the airline industry, distance learning technology has thus been in use for some time. In 2006, Etihad Airways installed a learning management system (LMS) for use in the training of their company personnel. The carrier, based in Abu Dhabi and serves 66 destinations around the world in 43 countries. The LMS was built to deliver training to their flight crews, cabin crews, and maintenance personnel working in their worldwide system. The system encountered both cultural and technical issues in its operation. In Pakistan, when the computer displayed an instruction to follow, users would ignore the message, not wanting to take direction from a machine. System design issues also impacted performance, using a single proxy server, for example. There were also instances of instantaneous high demand for a single piece of content. In the development of content, the company learned that the internal creation of courses was highly expensive; external development with strong quality control proved to be more cost effective (Bratengeyer, Albrecht, & Schwartz, 2010).

SUPPORTING SYSTEM SAFETY

In August 2009, a helicopter conducting a sightseeing flight collided with a single-engine aircraft in the skies above New York City. All nine passengers and crew aboard both aircraft were fatally injured in the event. The preliminary findings of the National Transportation Safety Board investigation expressed concern for flight procedures associated with the Hudson River airspace (NTSB, 2009). In response to these findings, the FAA established a Special Flight Rules Area in an effort to mitigate the risks associated with the accident (Federal Register, 2009).

The airspace over and around the New York City area is some of the most complex in the world. The environment is challenging for even the most experienced pilot to manage. The creation of a Special Flight Rules Area (SFRA), while addressing the identified risks associated with the airspace, added requirements that those operating in the airspace would need to be familiar with. Further complicating the issue was the highly diverse general aviation users of the airspace.

The campaign to educate pilots about the new requirements was facilitated, with distance learning playing a major role through the FAA Safety Team and their electronic learning system (FAA, 2009). This group within the FAA applies their resources toward general aviation operators. In this example, the focus was on developing training for pilots planning on using the airspace. Through the online resource, a course detailing the new rules and procedures associated with the SFRA, general aviation pilots or anyone with an interest could have the information necessary to operate in the new airspace.

Systems like the FAA Safety Team learning system also work to target available training to the desired audience. When new courses are added to the site, users are notified via e-mail of the offering. This proactive marketing of training available for consumption by pilots is unlike past practices. The notification system can advise subscribers of industry information and more critical or time-sensitive information such as safety alerts or notices to airmen (NOTAMs) on issues affecting flight.

CONCLUSIONS

The use of distance learning for training within the aviation industry will continue to grow. Technology has supported improved safety through training throughout the development of the industry and is likely to continue to do so. Distance method is the newest element that is becoming a common feature of training programs; many in aviation have been already exposed to some distance learning. This is during a time described as the safest in aviation history (Aviation Safety Oversight, 2007). Much discussion has been dedicated to the notion of delivering training when it is needed, "just in time." In this field, needs are often identified following an event—after the fact. Training is programmed based on experience and the known technical nature of the operation before a flight. Aviation professionals are trained in these areas prior to service; the goal becomes developing methods of predictive training, learning how to identify the hazards at all levels, and translating those into risk mitigation through timely training. Today the time between when a risk is identified and training is administered to mitigate that risk is too great. Adapting change management to analyze environmental interfaces and translating those findings into a training prescription has the potential to change how we think about all training.

The state of distance education in aviation, while resulting in many benefits, is also based on a determination that a distance education method will be as good as a traditional approach. As we become more comfortable with the application and capabilities of distance education, we will engage a form of "smart" distance education, employing the techniques because they are best practices and not merely because the capability exists.

COMPREHENSION AND APPLICATION QUESTIONS

1. This chapter discusses major changes in what and how people in the airline industry learn. Emphasis is on developing methods of predictive training. What are important topics that should be included in developing methods of such predictive training, and how can these be addressed in distance education?

2. Imagine that you have been asked to list the key areas for research on the training of pilots and its use of distance education. What are, in your opinion, the key questions to be asked?

RESOURCES FOR FURTHER EXPLORATION

Air Safety Foundation. (2009). *Interactive courses*. Available at http://www.aopa.org/asf

Lee, A. T. (2005). *Flight simulation: Virtual environments in aviation*. Burlington, VT: Ashgate.

Wensveen, J. G. (2007). *Air transportation: A management perspective* (6th ed.). Burlington, VT: Ashgate.

REFERENCES

Aviation Safety Oversight. (2007). *Testimony of the Federal Aviation Administration Assistant Administrator for Aviation Safety, Nicholas Sabatini.* Hearing before the Committee on Transportation and Infrastructure. 108th Congress.

Bratengeyer, E., Albrecht, C., & Schwartz, H. (2010). Deployment of elearning in the airline industry. Retrieved from http://aicc.org/joomla/dev/images/files/lms-deployment-final.pdf

Cohen-Bürki, J., Go, T. H., Chung, W. W., Schroeder, J., Jacobs, S., & Longridge, T. (2003, April). *Simulator fidelity requirements for airline pilot training and evaluation continued: An update on motion requirements research.* Proceedings of the 12th International Symposium on Aviation Psychology, Dayton, OH.

Daso, D. A. (2003). *Doolittle: Aerospace visionary.* Dulles, VA: Potomac.

Daly, K. (2009, May 28). Electronic flight bags set to deliver on their promise. *Flight International.* Retrieved from http://www.flightglobal.com/articles/2009/05/28/327074 /electronic-flight-bags-set-to-deliver-on-their-promise.html

DeAngelo, J. (2000). *The Link flight trainer: A historic mechanical engineering landmark.* Binghamton, NY: ASME International.

Directorate General of Civil Aviation, India. (2011). *Passengers carried by scheduled domestic airlines.* Retrieved from http://dgca.nic.in/reports/pass-ind.htm

Federal Aviation Administration. (2006). *Advanced qualification program* (Advisory Circular 120-54A). Washington, DC: Author.

Federal Aviation Administration. (2009). *FAA safety team.* Retrieved from http://www.faasafety.gov

Federal Register. (2009). *Proposed modification of the New York, NY, class B airspace area and proposed establishment of the New York class B airspace Hudson River and East River exclusion special flight rules area.* 74 Fed. Reg. 47495 (to be codified at 14 C.F.R. Part 93).

Flight Safety Foundation (FSF). (2009). Controlled flight into terrain (CFIT). Retrieved from http://flightsafety.org/current-safety-initiatives/controlled-flight-terrain-cfit

Glines, C. V. (1980). *The saga of the air mail.* Manchester, NH: Ayer.

MacCorkle, J., & Wong, T. (2009). *General aviation in China: Seizing growth opportunities.* Washington, DC: Booz.

National Transportation Safety Board (NTSB). (2009). *Safety recommendation A-09-82 through A-09-86.* Washington, DC: U. S. Government Printing Office.

Official Airline Guide (OAG). (2007). *OAG end of year review for 2007.* Bedfordshire, England: UMB Aviation.

Wiggins, M., & O'Hare, D. (2003). WeatherWise: Evaluation of a cue-based training approach for the recognition of deteriorating weather conditions during flight. *Human Factors, 45,* 337–445

CHAPTER 19

NEW TOOLS FOR LEARNING

The Use of Wikis

Evgeny Patarakin and Lya Visser

Although the wiki was introduced about 15 years ago, the role of wikis in education and training has been explored only in the last few years. In this chapter, we offer a limited overview of the uses of wikis in education and training. After a short introduction, the wiki as a knowledge-building tool is discussed, followed by information on how wikis can be used as learning tools and support strategies in instructional environments. By drawing on a number of examples of wiki use in education and training, we identify opportunities and obstacles of wikis for learning. The chapter concludes by asking whether wikis are a realistic option to improve the learning landscape or merely are a kind of luxurious add-on.

Trends and Issues in Distance Education:
International Perspectives, Second Edition, pp. 285–297
Copyright © 2012 by Information Age Publishing

INTRODUCTION

It is increasingly recognized that student interaction and communication is very important in learning (Visser, 2005), as is reflective thinking (Baron, 1981). In the last decade, the field of digital learning has improved in important ways, specifically with advancements in content, technology, and pedagogy. Autonomous and collaborative learning processes have received more attention and flexibility (INSPIRE, 2010).

An important goal of education is helping students learn to create ideas and to evaluate these in a critical way. This means that increasingly, attention is paid to opportunities and tools that allow students to participate in finding, creating, editing, and classifying digital learning objects. These activities are organized on the basis of networked communities and knowledge sharing. In such communities, facilitators and students work together with texts, photographs, diagrams, and programs. Various terms are used to describe this new pedagogy of network collaboration, such as metadesign and culture of participation and discussion.

In the last decade, many different forms of collaborative electronic communication have been launched. Some are based on instant messaging, others use e-mail or HTML-based content—the list of tools continues to increase. One form of communication that is showing great promise, and has grown impressively in recent years, is the wiki.

WHAT IS A WIKI?

A wiki (derived from the Hawaiian term for *quick*) is essentially a small piece of server software that allows users to freely create and edit Web content using any web browser with no special tools. A wiki is the simplest online database that could possibly work. No HTML or programming knowledge is needed to contribute to a wiki (Rupley, 2003). Wiki technology offers important opportunities for, among others, distance education, nonformal education, business training, and government decision-making processes. It makes collaboration around common projects possible, facilitates brainstorming, and is easy and cost-effective. A wiki is thus a collection of interconnected recorded items. The founder of the wiki technology, Ward Cunningham, named the environment wiki because of the fast hypertext interaction.

We can think about wikis as a learning management system (LMS), although some wikis look more like a personal learning environment. The majority of wiki software (also known as a wiki engine) is free and open-source software and is developed collaboratively. MediaWiki is the most popular of these and is also used to run Wikipedia, the world's largest online encyclopedia, as well as many other (nonprofit) educational projects.

Users of wikis do not need to know the programming commands of the hypertext language. The text of any article or page of recorded items is interpreted by the program as hypertext. The special wiki checking device looks through the texts of all the pages in search of patterns before they get to the browser. If a match is found, the device checks whether a page of that name already exists in the database; in that case, it makes a reference on that page; if such a page does not exist, then reference is made to the creation of a new page. The wiki user first makes a link to a new page and then creates the new page. Wikis can be used for various purposes, such as a personal information manager; a collaborative tool for organizing teamwork on collaborative projects; and a database, such as a repository of collective experience (Pearce, 2006).

WIKIS SUPPORTING LEARNING

Before we discuss practical uses of wikis, we should talk about one of the building blocks of the wiki as a learning tool: learning objects. Learning objects (LOs) facilitate the use of educational content online. They are interoperable, accessible, reusable, and durable (Rehak & Mason, 2003). Learning objects can be based on electronic text, simulations, Web sites, Java applets, or other sources that can be used in learning, and then have a profound impact (McGreal, 2004). These objects make it possible for students, individually and/or collaboratively, to tackle complex content. Learning object repositories contain the learning objects and provide access. One can compare their use to You-Tube or Flickr, which are also open, free, and reusable. Wiki pages and different types of images, audio, and other objects uploaded to wikis are reusable objects. There are many other types of digital learning objects, including Scratch projects (http://scratch.mit.edu), NetLogo models (http://ccl.northwester.edu/netlogo/models/index.cg), Alice objects (http://www.alice.org/index.php?page=gallery/index), and Google 3D Models (http://sketchup.google.com/)

Students are not only challenged to search information blocks, but also to create, write, and/or program their own new blocks, and then synthesize this information and evaluate it critically. Distance education provides an interesting opportunity to include digital objects as the learner hopefully operates in a self-responsible and collaborative learning environment. Wikis can greatly facilitate collaboration between members of a team, class, or study group and can be used to plan activities and to organize personal data to create a set of documents that reflect the shared knowledge of the learning group (Augar, Raitman, & Zhou, 2004).

Wikis are increasingly seen as an effective way of organizing training and teaching, offering an environment conducive to learning and support. Instructors, but also others, can look through collaborative writing and postings, and edit all existing pages, and identify partners who are working on the same topic, check how far they have come, and make suggestions on how they can collaborate. In the next section, we discuss examples of the use of wikis in learning environments and how they can enhance teaching and learning.

Wikis can be used in student teaching and learning situations in various ways. Teaching materials can be expanded and annotated, and teachers and students can leave notes and comments on lectures, projects, and/or exercises. Wikis can facilitate not only communication, but also the collaborative finding, shaping, and sharing of knowledge, all of which are essential properties in an educational context (Reinhold, 2006).

If we agree that knowledge work is essentially collaborative, wikis are a good way to learn to collaborate. According to Hooper and Hannafin (1991), collaborative and cooperative learning should be encouraged in order to facilitate constructivist learning. To make an impact on a wiki, real content should be offered; anything else will be removed. It means that anyone can play, but that only good players last.

Wikis are also great for encouraging critical thinking, defined by Paul and Elder (2008) as self-directed, self-disciplined, self-monitored, and self-corrective thinking. Critical thinkers ask vital questions and pose important problems that are precisely formulated. As critical thinkers should be open-minded, they communicate effectively and efficiently with others to find solutions to complex problems.

Bergin (2002) suggests a variety of uses for wikis, such as student homepages, anonymous feedback, frequently asked questions, and hints about the infrastructure of the course. Wikipedia's School and University Projects page proposes to use wikis in the classroom to provide students with exercises on how to edit and publish content on Wikipedia.

Evaluation of courses and instructors may also be considered a support strategy to help improve performance. In order to improve course evaluation, students at Brown University make use of CAW, the Course Advisor Wiki, a place for students to collaboratively write reviews of courses they have taken. CAW gives readers a flexibility to articulate their impressions and enables richer reviews that combine multiple impressions and perspectives (Wikis in Education, n.d.)

It is surprising that (business) training and higher (distance) education have been slow to explore the possibilities of wikis in the classroom (Evans & Nation, 2007; Majchrzak, Wagner, & Yates, 2006).

Publications on the use of wikis in (distance) education have only recently begun to appear. The main applications of wikis in distance learning relate to writing assignments, carrying out group projects, individual projects with peer review, group authoring, class/instructor reviews, and research tasks. Students can use a wiki to develop research projects, with the wiki serving as ongoing documentation of their work. No e-mail exchange is needed (http://www.wikinomics.com/blog/index.php/2008/03/26/wiki-collaboration-leads-to-happiness/). Effort is then necessary to coordinate these edits so that every participant's work is equally represented. In this endeavor, collaboration (but also coordination and management skills) are important. Finally, the edited document may appear on a single central wiki page. Hegarty et al. (2006) identified adoption as the basic measurement of successful realization of specific e-learning strategies. One effective way to measure implementation is diffusion—how many users, courses, faculties, and training groups have adopted the new tools—this, combined with sustainability, seen as how many courses, programs, companies, and/or organizations make the technology an integral part of their teaching, training, and learning objectives. In the next section, we offer a few examples of the use of wikis in education and training.

APPLICATION OF WIKIS

Collaborative Work on a Virtual Study

Schoolchildren in Nizhniy Novgorod, Russia, read an article by Russian naturalists about rare and disappearing breeds of animals and plants. In the article, they found information about a butterfly named Apollo. They learned that it lays its eggs on a large crassula, or "harel cabbage" (Sedum telephium L.). To find out more about this, they clicked on the reference to the harel cabbage to see what it looks like. When they then read that Apollo lives in the Pustinskiy nature reserve in a Russian swamp, they looked up this swamp. It is very helpful that they only needed to select as internal references the basic words about which they wish to learn more.

This example shows us how a wiki can be used to elaborate a project in a variety of ways. We may select those words/concepts that we want to use as a basis and about which we wish to learn more; MediaWiki dictates that we include the key words in two square brackets. Following up on the example given, we can use [[crassula]] or [[Pustinskiy nature reserve]]. If a botanist has already written and placed an article about [[crassula]] in a wiki, the reference will work immediately and will lead us to the text. If he or she intends to write an article in the future, there will be a deferred reference that can be activated in the future. The beauty of wikis is that we do not have to bother a botanist with questions about how to find the file containing his or her article on the crassula or to ask a geographer about the name of the swamp. We just abide by the way wikis work—the article is named and has a reference. And if a geographer then writes another article about the swamp in question, the link becomes activated automatically—nothing else has to be done.

The Letopisi Encyclopedia

Another project from Russia is the Letopisi project, created in 2006. It initially aimed at setting up a hypertext educational encyclopedia based on MediaWiki. It is open and accessible to all interested participants. The project is based on modern theories of collective knowledge acquisition and teaching, and strongly supports Papert's (1991) constructionism theory: that people study better when they are involved in the creation of something specific and have objectives for activity that they can reflect on. The result of the project is open and accessible to all interested learners (http://letopisi.ru).

Letopisi promotes the use of new technology and networked open-access web services in Russian education and has established "hubs" in more than 30 regions using wiki technology.

The use of wikis for combined activity does not necessarily imply an environment in which people work closely together or closely interact with what others on the site are doing. To keep participants motivated, facilitators can look through all the existing pages, find general themes and references, show participants what potential partners are working toward, and make suggestions on how to cooperate. Not all projects were

Table 19.1. Example of "Movement" in the Letopisi Project Between 2006 and 2010

Year	Users	Pages	Articles	Edits	Files
2006	1,358	9,236	3,236	35,251	2,488
2007	5,024	50,627	20,022	200,550	5,030
2008	23,033	105,697	32,455	436,660	42,318
2009	31,682	146,433	38,673	665,964	60,797
2010	43,150	172,551	41,553	809,681	71,023

equally successful; some were discontinued soon after take-off. The following features of successful projects have been identified:

- A large and stable audience, combined with more than one leader, from different regions of the area to increase stability.
- A simple start, but adding "building blocks" of knowledge to facilitate constructing a larger-scale project.
- Stimulating and collaborative activities in which to engage wiki participants.
- A constant refining of learning objects and of constructing "new" articles from existing ones.

WIKIS IN OPEN AND DISTANCE LEARNING ENVIRONMENTS

Icaza, Heredia, and Borch (2005) describe the use of wikis in an online graduate course using project-oriented immersion learning. Distance learners were immersed in the environment of a fictional online publishing house that hired them to develop e-books, tutorials, and websites online. Collaboration was a first condition, and students faced a number of challenges to work together and to design, develop, and create an interesting product.

Collaborative activities play a crucial role in finding errors and testing hypotheses. Discussions, feedback, collaborative work, and knowledge sharing create conditions for the development of critical-thinking skills. Students can be told what critical thinking is or can be put in an environment in which critical thinking is an indispensable condition. The existence within the hypertext of different points of view makes wikis an important tool for developing critical-thinking skills. Tools for creating collective hypertexts facilitate, provoke, and encourage joint writing, annotating, and discussion of articles. It is often found that it is necessary to constantly negotiate, refine, and improve the titles of articles and the category tags.

This short overview is not complete without mentioning what Lamb (2004) calls the most common pedagogical application of wikis, namely, as a teaching and writing tool both in traditional and distance education. Lamb asserts that wikis

- stimulate writing ("fun" and "wiki" are often associated);
- provide a low-cost but effective communication and collaboration tool;

- promote the close reading, revision, and tracking of preliminary work;
- discourage product-oriented writing while facilitating writing as a process; and
- ease students into writing for a wider audience.

Lamb is seconded by Barton (2004), who offers excellent examples of use and misuse of wikis: *Joe plans to write his entire novel in a wiki. He will then seek to publish it with a commercial publisher.* According to Barton, this is doomed to failure. A novel is not a collaborative project, and Joe will probably get upset if someone starts changing his text. Then, will it really be his novel if other people make changes to it? NOT a suitable project for a wiki. Another example: *Hubert plans a wiki reference guide. His hobby is making model aircraft. He thinks it would be helpful to create a wiki to get in touch with other hobbyists and learn something himself.* This is, according to Barton, an IDEAL project for a wiki. Hubert can invite everyone he knows to visit and contribute to this tightly focused wiki. Most hobbyists will probably have special information or advice that could easily be organized and edited to build an effective and highly useful wiki.

Wikis have made brainstorming easier. The ease of revising different editions, the quick way of retrieving information, and the possibility of quickly improving instruction in wiki environments is promising and may be explored in more depth.

WIKIS IN BUSINESS

Corporate environments also have identified wikis as a knowledge-sharing and learning tool. There has, however been little research to find out how corporate wikis are used; what, if any, are the benefits of their use; and how sustainable they are. Majchrzak et al. (2007) conducted a survey involving 168 corporate wiki users. Their findings revealed that the older the wiki is, the more frequent the access, the greater the number of lurkers, and also the greater the number of participants. It seems that companies succeed at using wikis if they get beyond a pilot project of a couple months. After this, corporate wikis seem to be sustainable. Respondents to the survey also indicated that wikis helped to improve work processes and knowledge reuse. Benefits of using wikis included improved communication processes, as the more expert participants "taught" novel participants how to carry out tasks that required novel solutions. Learning was also created through sharing opinions, participating in discussions and tasks, and through the recognition that added knowledge must be credible and used.

Among the possible uses of wikis is distribution of standards, guidelines, and progress reports shared by large groups of employees, often employed in different countries. In an interesting article, Hendrix and Johannsen (2008) describe how Shell International introduced a wiki in 2007. Its goal was to be a community-managed internal encyclopedia aimed at sharing information and collaborative activities and to make up-to-date knowledge from Shell's different disciplines easily available to staff all over the world. It now contains training materials, technical handbooks, and a number of nontechnical subjects. By March 2008, there were about 30,000 registered ShellWiki users, and between 550 and 700 new users register every month. ShellWiki captures large parts of Shell's knowledge and information. Shell considers the ease of interaction an effective and efficient tool for sharing knowledge and for encouraging learning. ShellWiki's program leader mentioned that users like ShellWiki because it's accessible, easy to update, and the content promotes learning and knowledge sharing. The Global Knowledge Management team at Shell is offering wiki training sessions, but most wiki contributors seem to be able to train themselves.

Wikis are gradually rewriting the rules of collaboration in a variety of companies such as Xerox, Disney, and Sony. Aside from project management, companies use wikis for wide-ranging activities such as tracking industry news, setting meeting agendas, posting corporate policies, and even creating strategy documents.

WIKIS IN GOVERNMENT

Wikis can also play a role in improving government functioning, strengthening democracy, and empowering citizens (Noveck, 2009). The Russian Ministry of Education decided in April 2010 to use a crowd-sourcing platform for evaluating and editing the draft for the new Law on Education. The chapter, consisting of 11 articles and 71 items, was used for testing. The objective was to invite Russian experts, teachers, and parents to participate in an in-depth analysis of the proposed law by evaluating and discussing its overall concept and the various sections, thereby soliciting ideas and suggestions for improvement. Each law item was posted on the site as a separate page. After registration, users could vote in favor or against the draft, make comments or suggestions, and propose their own versions. User-created item versions were also open for comments and evaluation. During the testing period from June to August 2010, a total of 512 users, more than enough for realizing the goals, joined the community and participated in discussing and evaluating the law.

EDUCATIONAL OPPORTUNITIES OF WIKIS

In the examples of wiki use, we noted the following advantages. These are only some of the opportunities wiki offers.

1. Interaction. Contrary to a blog, usually written by one person and available to many people, a wiki is a website that is interactive, meaning that a user can add postings and permits the content to be edited by other users (unless the wiki is only available for a specific community).
2. Ease of access: Creating websites is simple. No prior knowledge of HTML programming is necessary.
3. Ongoing development of documentation and summaries of readings and discussion: Prescribed readings, group projects, and discussions can be stored and consulted by others.
4. Knowledge base: Instructors and trainers can share reflections, documentation, and course evaluations.
5. Evolving documents and publications: Wikis make it possible for instructors and learners to follow the development of a given task or a project, post feedback, and make the task a learning project and not a one-time product.
6. Facilitating international cooperation: People from all over the world can work on the same document, publishing effort, report, or group assignment.

EDUCATIONAL OBSTACLES OF WIKIS

The use of wikis has, next to a variety of advantages, also drawbacks. In this chapter we identified the following:

1. Easy edit: If access is not regulated, everyone can edit, leading to chaos and a decrease in quality. Obligatory registration is thus recommended.
2. Spam and other negative practices: Using a log-in for editing, as WikiEducator does, is good practice.
3. Access: Wikis require reliable Internet connectivity in order to participate. Internationally, important groups may thus be excluded.

CONCLUSIONS

We have explored the use of wikis in several contexts and how they can be used to support learning and teaching. In summary, wikis

- reinforce the search for and the sharing of knowledge;
- increase interactions;
- provide opportunities for two-way learning;
- require thoughtful planning, creativity, and enthusiasm from participants;
- have the potential to improve efficiency in a variety of environments; and
- are particularly suited for tasks that require negotiated meaning.

We also noted that wikis may still be underused in distance/e-learning environments, in some sections of training, in nonformal education, in out-of-school learning, and in literacy programs. We concluded that more research should be done. We do, however, expect that use of wikis will increase the coming years.

COMPREHENSION AND APPLICATION QUESTIONS

One of the tasks of educators is reducing the diffusion of useless or misinformation. Wikis often allow for quick page creation, which may promote loose interlinking and as such, can cause confusion or leading students in the wrong direction.

1. To what extent do you agree with this statement? Is there a way to avoid such confusion?
2. "Bob Dylan once said: 'I accept chaos. I am not sure whether it accepts me.' Moving instruction into the chaotic wiki medium presents challenges on a number of fronts. Tracking work created in wiki spaces can become a logistical nightmare, and course management can spin out of control quickly if pages are allowed to spawn without some set of protocols to regulate or index them. Attribution of individual work can be difficult, and an environment in which students (or even nonstudents) are invited to rework content further complicates matters. Seemingly minor contributions to a collaborative document may have major effects, effects that may be near impossible to assess fairly or even to detect" (Brian Lamb [2004] in EDUCAUSE Review Magazine). How is this a pessimistic view of Wiki use in instruction? What can be done to create order in what Lamb calls the "chaos"?

RESOURCES FOR FURTHER EXPLORATION

Bower, M., Woo, K., Roberts, M., & Watters, P. (2006, July). *Wiki pedagogy: A tale of two wikis*. Paper presented at the 7th International Conference on Information Technology Based Higher Education and Training, Sydney, Australia.

REFERENCES

Augar, N., Raitman, R. & Zhou, W. (2004, December). *Teaching and learning online with wikis* (pp. 95–104). Proceedings of the 21st Australasian Society for Computers in Learning in Tertiary Education (ASCILITE) Conference, Perth, Australia. Retrieved from http://www.ascilite.org.au/conferences/perth04/procs/pdf/augar.pdf

Baron, J. (1981). Reflective thinking as a goal of education. *Intelligence, 5*(4), 291–309

Barton, M. (2004). *Embrace the wiki way!* Retrieved from http://www.mattbarton.net/tikiwiki/tiki-print_article.php?articleId=4

Bergin, J. (2002, June). *Teaching on the wiki web.* Proceedings of the 7th Annual Conference on Innovation and Technology in Computer Science Education, ITICSE'02, Aarhus, Denmark, 195. Retrieved from http://portal.acm.org/citation.cfm?id=637610.544473

Evans, T., & Nation, D. (2007). Globalization and emerging technologies. In M. G. Moore, (Ed.), *Handbook of distance education* (pp. 649–660). Mahwah, NJ: Erlbaum.

Hegarty, B., Penman, M., Coburn, D., Kelly, O., Brown, C., Gower, B., … Suddaby, G. (2006). E-learning adoption: Staff development and self-efficacy. Retrieved from http://www.ascilite.org.au/conferences/sydney06/proceeding/pdf_papers/p156.pdf

Hendrix, D., & Johannsen, G. (2008). *A knowledge sharing and collaborative platform.* Retrieved from http://www.ikmagazine.com/xq/asp/sid.0/articleid.0A6EF1DD-1D6A-4CD0-94EA-DC872A5A708E/eTitle.Case_study_Shell_Wiki/qx/display.htm

Hooper, S., & Hannafin, M. J. (1991). Psychological perspectives on emerging instructional technologies: A critical analysis. *Educational Psychologist, 26,* 69–95.

Icaza, J. I., Heredia, Y., & Borch, O. (2005, July). *Project oriented immersion learning: Method and results.* Proceedings of ITHET 6th Annual International Conference, Juan Dolio, Dominican Republic.

INSPIRE. (2010). [Web site]. Retrieved from http://www.virtuelleschule.at/wiki-inspire/index.ppphp/Home

Lamb, B. (2004. September/October). Wide open spaces: Wikis, ready or not? *EDUCAUSE Review, 39*(5), 36–48.

Majchrzak, A., Wagner C., & Yates D. (2006, August 21–23). *Corporate wiki users: Results of a survey.* Proceedings of the 2006 International Symposium on Wikis, Odense, Denmark.

McGreal, R. (2004). Learning objects: A practical definition. *International Journal of Instruction and Distance Education, 1*(9), 21–32.

Noveck, B. S. (2009). *Wiki government: How technology can make government better, democracy stronger, and citizens more powerful.* Washington, DC: Brookings Institution.

Papert, S. (1991). Preface. In I. Harel & S. Papert (Eds.), *Constructionism, research reports and essays, 1985–1990* (p. 1). Norwood, NJ: Ablex.

Paul, R., & Elder, L. (2008). *The analysis and assessment of thinking.* Retrieved from http://www.criticalthinking.org/page.cfm?PageID=497&CategoryID=68

Pearce, J. (2006). Using wiki in education. *The science of spectroscopy.* Retrieved from http://www.scienceofspectroscopy.info/edit/
index.php?title=Using_wiki_in_education

Rehak, D., & Mason, R. (2003). Keeping the learning in learning objects. In A. Littlejohn (Ed.), *Reusing online resources: A sustainable approach to e-learning.* London, England: Kogan Page.

Reinhold, S. (2006). WikiTrails: Augmenting wiki structure for collaborative, interdisciplinary learning. *Proceedings of the 2006 International Symposium on Wikis* (pp. 47-58). New York, NY: ACM 47-58.

Rupley, S. (2003). *What's a wiki?* Retrieved from http://www.extremetech.com/
article2/0,3973,1072778,00.asp

Visser, L. (2005). The promise of m-learning for distance education in South Africa and other developing nations. In Y. L. Visser, L. Visser, M. Simonson, & R. Amirault (Eds.) *Trends and issues in distance education: International perspectives* (1st ed.). Greenwich, CT: Information Age.

Wikis in Education. (n.d.). Retrieved from http://www.scienceofspectroscopy.info/
edit/index.php?title=Using_wiki_in_education

CHAPTER 20

FORMALIZING VIRTUAL LEARNING SPACES FOR REFUGEE YOUTH

Barbara Zeus

This chapter highlights the educational needs of refugees trapped in long-term encampment and presents viable solutions. It argues that while much has been achieved regarding the provision of basic education for refugee children, refugee youth, although showing the necessary commitment and having the time to attain higher education, are often left without the resources, opportunities, and freedom their nonrefugee peers enjoy as they transition into adulthood and look for meaningful ways to support themselves. Refugees' right to higher education has been largely ignored on the basis of such a provision, presenting insurmountable practical and political challenges. The chapter also shows how distance education has been employed in numerous nonformal settings such as refugee camps, creating hope and self-esteem for young refugees. It will present case studies from Palestinian refugee camps, from Somalia, Chad, Kenya, and the Thai-Burmese border where higher educational needs of refugee youth have been addressed in different forms, from vocational training to academic secondary and tertiary education. It will be argued that modern technology can create virtual spaces to access higher education for neglected and marginalized groups such as refugees who are living in resource-poor and remote areas. Despite some obvious challenges, successful distance education programs could be impulsive for rethinking refugee higher education and could mark the beginning of an innovative discourse on a global system of accreditation through a formalized distance mode.

Trends and Issues in Distance Education:
International Perspectives, Second Edition, pp. 299–309
Copyright © 2012 by Information Age Publishing
All rights of reproduction in any form reserved.

REFUGEES AND REFUGEE EDUCATION

Refugees often spend their time in exile in specially designed and separately administered camps where they are dependent upon external humanitarian agencies for the most basic needs. They have limited access to employment and services such as health care and education. Although education has been a fundamental operational aspect of the United Nations High Commissioner for Refugees (UNHCR) since the 1960s, only the last two decades have seen a tremendous push in implementation. The World Declaration on Education for All (EFA), adopted in 1990, highlighted the right to education for the excluded. It helped move education to the center of the international development agenda and on the priority list of governments. A growing pool of research and a gradual reorientation among governments and agencies have generated recognition for education as the "fourth pillar" of humanitarian response alongside food, shelter, and health.

The vast majority of refugees in the world, an estimated 10 million, are trapped in protracted refugee situations with no prospect of a solution, and mostly in developing-nation host states (Loescher, Milner, Newman, & Troeller, 2007; UNHCR, 2009). UNHCR defines such a situation as "one in which 25,000 or more refugees of the same nationality have been in exile for five years or more in a given asylum country" (2009, p. 7). The average length of displacement is now 17 years. Surveys show that education is valued and prioritized by crisis-affected communities themselves because of its stabilizing effects (INEE, 2009a; Sinclair, 2002). In long-term crises, education efforts can play a role in helping communities understand and cope with their fate and can be a critical part of providing meaning in life (Alzaroo & Hunt, 2003; Nicolai, 2003; Smith & Vaux, 2003). Lack of education, on the other hand, can lead to further destabilisation (Davies, 2004) and make young people more vulnerable to criminal activity (Women's Refugee Commission, 2000).

The realization that only with education can refugees be expected to adapt themselves to their new surroundings, to integrate into their host society, and to become self-reliant is not a recent one (Dodds & Inquai, 1983). And yet, it is clear that education, like any other intervention, cannot be a panacea. When education does not lead to further studies or employment opportunities, it may raise false expectations, and this frustration can similarly drive youth into the arms of military recruiters (Boyden & Ryder, 1996). Holistic approaches to refugee education and well-being are thus essential.

In the next sections, the gaps in the education in emergencies sector that are to be found in an imbalanced emphasis on different educational levels and beneficiaries are discussed, followed by a potential role for distance education to counteract this imbalance. Then, case studies from different countries on vocational and secondary as well as tertiary education are analyzed, while the last section highlights the challenges ahead.

TIME TO ADDRESS EDUCATIONAL NEEDS OF REFUGEE YOUTH

While great achievements can be celebrated in moving the issue of refugee education forward, millions of children in situations of conflict and crisis are still left without access to quality education. These children grow up to be young adults in refugee camps with few opportunities to find employment or further their studies. Youth (between 12 and 24 years) account for approximately 35% of the world's refugees. Yet only 5% of UNHCR-supported education programs are at the secondary level, 6% at nonformal, and 3% at vocational and tertiary levels (UNHCR, 2003) (some 10% are at preschool and 76% at primary level). This is a severe neglect of refugee youth's needs. Youth make the transition into adulthood in camps where they lack the freedom and opportunities their non-refugee peers enjoy. As they make this transition, they look for meaningful ways to support themselves and their families, often finding they are "constrained by camp boundaries and forced to remain idle" (Berg, Stern, & Rajkotia, 2009, p. 1).

Donors' rationale for a lack of support for higher education often has been that these refugee youth live in temporary shelters and are better off searching for further education opportunities once their lives have stabilized and a durable solution for the refugee "problem" has been found. This, however, is usually subject to regional and world politics. Scholarships for refugees are scarce. Upon resettlement to third countries, youth are often forced to shoulder great responsibility in taking up adult roles and pursue livelihood activities to sustain their families. This again leaves them with few opportunities to resume or take up further studies (Zeus, 2009).

While there seems to be general agreement that higher education can serve the refugee community and contribute to the qualification of human resources needed in all three durable solutions (voluntary repatriation, local integration, and resettlement) alike (UNHCR, 2007), the paradox is that while time for study during protracted encampment is abundant, there are few opportunities and little financial means for youth to access learning opportunities that would allow them to prepare for different future scenarios (Zeus, 2009).

This underlines the need to create higher-learning opportunities for refugee youth. How distance education can assist is discussed in the next section.

A ROLE FOR DISTANCE EDUCATION IN REFUGEE SITUATIONS

The unsustainable character of refugee situations often makes traditional higher education an impossible endeavor. This generates room for a potential role for distance education. Its flexibility allows students to continue their education without leaving their homes or their social and family responsibilities. Distance education becomes a popular option, particularly for young people, as through it, higher education can be made more accessible and inclusive. It has been described to have the potential to "democratize education" (Dodds, 2005, p. 118). Young refugee students studying via distance education may develop valuable human capital and take on social and economic leadership roles in crisis-affected communities.

While teachers and learners are no longer necessarily divided through an asynchronous mode (Thomas, 1996), there is often not only a spatial separation, but also a sociocultural one. Existing face-to-face materials have often been adopted and adapted to different contexts. This, however, demands great care and skill in the adaptation process and requires a participatory approach to be able to design and develop culturally appropriate, high quality, and relevant course materials. Students should be able to be in touch with administrators and counselors about course duration, admission procedures, and choices of programs and courses. Appropriate assessment and evaluation processes are also very important. Logistical challenges to distance courses for refugees still exist, but the technological revolution (Bates, 2008; Dodds, 2005) has brought radio, television, and even Internet access close to refugee camps and displaced populations.

UNESCO (2006) suggests possible steps and provides guidance for the development and implementation of distance education programs in challenging situations. These steps reach from conducting surveys of existing programs to determining relevant forms and methods of open and distance learning, deciding on target groups, reviewing and adapting existing materials for piloting and revising, and finally implementing and monitoring the program.

The next section presents some examples of distance education opportunities in protracted refugee situations.

SOME EXAMPLES OF REFUGEE DISTANCE EDUCATION

Distance Education in the Palestinian Territories

The first large-scale application of distance education in a refugee situation was for Palestinian refugees beginning in the 1960s (Inquai, 1993).

The idea to establish a regional Open University was born in 1975 based on the needs of the Palestinians for higher education and taking into consideration that students are often unable to reach campuses due to unpredictable checkpoints, closures, and curfews restricting travel. In 1991, Al-Quds Open University began its educational services as an independent public university headquartered in Jerusalem. It now caters to around 60,000 students in 24 educational regions and centers distributed all over the West Bank and Gaza Strip. It is the biggest noncampus university in the Palestinian territories (QOU, 2010).

Vocational Training Through Distance Education in Somalia

Distance education programs are used at various educational levels in refugee contexts around the world, but remain an underused tool (INEE, 2009b). It has been a popular option for refugees in teacher training (Moran & Rumble, 2004; Robinson & Latchem, 2003). One example is the Institute for In-Service Teacher Training (IITT) in Somalia, which provided basic and advanced teacher training programs to refugees, using print materials, audio tapes, self-help study groups, and face-to-face tutorials (Bradley, 2001). Based on these experiences, new programs have been developed (UNESCO, 2006), and there is evidence that young women, particularly, benefit from such courses (Burge, 2009).

Secondary Distance Education in Chad

For postprimary education, a successful program has been developed for Sudanese refugee students in Eastern Chad by the Refugee Education Trust (RET) in collaboration with the International University of Africa (IUA, Khartoum). Secondary Education through Distance Learning (SEDL) stands out as a program that provides both refugee and local young people with accredited secondary education and options to specialize in the arts or sciences. Since the launch of the program in 2007, a total of 357 students have completed their secondary education, which they had to discontinue because of war in Darfur. The students engage in self-study with the help of manuals provided by the IUA and meet to get learning support from subject animators and to share knowledge. In recognition of the students' excellent results, the IUA has reduced fees, offered scholarships to the best students, and opened examination centers in towns near the refugee camps (RET, 2009). This is an example of a certification initiative by an NGO-university partnership, which proves how complicated negotiations can bear fruit and allow refugee youth to gain accredited education on which to build their futures (Kirk, 2009).

Tertiary Distance Education in Kenya

Another such example is the Jesuit Refugee Service's (JRS) Tertiary Distance Learning program in the Kakuma refugee camp in Kenya through the distance learning program of the University of South Africa (UNISA). It started in 1998 aiming at fulfilling higher education needs of students whose university education was interrupted due to displacement. Despite logistical challenges related to delivery of materials and the harsh conditions in Kakuma, refugee students are reported to do very well academically (JRS, 2005).

Tertiary Distance Education in Thailand

A further encouraging example is that of Burmese refugees in Thailand studying for tertiary degrees from the Australian Catholic University (ACU) since 2004. The program follows a mixed mode, combining online learning with on-site tutorial support. Approximately 20 students, one fifth of the initial applicants, are studying for a diploma in liberal studies. Among previous cohorts, 17 graduated in business studies and 5 in theology, allowing them to gain an internationally recognized qualification.

Students show a great desire to further their education and extend their horizons despite some obstacles. An evaluation of the pilot project (Purnell, 2006) raised concerns about the relevance of course content for camp students, who are largely unfamiliar with Western cultural concepts and learning techniques, if the material is taken out of the Australian context with little prior modification and adjustments to the sociocultural context of refugee camps. Changes suggested by this evaluation have been implemented as far as possible. Further, offering a liberal-studies degree reflects a rapprochement to students' preference for social science-related subjects and a more participatory approach that is often missing in educational programming for refugees.

Having lost some students to resettlement, it has been argued that educational programs at such a high level facilitate and encourage brain drain. This, however, goes hand-in-hand with a brain gain for the local community. Research into ways that past graduates have used their qualifications revealed that all respondents are working for the common good in the camps, while three graduates received scholarships for entry into universities in the United States and Australia on the basis of their ACU qualification (D. MacLaren, personal communication, March 2010).

Purnell (2006) found a high degree of student motivation, a necessary component of a successful distance education course. Internal reviews state the impact of the project on the students was both psychological and life-transforming. Students' self-esteem and confidence grew as they had improved their English language skills and become a vital link between local communities, host country authorities, and the international donor community. This has empowering effects not only for the graduates but the refugee community at-large (Zeus, 2009). Being awarded an internationally recognized degree also bestows upon refugee students a lost sense of official personal identity. The provision of higher education via distance learning out of the nonformal refugee camp context has thus been effectively formalized.

The success of this pilot program has taken the world community one step closer to being able to provide long-term refugees around the world with accredited tertiary education. Research is under way to ascertain the feasibility of setting up similar programs assisting refugees in other contexts to access tertiary education online.

THE NEED FOR A GLOBAL SYSTEM OF REFUGEE DISTANCE EDUCATION

We have seen how distance learning can take on a powerful role, and these "remote" degrees present a way toward ensuring equal opportunities for camp students in accessing higher education and could be a feasible, low-cost education option for refugees. However, distance education is not a panacea and cannot be a quick and inexpensive fix to silence refugees' quest for higher education, but needs to be carefully planned, implemented, and supported on a continuous basis (Bayham, 2008; Dhanarajan, 2008; Saint, 2003). It offers a realistic and practical alternative, but should go alongside other efforts. Learning and teaching materials have to be relevant and adapted to the specific sociocultural context of the refugee situation if efforts are to have a positive sustainable impact upon the lives of young refugees. The quality component in refugee situations is as important as in other contexts (Kirk & Winthrop, 2007).

Unable to leave the camps to broaden their intellectual horizons, refugees can access a whole new range of experience and knowledge through distance education. Courses may contribute to making refugee youth critical thinkers, and alongside increased livelihood opportunities, can provide them with an area of initiative to attain self-reliance rather than presenting a burden to host nations and the international community. Youth are a powerful force within refugee and displaced communities. Displaced young people face all the complexities and uncertainties of any adolescent, but with very few opportunities to gain the knowledge, skills, and experiences required for a healthy transition to adulthood.

With few options and prospects for the future, young people are vulnerable to recruitment into armed groups, one of the few viable options for employment, or they may resort to dangerous jobs, criminal activity, and drug and alcohol abuse (Perlman Robinson & Alpar, 2009). The skills youth develop and positive activities they participate in during displacement will prove useful once the community finds a durable solution. With the time refugees spend in exile increasing, we cannot afford to put young refugees' education on hold until such solutions are found. If the developmental needs of youth in protracted displacement are not duly addressed, we risk losing a whole generation not only to idleness but also to poverty and instability (Berg et al., 2009).

The provision of higher education to long-term refugee youth has for too long been a low-profile activity. Despite distance education being promoted by UNESCO, its potential remains relatively unexplored (INEE, 2009). More robust research on the impacts of higher educational programming for refugee youth, and in particular the role distance education could play, is needed. It is time for the international humanitarian aid regime to acknowledge refugees' right to higher education and their right to develop to their fullest potential. This is the prerequisite for establishing a global system of refugee higher education at a distance. Lessons learned from distance education programs like the ones presented in this chapter could stimulate an innovative discourse on refugee higher education, alternative accreditation mechanisms through a formalized distance mode, and for finding a long-needed balance in the education in the emergencies sector. Applying a holistic approach to educational programming in protracted displacement will improve the quality of life for all.

COMPREHENSION AND APPLICATION QUESTIONS

1. To what extent do you think refugees have the unconditional right to higher education?

2. In your view, what is the role of education in crisis contexts? What do you think would be the impacts of excluding refugees and other crisis-affected populations from higher education?

3. Are you familiar with any of the refugee contexts described in this chapter? Choose an example of a refugee situation and try to find out more about refugees' lives and living conditions.

4. Work in groups on a project designing a distance learning program in that refugee context. You could think of teacher training or university undergraduate programs. What are the main conditions of designing such a program (in terms of actors, processes,

and environment)? What would be key components of your educational program? Would you integrate face-to-face components? How would you integrate cultural awareness and soft skills such as critical thinking or peace-building components in your distance education program?

RESOURCES FOR FURTHER EXPLORATION

Bates, T. (2001). *National strategies for e-learning in post-secondary education and training*. Paris, France: UNESCO.

McKay, V., & Makhanya, M. (2008). Making it work for the south: Using open and distance learning in the context of development. In T. Evans, M. Haughey, & D. Murphy (Eds.), *International handbook of distance education* (pp. 29–50). Bingley, England: Emerald Group.

Newby, L. S. (2009). *Education, technology and conflict: The use and perceptions of the Internet in Palestinian higher education*. Oxford, England: University of Oxford, MSc Education (e-learning).

REFERENCES

Alzaroo, S., & Hunt, G. L. (2003). Education in the context of conflict and instability: The Palestinian case. *Social Policy & Administration, 37*(2).

Bates, T. (2008). Transforming distance education through new technologies. In T. Evans, M. Haughey, & D. Murphy (Eds.), *International handbook of distance education* (pp. 217–236). Bingley, England: Emerald Group.

Bayham, L. (2008). *Opening windows to success: Improving Liberian refugees' access to higher education*. Durham, NC: Duke University, Hart Leadership Program, Sanford School of Public Policy.

Berg, C., Stern, L., & Rajkotia, R. (2009). *Youth livelihoods in protracted displacement: Approaches and challenges*. Washington, DC: Youth and Livelihoods Team, International Rescue Committee.

Boyden, J., & Ryder, P. (1996). *The provision of education to children affected by armed conflict*. Unpublished paper. Oxford, England: Refugee Studies Centre.

Bradley, J. (2001, July 18). *Distance education for refugees: The IEC experience*. Paper presented at the NGO Education forum, Cambridge, England.

Burge, R. (2009). *Impact study: People affected by conflict*. London, England: Comic Relief.

Davies, L. (2004). *Education and conflict: Chaos and complexity*. New York, NY: RoutledgeFalmer.

Dhanarajan, G. (2008). *Open distance learning in the Asia-Pacific region: A snapshot*. Paper presented at the Asia Pacific Sub-regional Preparatory Conference for the 2009 World Conference on Higher Education "Facing Global and Local Challenges: The New Dynamics for Higher Education," Macao SAR, China.

Dodds, T. (2005). Open and distance learning for developing countries: Is the cup half full or is it still half empty? In Y. L. Visser, L. Visser, M. Simonson, & R. Amirault (Eds.), *Trends and issues in distance education: International perspectives* (1st. ed., pp. 117–130). Greenwich, CT: Information Age.

Dodds, T., & Inquai, S. (1983). *Education in exile: The educational needs of refugees.* Cambridge, England: International Extension College.

INEE. (2009, June 20a). *INEE Newsletter: Celebrating World Refugee Day.* Retrieved June 20, 2009, from www.ineesite.org

INEE. (2009b). *Strategic research agenda for education in emergencies, chronic crises, early recovery & fragile contexts: Draft.* Oxford, England and New York, NY: The Conflict and Education Research Group at Oxford University & The Teachers College International Education Research Group.

Inquai, S. (1993). Refugees and distance education. In K. Harry, M. John, & D. Keegan (Eds.), *Distance education: New perspectives.* New York, NY: Routledge.

JRS. (2005). *Horizons of learning: 25 years of JRS education.* Rome, Italy: Jesuit Refugee Service.

Kirk, J. (Ed.). (2009). *Certification counts: Recognising the learning attainments of displaced and refugee students.* Paris, France: UNESCO, IIEP.

Kirk, J., & Winthrop, R. (2007). Promoting quality education in refugee contexts: Supporting teacher development in northern Ethiopia. *International Review of Education, 53,* 715–723.

Loescher, G., Milner, J., Newman, E., & Troeller, G. (2007). *Protracted refugee situations and peacebuilding.* Tokyo, Japan: United Nations University.

MacLaren, D. (2010). Tertiary education in pursuit of the common good: The Thai-Burma border experience (Unpublished manuscript). Faculty of Arts and Sciences, Australian Catholic University, MacKillop Campus.

Moran, L., & Rumble, G. (Eds.). (2004). *Vocational education and training through open and distance learning.* London, England: Routledge.

Nicolai, S. (2003). *Education in emergencies: A tool kit for starting and managing education in emergencies.* London, England: Save the Children.

Perlman Robinson, J., & Alpar, S. (2009). Hope and opportunities for young people. *Forced Migration Review, 33,* 50–52.

Purnell, S. (2006). *RTEC/ACU evaluation.* Mae Sot, Thailand: ZOA Refugee Care Thailand.

QOU. (2010). *QOU establishment, history, mission, general goals.* Retrieved from http://www.qou.edu/homePage/english/index.jsp?pageId=4

RET. (2009). *The success of the RET secondary education through distance learning (SEDL) as exemplified through exams.* Geneva, Switzerland: The Refugee Education Trust.

Robinson, B., & Latchem, C. R. (Eds.). (2003). *Teacher education through open and distance learning.* London, England: Routledge.

Saint, W. (2003). Tertiary distance education and technology in sub-Saharan Africa. In T. Damtew & P. Altbach (Eds.), *African higher education: An international reference handbook* (pp. 93–110). Bloomington: Indiana University Press.

Sinclair, M. (2002). *Planning education in and after emergencies.* Paris, France: UNESCO, International Institute for Educational Planning.

Smith, A., & Vaux, T. (2003). *Education and conflict*. London, England: Department for International Development.

Thomas, J. H. (1996). *Distance education for refugees: The experience of using distance and open learning with refugees in Africa, 1980–1995, with guidelines for action and a directory of in formation*. Cambridge, England: International Extension College.

UNESCO. (2006). Open and distance learning. In UNESCO (Ed.), *Guidebook for planning education in emergencies and reconstruction*. Paris, France: UNESCO - International Institute for Educational Planning.

UNHCR. (2003). *World Refugee Day 2003: Information Kit*. Geneva, Switzerland: UNHCR.

UNHCR. (2007). *The Albert Einstein German academic refugee initiative fund (DAFI)*. Retrieved from http://www.ofadec.org/CRITERES-DAFI.pdf

UNHCR. (2009). *2008 global trends: Refugees, asylum-seekers, returnees, internally displaced and stateless persons*. Geneva, Switzerland: UNHCR.

Women's Refugee Commission. (2000). *Untapped potential: Adolescents affected by armed conflict—A review of programs and policies*. New York, NY: Women's Refugee Commission.

Zeus, B. (2009). *Exploring paradoxes around higher education in protracted refugee situations: The case of Burmese refugees in Thailand*. Unpublished master's dissertation, Institute of Education, London, England. Retrieved from http://www.ineesite.org/uploads/documents/store/ZEUS_B-MADiss-FINAL.pdf

CHAPTER 21

LEARNING LANDSCAPES

European Perspectives on
Distance Learning in Prisons

Anita Wilson

This chapter offers an overview of some of the issues, successes, and concerns related to distance learning for prisoners. It refers to the practices and philosophies of various nation-states across Europe and draws in particular on the experiences of prisoners in England and Scotland. It begins with an overview of educational provision in prison prior to teasing out some of the reasons that may force reluctance on the part of prison authorities to offer distance learning to inmates. This is followed by an overview of some pan-European initiatives, including vignettes from contrastive systems. By drawing on the lived experiences of prisoner-students, obstacles and opportunities related to distance learning they encounter are discussed. The chapter concludes by asking whether distance learning is a realistic option or merely a luxurious add-on to the educational package offered to prisoners.

Trends and Issues in Distance Education:
International Perspectives, Second Edition, pp. 311–323
Copyright © 2012 by Information Age Publishing

INTRODUCTION

> Landscapes, then, are not just superficial visual expressions of relationships
> between society and nature, but the creative products of specific social con-
> texts and power relations. They may thus be the result of historical and
> ongoing struggle, and indeed certain landscapes may come to symbolize
> struggle between certain groups. (Holloway & Hubbard, 2001, p. 114)

The learning landscapes of people in prison are not particularly scenic.
They are often sites of struggle and fraught with problems. For the majority of prisoners, the view is barren and unappealing. Available alternatives
are limited. For those who set out on prison learning journeys, their path
can be littered with obstacles: lack of appropriate courses, insufficient
resources, or the threat of sudden transfers between prisons. For some,
negative or uncomfortable memories, such as childhood difficulties in
school or home life, have to be overcome before they can progress further
along their chosen academic path. For those who persevere, their efforts
may be rewarded, not only enhanced by certification and accreditation,
but also with a broadened philosophical perspective that can impact on
their current and future life.

The road trodden by distance learners, however, is particularly underused and difficult to find—off the beaten track—and strewn with its own
particular difficulties, such as lack of information, support, funds, and
appropriate technologies. Those who make this journey do so for a variety of reasons, in a variety of ways. However, despite various "boulders in
the road," some prison systems and related organizations help to clear the
path, find innovative ways to assist such a journey, and encourage students to persevere and reach a broader view of the world.

In this chapter, I focus on issues that relate primarily to the United
Kingdom, but also on examples from Scandinavia and Eastern Europe,
and draw on the real-world experiences of prisoner students themselves.

AN OVERVIEW OF EDUCATION AND LEARNING IN PRISON

For students in the outside world, the path to education, at least in
Europe, is relatively easy. Governments encourage and support students
to continue with their education by making grants and loans available.
The need for qualifications is driven home as a protective factor in the
current climate of limited jobs and unequal opportunities. For students in
prison, Council of Europe Recommendations (1989) state that their right
to education is fundamental, that access should be the equivalent to that

in the outside world, and that prison education should aim to develop the whole person.

In England and Wales, education and training are seen as possible pathways out of re-offending (National Offender Management Services, 2005). This view is reflected in many other parts of Europe (ISOFOL, 2010). Nevertheless, in many countries, less than 25% of prisoners have access to education. Moreover, in England and Wales, capacity to offer education and training is limited, as is the range of courses offered (Prisoners Education Trust, 2009a). Further and higher education provision is eclipsed by a continued focus on improvement of prisoners' basic skills, and higher-level programs have been the first to fall in the drive to cut costs (Duguid, 2000).

Distance learning in prison ranges across Open University (OU) academic courses, through vocational training such as Stonebridge Associated Colleges, to Learndirect, one of the U.K.'s biggest providers of distance learning. Both Open University and Learndirect have had considerable success in U.K. prisons. According to the OU (2010), in 2009, around 1,400 prisoners were taking OU courses, while a recent Ufi/Learndirect report (2009) suggests that, between 2008 and 2009, almost 5,000 offenders took almost 10,000 Learndirect courses. The current prison population in the U.K. is around 85,000 (National Offender Management Services, 2005).

It seems logical to assume that distance learning would be well-suited to the prison landscape. Prisoners have time on their hands, come from an eclectic range of educational backgrounds, and have a variety of needs and interests. However, few countries take the view that prison education should be comprehensive enough to integrate distance learning into their provision.

Within Europe, in documentation such as the Report on the Right to Education for Persons in Detention by the UN Special Reporter (Munoz, 2009), distance learning is barely mentioned. It is often restricted to provision for higher level learners and those wishing to take university-level courses (Prison Service Order 4201, 1999). Moreover, higher education in prison is rarely included in prison education budgets. Scotland is a notable exception; higher level learning such as Open University courses undertaken by modular distance learning units, are paid for by the Scottish government. South of the border in England, however, the Offender Learning and Skills Service for England and Wales is not tasked to fund distance learning. Prisoners with no personal funds must apply to an outside agency such as the Prisoners Education Trust for support. While this agency does everything in its power to assist—awarding 2,300 grants per year for a variety of distance learning courses—demand far exceeds supply, with 200–300 applications per month (Prisoners Education Trust,

2009b). To be fair, however, there are a number of understandable inter-related reasons why prisons are often unable to be supportive of distance learning.

THE RELUCTANCE OF PRISONS TO SUPPORT DISTANCE LEARNING

Across Europe, penal policy is currently focused on the prevention of re-offending and on the rehabilitation of the offender. The success of such policy rests on the premise that learning should relate primarily to training, which in turn can lead to employment. Interventions thus take employability and employment-related skills as their objectives. Courses focus on CV writing, interview skills, and vocational training such as bricklaying, plastering, and joinery. Many prisoners have low levels of literacy and numeracy (European Parliament, 2001), and most emphasis and financial backing is given to addressing and rectifying these gaps and needs.

However, the two issues of employability and low level of skill seem to presume that, on release, most prisoners will be placed on the outer limits of the employment landscape, taking up what might be termed lower level manual employment. This effectively deflects attention and resources away from more academic or specialist employment-related studies that prisoners might want to take.

Second, prisons, understandably, have security as their priority, and this has an impact on approved, and increasingly essential, technology. In the United Kingdom, for example, Internet access is still considerably limited for prison personnel, with restrictions on degrees of access and availability of computers. Often, even when access is available, prison staff are prohibited from moving beyond the first page on many websites, or from downloading pdf files. In many prisons in the United Kingdom, education staff are forbidden from bringing in memory sticks, CDs, cameras, or DVDs, often the most suitable way of providing supplementary materials and resources for distance learners. For prisoners, Internet access varies. As shown in the vignettes below, some European systems allow access, while others use satellite technology to overcome security difficulties. Other systems, for instance in Sweden, use distance learning through secured platforms for a large proportion of prisoner learning.

In the United Kingdom, Internet access remains extremely limited and terminology currently required to describe e-mail (as "electronically transmitted messages") reflects the fear of reprisal if the media circulated reports that prisoners have e-mail access. The website Email a Prisoner (http://www.emailprisoner.com/) contains the following strong statement:

"Please note—Prisoners do not have access to email and we are NOT developing our service in that direction."

For higher level learners, however, steps are being taken in the U.K. to link prisoners to web-based learning such as the Virtual Campus, with the capacity to secure access to sites that have internal but no external hyperlinks. In addition to offering access to some distance learning courses, material continues to reflect the current focus on employment, with job-related materials, CV writing, and access to information on housing, health, finance, and debt (Pike, 2009). It is also seen that access to the Internet does not guarantee a positive learning experience. While in parts of Scandinavia, the perceived problems of Internet access have mostly been overcome, this does not ensure that learners automatically feel part of a learning community.

Third, while prisoner access to the outside world is rigorously controlled, access to the prison by the outside world is equally constrained. Prolonged in-depth security training must be undertaken, and although distance learning tutors may only be supporting one prisoner, for a short amount of time, they still require supervised contact and thus intensive manpower, which may be seen as a drain on resources and considered impractical. This should not be seen as a criticism of the prison, which has a duty to protect the public, or of the tutors who come into prison to support a student.

Finally, there is the question of funding. In U.K. prisons, for example, prison governors are required to cut their budgets for the next 3 years by 3% (HM Treasury, 2009). While distance learning is funded primarily either by the prisoner or by an outside organization, it still requires some financial input from the prison (usually 10% of the course fee).

In summary, distance learning in prison is complex, and there are understandable reasons why prisons might appear to be unsupportive. Education per se has to be set against other priorities. In parts of Eastern Europe such as Estonia, a high migrant prison population often means that prison tutors must be bilingual, and additional teaching staff who speak other languages may have to be involved. This takes resources away from distance learning. There are some promising developments and productive partnerships illustrating that it is possible to overcome the difficulties presented by dominant policy, security and finance, and offer alternative pathways on prisoners' learning landscapes. While it is not possible to give a comprehensive account of distance learning in prisons across Europe, there is merit in giving a brief overview of some distance learning initiatives before listening to the voices and journeys of learners themselves.

PARTNERSHIPS AND POLICIES:
DISTANCE LEARNING ACROSS EUROPE

At the pan-European level, there have been a number of successful transnational projects focusing on prison education, some of which have included distance learning and the related issue of Internet access. Supported by the European Prison Education Association, and funded through the EU Grundtvig program, the PIPELINE project (http://www.epea.org/) set out to create an e-learning platform that was both secure enough to satisfy prison security requirements and accessible enough for students. It was formed through collaboration between Norway, Denmark, Sweden, the Czech Republic, Slovenia, Germany, Greece, the UK, and Romania. A second project, the Virtual European Prison School (VEPS; www.prisoneducation.org), was a collaboration between Ireland, Greece, Sweden, the Czech Republic, England, Bulgaria, and Norway, and transferred existing good practice around learning from one system to another. It also created a repository of materials in various languages that could be accessed by prisoner learners in countries other than their homeland. A compendium of successful projects has also been collated across Italy (ISOFOL, 2010), including one that linked prisoners in Lazio prison to university lectures.

There are various models of distance learning across Europe that are proving to be successful in overcoming the difficulties presented by lack of Internet access. The two vignettes illustrate this point. Of significance is the approach taken by Russia, which adapted its distance learning technologies to the prison environment (in rather the same way as the SFIDE project referred to earlier). A campus-based college approach to university level education at the Moscow University of the Humanities has meant that students from across Russia and beyond (including prisoners) can meet up virtually, enjoying shared seminars and discussions with their fellow learners. It means that prisoners can feel they belong to an academic "community of practice." Although open to only a small subsection of prisoners, the Russian experience reflects a phenomenon noted elsewhere: that prisoner students are prepared to make the effort, often at considerable personal cost, in order to expand their academic knowledge.

Vignette 1

Distance Learning for Russian Prisoners

Moscow University of the Humanities (MUH) is a state-accredited higher education institution. International recognition of the MUH's diplomas is ensured by issuing of appropriate certificates.

Currently, there are more than 950 branches within the framework of MUH in the territory of the Russian Federation and the CIS countries. There are also branches in the Czech Republic and Bulgaria.

MUH is the only Russian higher education institution possessing satellite information educational technology, which gives an opportunity to arrange a top-quality process of higher education in every geographic destination in the Russian Federation and in a number of other countries. MUH possesses satellite educational television with its own teleport for 24-hour four-channel broadcasting throughout the territory of Russia and the CIS countries. These channels are also used for data transmission. In the near future, 400 of MUH's branches will be equipped with VSAT-teleports (now already 205). This allows organizing high quality broadcasting using two-way satellite connection between branches and Moscow headquarters.

Multimedia computer-based learning products play an important role in the educational process at MUH. For the last 4 years, MUH has designed and developed over 10,000 volumes of learning products.

Currently, there are around 1,600 prisoners studying with MUH in 30 major prisons all over Russia. Each of these major prisons has its own center. We cannot say what are the most popular courses, but we know that law is the most unpopular. Taking into account that in Russia there are around 900,000 prisoners, we can facilitate study for about 10% of them, so the potential is huge.

Information provided by Dmitri Nersesyan, MUH

Vignette 2

Internet Access for Inmates in Norwegian Prisons: IFI

By the end of 2009, a total of 25 prisons got access to the Internet through a national network. By the end of 2010, the other Norwegian prisons joined. According to the Educational and Sentence Act, all prisoners in Norway have a legal right to education. The use of digital tools such as the Internet is an integrated part of the competence aim in the Norwegian subject curriculum. Internet access is also necessary in connection with preparing and writing exams.

We aim at giving access to all sites relevant for educational reasons. The web contains many different ways to communicate. These are the main challenges in the prison such as dealing with surveillance of all traffic.

The solution is based on an Internet divided in categories. An international company is responsible for putting websites into categories. For example, the CNN website (http://www.cnn.com/) would be in the news category and the Google website (http://www.google.com) would be in the category of search engines. The Internet that prisoners in high security have access to is restricted to categories that are considered safe. Other websites are blocked. There is also a communication filter that blocks attempts to send messages out—all plug-ins are blocked. This makes the Internet less interactive.

To make the Internet more useful, we open up for interaction with pedagogical websites by turning on scripts, plug-ins, or other features that block the interactivity. This interactivity is communication with a website and not with people outside the prison wall.

Prisoners in a prison with low security are allowed Internet access without the communication filter, allowing them to follow the normal school outside the prison walls using the learning management system (LMS) of the school in question.

All prisons are connected to a national center from which the correctional service controls the Internet traffic, users, and computers. The center logs who has been surfing, what the prisoner has been viewing, when he visited each website, and on what computer he worked. Even though the center carries out the logging, it is the local security officer at the local prison who reads the logs. The local prison officer knows the prisoners and knows who needs special security attention.

Information provided by Bent Dahle Hansen and Paal Chr Breivik.

LEARNING LANDSCAPES: OBSTACLES AND OPPORTUNITIES

To obtain a more complete picture of the situation, it is important to look beyond partnerships and policies and extend our view to the more detailed learning landscapes of individual prisoners and the journeys they make. I want to draw on the perspectives of prisoners who are engaged or would like to be engaged in distance learning, who have been part of recent prison ethnographies that I have conducted in prisons in the United Kingdom and parts of Europe (Wilson, 2010). There is no question that obstacles stand in the way, but the opportunities offered by distance learning are not underestimated by prisoners.

Obstacles

The obstacles and tensions of competing institutional priorities touched on above are some of the broader issues that impact prisoners who wish to engage in distance learning. The personal experience of individual prisoners illuminates how these obstacles impact on "real life" learning, shedding additional light on some of the more nuanced factors that work for and against. Obstacles include the ever-present security issues and issues of transience, loneliness, and ignorance.

Security: "I Waited Three Months for My Books"

While distance learning is seen by many prisoners as a useful way of occupying their minds as well as their time, the prison—by putting security before well-being—adds additional (and often dispiriting) obstacles. Stuart, for example, had begun a distance learning course in prison. He was subsequently released and took his course books with him. He was then returned to prison, wanted to take up his course once more, but found that because his materials had left the system, they had to be resubjected to rigorous security screening before they were allowed back in the prison and into his possession. This took 3 months to take effect.

Transience: "And Then I Got Transferred Out"

Stories abound of prisoners being "transferred out" to different jails just prior to starting courses, completing courses, or taking exams. The disruptive force of the system for young prisoners has been rigorously documented (Wilson, 2009). Adult prisoners recount similar stories. Moving to a different prison can be a difficult and unsettling time, and be a disruptive force on attitudes to learning.

Loneliness: "I Don't Know if I'm Saying the Words Right"

Distance learning in the "outside world" assumes that students will be able to be online (Finkelstein, 2006), thus becoming part of "virtual" communities. Distance learners in Norwegian, English, and Scottish prisons emphasized that they want to feel part of "something more"—beyond electronic resources. Even though they appreciated being allowed to use a computer, each of them was engaged in individualized study, and they thus formed only a physical community. Opportunities for collaborative discussion—a shared landscape—were limited.

Ignorance: "How Do I Hand In the Assignments?"

Discussions with providers revealed prisoners' ignorance about how learning materials made their way to and from the prison. The process and protocol of learning how to submit an assignment would test the patience, resolve, and ability of any prisoner, no matter how keen. Prisoners often have to write out their assignment by hand, hopefully copy it onto a computer, get it printed out, have a photocopy made for safe-keeping, have enough money to pay for postage, and finally wait for the system to return it.

Opportunities

Given the significant obstacles prisoners who wish to engage in distance learning face, the obvious question is "Why do they still persevere?" Encouraging factors seem to be stability, self-determination, the negation of past experience, and imagined futures.

Stability: "Keeps Your Head Busy"

Prisoners constantly have to respond to the commands of others—when to wake, eat, work, sleep. There is little opportunity to make personal decisions, and there are few articles that prisoners can truly call their own. Thus, intellectual decisions and personal possessions become extremely important. Decisions to take a distance learning course, to study, make assignments take on a particular significance and position the prisoner as a student, that is, "someone other than a prisoner."

Self-Determination: "I Get No Help—I Don't Tick Any of the Boxes"

Prison has its own agenda and its prescribed view of prisoners. It sees them as needing to do certain courses such as training for employment or needing basic education. A higher level distance learner recently said, "I don't do drugs, I don't need literacy, I don't have mental health problems, so I get no courses and no help … I don't tick any of the boxes." Others have the self-determination to apply for courses with seemingly little or no help, such as Stuart who said, "I just filled the forms in myself." Self-determination is part of prison life. Given the barriers that are sometimes put in their way, it requires a special kind of persistence for prisoners to apply for a course and finish it while having limited time, sharing a cell with an often noisy or intrusive mate, and negotiate the submission procedures from a distance.

Negation of Past Negativity: "School was a Nightmare"

Although not all prisoners have poor educational histories, there is no question that some have experienced fragmented schooling, bullying, and trauma, resulting in an incomplete education. This seems to be the case in the UK, for juveniles, young people, and adults alike (Social Exclusion Unit, 2002; Wilson, 2009). Being accepted, undertaking, and completing a distance learning course seems to go some way toward ameliorating these difficult histories. The system, however, through its obsession with testing and targets, appears to do little to decrease past negativity. Prisoners participating in distance learning appear to use their negative experiences as a way of negating past difficulties through present development,

Imagined Futures: "An Entirely New Career Path"

Danny told me that this was his first time in prison. By his own admission he had been affected badly and found it difficult to adjust. He had been grateful for the services of a prison mentor and had decided that he would like to be trained to become one himself. From there, he progressed to taking a distance learning course on counseling. He said it was not something he had "just jumped into" but wanted to go on to help people through "what I've been through," a sentiment echoed by Paul, another prisoner with a difficult history. Danny and Paul's distance learning course had been a catalyst for a desire to set off on an entirely new career path.

DISTANCE LEARNING: A REAL OPTION OR A LUXURY ADD-ON?

Increase in personal development, the widening of experience, and the opportunity for positive self-application, reflected in prisoners' experiences and views above, suggest that distance-learning has the potential to be a real option for prison education, which would contribute significantly to one of the aims of prison, which is to place prisoners within the wider landscape occupied by civil society. However, across Europe, systems still remain somewhat ambivalent toward distance learning in prison and to how much support or profile it should be given. The question remains as to whether distance learning can be given a more central place in the rehabilitative process or whether it will always be seen as a luxury add-on.

Even within the brief discussion presented here, it becomes apparent that distance learning in prison has a wide variety of interpretations and manifestations. It requires the will and collaboration of many different systems and professionals before it filters down to prisoners themselves. In the provision for prisoner students in Russia and Italy, it is an option that links learning to the wider community (albeit available to only a small proportion of prisoners). For other distance learners in prison, it would seem that it is only by good will and good fortune that they succeed in getting prisons to acknowledge that distance learning is a valid option (Wilson, 2010). It is important to keep a perspective and remember where education is situated in the overall prison landscape. Prison education per se, and distance learning in particular, is rarely given precedence, taking its place within a hierarchy that prioritizes security, economics, and competing policies over the benefits and wider purpose of education. However, if distance learning helps to, as prisoners say, "keep your head straight," then it has the potential for wider impact on the emotional health of the entire prison.

If we agree that re-offending can indeed be reduced by employment, education, and improved life chances, the marginalization of distance learning is counterproductive. What better way to fulfill this aim than by encouraging prisoners to engage in learning that is relevant, motivating, rewarding, and encourages positive decision making?

Additionally, if we are truly to subscribe to European recommendations and agree that education is a right, that learning should be appropriate to the individual and be as available as that offered to the wider community, then distance learning should be recognized as bridging a gap that conventional prison education currently does not fill.

Doing nothing in prison is dangerous. As one prisoner, Colin, said, "If you keep pressing the 'off' button, eventually it will stay off." Distance learning offers the chance for prisoners to appraise their learning landscape, identify the various and eclectic educational buttons that distance learning can offer, and as Colin would suggest, keep pressing them "on"!

ACKNOWLEDGMENTS

The author wishes to thank all prisoners and staff who were generous enough to contribute the experiences that informed this chapter and to the Prisoners' Education Trust Learning Matters project for their support.

COMPREHENSION AND APPLICATION QUESTIONS

1. To what extent does "distance" in distance education get another meaning for prison inmates?
2. To what extent can we state that learners in prison are still part of a learning community?
3. What suggestions, not given in the chapter, do you have to improve the academic situation of learners in prison?

REFERENCES

{ref}Council of Europe. (1989). *Recommendations No R (89) 12 of the Committee of Ministers to Member States on Education in Prison*. Retrieved from http://www.epea.org/
index.php?option=com_content&task=view&id=53&Itemid=66

Duguid, S. (2000). *Can prisons work? The prisoner as object and subject in modern corrections*. Toronto, Canada: University of Toronto Press.

European Parliament. (2001). *Meeting of the Committee on Culture, Youth, Education, the Media and Sport for the Committee on Employment and Social Affairs on Illiteracy and Social Exclusion* (2001/2340 [INI]). Retrieved from http://www.europarl.europa.eu/meetdocs/committees/empl/20020107/449043EN.pdf

Finkelstein, J. (2006). *Learning in real time: Synchronous teaching and learning online*. San Francisco, CA: Jossey-Bass.

HM Treasury. (2009). *Budget 2009—Building Britain's future*. London, England: Stationery Office. Retrieved from http://www.hm-treasury.gov.uk/d/bud09_completereport_2520.pdf

Holloway, L., & Hubbard, P. (2010). *People and place: The extraordinary geography of everyday life*. London, England: Prentice-Hall

ISOFOL. (2010). *Results from the national survey on projects supporting the integration of (ex)offenders*. Rome, Italy: Ministero del Lavoro, della Salute E Politiche Sociali.

Munoz, V. (2009). The right to education of persons in detention. *United Nations General Assembly Promotion and Protection of Human Rights, Civil, Political, Economic, Social and Cultural Rights, Including the Right to Development*. Retrieved from http://www2.ohchr.org/english/bodies/hrcouncil/docs/11session/A.HRC.11.8_en.pdf

National Offender Management Services. (2005). *The government's national reducing re-offending delivery plan*. London, England: Home Office.

Open University. (2010). *Online*. Retrieved from http://www.open.ac.uk/platform/news/society

Pike, A. (2009). Virtual Campus: Is this the future? *Inside News, 6*, 1.

Prisoners' Education Trust. (2009a). *NIACE inquiry into lifelong learning: Submission from prisoners education trust*. Retrieved from http://pet.netefficiency.co.uk/fileadmin/user_upload/doc/offender_learning_matters/NIACE_LL_Inquiry_PET_Submission_Sept_08.pdf

Prisoners Education Trust. (2009b). *Annual review*. Mitcham, England: Author.

Prison Service Order 4201. (1999). *Open university: Operation of the Prison Service Scheme*. London, England: HMSO

Social Exclusion Unit. (2002). *Reducing re-offending by ex-prisoners*. London, England: SEU.

Ufi/learndirect. (2009). *Ufi/learndirect response to the National Skills Forum inquiry into skills and inclusion*. Retrieved from http://www.skillsandinclusion.org.uk/downloads/Learn%20Direct.pdf

Wilson, A. (2009). *Interrupted education—interrupted: The criminal justice system as a disruptive force on the educational progress of young people in prison*. Retrieved from www.interruptededucation.org

Wilson, A. (2010). *Goodwill and good fortune: Obstacles and opportunities for level 2 learners in local jails*. Retrieved from http://www.prisonerseducation.org.uk/fileadmin/user_upload/doc/offender_learning_matters/Good_Will__Good_Fortune._Summary_Report._July_2010.pdf

ABOUT THE
SECTION AUTHORS

Lya Visser, PhD, is currently the director of Human Resource Development at the Learning Development Institute and adjunct professor at The George Washington University. Lya earned her master's degree in distance education via distance learning from the University of London. She holds a PhD in educational science and technology from The University of Twente, The Netherlands. Visser's research and publication interests are in the areas of learner support, critical thinking, motivational communication, and performance improvement. She is an international editor of the

Quarterly Review of Distance Education and an adviser to the International Board of Standards for Training, Performance and Instruction (ibstpi). She lived and worked for some 20 years in a number of developing countries. This experience has helped her to see that international cooperation and collaboration, and a spirit of wanting to learn from and with each other, is crucial to living in a more peaceful and just world. Her other areas of interest are English literature, music, and sculpting in stone.

Yusra Laila Visser, PhD, is a faculty member at Florida Atlantic University, teaching instructional technology courses and coordinating the Digital Education Teacher's Academy (DETA). Visser is also an adjunct instructor for the international doctoral program in Instructional Technology and Distance Education, delivered online in Spanish, by Nova Southeastern University. She has served as researcher and vice president for the Learning Development Institute since 2001. Previously, she was an assistant professor in instructional technology at Wayne State University and Florida Atlantic University. She served as project manager for a major distance learning initiative at Florida State University's Distance Learning Office and as program associate for International Programs at Education Development Center. As a consultant, she has served clients including the World Bank, Verizon, the U.S. Department of Homeland Security, and the Netherlands Ministry of Foreign Affairs. Yusra holds a PhD and Master of Science in instructional systems from Florida State University. Her bachelor's degree in international relations is from American University. She has a deep appreciation for art and is a committed amateur photographer.

Ray J. Amirault, PhD, is an assistant professor of instructional technology at Florida Atlantic University (FAU). He holds a BS in computer science from the University of West Florida, and an MS and a PhD in instructional systems from Florida State University. Amirault has an extensive background in both instructional design and instructional technology that spans some two decades. Before assuming an academic role, he held a variety of technical positions in both state and private organizations. Using this technical background to inform his thinking on the role of technology in learning, he subsequently worked on instructional design projects for a wide array of institutions, including the Learning Systems Institute, Verizon, the U.S. Navy, the World Bank, IBM, and many others. Ray currently teaches instructional design and instructional technology courses in FAU's instructional technology program, often in online format. Ray's area of research involves the historical evolution of the university and the manner in which technology has affected, and continues to affect, that history. Ray maintains an active interest in history, is often an "early adopter" of technology innovation, and regularly enjoys reading *The Economist*.

Michael Simonson, PhD, is a program professor at Nova Southeastern University in the Instructional Technology and Distance Education program. He earned his PhD from the University of Iowa in instructional systems. He works with schools, organizations, and corporations to assist them in integrating instructional technology and distance education into teaching and training, and on the development of virtual schools. Simonson has authored four major textbooks dealing with distance education, instructional technology, instructional computing, and instructional media. Simonson has over 150 scholarly publications and in excess of 200 professional presentations dealing with distance education and instructional technology. He is editor of the *Quarterly Review of Distance Education*, *Distance Learning* journal, and *Proceedings of Selected Research and Development Papers* presented at the annual conventions of the Association for Educational Communications and Technology. Most recently he has been an external evaluator of South Dakota's Connecting the Schools and Digital Dakota Network projects, and is a consultant for the U.S. Army Research Institute. Simonson was honorably discharged as a Captain from the United States Marine Corps (R).

ABOUT THE AUTHORS

Ray J. Amirault (ray.amirault@gmail.com) received his PhD and MS degrees in instructional systems from Florida State University, Tallahassee, and his BA in computer science from the University of West Florida, Pensacola. He has worked in the instructional systems field for some 15 years, before which he held a number of technical and computer programming positions. He has authored or co-authored a number of chapters and articles on technology within the university setting and was also a section editor for the first edition of the *Trends* volume. He is interested in the historical development of the university, particularly as regards technology's use in various historical periods of the institution. He is currently an assistant professor in instructional technology at Florida Atlantic University in Boca Raton, FL.

Gary J. Anglin (ganglin@uky.edu) earned graduate degrees in mathematics and instructional systems technology (doctorate) from Indiana University and is currently a faculty member and program coordinator in the Instructional Systems Design Program at the University of Kentucky. He teaches graduate classes in the areas of instructional design, instructional theory, distance learning, and foundations of instructional technology. His research interests include visual representations and learning, distance education, and formative assessment for student learning. He is co-author of two forthcoming book chapters: *Instructional Design for Technology-based Systems*, and *An Analysis of Success and Failures: Focusing on Learner-Content Interactions for the Next Generation of Distance Education*. He is also editor of the book, *Instructional Technology: Past, Present and Future* (3rd ed.).

Zane L. Berge (berge@umbc.edu) is a professor and former director of the training systems graduate program at the University of Maryland, Baltimore County. His scholarship, teaching, and consulting involves distance education and learning in virtual schools, higher education, and the workplace.

Tom Clark (tom@taconsulting.net), president of TA Consulting, provides evaluation and research services for state and federal agencies, universities, museums, school districts, and other organizations. His U.S. Department of Education-funded projects include evaluations for a $9.1 million Star Schools grant (2000–2005) and a FIPSE grant (2010–2012). He served as contractor for team-based evaluations of state virtual schools in Missouri (2007–2009), Mississippi (2008), Georgia (2007), and Illinois (2002), as well as the Chicago Public Schools Virtual High School (2005–2006). Dr. Clark has many related publications, and co-edited *Virtual Schools: Planning for Success* (Teachers College Press, 2005) with Dr. Zane Berge.

Michael Crudden (crudden@fttpartners.com) has been part of the aviation community for the past 20 years. He has worked in both the airline industry and general aviation as an instructor and in corporate aviation as a manager. Crudden is a licensed airline transport pilot and flight instructor. He is currently working in Alaska, focusing on the reduction of aircraft accidents and incidents through safety education and outreach. His interest in performance improvement and training has led to a master's degree in educational technology leadership from The George Washington University. He lives with his family outside of Anchorage.

Palitha Edirisingha (pe27@leicester.ac.uk) is a lecturer in e-learning at the University of Leicester, England. Edirisingha's research and supervision interests include the potential of digital devices and emerging Web-based technologies to support formal and informal learning, and harnessing technologies to improve open and distance learning in developing countries. Edirisingha's research projects include IMPALA (podcasting), WoLF (m-learning), MOOSE (3D virtual worlds), GIRAFFE (wikis), and PELICANS (Web 2.0) (www.le.ac.uk/mediazoo). Edirisingha teaches on the ICT module of the MA in International Education at Leicester, and coordinates BDRA's E-Learning and Knowledge Sharing (ELKS) Community. Edirisingha is an organizing committee member of the Evaluation of Learners' Experiences of e-learning Special Interest Group (ELE SIG). Edirisingha previously taught agricultural extension, and designed low-cost educational material for development in Sri Lanka.

Jennifer Ho (jennifereho@ucla.edu) received her MA in international education policy from the Harvard Graduate School of Education. Following her work in education in China, the United States, and Thailand, she is currently an international technical associate at Education Development Center Inc. (EDC). Her portfolio includes monitoring and evaluating the $79 million USAID-funded Decentralized Basic Education 2 (DBE 2) project in Indonesia, covering programming in teacher professional development, the improvement of school learning environments, student assessment, ICTs, distance learning, interactive audio instruction, and primary-level reading. In addition, Ho conducts cross-country research for EDC's international programming, most recently with respect to the use of ICTs in education and teacher beliefs about early-grade reading instruction.

Andrea Hope (ahope@hksyu.edu) is the associate academic vice-president of Hong Kong Shue Yan University, where she has particular responsibility for academic accreditation and quality assurance. Prior to taking up her present position, she served as education specialist (higher education) at the Commonwealth of Learning in Vancouver, British Columbia, Canada. After more than 20 years of international experience in both distance and face-to-face institutions of higher education, she continues to research and write on quality assurance in higher education and to seek new ways to support the development of an affordable institutional-quality culture that responds to the expectations of internal stakeholders and external accreditors, and ensures the delivery of an educational experience that fits students to excel in a globalized world.

Ansie Minnaar (minnaa@unisa.ac.za) is a staff member in the Institute for Open Distance Learning (IODL) at the University of South Africa in Pretoria, South Africa. With more than 20 years of experience in higher education and research supervision, she is responsible for the postgraduate research program at IODL. Minnaar's research interests include student support in ODL, technological innovations in learning, metacognition, research mentoring, and supervision of postgraduate students. She has authored various articles regarding job satisfaction, management of health services, HIV and AIDS in the workplace, and online learning. She has also published a number of academic books on related topics.

Josep Monguet (jm.monguet@upc.edu) is an engineer and industrial designer, and is professor at Barcelona Tech-UPC (Universitat Politècnica de Catalunya), a researcher at the i2Cat Foundation (Advanced Internet), an associate researcher at SICTA s.l., member of the executive board of

BCD (Barcelona Centre for Design) and the executive board of ADP (Association of Professional Designers), as well as a guest lecturer at universities in Mexico, Colombia, Venezuela, and Portugal. He was previously vice chancellor at Universitat Politècnica de Catalunya, director of the Industrial Design Programme and the Multimedia Programme at the UOC (Open University of Catalonia) and UPC, and director of the multimedia laboratory at UPC. He is the coordinator of the design and systems PhD program. His professional and research activity is focused on innovation in business models based on the application of ICT and design.

Cynthia Moos (cynthia.moos@gmail.com) recently earned an MA in project management of humanitarian and cultural affairs form Université de Provence, France, after a specialization in communications (Exchange program—Loyola University of Chicago). She gained knowledge about developing countries' issues during her master's program as she participated in organizing a conference on education and training of teachers in sub-Saharan Africa. She loves traveling, discovering other cultures, and experiencing intercultural communications. Moos has just started to work in a communication agency and works with Muriel Visser-Valfrey on some thrilling international development projects.

Gary R. Morrison (gmorriso@odu.edu) received his doctorate in instructional systems technology from Indiana University and is a professor and graduate program director in the instructional design and technology program at Old Dominion University. His research focuses on cognitive load theory, instructional strategies, K–12 technology integration, and distance education. He is author of two books: Morrison, Ross, & Kemp's *Designing Effective Instruction* (6th ed.) and Morrison & Loather's *Integrating Computer Technology into the Classroom* (4th ed.). He has written over 25 book chapters and over 40 articles on instructional design and educational technology. Morrison is the editor of the *Journal of Computing in Higher Education* and is on the editorial boards of *Computers in Human Behavior,* and *Quarterly Review of Distance Education.*

Wai-Kong Ng (ngwkong_1@yahoo.com.sg) was a professor of instructional technology at the University Sains Malaysia for over 20 years, after which he joined the Wawasan Open University Malaysia as the Director of Educational Technology. He heads a team of instructional designers that work with course coordinators and course writers to develop print and digital-learning course materials. He is an active researcher in supports for enhancing learner experiences and retention in a distance education environment. He participates in capacity building of instructional design skills and ICT applications for all modes of instruction in a variety of locations in Asia. Wai-Kong has been an active presenter and has published in a variety of international journals.

Evgeny Patarakin (patarakin@gmail.com) is an associate professor in the department of science education of the Nizhny Novgorod Pedagogical University in Nizhny Novgorod, Russia. His research interests are in the area of hypertext, collaborative activities, and using of multi-agent models in education. Dr. Patarakin is also a coordinator of Letopisi, an educational network, and of Mobile and ubi-learning, a scientific project. In addition to having authored two books on education in Russian: *Social Interaction and Learning*, and *Network Communities and Learning*, Patarakin has published a number of articles in English. He received awards for his work from the Heritage Foundation Mendeleev and from the Soros Foundation.

Pedro Reis (preis@ufp.edu.pt) is an associate professor at the Faculty of Human and Social Sciences at Fernando Pessoa University, Porto, Portugal, pedagogic coordinator of UFP-UV (Virtual University), co-founder and researcher at the Centre for Computer-produced Texts and Cyberliterature Studies, and researcher of the project Literature, financed by the Portuguese Foundation for Science and Technology. He developed a postdoctoral research project on e-learning with the cooperation of the Program in Instructional Technology and Distance Education at Nova Southeastern University, Florida. He is currently a consultant on e-learning for the United Nations organizations UNITAR and IAEA. He is subdirector of the magazine *Cibertextualidades* (Edições UFP). His main research interests are cyberliterature, humanities computing, and e-learning.

J. Michael Spector (jmspector007@gmail.com) is chair of learning technologies at the University of North Texas. His recent research is in the areas of intelligent support for instructional design, system dynamics-based learning environments, assessing learning in complex domains, distance learning, and technology integration in education. Dr. Spector served on the International Board of Standards for Training, Performance and Instruction (ibstpi) as executive vice president; he is on the executive committee of the IEEE Learning Technology Technical Committee and is past president of the Association for Educational and Communications Technology (AECT). He is the editor of the Development Section of *Educational Technology Research & Development*, and he serves on numerous other editorial boards. He co-edited the third and fourth editions of the *Handbook of Research on Educational Communications and Technology*, and has more than 100 journal articles, book chapters, and books to his credit.

Hetal Thukral (hthukral@edc.org) received her MA in international education from The George Washington University. Since then, Thukral has worked to implement technology-based education projects in India, Pakistan, and Guyana for over 8 years, including over 6 years of experience in monitoring and evaluation. In this capacity, Thukral has conducted student and teacher assessments for a variety of technology-based teacher and student interventions, which deliver high-quality instructional materials via radio, television, and computer. Thukral is currently pursuing a doctorate degree at the University of Maryland, College Park, in measurement and statistics with an applied focus on education policy. Thukral has also co-taught a graduate-level course on quantitative research methods at the University of Maryland, College Park.

Ricardo Torres Kompen (rtorres@citilab.eu) is a researcher in the field of technology-enhanced learning and multimedia. He holds both a BS (1991) and an MS (2000) in chemical engineering, and has been working as a teacher in higher education institutions since 1996. Currently a PhD candidate in multimedia engineering at the Universitat Politècnica de Catalunya, his thesis focuses on the personalization of learning through the use of multimedia and technology. He works as e-learning cluster coordinator for Citilab, a foundation based in Cornellà-Barcelona, Spain, where he coordinates the Digital Orchard project, whose aim is helping teachers implement ICT-based methodologies in the classroom. He was the local organizer for the PLE Conference 2010 (Barcelona, Spain).

Jennifer A. Linder-VanBerschot (Jennifer.vanberschot@ucdenver.edu) is an instructional designer for a large contractor and is an adjunct professor for University of Colorado, Denver. She received her PhD degree from the University of New Mexico in the Organizational Learning and Instructional Technology (OLIT) Program. She is interested in the use of social software to promote interaction across cultures and between international learning communities. She has also conducted educational research and evaluation on the topics of leadership, English language learners, instructional design, and classroom instruction.

Ai Ping Teoh (apteoh77@hotmail.com) is a senior lecturer at the Graduate School of Business, Universiti Sains Malaysia (USM). Her current research and expertise areas include e-learning, enterprise risk management, quality assurance, e-business, and cloud computing. She has presented papers at conferences and published research articles in journals. Prior to joining USM, she was one of the pioneer academics of Wawasan Open University and has served as the deputy dean and senior lecturer for the School of Business and Administration. She has about 10 years of experience in the industry, previously working in multinational corporations and a consulting firm dealing with the SAP R/3 ERP system. She was the recipient of the Asian Association of Open Universities Conference Best Paper Award in 2008, the Asian Association of Open Universities Research Fellowship in 2009, and the Asian Association of Open Universities Young Innovator Award in 2010.

Jan Visser (jvisser@learndev.org) is president and senior researcher at the Learning Development Institute and professor extraordinary at Stellenbosch University, South Africa. He is a lifetime fellow and former director of the International Board of Standards for Training, Performance and Instruction. He is also UNESCO's former Director for Learning Without Frontiers, a global program of which he was the principal architect. Originally a theoretical physicist who graduated from the Delft University of Technology in The Netherlands, he strayed into other areas, including filmmaking and instructional design. In the latter area he obtained his degrees from Florida State University. Working in different fields around the world, he developed a career in international development that lasted four decades. Dr. Visser is also a musician (who built some of his own instruments) and an avid walker.

Lya Visser (lvisser@gwu.edu) is a part-time professor in the Educational Technology Leadership Program of The George Washington University and is director of training of the Learning Development Institute. Her main professional interest themes are motivational communication and performance improvement; English literature and sculpturing in stone are also passionate pursuits for her. Lya holds a PhD in educational science and technology from the The University of Twente (The Netherlands), and a master's degree in distance education from the University of London.

Muriel Visser (mvisser@learndev.org) has an academic background in rural sociology, distance education (MA, University of London, Cambridge), and mass communication (PhD, Florida State University). Her professional experience has focused on the design and management of international development projects, particularly in Africa and more recently on supporting education systems in developing an effective response to the threat of HIV/AIDS. Visser currently works as an independent consultant in health communication and education. Her research interests focus on promoting human learning and change within the wider context of development. Muriel is associated with the Learning Development Institute as a researcher. For more about the institute and about the projects Muriel has been involved in see http://www.learndev.org

Yusra Laila Visser (yvisser@learndev.org) is a faculty member at Florida Atlantic University (FAU), coordinating the Digital Education Teacher's Academy (DETA). Previously, she held positions as an assistant professor in instructional technology at FAU and Wayne State University. She was project manager for a major distance learning initiative at Florida State University and a program associate for international programs at Education Development Center. As a consultant, she served clients including the U.S. Department of Homeland Security, the Netherlands Ministry of Foreign Affairs, the U.S. Navy, the World Bank, and the United Nations. Her PhD in instructional systems is from Florida State University.

Anita Wilson (anita@wilsonhmp.freeserve.co.uk) is a prison ethnographer who has spent the last 20 years researching alongside members of the prison community. Her interest is in how people in prison develop coping strategies in order to "do the time," and her findings illustrate that holding on to one's creative intellect is a top priority. Anita has undertaken commissions from various government departments and third-sector agencies in the UK, and she has held a Spencer Postdoctoral Fellowship from the NAE/Spencer Foundation, New York in order to extend her work across Europe and North America. She is currently the chairperson of the European Prison Education Association. She has published widely.

Brent G. Wilson (brent.wilson@ucdenver.edu) is a professor of information and learning technologies at the University of Colorado, Denver. He has published four books and more than 120 articles and chapters, with a focus on foundations of professional practice: How can we better support instructors and designers in creating outstanding instruction? How can we encourage appropriate use of learning technologies and resources? What do we know about professional expertise, and how can we advance it and encourage outstanding work in the profession? His most recent work explores how we can help learners have more impactful learning experiences as they complete our courses and programs.

Barbara Zeus (zeus.barbara@gmail.com) works as education manager with the Foundation for the Refugee Education Trust (RET) in Burundi. With a BA in regional studies Asia/Africa and social sciences, and an MA in education and international development, she has worked in diverse contexts from grassroots to national policymaking-level on four continents. Most recently she has worked with the Inter-Agency Network for Education in Emergencies (INEE) Adolescent and Youth Task Team and a private company serving the education sector in the UK. She has done research and published on higher education in protracted refugee situations, educational opportunities for refugee youth, and issues surrounding refugeehood.

ABOUT THE REVIEWERS

Gamin Bartle (gbartle@gwmail.gwu.edu) is Director of Instructional Technology Services at Drew University in Madison, New Jersey. She taught German for over a dozen years at the graduate and undergraduate levels and directed Language Resource Centers at the University of Alabama at Birmingham and at Tuscaloosa before expanding the scope of her work to a broader array of instructional technology in her current position. Dr. Bartle is currently pursuing a Graduate Certificate in Educational Technology.

Jennifer Glennie is the founding director of the South African Institute for Distance Education (SAIDE), which plays an important role in advocating and supporting innovative educational methods to increase access to quality education in the sub-Saharan region. In recognition of her contributions, she was named an Honorary Fellow of the Commonwealth of Learning in 2002.

Greg Kearsley (gkearsley@earthlink.net) has been involved in the design, teaching, and administration of online learning courses for over 30 years. He is the author of more than 20 books about education and technology, including the textbook, *Distance Education: A Systems Approach*, co-authored with Michael Moore.

Peter Mortimer (elearning.france@gmail.com) works in the Innovation Department of France's National Distance Learning Centre (CNED). His primary focus is in the field of networked learning, with a concentration in the role of Personal Learning Environments (PLE's) in networked learning.

J. Michael Spector (jmspector007@gmail.com) is Chair of Learning Technologies at the University of North Texas. His recent research is in the areas of intelligent support for instructional design, system dynamics-based learning environments, assessing learning in complex domains, distance learning, and technology integration in education. Dr. Spector served on the International Board of Standards for Training, Performance and Instruction (ibstpi) as Executive Vice President; he is on the executive committee of the IEEE Learning Technology Technical Committee and is past president of the Association for Educational and Communications Technology (AECT). He is the editor of the Development Section of *Educational Technology Research & Development*, and he serves on numerous other editorial boards. He co-edited the third and fourth editions of the *Handbook of Research on Educational Communications and Technology* and has more than 100 journal articles, book chapters, and books to his credit.

Rosita Ulate (rositaulate@gmail.com) has served as director for academic programs in management and administration at several private institutions in Costa Rica, including the International University of the Americas (UIA) and the Latin-American University of Science and Technology (ULACIT). For 10 years, she has worked for the National Distance Education University (UNED) as professor and program leader for management and administration. She currently works as academic assessor for the School of Natural Sciences at UNED. Rosita holds a bachelor's and master's in business administration with an emphasis in marketing, and a doctorate in instructional technology and distance education from Nova Southeastern University